"WATASE HAS A GIFT FOR INVOLVING CHARACTERIZATION. THOUGH SHE SOMETIMES USES MIAKA FOR LAUGHS, SHE ALSO LETS US SEE HER HEROINE'S COMPASSION AND COURAGE. THE EMPEROR HOTOHORI IS NOT QUITE AS NOBLE AS HE SEEMS, NOR IS THE WILY TAMAHOME AS SELF-CENTERED AS HE WOULD HAVE OTHERS BELIEVE HIM TO BE. EVEN TREACHEROUS EMPRESS-CANDIDATE NURIKO HAS MANY LEVELS. WATASE'S STORYTELLING IS AN ENGAGING ONE. SHE PACES HER STORY WELL AND KNOWS WHEN TO PUMP UP THE ENERGY."

—TONY ISABELLA

"ONE OF THE BEST MANGA EVER, IT CAN BE ENJOYED BY FEMALE AND MALE READERS ALIKE."

—PROTOCULTURE ADDICTS

"THERE ARE TWO POINTS IN FUSHIGI YÛGI'S FAVOR. THE FIRST IS WATASE HERSELF, WHO HAS WRITTEN MARGIN NOTES FOR THE COMPILATION. UNLIKE MANY CREATORS WHO RABBIT ON ABOUT TRIVIA, SHE WANTS TO TALK ABOUT HER CRAFT, AND HAS INTERESTING POINTS TO MAKE ABOUT RESEARCH AND THE CREATIVE PROCESS. THE SECOND IS THAT THE STRIP SUCCEEDS IN BEING QUITE CHARMING; IN SPITE OF ITS DERIVATIVE STORYLINE—AT ONE POINT A CHARACTER ADMITS THE SIMILARITIES TO AN RPG! BUT ANY COMIC THAT LEAVES ME WANTING TO KNOW WHAT HAPPENS NEXT DEFINITELY DELIVERS VALUE FOR MONEY."

—MANGA MAX

ANIMERICA EXTRA GRAPHIC NOVEL

fushigi yûgi™

The Mysterious Play
VOL. 6: SUMMONER

Fushigi Yûgi™
The Mysterious Play
VOL. 6: SUMMONER

This volume contains the FUSHIGI YÛGI installments from Animerica Extra
Vol. 4, No. 6 through Vol. 4, No. 11 in their entirety.

STORY & ART BY YÛ WATASE

English Adaptation/Yuji Oniki
Touch-Up Art & Lettering/Bill Spicer
Cover Design/Hidemi Sahara
Layout & Graphics/Carolina Ugalde
Editor/William Flanagan

Managing Editor/Annette Roman
V.P. of Sales & Marketing/Rick Bauer
V.P. of Editorial/Hyoe Narita
Publisher/Seiji Horibuchi

Printed in Canada

10 9 8 7 6 5 4 3 2
First printing, February 2002
Second printing, October 2002

Published by Viz Communications, Inc.
P.O. Box 77010, San Francisco, CA 94107

ANIMERICA EXTRA GRAPHIC NOVEL

fushigi yûgi™

The Mysterious Play
VOL. 6: SUMMONER

Story & Art By
YÛ WATASE

CONTENTS

STORY THUS FAR

Chipper junior-high-school girl Miaka and her best friend Yui are physically drawn into the world of a strange book—*The Universe of the Four Gods*. Miaka is offered the role of the lead character, the Priestess of the god Suzaku, and is charged with a mission to save the nation of Hong-Nan, and in the process grant her any wish she wants. Yui suffers rape and manipulation which drives her to attempt suicide. Now, Yui has become the Priestess of the god Seiryu, the bitter enemy of Suzaku and Miaka.

The only way for Miaka to gain back the trust of her former best friend is to gather all seven Celestial Warriors of Suzaku together, summon the god, and wish to be reconciled with Yui. Now that Miaka seems to have found all seven, she only needs to retrieve her love and Celestial Warrior of Suzaku, Tamahome. But he has been drugged by love-struck Yui and her Warrior Nakago in Seiryu's kingdom of Qu-Dong, and when Miaka, mystical Chichiri, and rambunctious Tasuki go to rescue Tamahome, they find that the drug's hold on Tamahome's mind is too powerful. They are forced to escape, leaving the traitorous Tamahome behind.

THE UNIVERSE OF THE FOUR GODS *is based on ancient China, but Japanese pronunciation of Chinese names differs slightly from their Chinese equivalents. Here is a short glossary of the Japanese pronunciation of the Chinese names in this graphic novel:*

CHINESE	JAPANESE	PERSON OR PLACE	MEANING
Hong-Nan	Konan	Southern Kingdom	Crimson South
Qu-Dong	Kutô	Eastern Kingdom	Gathered East
Diedu	Kodoku	A Potion	Seduction Poison
He-Yan	Waen	A Palace Room	Eternal Peace
Bei-Jia	Hokkan	Northern Kingdom	Armored North
Wong Tao-Hui	Ôdokun	A Chinese Name	King Bright Path
K'o-Ju	Kakyo	Bureaucracy Exam	Department Trial
Hsing-Shin	Shôshi	A Second Exam	Ministry Test
Tai Yi-Jun	Tai Itsukun	An Oracle	Preeminent Person
Shentso-Pao	Shinzahô	A Treasure	God's Seat Jewel

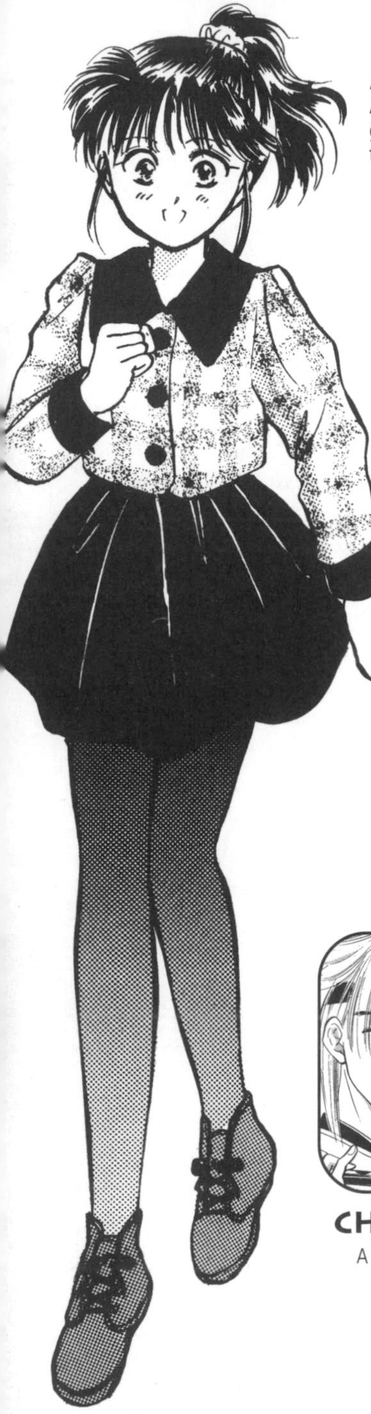

MIAKA
A chipper junior-high-school glutton who has become the Priestess of Suzaku.

THE CELESTIAL WARRIORS OF SUZAKU

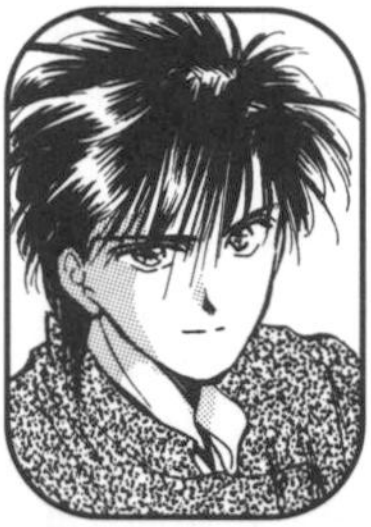

TAMAHOME
A dashing miser.

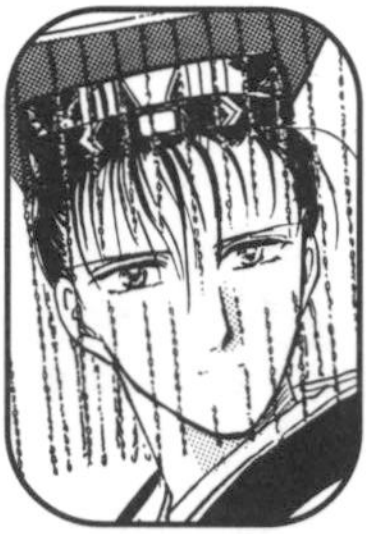

HOTOHORI
The beautiful emperor of Hong-Nan.

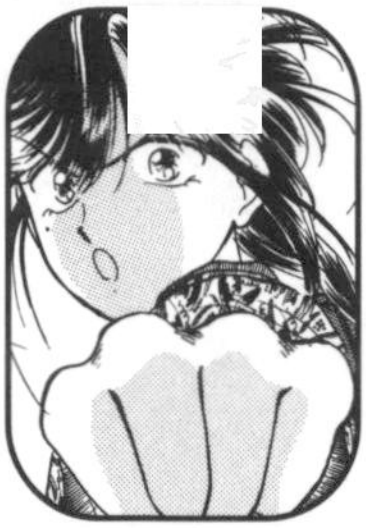

NURIKO
An amazingly strong cross-dresser.

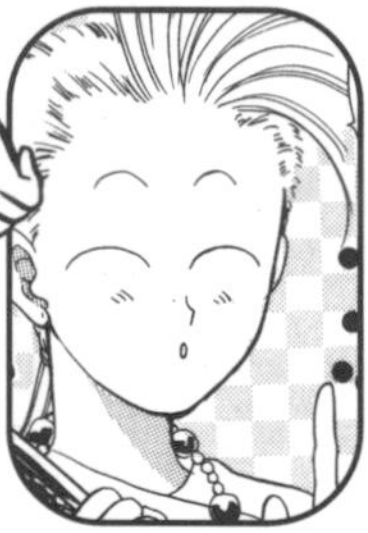

CHICHIRI
Former disciple of the oracle.

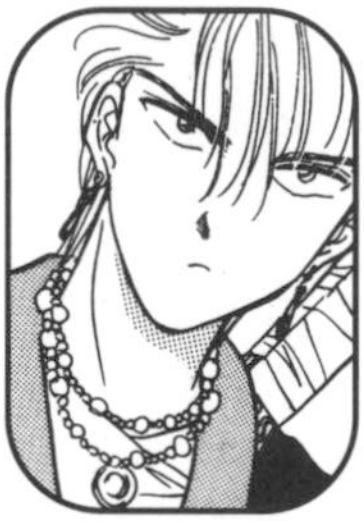

TASUKI
An ornery ex-bandit.

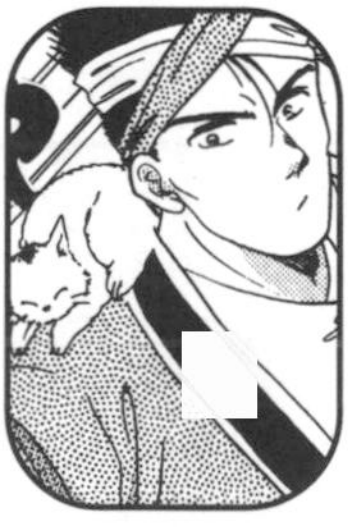

MITSUKAKE
A silent healer.

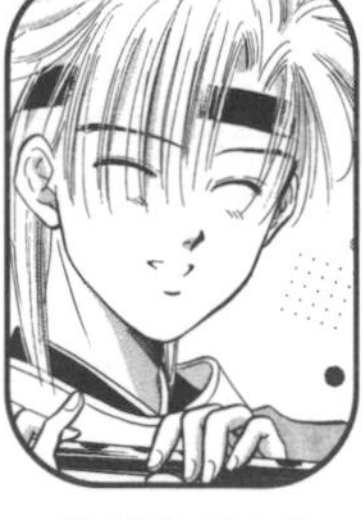

CHIRIKO
A flutist with a secret.

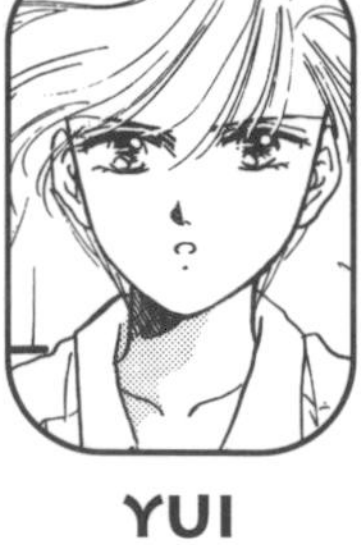

YUI
Miaka's former best friend, but now her enemy and the Priestess of Seiryu.

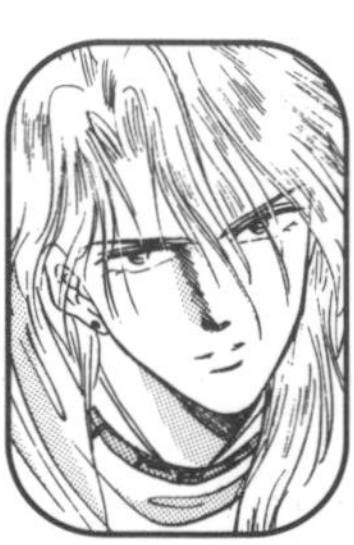

NAKAG
A general of Qu-Dong and a Celestial Warrio of Seiryu.

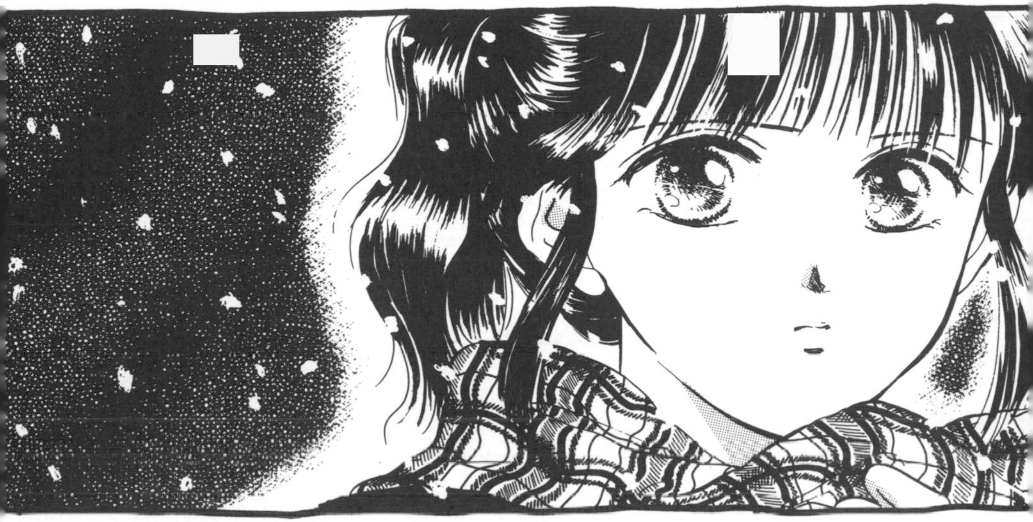

CHAPTER THIRTY-ONE

THE WAY TO GOODBYE

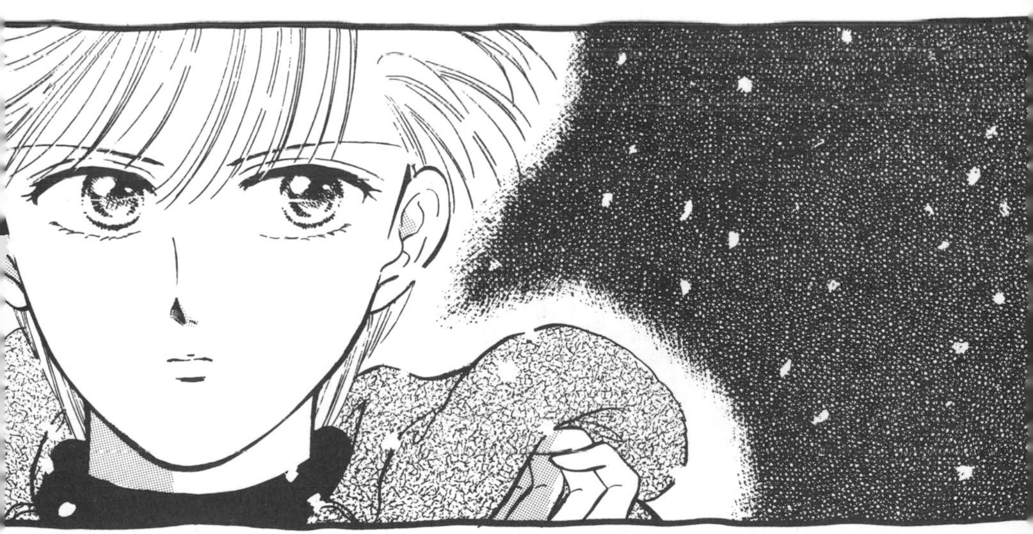

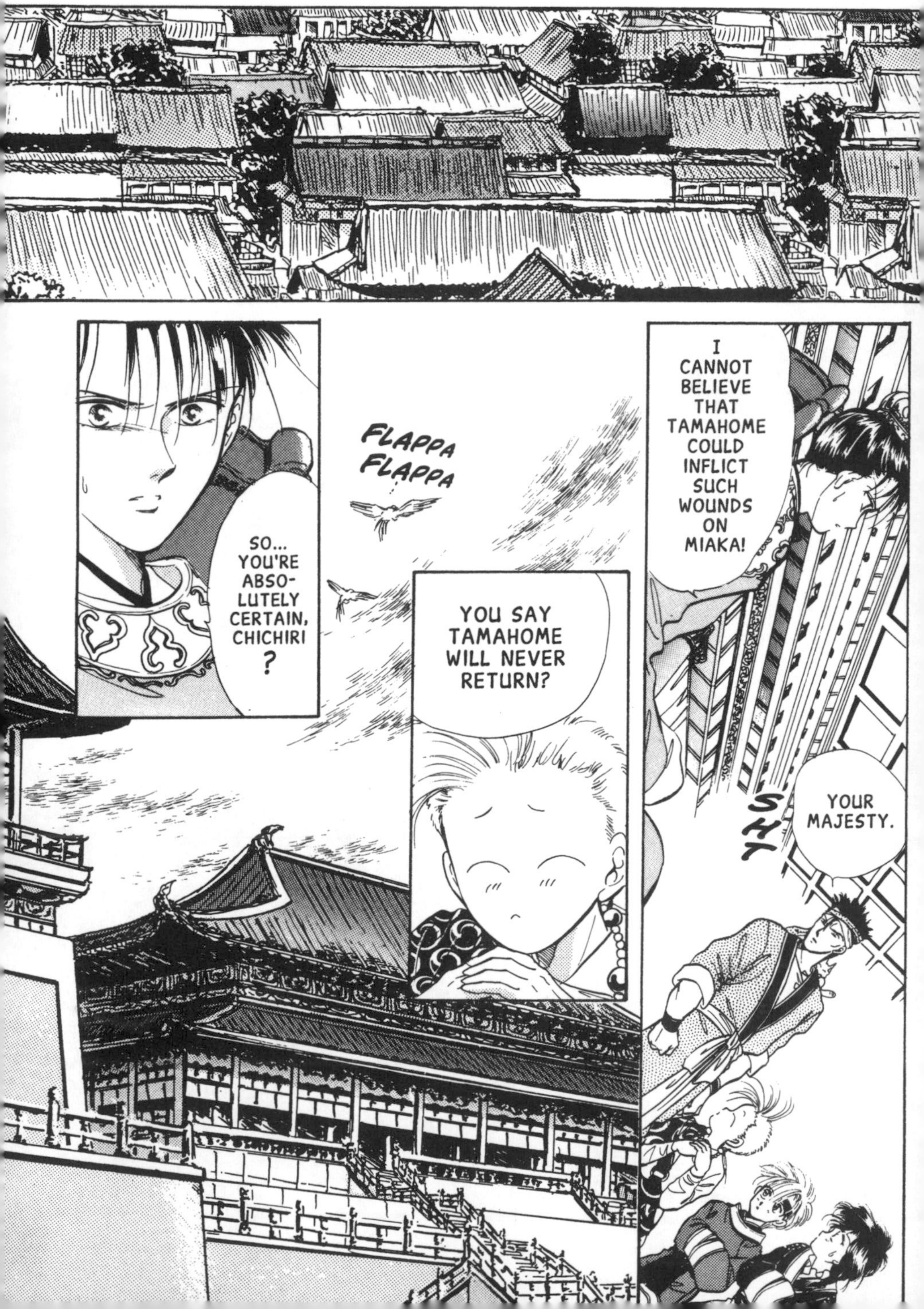
SO... YOU'RE ABSO-LUTELY CERTAIN, CHICHIRI?
FLAPPA FLAPPA
YOU SAY TAMAHOME WILL NEVER RETURN?
I CANNOT BELIEVE THAT TAMAHOME COULD INFLICT SUCH WOUNDS ON MIAKA!
SHT
YOUR MAJESTY.

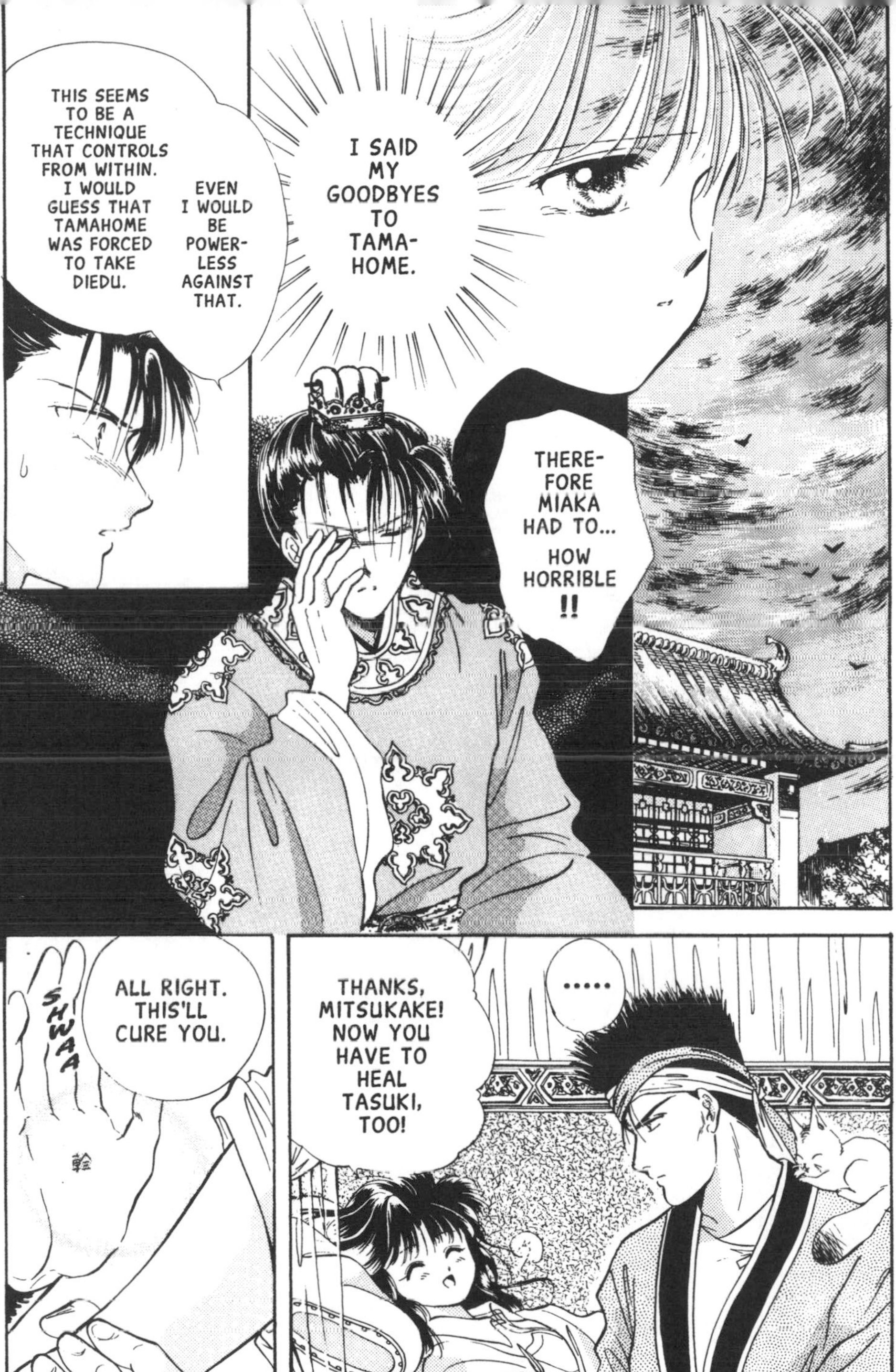
THIS SEEMS TO BE A TECHNIQUE THAT CONTROLS FROM WITHIN. I WOULD GUESS THAT TAMAHOME WAS FORCED TO TAKE DIEDU.
EVEN I WOULD BE POWER-LESS AGAINST THAT.
I SAID MY GOODBYES TO TAMA-HOME.
THERE-FORE MIAKA HAD TO... HOW HORRIBLE!!
SHWAA
ALL RIGHT. THIS'LL CURE YOU.
THANKS, MITSUKAKE! NOW YOU HAVE TO HEAL TASUKI, TOO!
.....

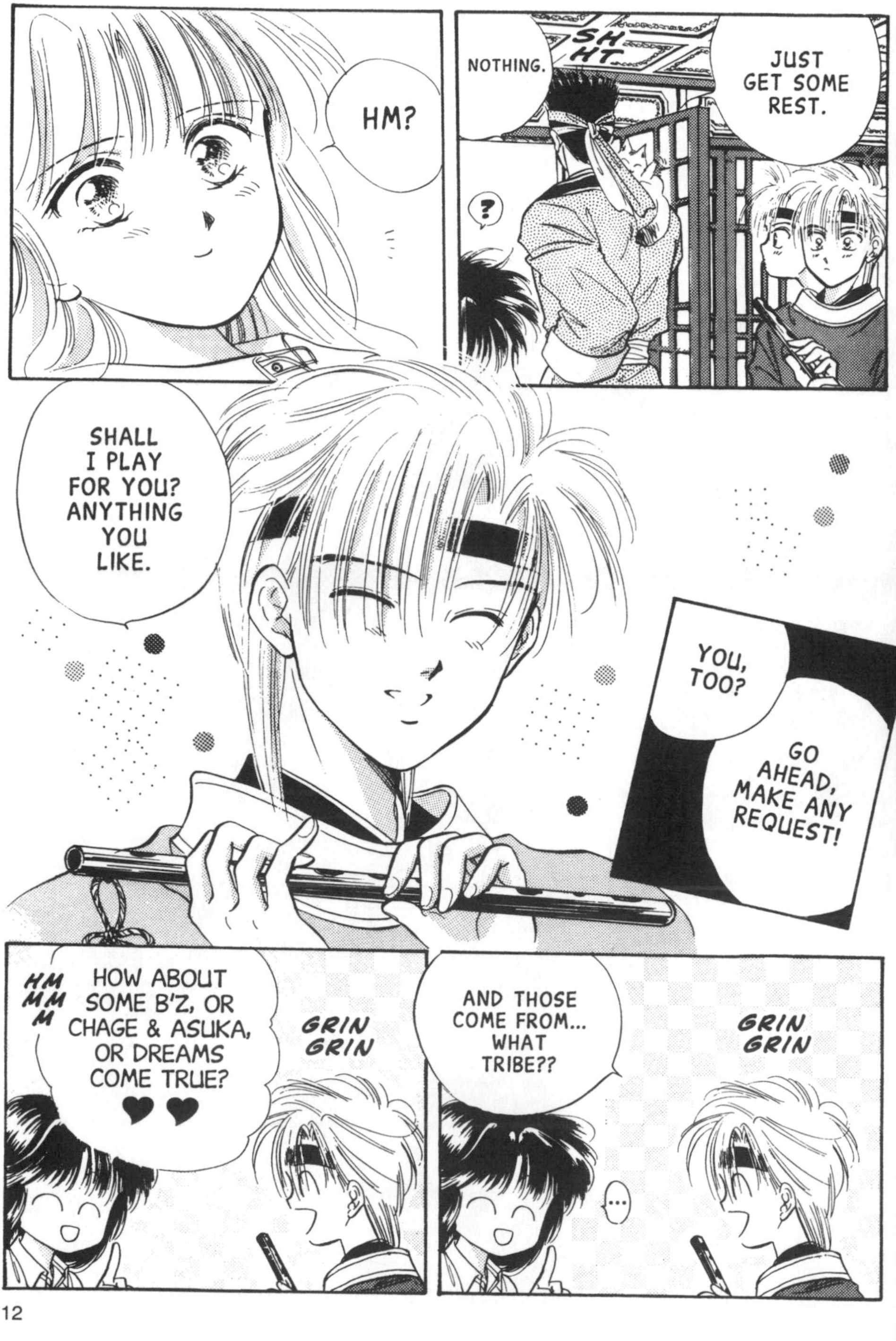
HM?
NOTHING.
SH HT
JUST GET SOME REST.
?
SHALL I PLAY FOR YOU? ANYTHING YOU LIKE.
YOU, TOO?
GO AHEAD, MAKE ANY REQUEST!
HMMMM
HOW ABOUT SOME B'Z, OR CHAGE & ASUKA, OR DREAMS COME TRUE? ♥ ♥
GRIN GRIN
AND THOSE COME FROM... WHAT TRIBE??
GRIN GRIN
...

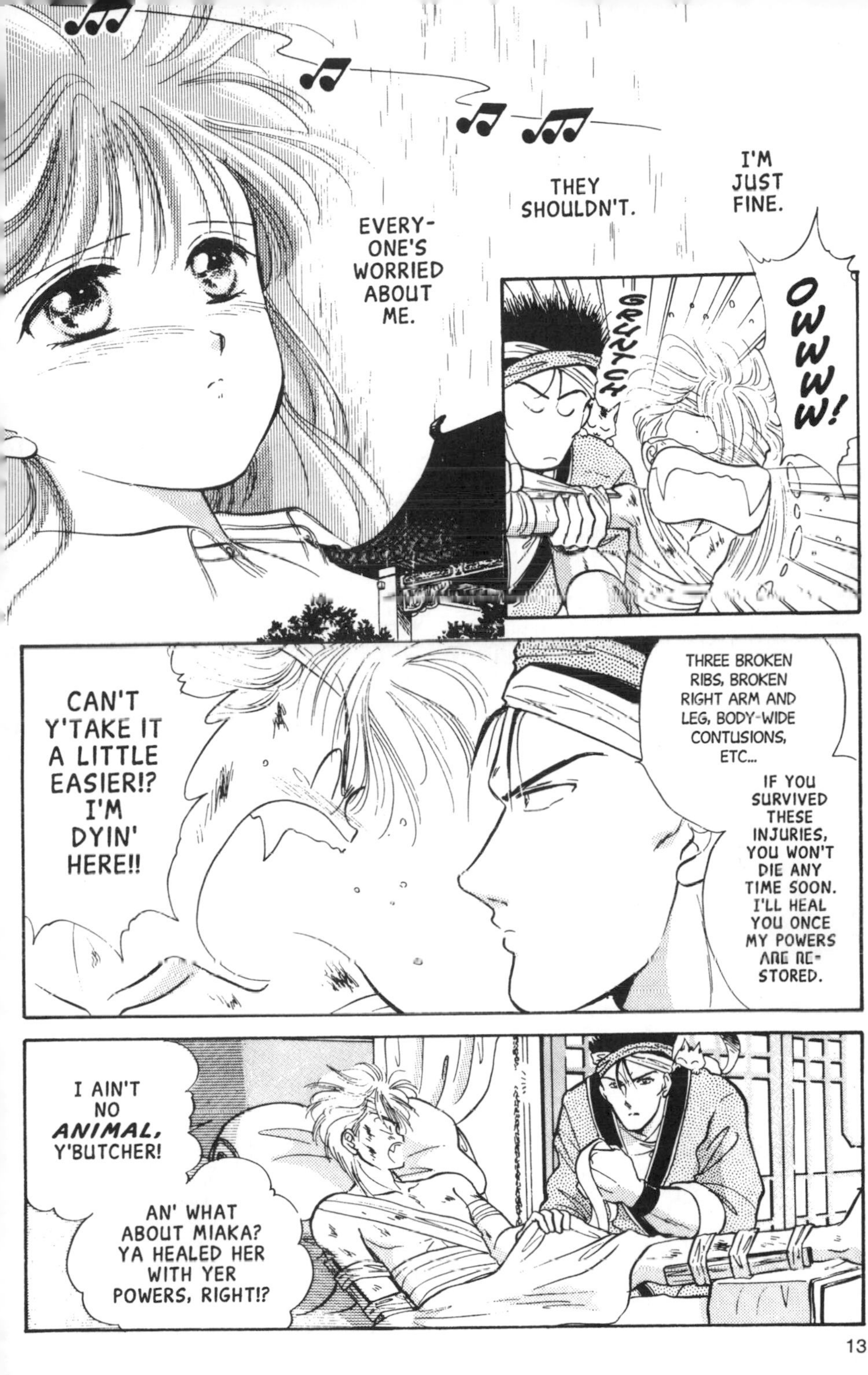

EVERY-ONE'S WORRIED ABOUT ME.
THEY SHOULDN'T.
I'M JUST FINE.
GRUNCH
OWWWWW!
CAN'T Y'TAKE IT A LITTLE EASIER!? I'M DYIN' HERE!!
THREE BROKEN RIBS, BROKEN RIGHT ARM AND LEG, BODY-WIDE CONTUSIONS, ETC...
IF YOU SURVIVED THESE INJURIES, YOU WON'T DIE ANY TIME SOON. I'LL HEAL YOU ONCE MY POWERS ARE RE-STORED.
I AIN'T NO ANIMAL, Y'BUTCHER!
AN' WHAT ABOUT MIAKA? YA HEALED HER WITH YER POWERS, RIGHT!?

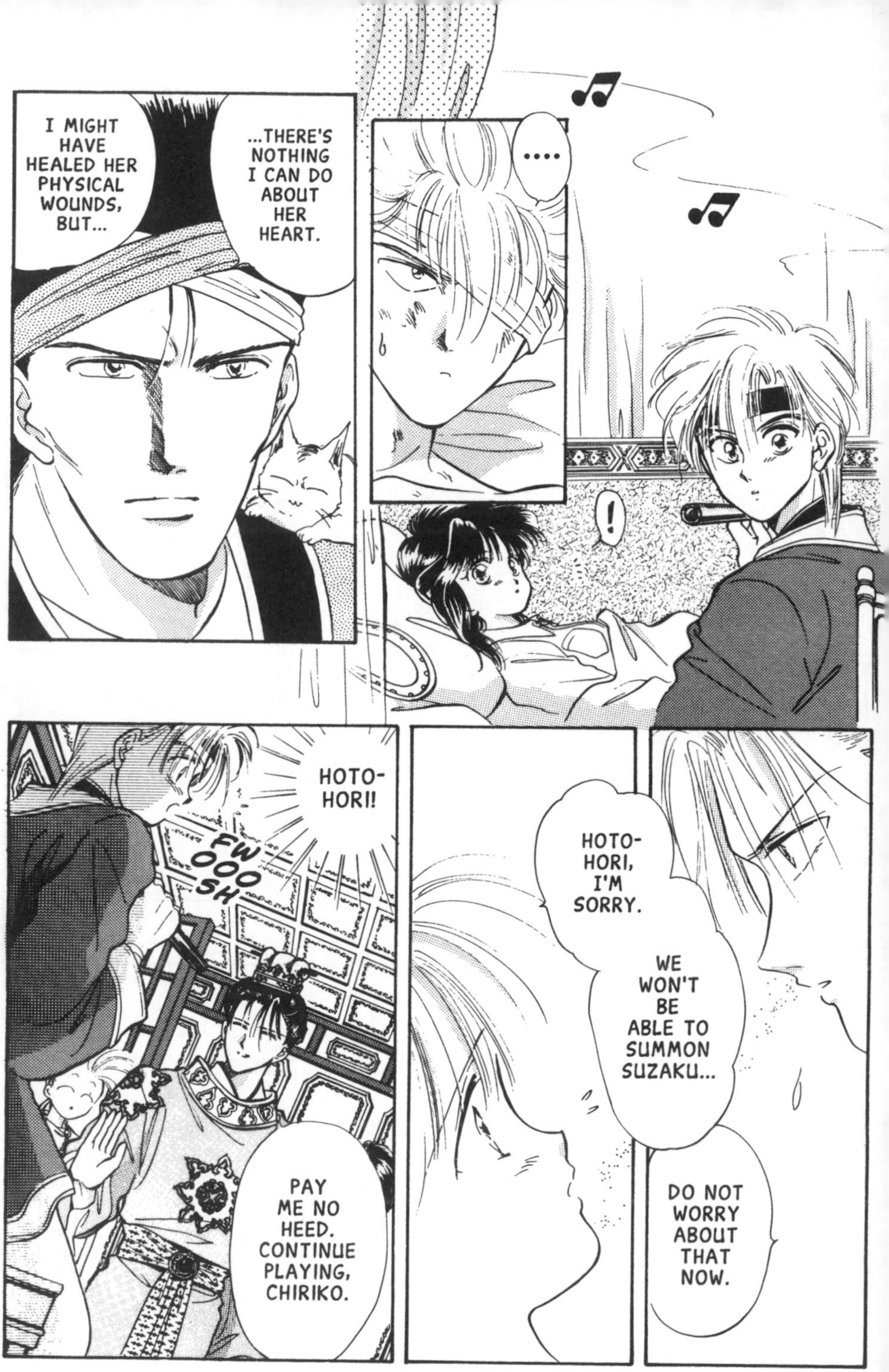
I MIGHT HAVE HEALED HER PHYSICAL WOUNDS, BUT...
...THERE'S NOTHING I CAN DO ABOUT HER HEART.
....
!
HOTO-HORI!
FWOOOSH
PAY ME NO HEED. CONTINUE PLAYING, CHIRIKO.
HOTO-HORI, I'M SORRY.
WE WON'T BE ABLE TO SUMMON SUZAKU...
DO NOT WORRY ABOUT THAT NOW.

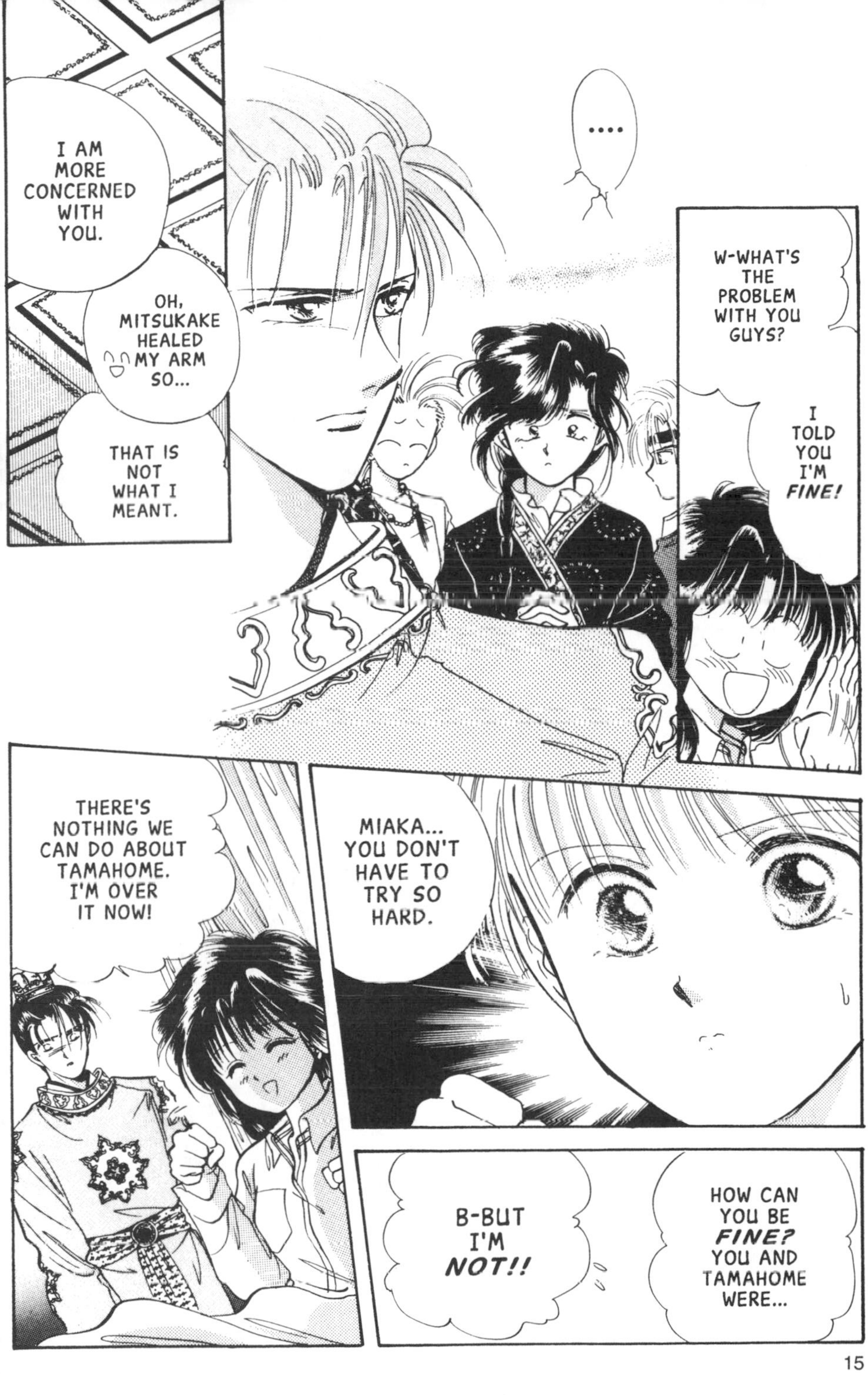
I AM MORE CONCERNED WITH YOU.
OH, MITSUKAKE HEALED MY ARM SO...
THAT IS NOT WHAT I MEANT.
....
W-WHAT'S THE PROBLEM WITH YOU GUYS?
I TOLD YOU I'M *FINE!*
THERE'S NOTHING WE CAN DO ABOUT TAMAHOME. I'M OVER IT NOW!
MIAKA... YOU DON'T HAVE TO TRY SO HARD.
B-BUT I'M *NOT!!*
HOW CAN YOU BE *FINE?* YOU AND TAMAHOME WERE...

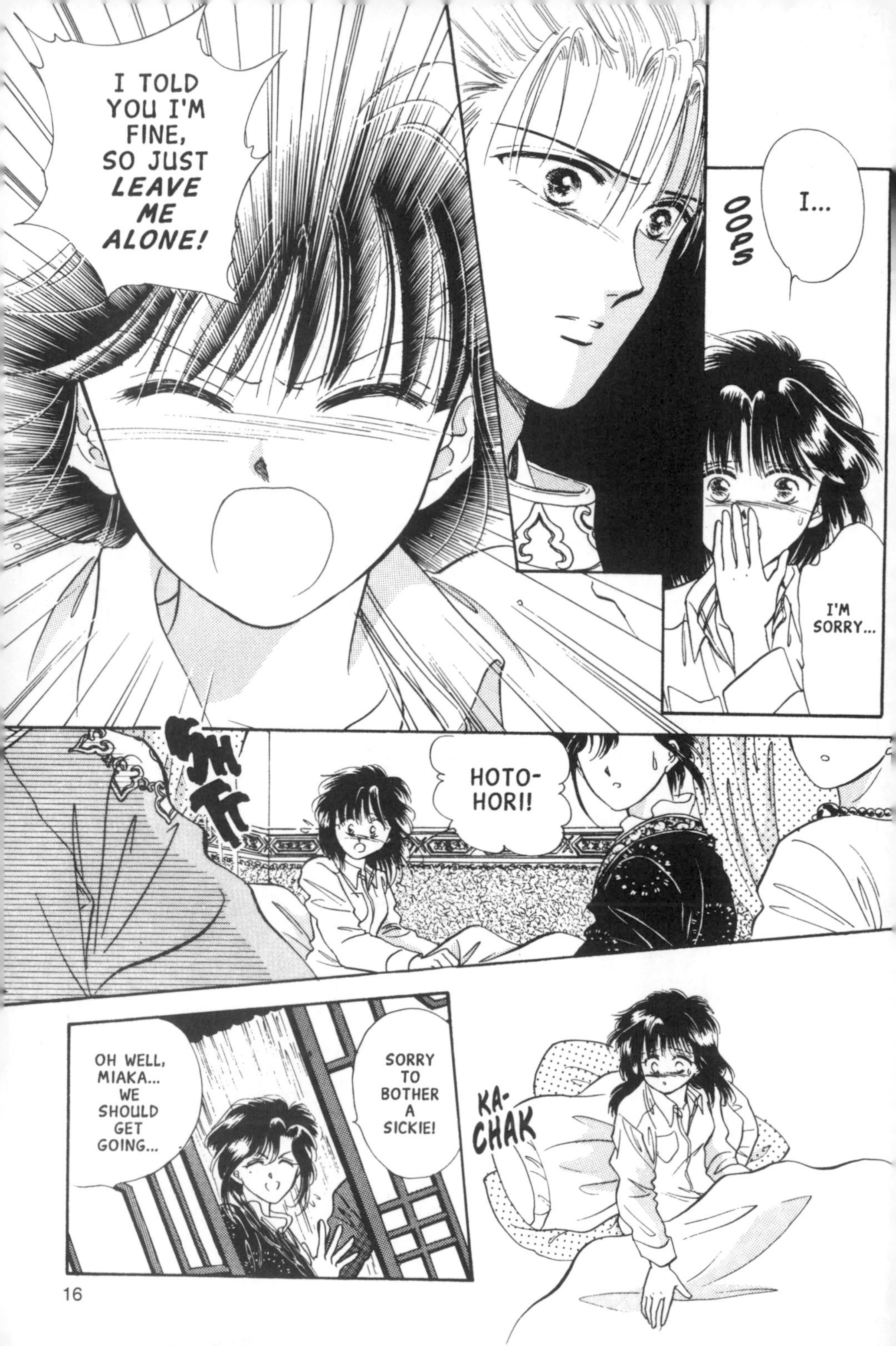
I TOLD YOU I'M FINE, SO JUST LEAVE ME ALONE!
OOPS
I...
I'M SORRY...
SHFF
HOTO-HORI!
OH WELL, MIAKA... WE SHOULD GET GOING...
SORRY TO BOTHER A SICKIE!
KA-CHAK

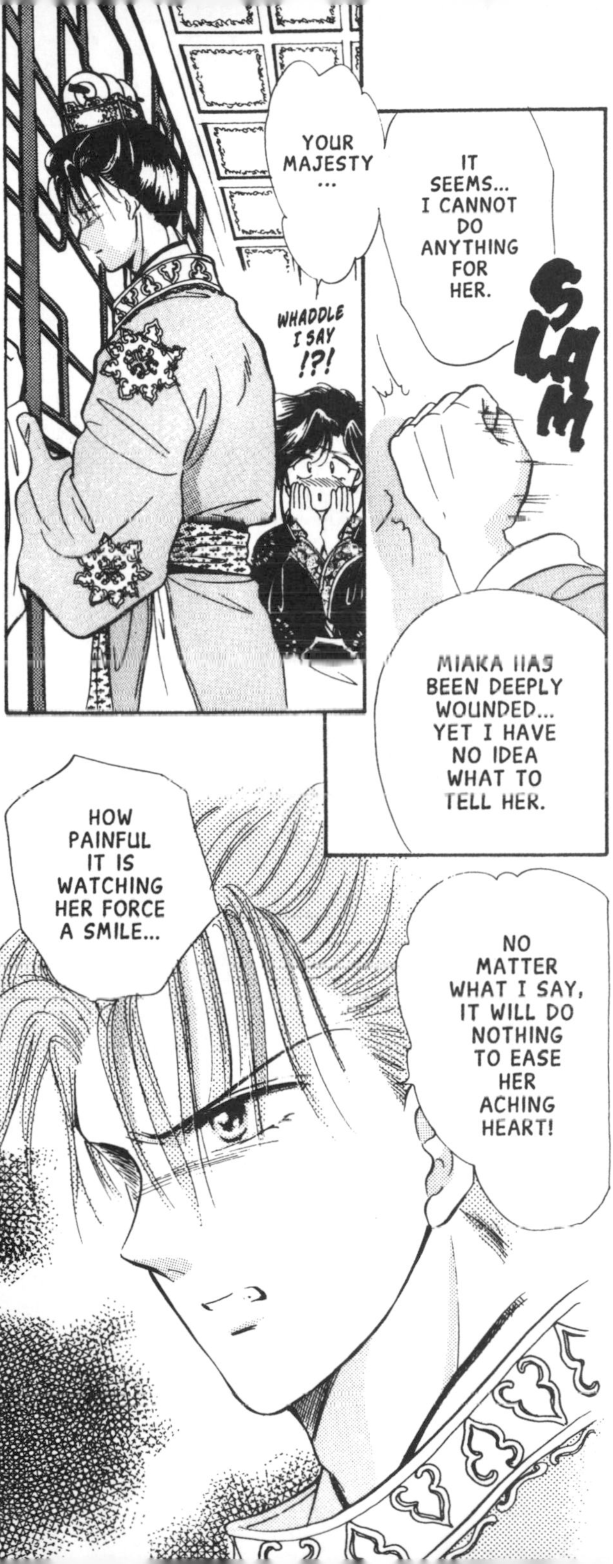
YOUR MAJESTY ...
WHADDLE I SAY !?!
IT SEEMS... I CANNOT DO ANYTHING FOR HER.
SLAM
MIAKA HAS BEEN DEEPLY WOUNDED... YET I HAVE NO IDEA WHAT TO TELL HER.
HOW PAINFUL IT IS WATCHING HER FORCE A SMILE...
NO MATTER WHAT I SAY, IT WILL DO NOTHING TO EASE HER ACHING HEART!

Hello. Thanks to you, we've reached volume 6! As a matter of fact, I currently feel pretty normal, which is unusual for me while I'm writing these free-talk sections. So what state of mind was I in previously?

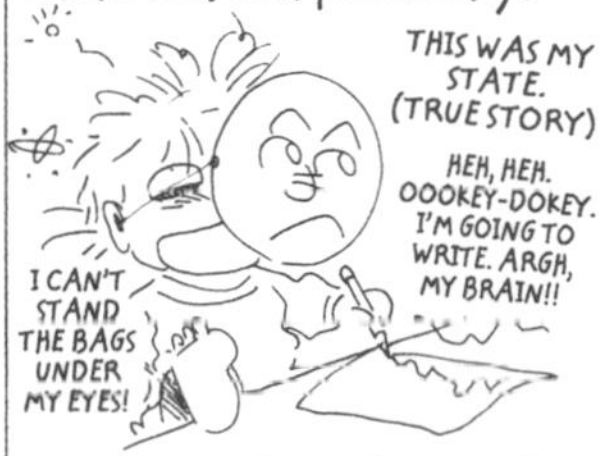
THIS WAS MY STATE. (TRUE STORY)
HEH, HEH. OOOKEY-DOKEY. I'M GOING TO WRITE. ARGH, MY BRAIN!!
I CAN'T STAND THE BAGS UNDER MY EYES!

That's right. I was sleepy and tired, stressed, overworked and fed up completely! A person has to have some free time once in a while! *Not that I have free time now, though.* So from now on I'll throw away that ugly, overworked-looking mask, and put on a different bright-eyed, cheery Watase mask.

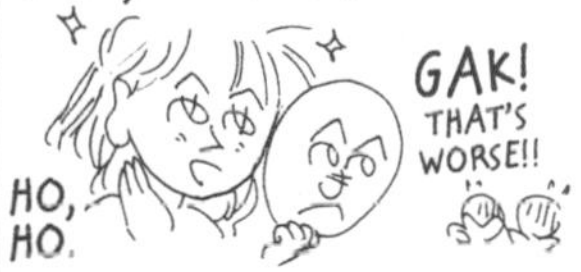
HO, HO.
GAK! THAT'S WORSE!!

All right, enough with the boring banter. Well, it's summer, so I'm thinking of sharing a real-life horror story I actually experienced. Those of you who don't like horror can skip these sections and just read the manga. *I won't be put out. Promise!* Those of you who do, it's not a great story, but you should check it out. Actually, it was worse on my assistants than it ever was on me.
All I know is that I'm grateful we finally moved.

To be continued...

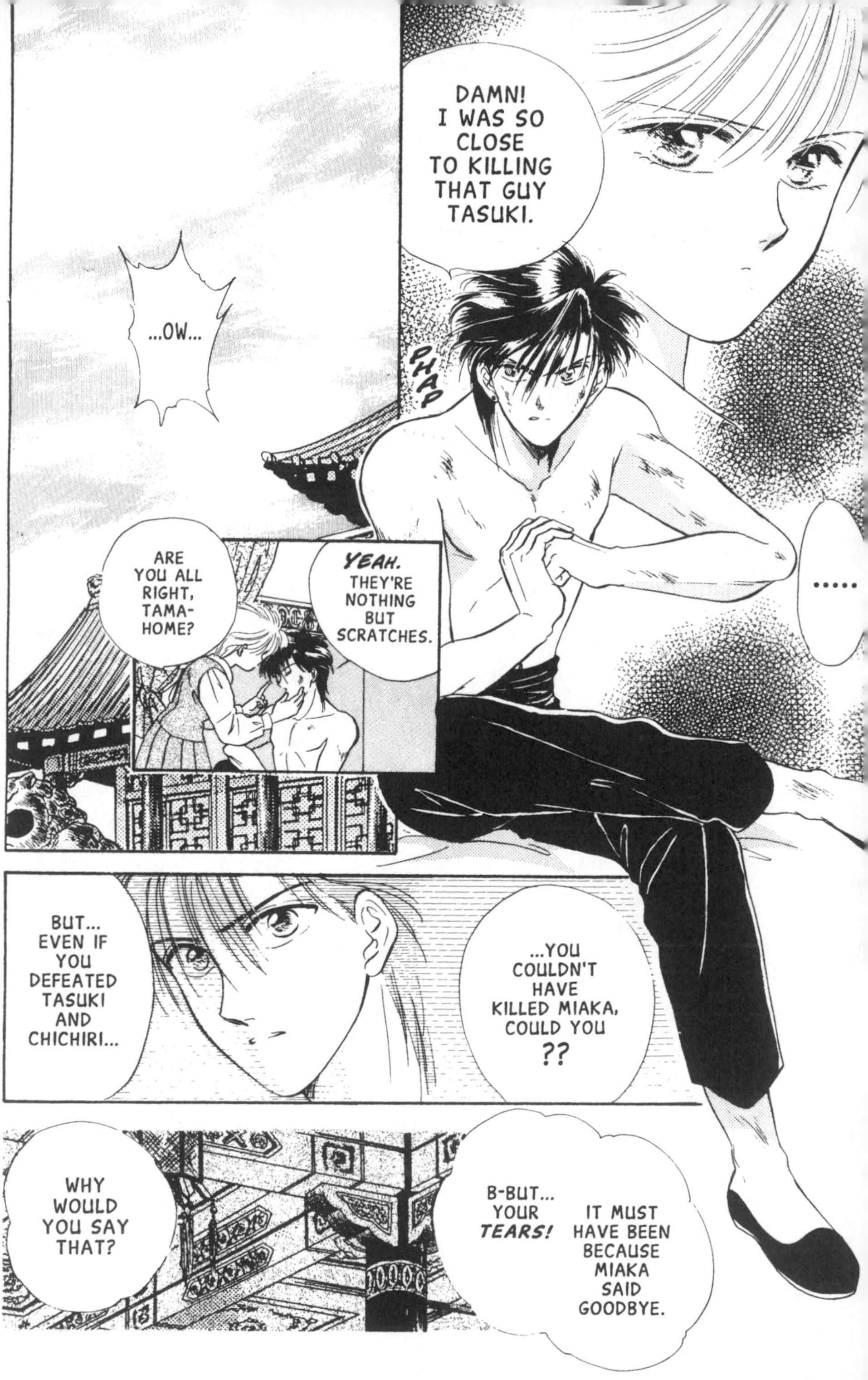
...OW...
ARE YOU ALL RIGHT, TAMA-HOME?
YEAH. THEY'RE NOTHING BUT SCRATCHES.
DAMN! I WAS SO CLOSE TO KILLING THAT GUY TASUKI.
PHAP
.....
BUT... EVEN IF YOU DEFEATED TASUKI AND CHICHIRI...
...YOU COULDN'T HAVE KILLED MIAKA, COULD YOU ??
WHY WOULD YOU SAY THAT?
B-BUT... YOUR TEARS!
IT MUST HAVE BEEN BECAUSE MIAKA SAID GOODBYE.

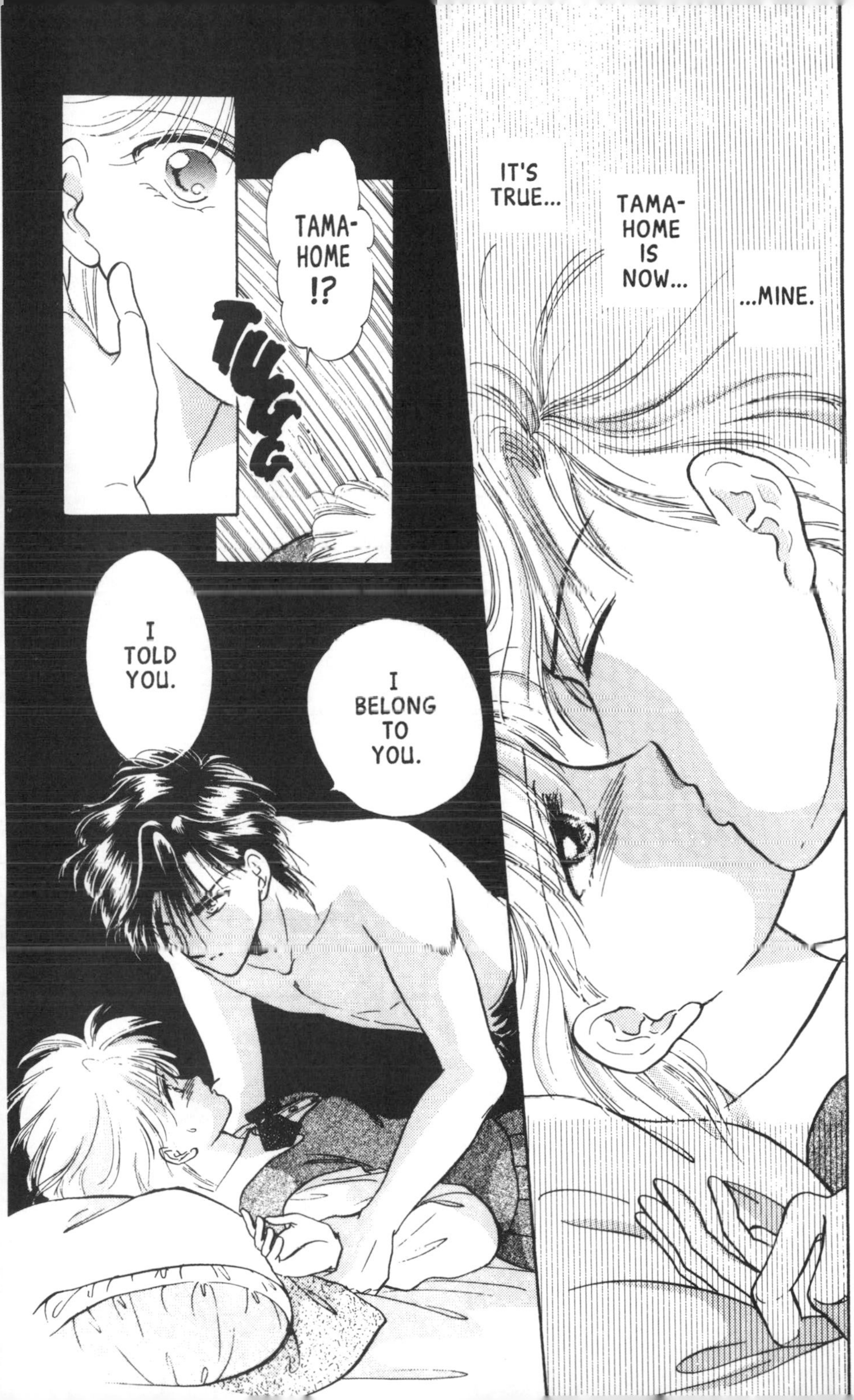
TAMA-HOME!?
TUGG
I TOLD YOU.
I BELONG TO YOU.
IT'S TRUE...
TAMA-HOME IS NOW...
...MINE.

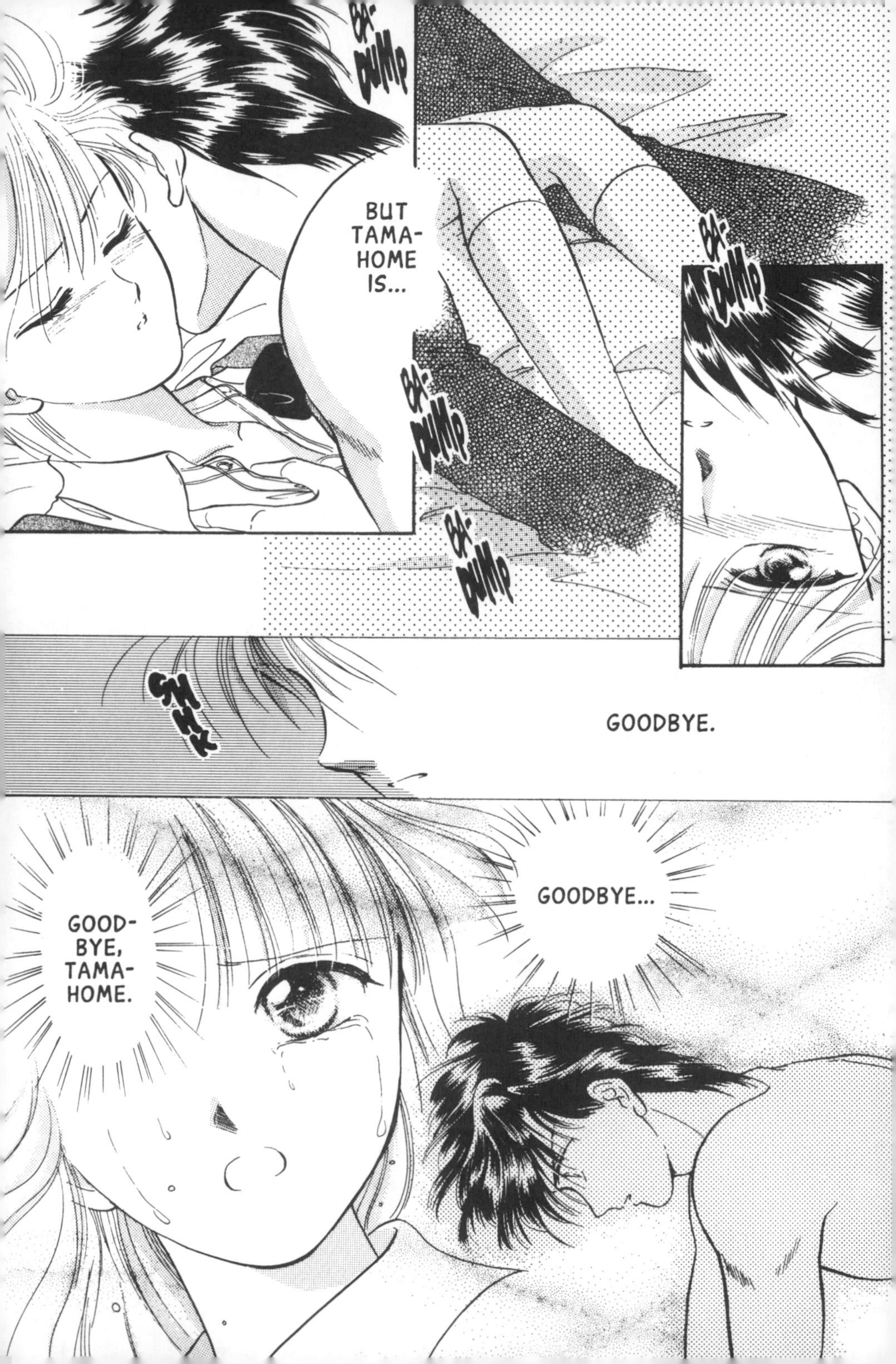
BA-DUMP
BUT TAMA-HOME IS...
BA-DUMP
BA-DUMP
BA-DUMP
BA-DUMP
SHHK
GOODBYE.
GOOD-BYE, TAMA-HOME.
GOODBYE...

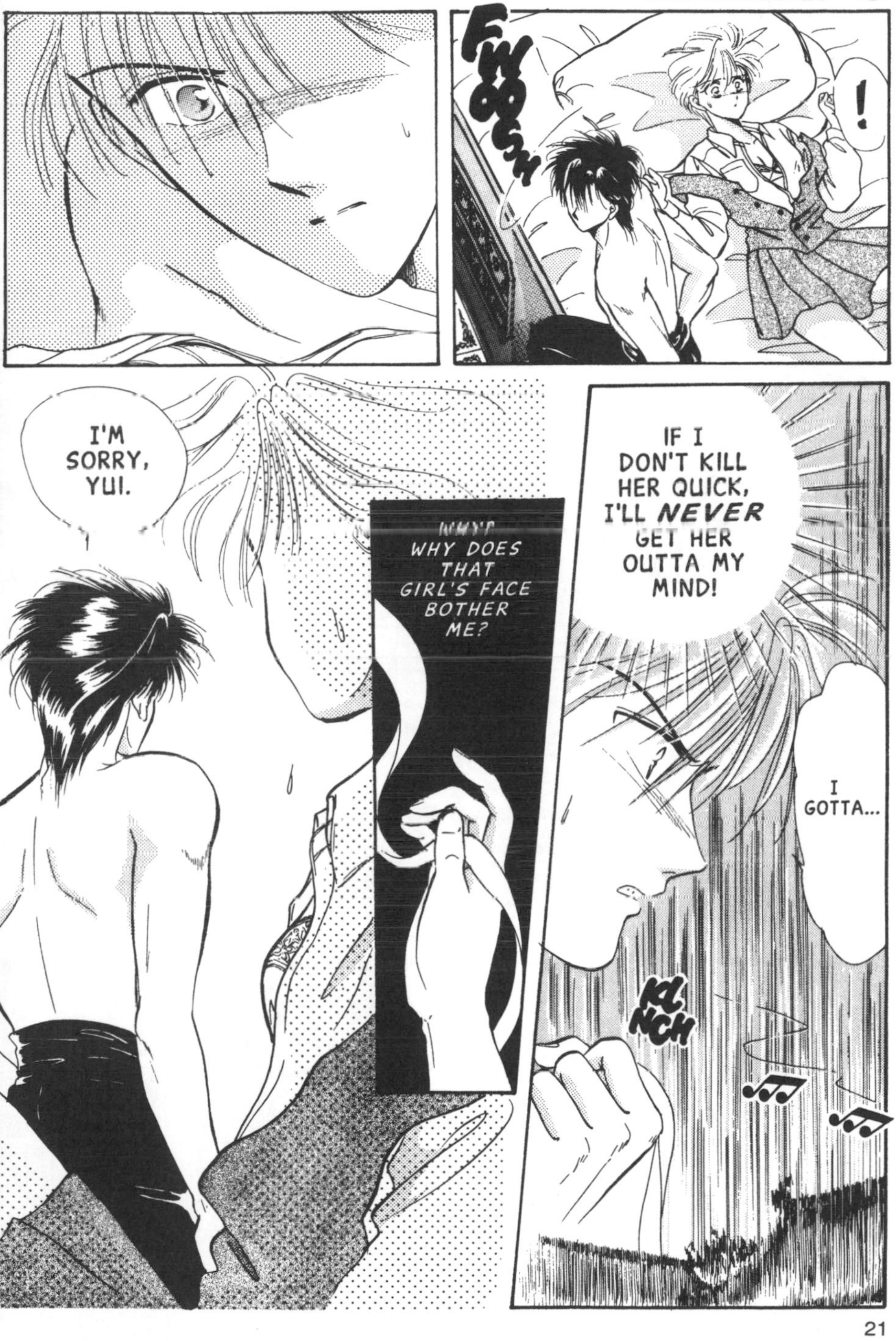
FWOOSH
!
I'M SORRY, YUI.
WHY? WHY DOES THAT GIRL'S FACE BOTHER ME?
IF I DON'T KILL HER QUICK, I'LL ***NEVER*** GET HER OUTTA MY MIND!
I GOTTA...
KLNCH

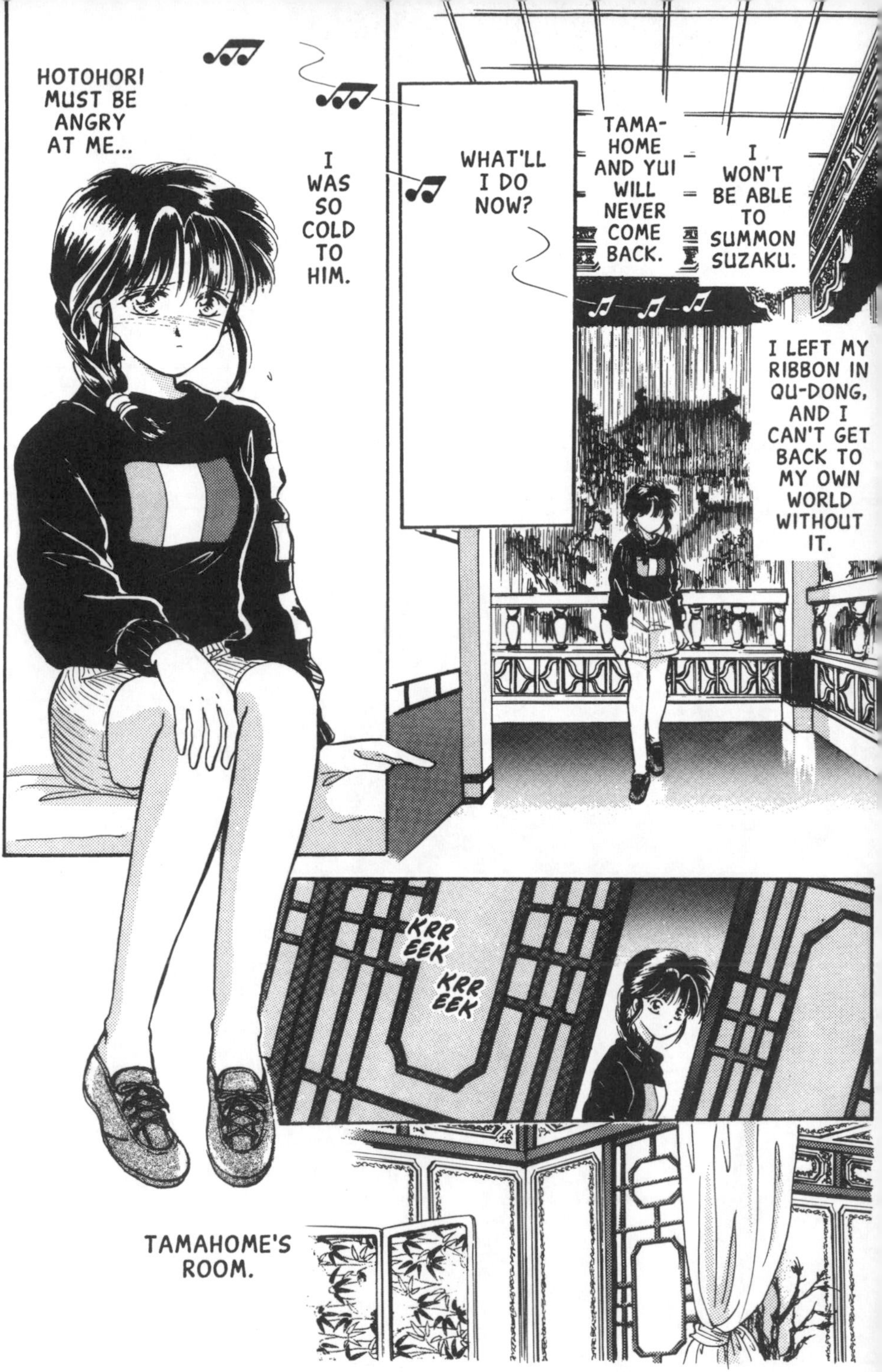
HOTOHORI MUST BE ANGRY AT ME...
I WAS SO COLD TO HIM.
WHAT'LL I DO NOW?
TAMA-HOME AND YUI WILL NEVER COME BACK.
I WON'T BE ABLE TO SUMMON SUZAKU.
I LEFT MY RIBBON IN QU-DONG, AND I CAN'T GET BACK TO MY OWN WORLD WITHOUT IT.
KRR EEK
KRR EEK
TAMAHOME'S ROOM.

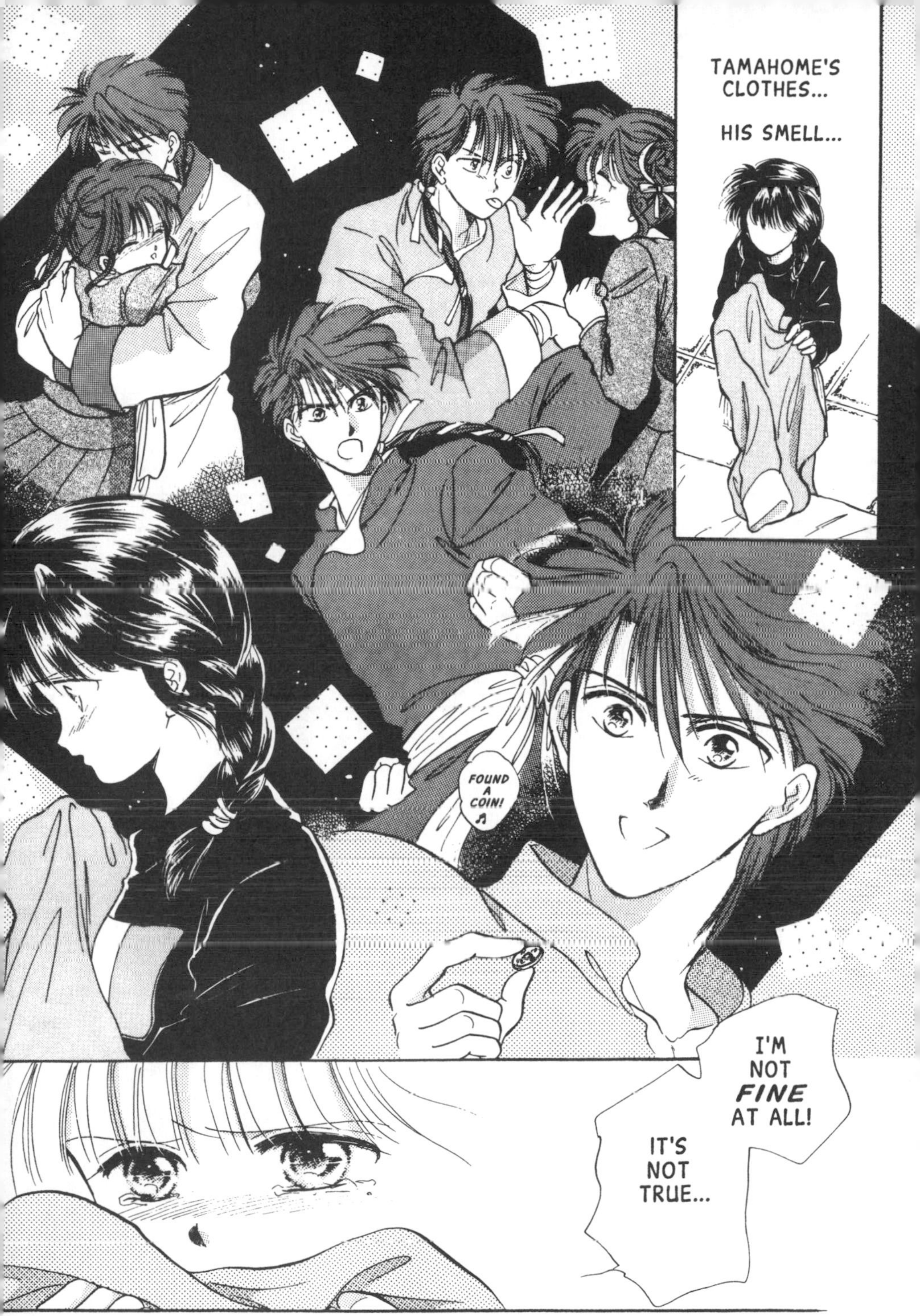
FOUND A COIN! ♪
TAMAHOME'S CLOTHES...
HIS SMELL...
I'M NOT *FINE* AT ALL!
IT'S NOT TRUE...

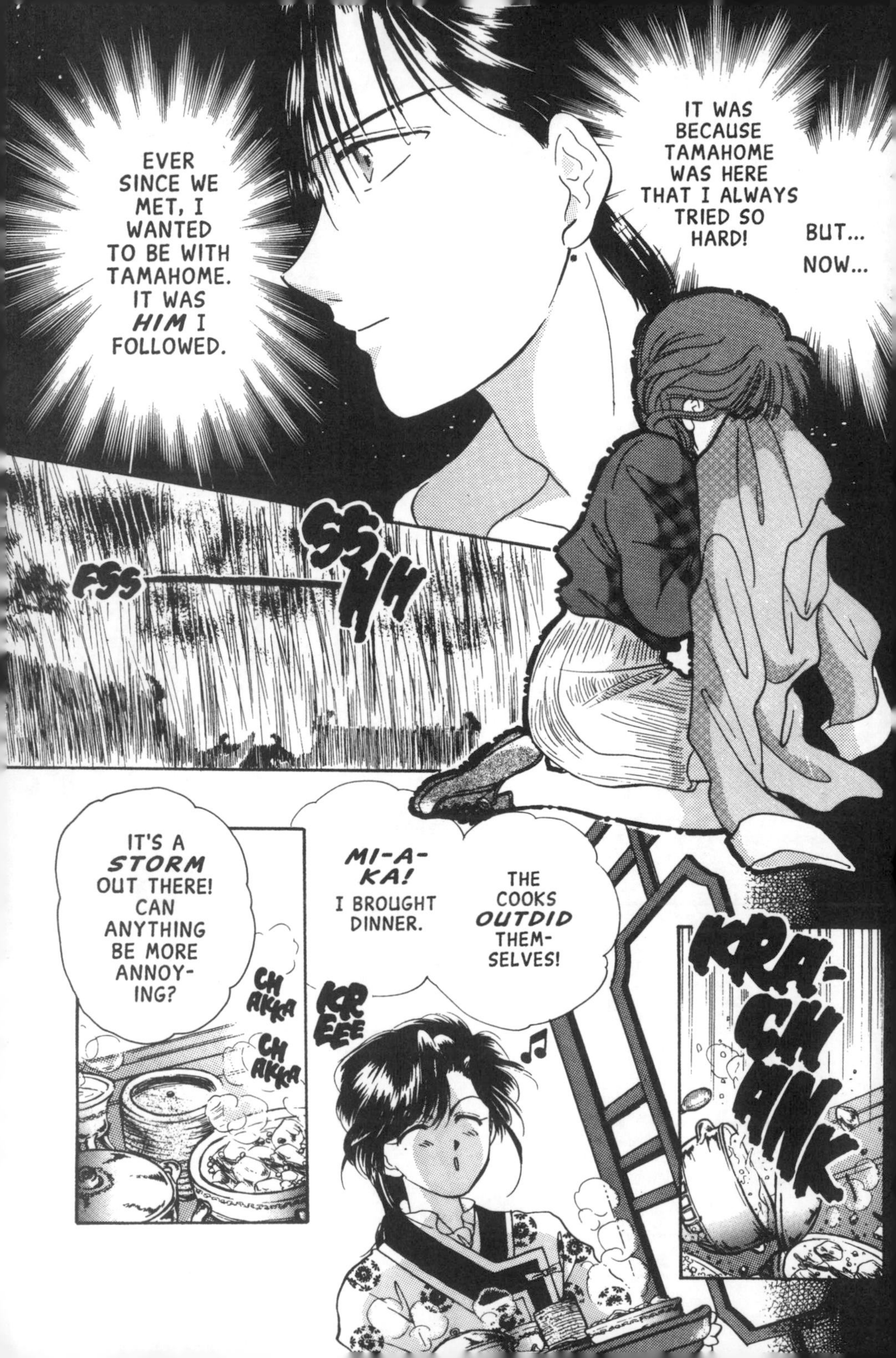

EVER SINCE WE MET, I WANTED TO BE WITH TAMAHOME. IT WAS *HIM* I FOLLOWED.
IT WAS BECAUSE TAMAHOME WAS HERE THAT I ALWAYS TRIED SO HARD!
BUT... NOW...
FSS
SSHH
IT'S A *STORM* OUT THERE! CAN ANYTHING BE MORE ANNOY-ING?
CHAKKA
CHAKKA
MI-A-KA! I BROUGHT DINNER.
THE COOKS *OUTDID* THEM-SELVES!
KREEE
KRA-CHANK

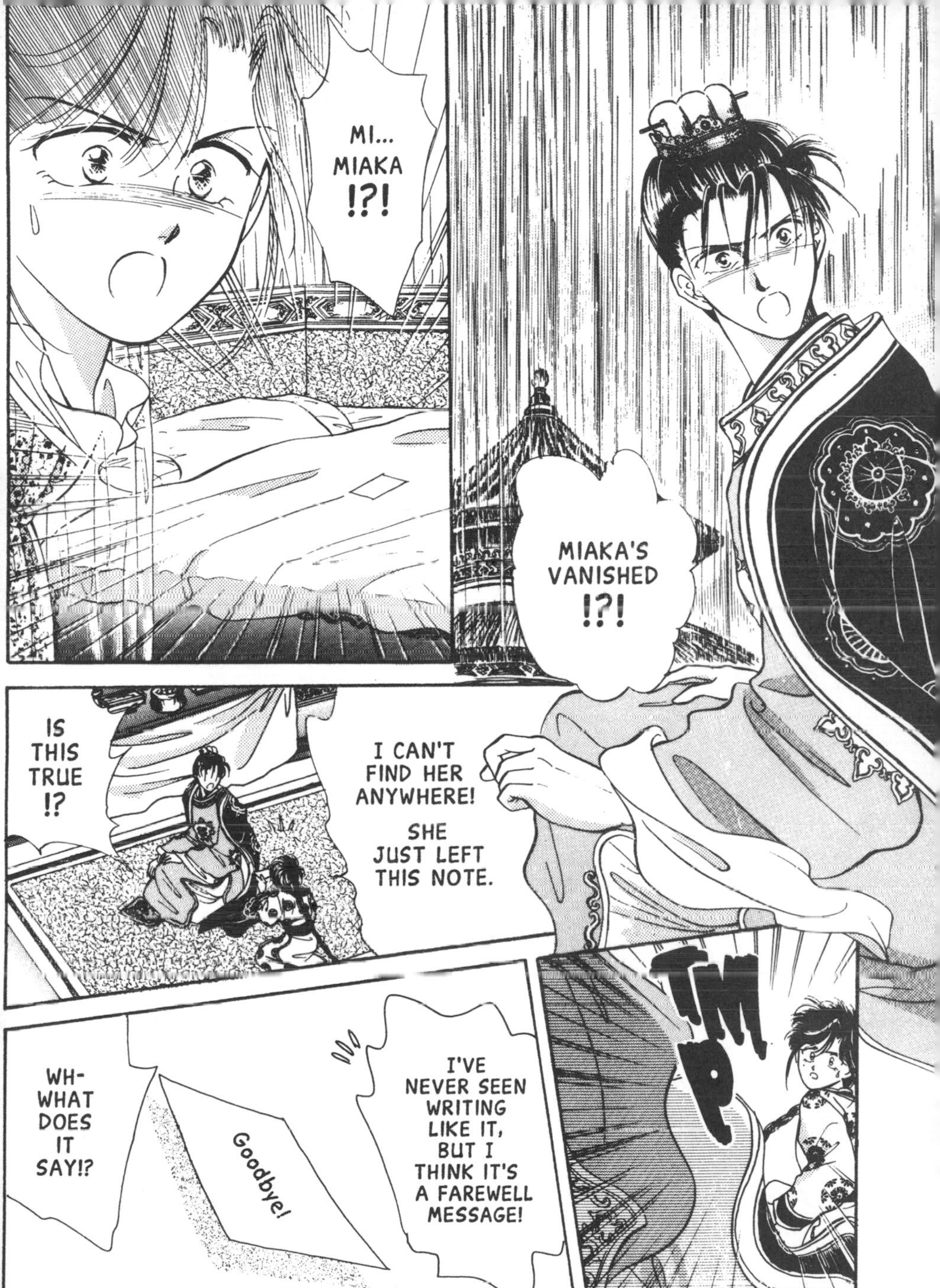
MI... MIAKA !?!
MIAKA'S VANISHED !?!
IS THIS TRUE !?
I CAN'T FIND HER ANYWHERE!
SHE JUST LEFT THIS NOTE.
TMP
WH- WHAT DOES IT SAY!?
Goodbye!
I'VE NEVER SEEN WRITING LIKE IT, BUT I THINK IT'S A FAREWELL MESSAGE!

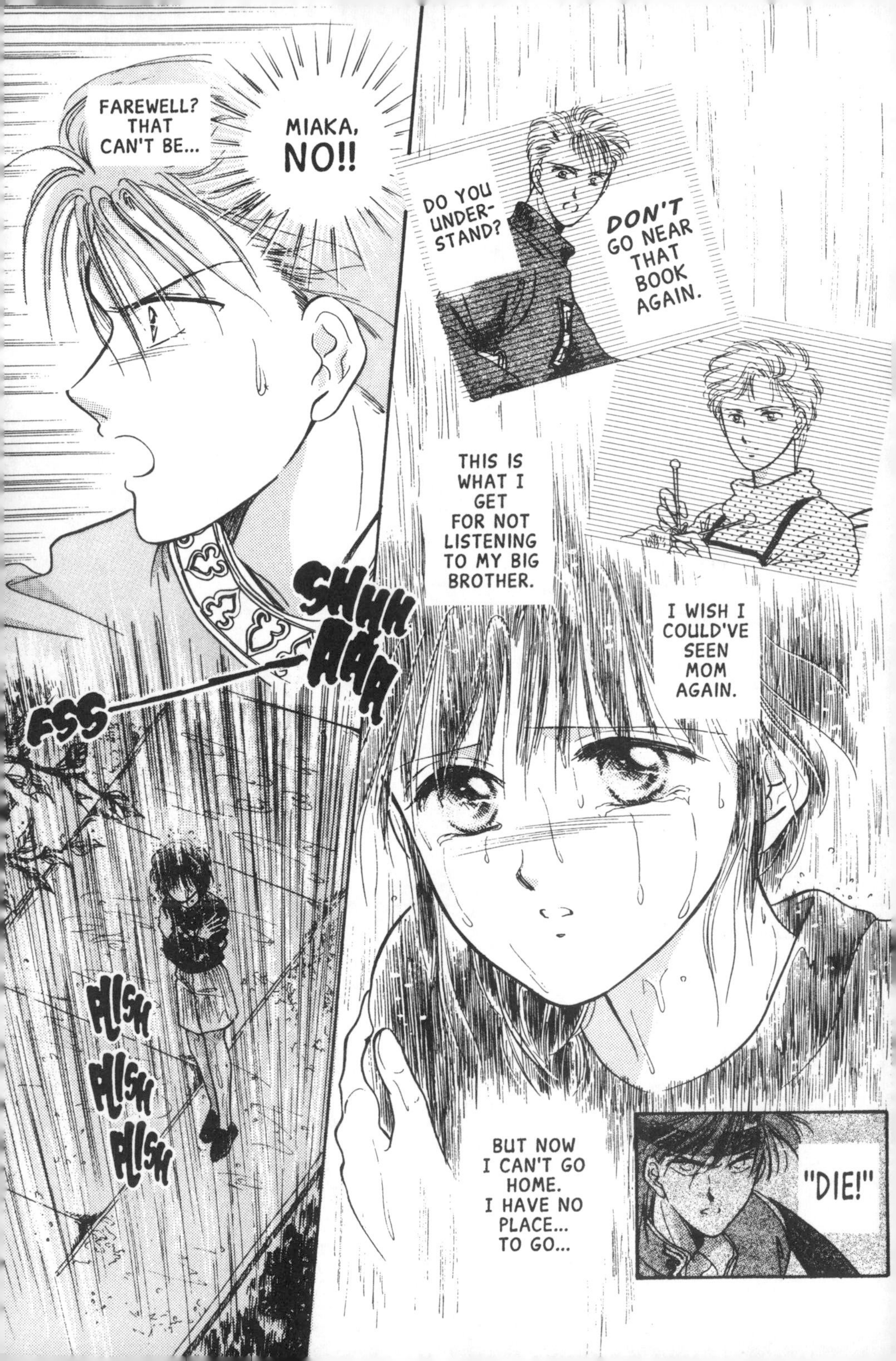

FAREWELL? THAT CAN'T BE...
MIAKA, NO!!
SHUHH AAA
FSS
PLISH PLISH PLISH
DO YOU UNDER-STAND?
DON'T GO NEAR THAT BOOK AGAIN.
THIS IS WHAT I GET FOR NOT LISTENING TO MY BIG BROTHER.
I WISH I COULD'VE SEEN MOM AGAIN.
BUT NOW I CAN'T GO HOME. I HAVE NO PLACE... TO GO...
"DIE!"

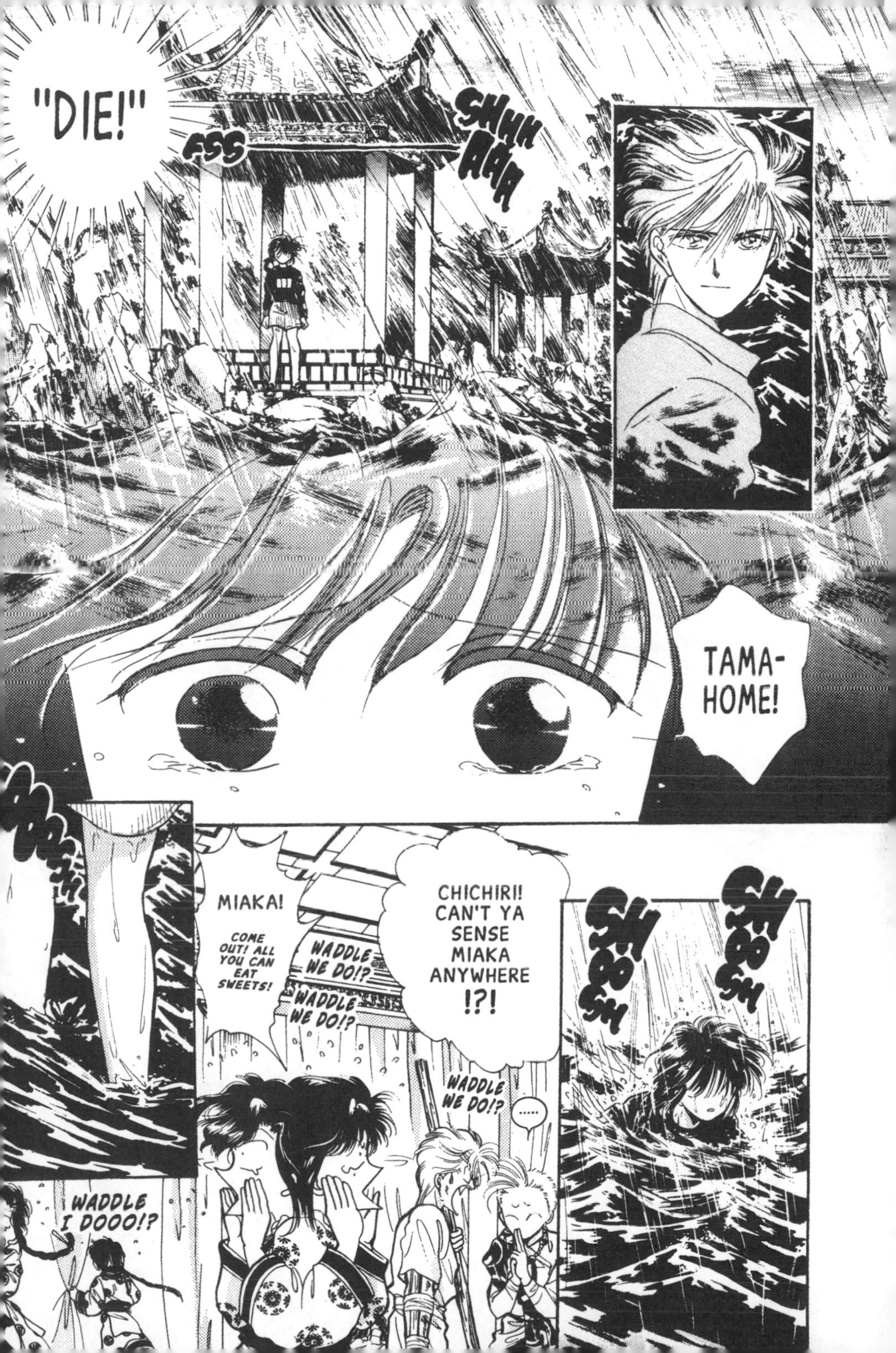
"DIE!"
FSS
SHHHAAA
TAMA-HOME!
MIAKA!
COME OUT! ALL YOU CAN EAT SWEETS!
WADDLE WE DO!?
WADDLE WE DO!?
CHICHIRI!! CAN'T YA SENSE MIAKA ANYWHERE !?!
WADDLE WE DO!?
.....
SHOOSH
SHOOSH
WADDLE I DOOO!?

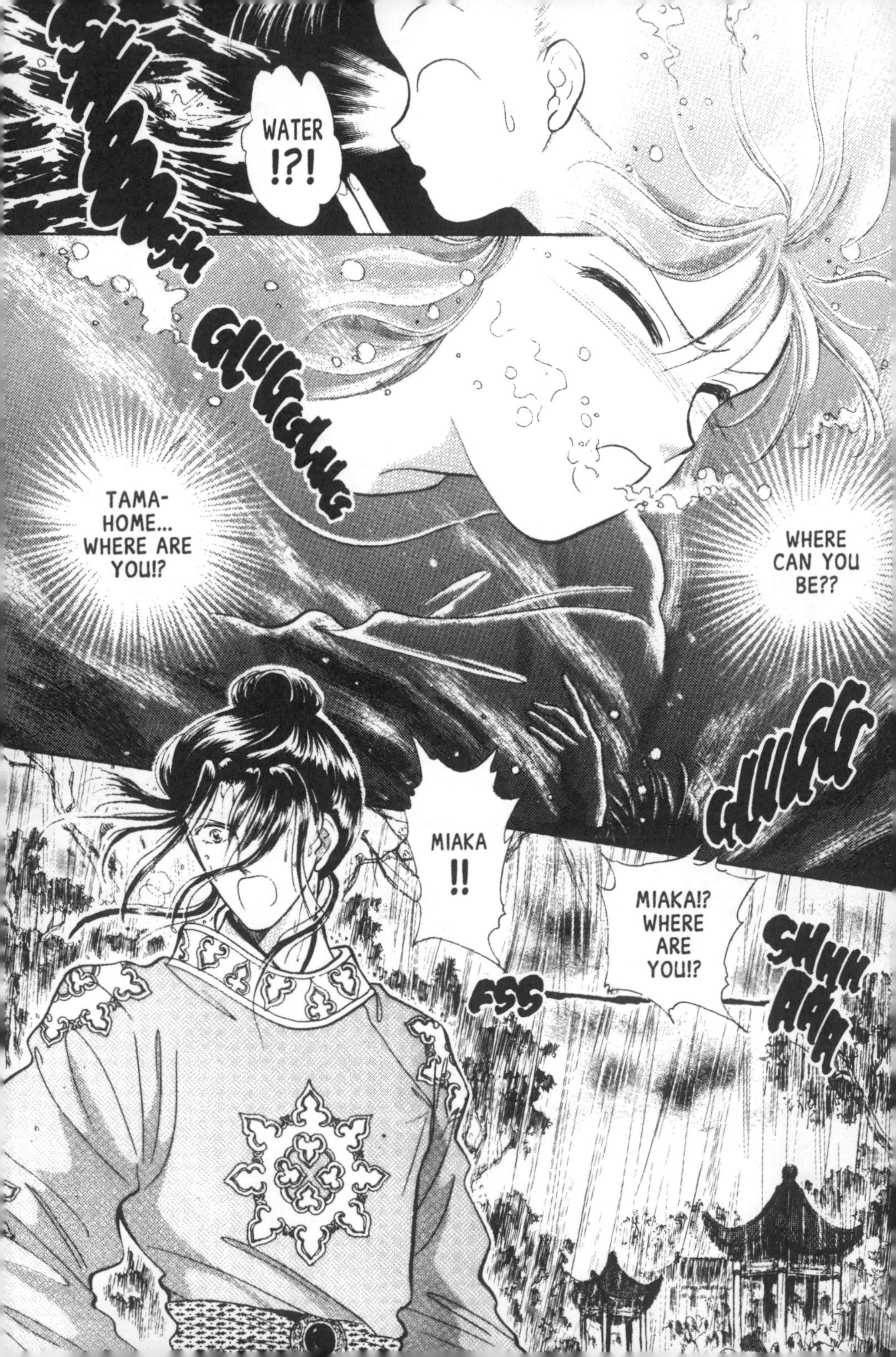
WATER !?!
TAMA-HOME... WHERE ARE YOU!?
WHERE CAN YOU BE??
MIAKA !!
MIAKA!? WHERE ARE YOU!?
FSS
SHHH AAA

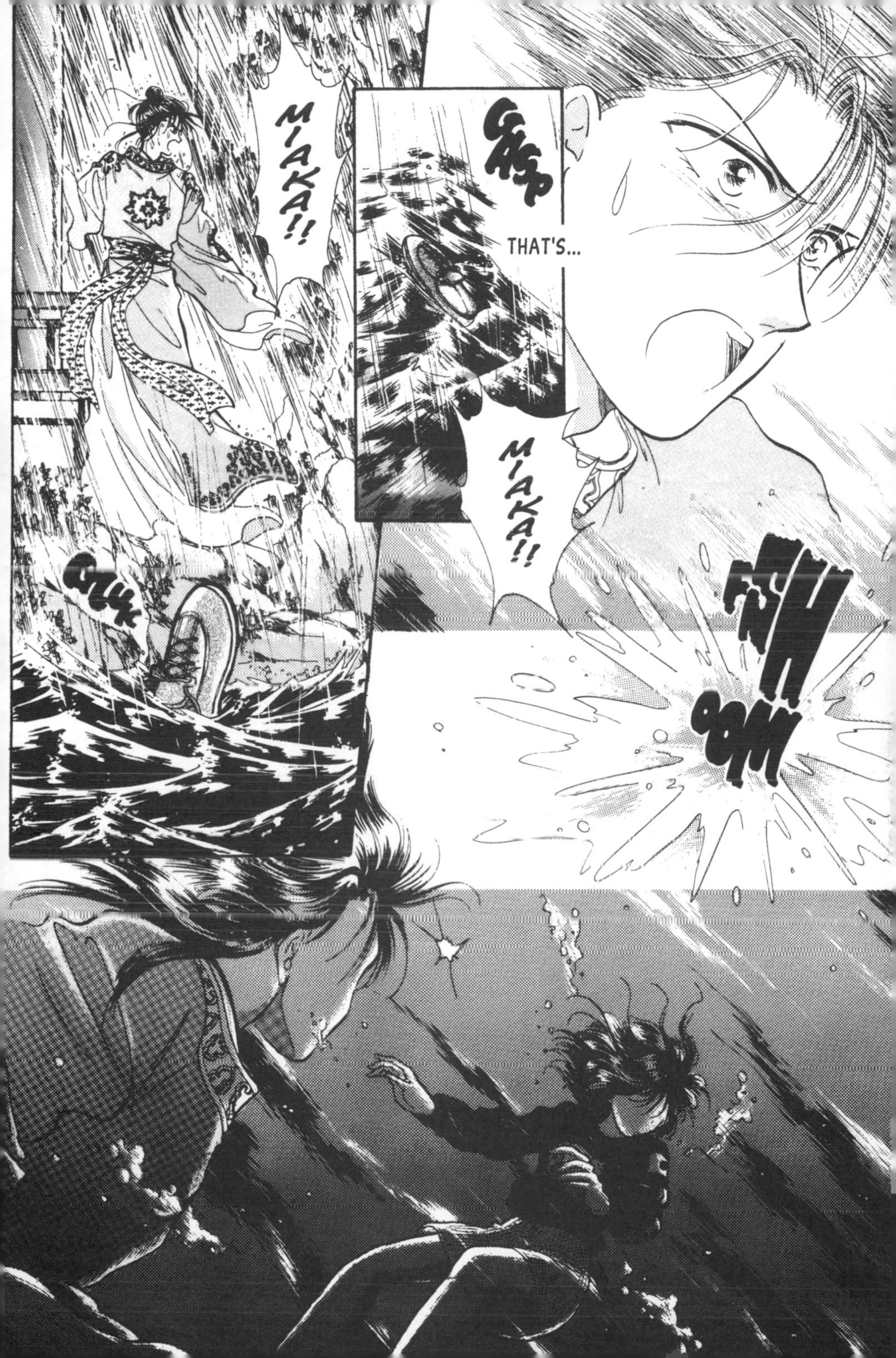
MIAKA!!
GASP
THAT'S...
MIAKA!!
FWHOOM

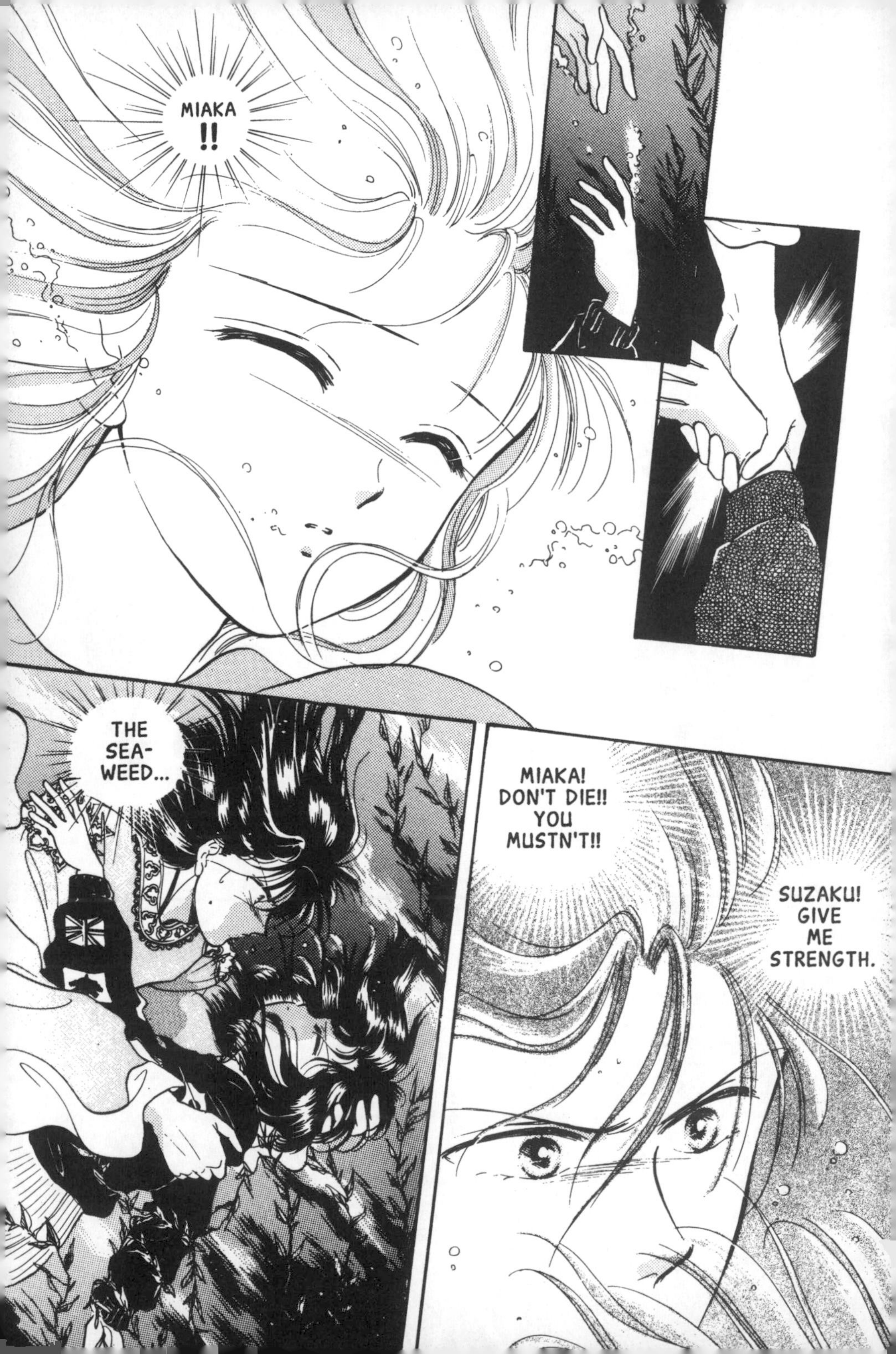
MIAKA !!
THE SEA-WEED...
MIAKA! DON'T DIE!! YOU MUSTN'T!!
SUZAKU! GIVE ME STRENGTH.

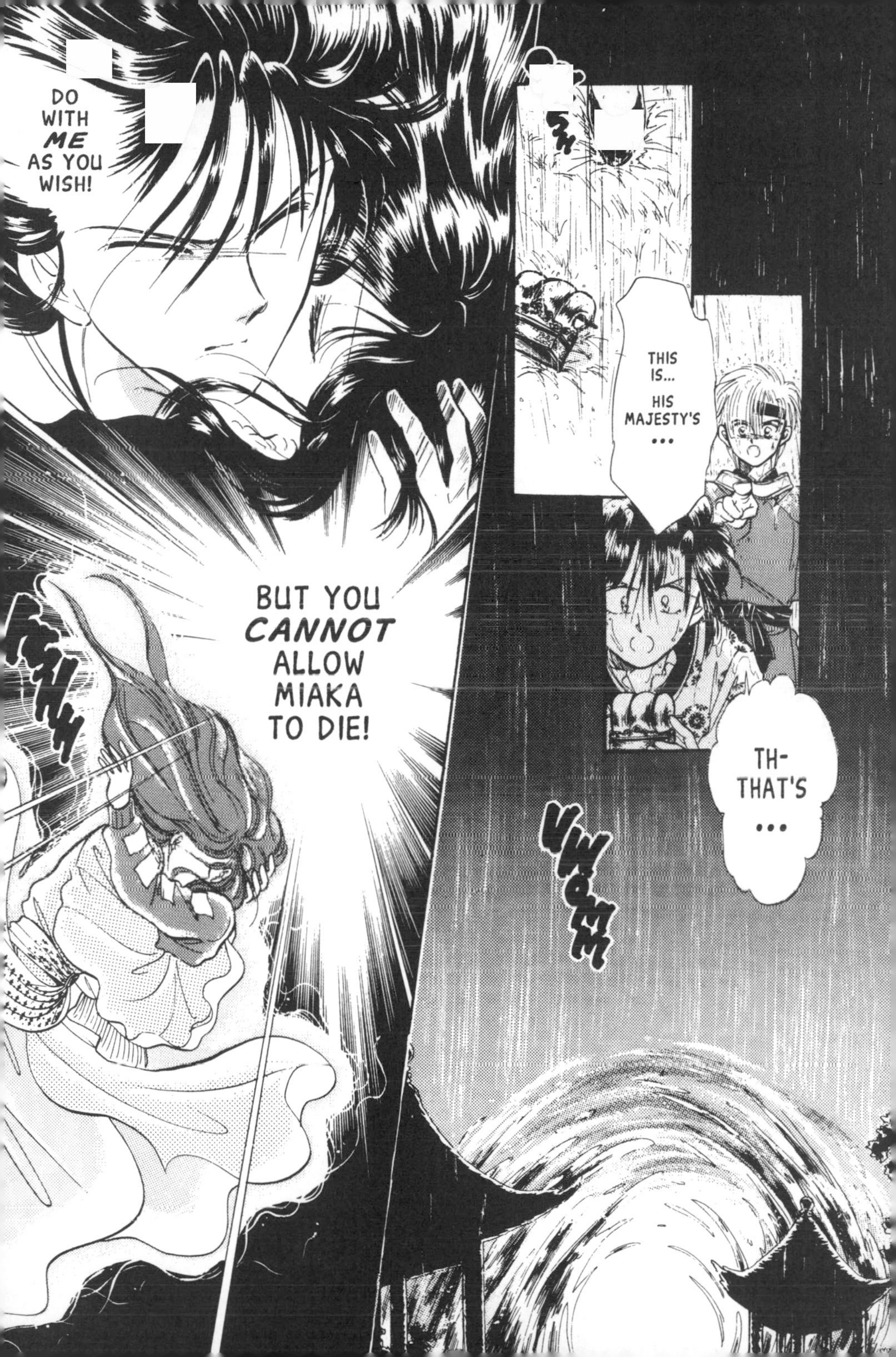
DO WITH *ME* AS YOU WISH!
BUT YOU *CANNOT* ALLOW MIAKA TO DIE!
THIS IS... HIS MAJESTY'S ...
TH- THAT'S ...

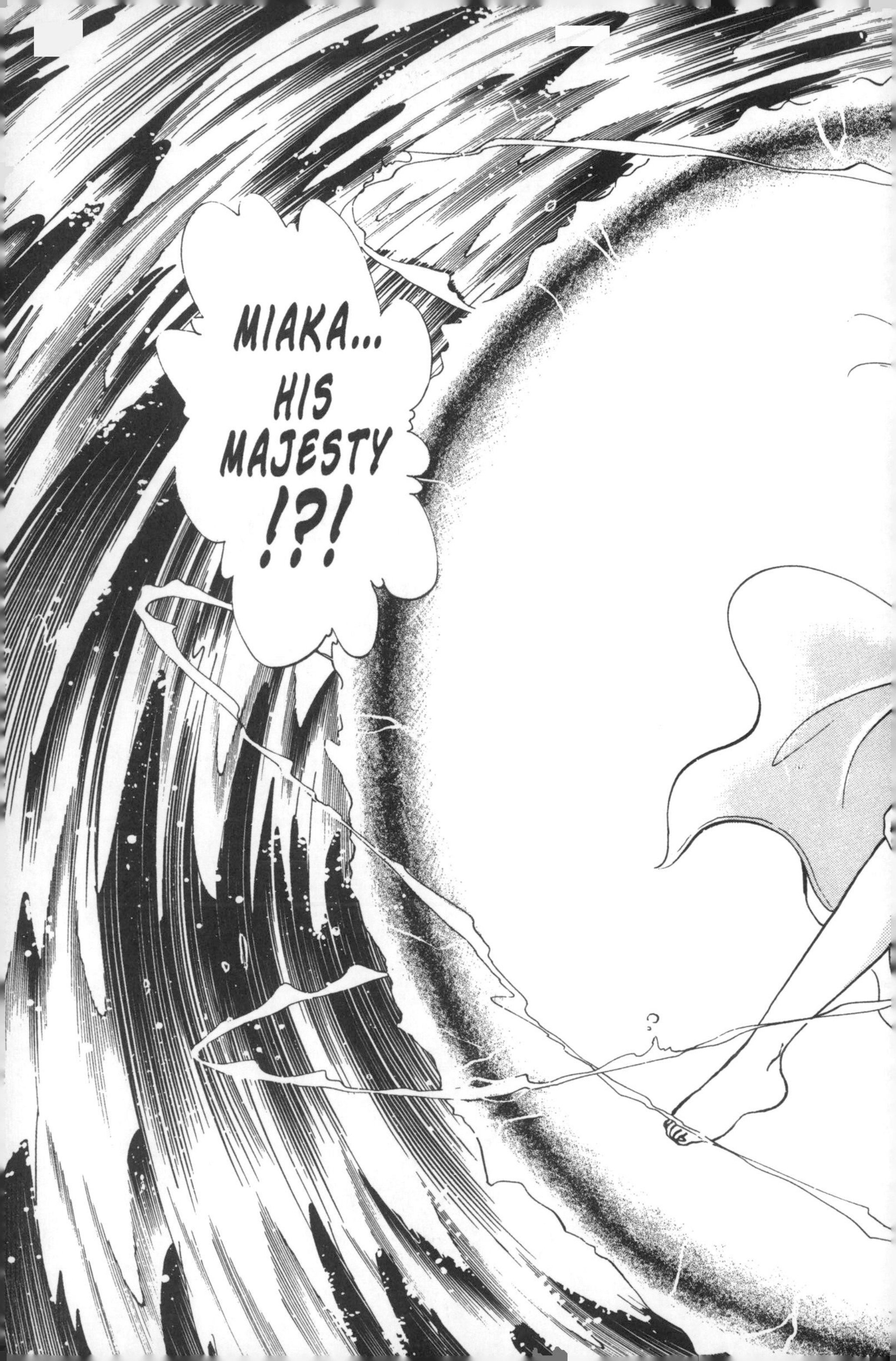
MIAKA... HIS MAJESTY !?!

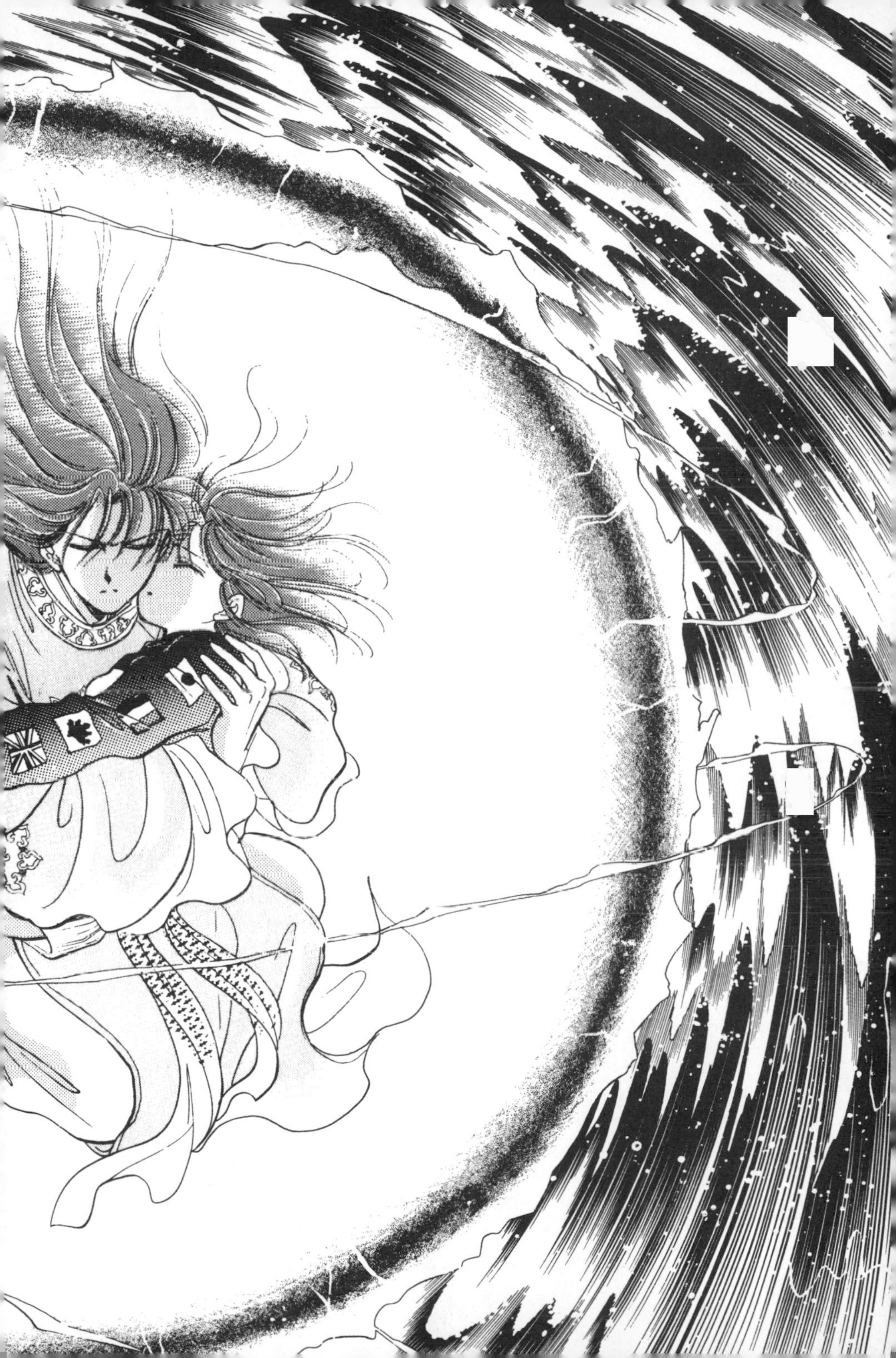

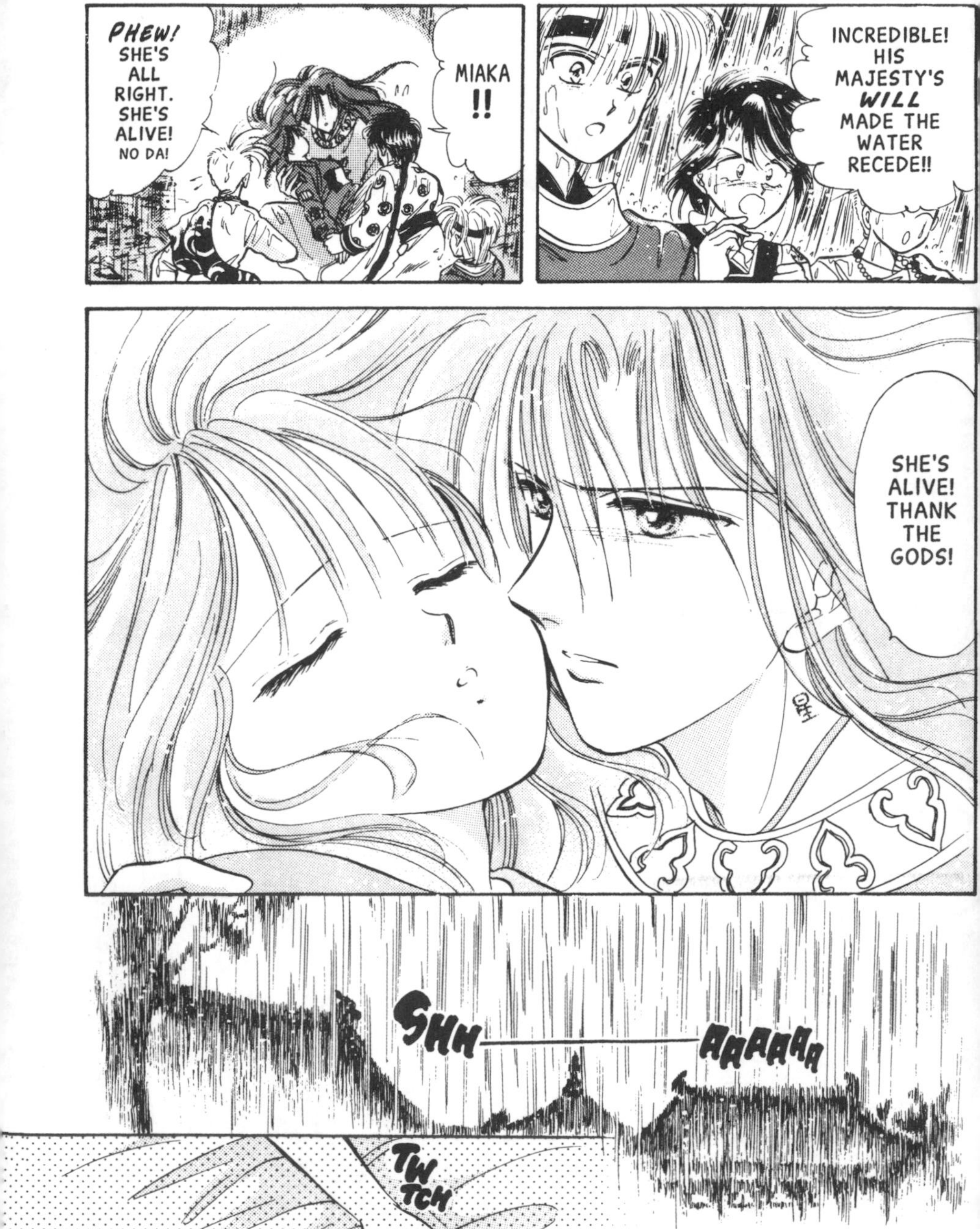
PHEW! SHE'S ALL RIGHT. SHE'S ALIVE! NO DA!
MIAKA !!
INCREDIBLE! HIS MAJESTY'S WILL MADE THE WATER RECEDE!!
SHE'S ALIVE! THANK THE GODS!
SHH——AAAAAA
TWTCH

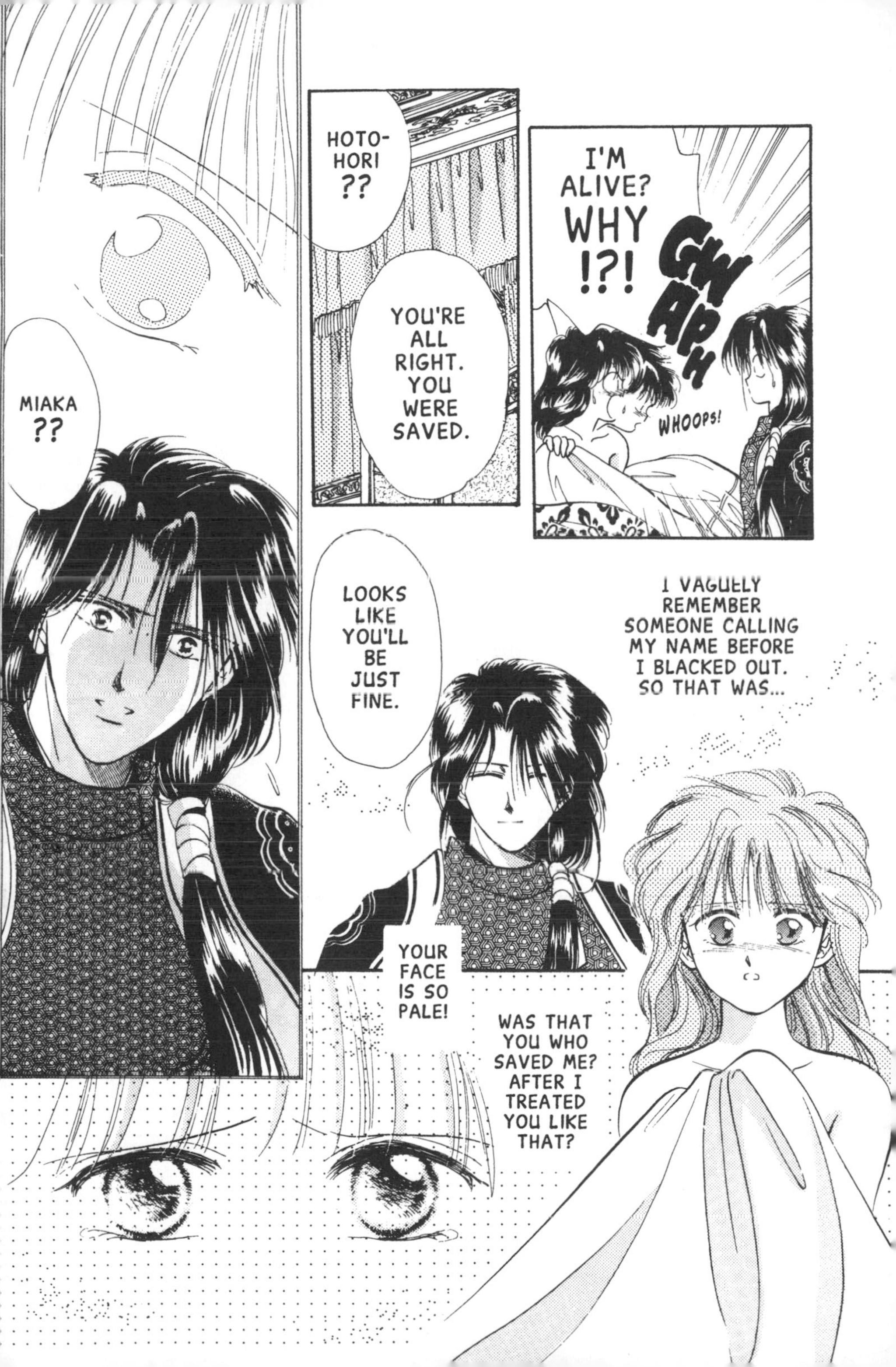
MIAKA ??
HOTO-HORI ??
YOU'RE ALL RIGHT. YOU WERE SAVED.
I'M ALIVE? WHY !?!
GWAPH
WHOOPS!
LOOKS LIKE YOU'LL BE JUST FINE.
I VAGUELY REMEMBER SOMEONE CALLING MY NAME BEFORE I BLACKED OUT. SO THAT WAS...
YOUR FACE IS SO PALE!
WAS THAT YOU WHO SAVED ME? AFTER I TREATED YOU LIKE THAT?

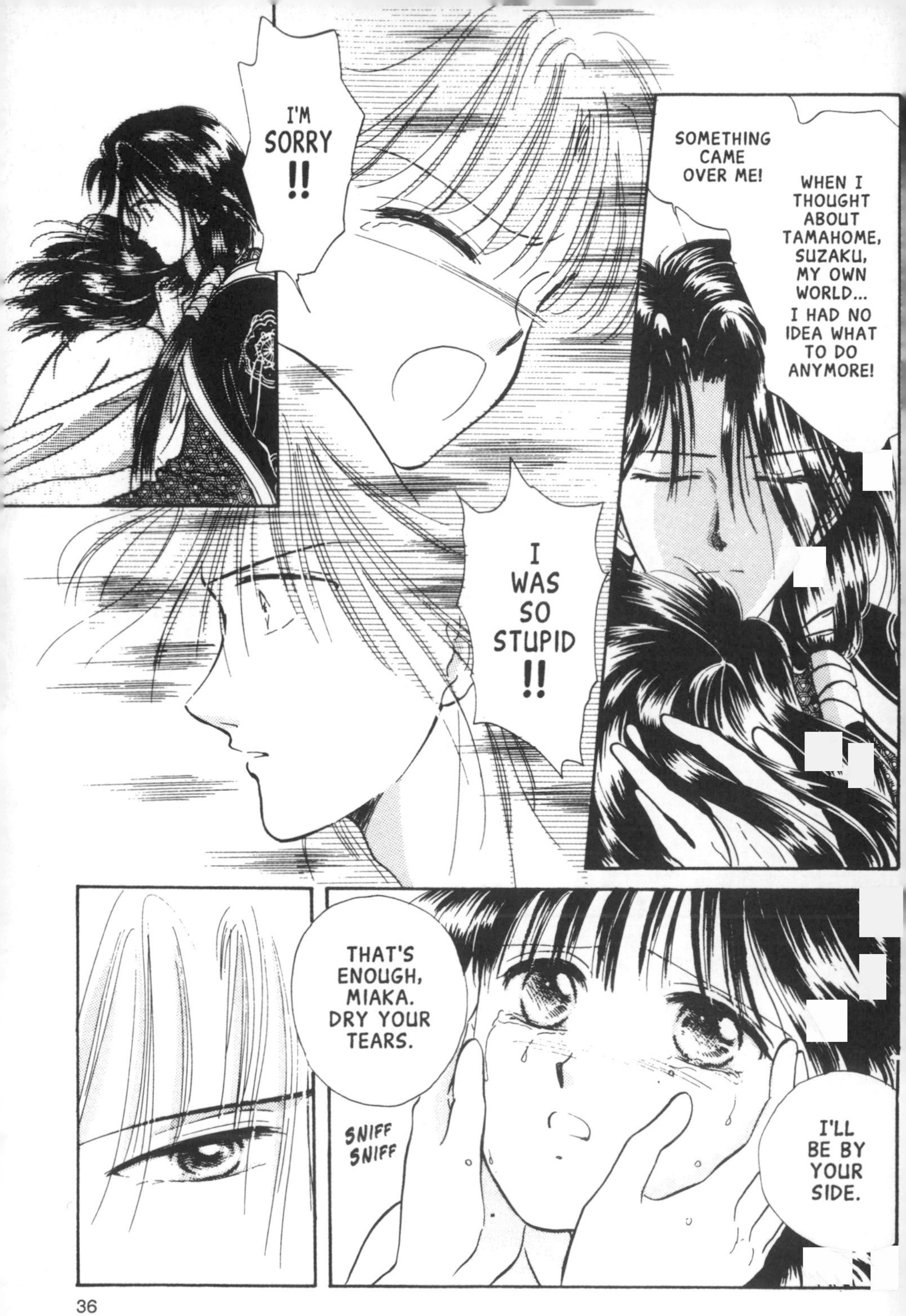
I'M SORRY!!
I WAS SO STUPID!!
SOMETHING CAME OVER ME!
WHEN I THOUGHT ABOUT TAMAHOME, SUZAKU, MY OWN WORLD... I HAD NO IDEA WHAT TO DO ANYMORE!
THAT'S ENOUGH, MIAKA. DRY YOUR TEARS.
SNIFF SNIFF
I'LL BE BY YOUR SIDE.

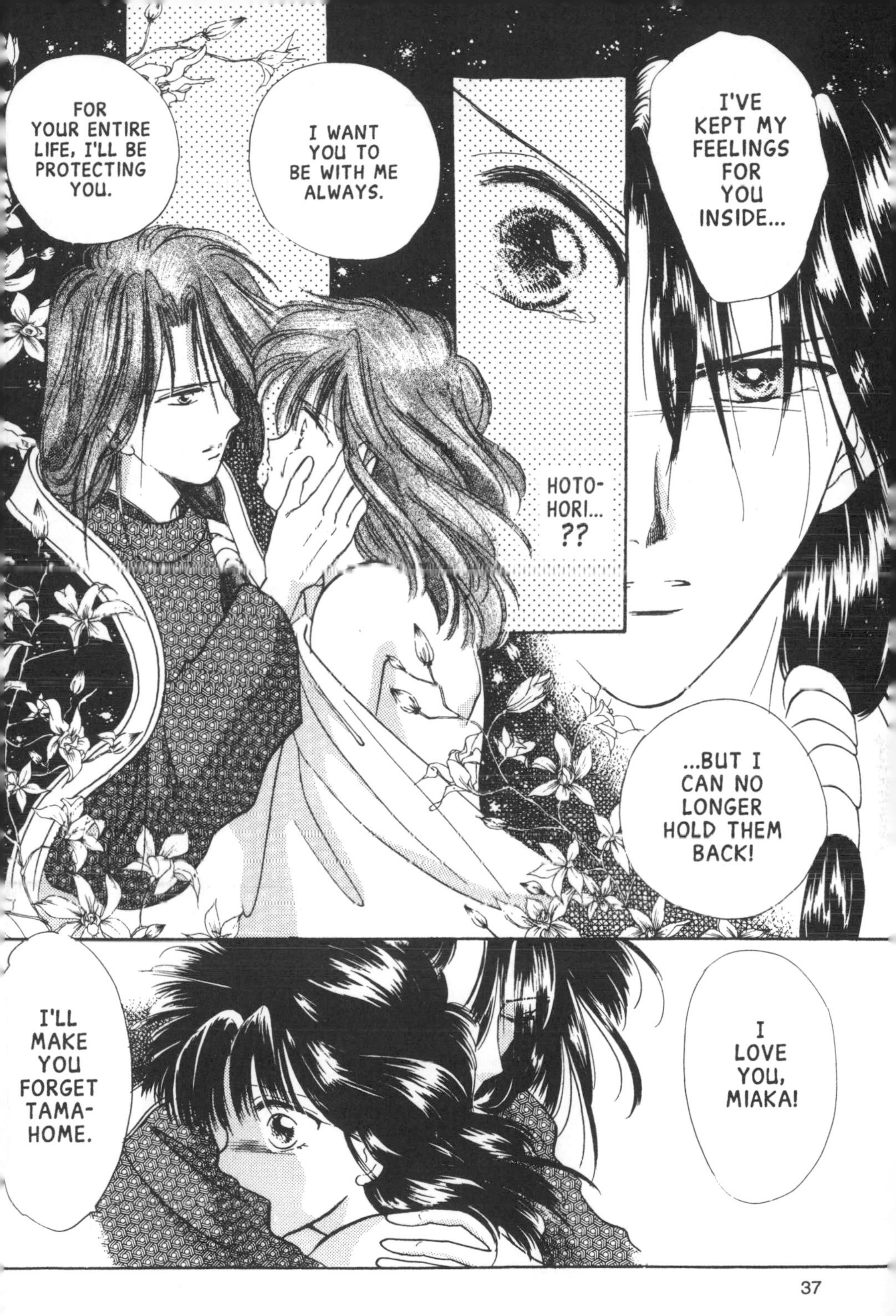

FOR YOUR ENTIRE LIFE, I'LL BE PROTECTING YOU.
I WANT YOU TO BE WITH ME ALWAYS.
HOTO-HORI... ??
I'VE KEPT MY FEELINGS FOR YOU INSIDE...
...BUT I CAN NO LONGER HOLD THEM BACK!
I'LL MAKE YOU FORGET TAMA-HOME.
I LOVE YOU, MIAKA!

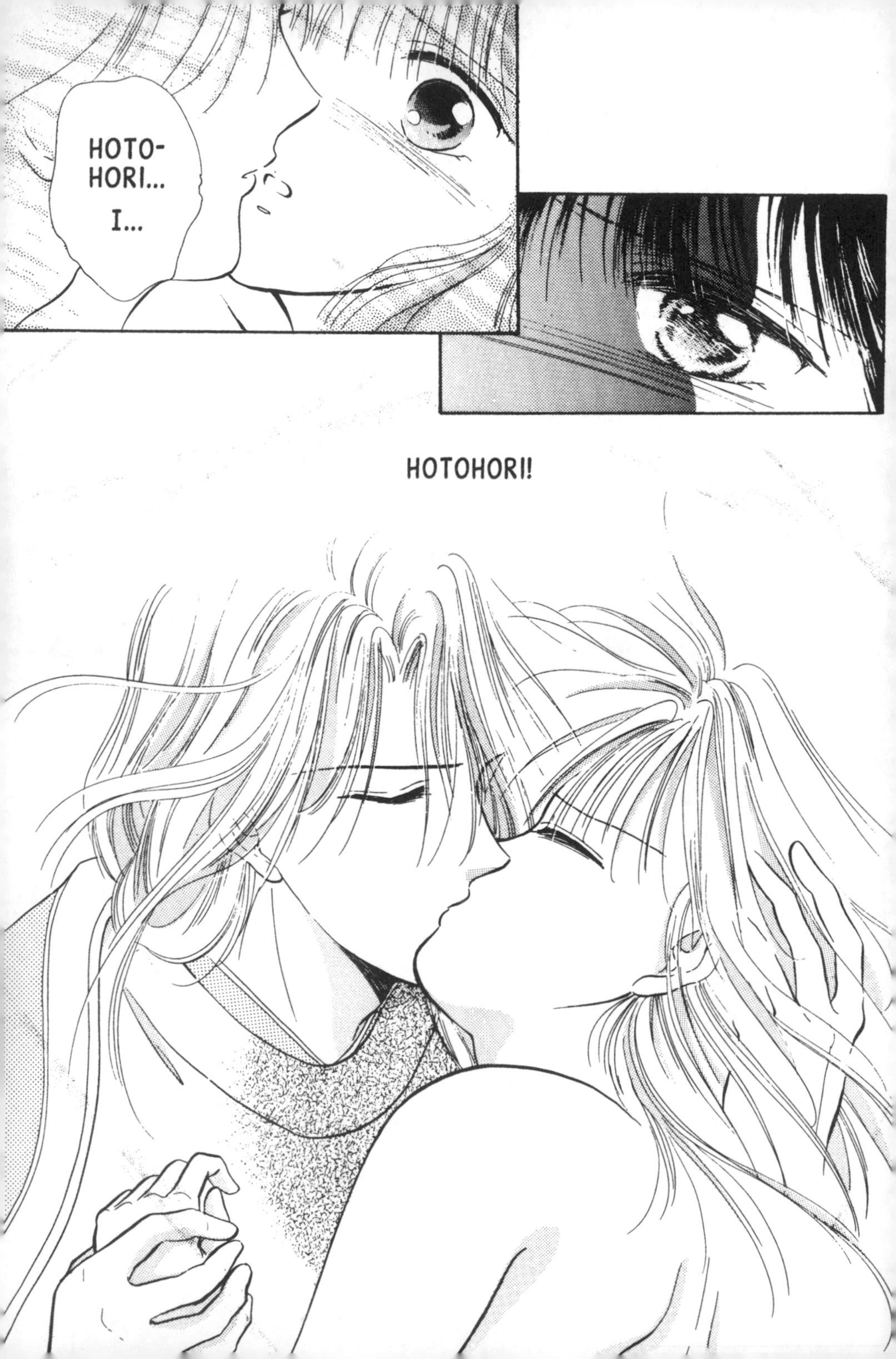
HOTO-
HORI...
I...
HOTOHORI!

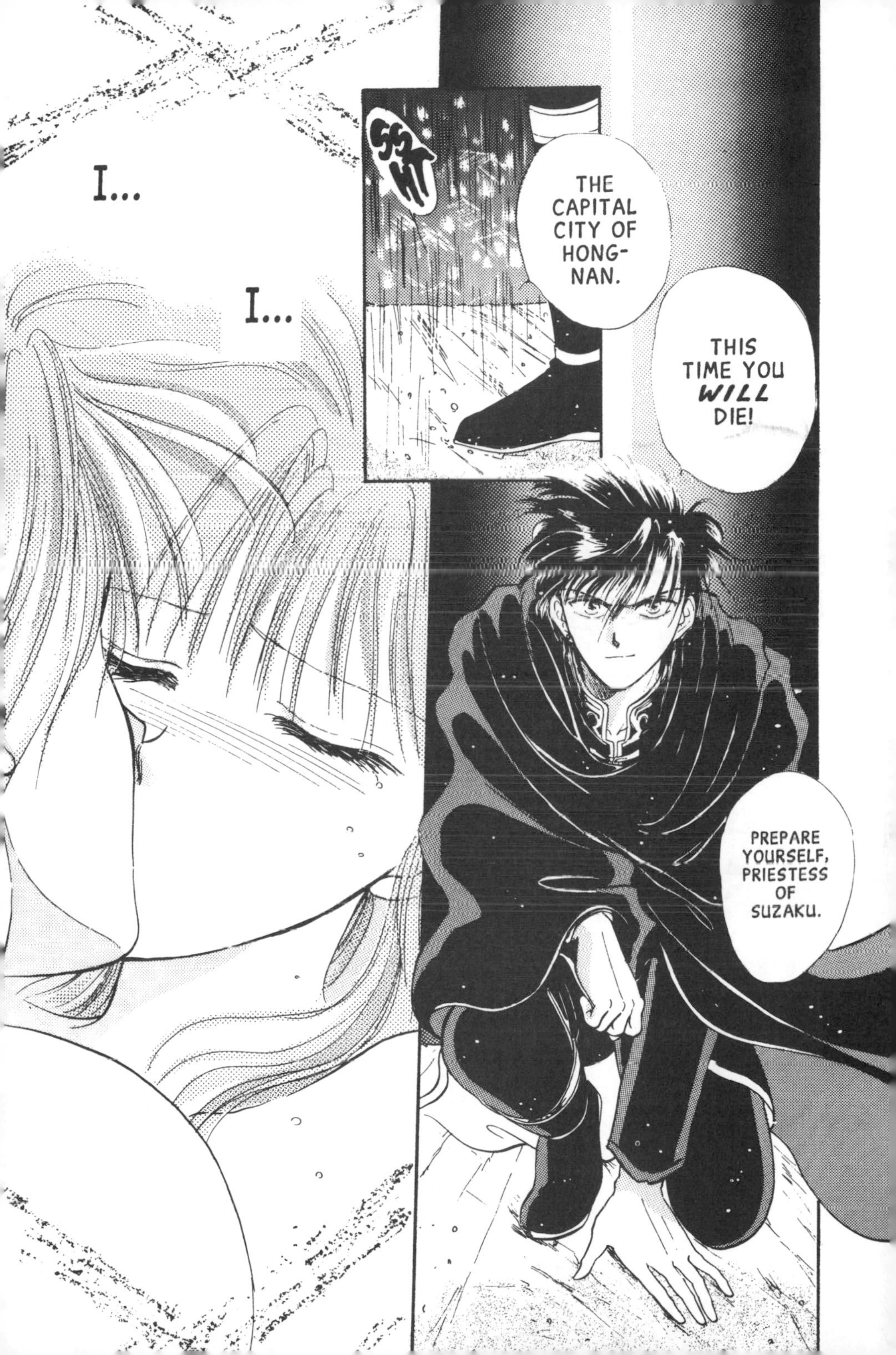
I...
I...
THE CAPITAL CITY OF HONG-NAN.
THIS TIME YOU WILL DIE!
PREPARE YOURSELF, PRIESTESS OF SUZAKU.

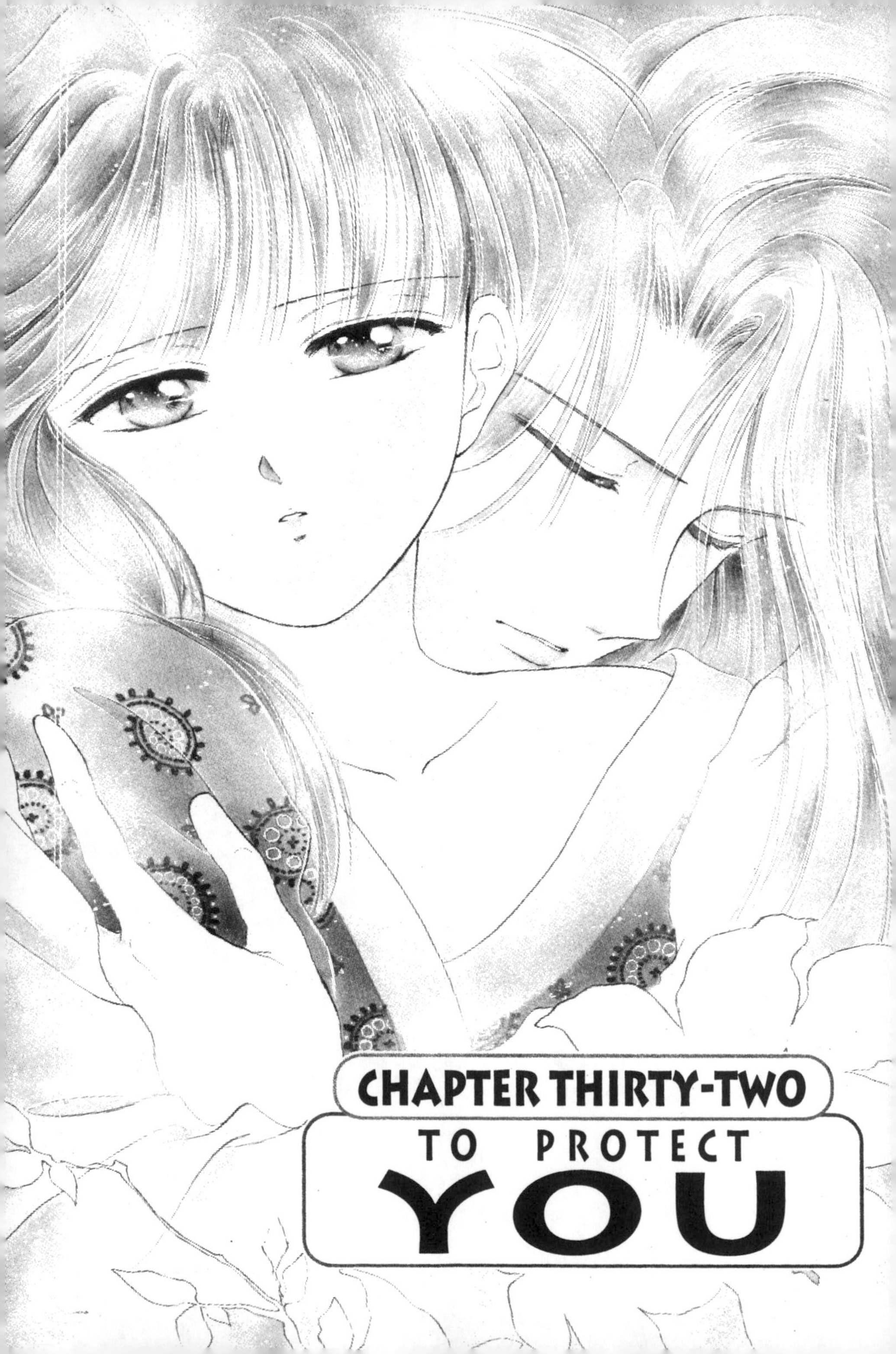
CHAPTER THIRTY-TWO
TO PROTECT
YOU

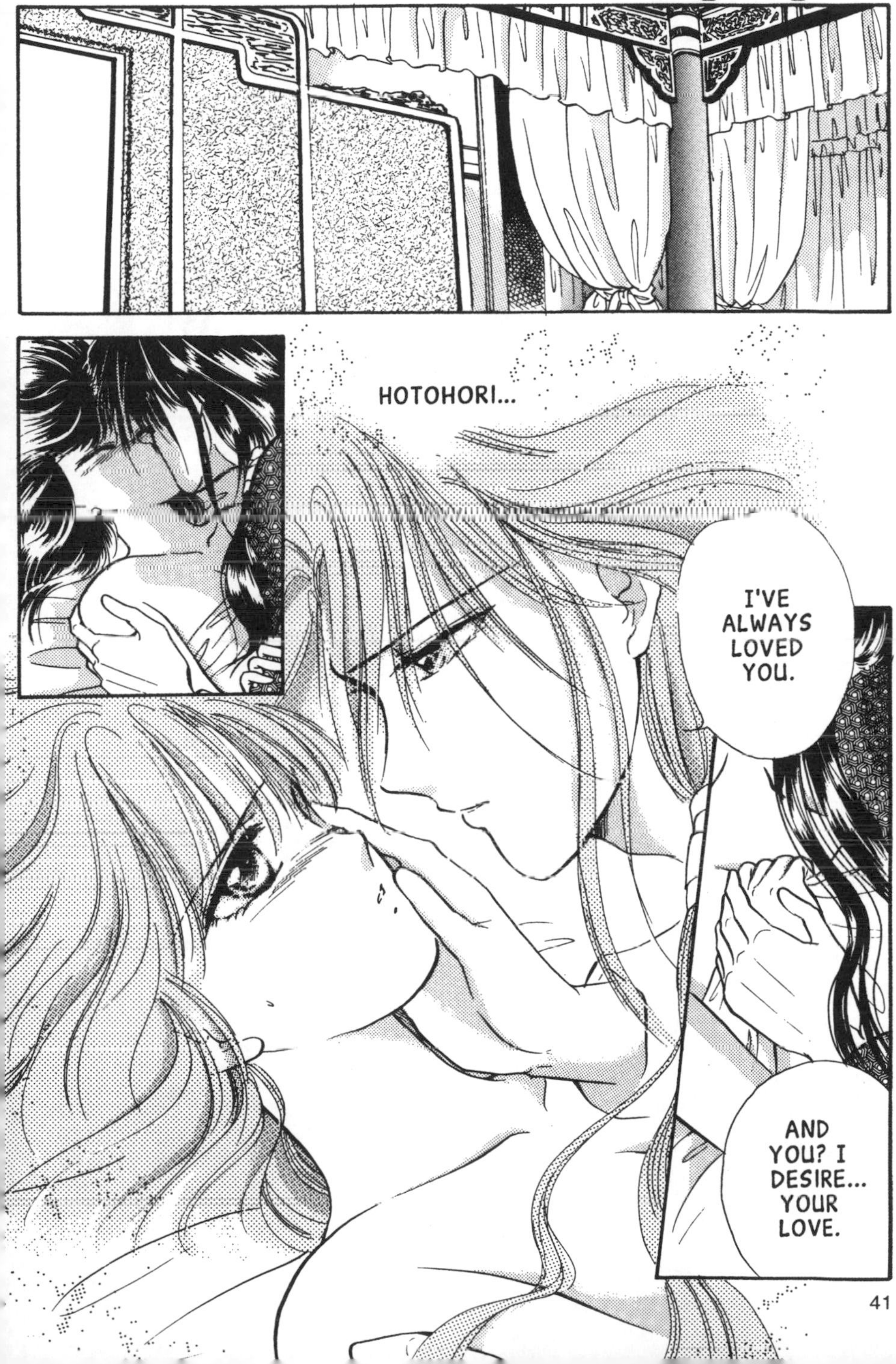
HOTOHORI...
I'VE ALWAYS LOVED YOU.
AND YOU? I DESIRE... YOUR LOVE.

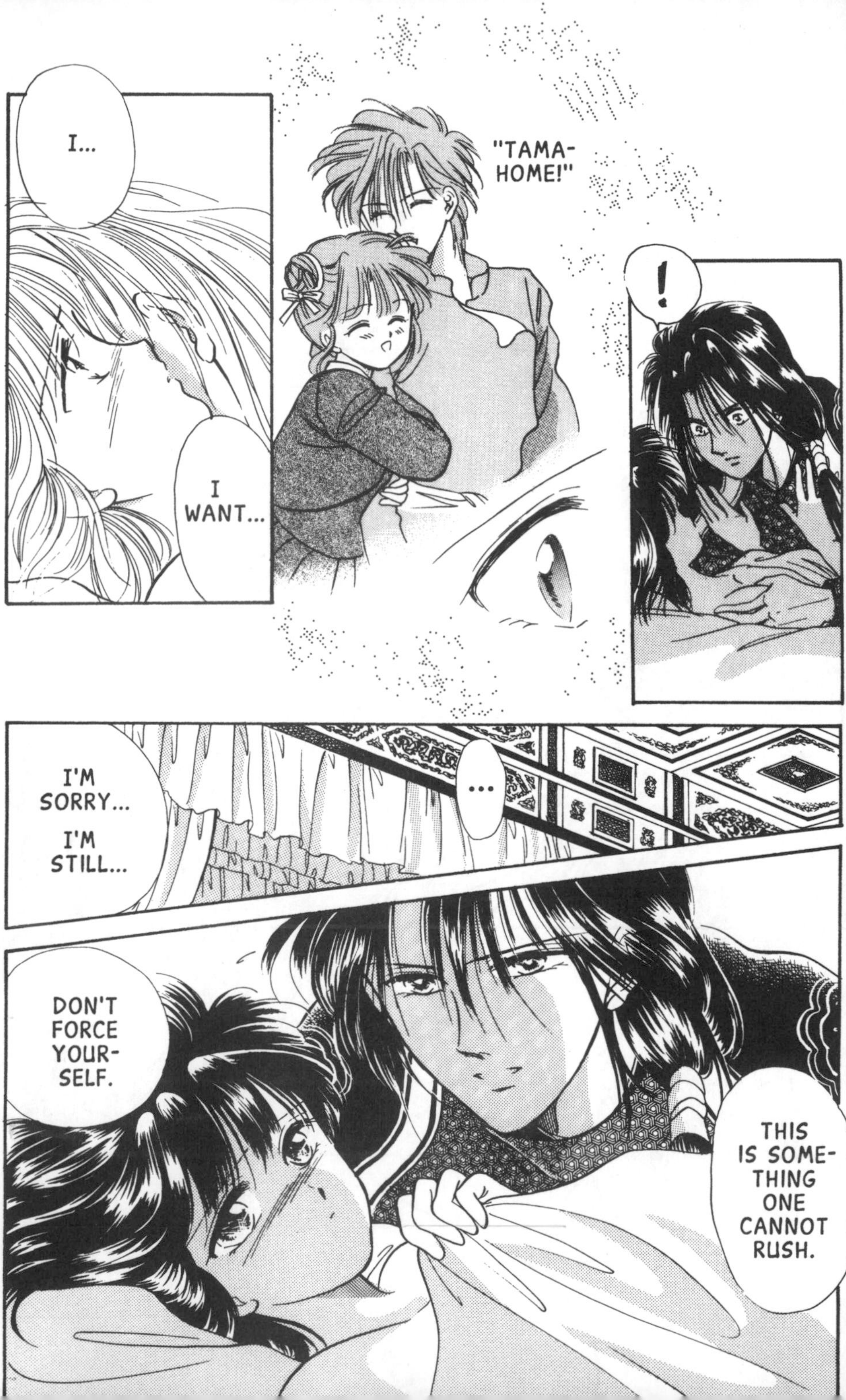
I...
I WANT...
"TAMA-HOME!"
!
I'M SORRY...
I'M STILL...
...
DON'T FORCE YOURSELF.
THIS IS SOMETHING ONE CANNOT RUSH.

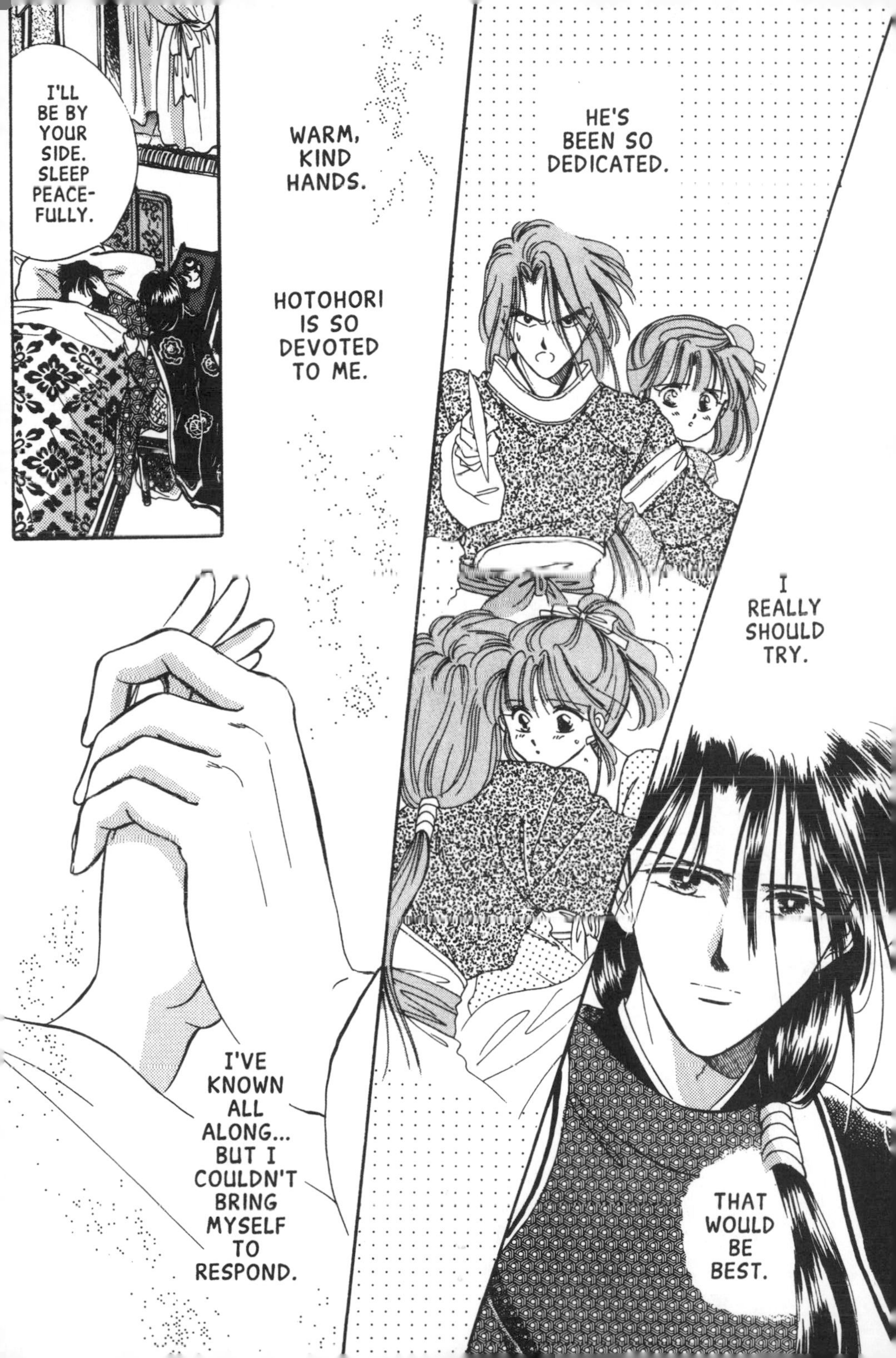
I'LL BE BY YOUR SIDE. SLEEP PEACE-FULLY.
WARM, KIND HANDS.
HOTOHORI IS SO DEVOTED TO ME.
I'VE KNOWN ALL ALONG... BUT I COULDN'T BRING MYSELF TO RESPOND.
HE'S BEEN SO DEDICATED.
I REALLY SHOULD TRY.
THAT WOULD BE BEST.

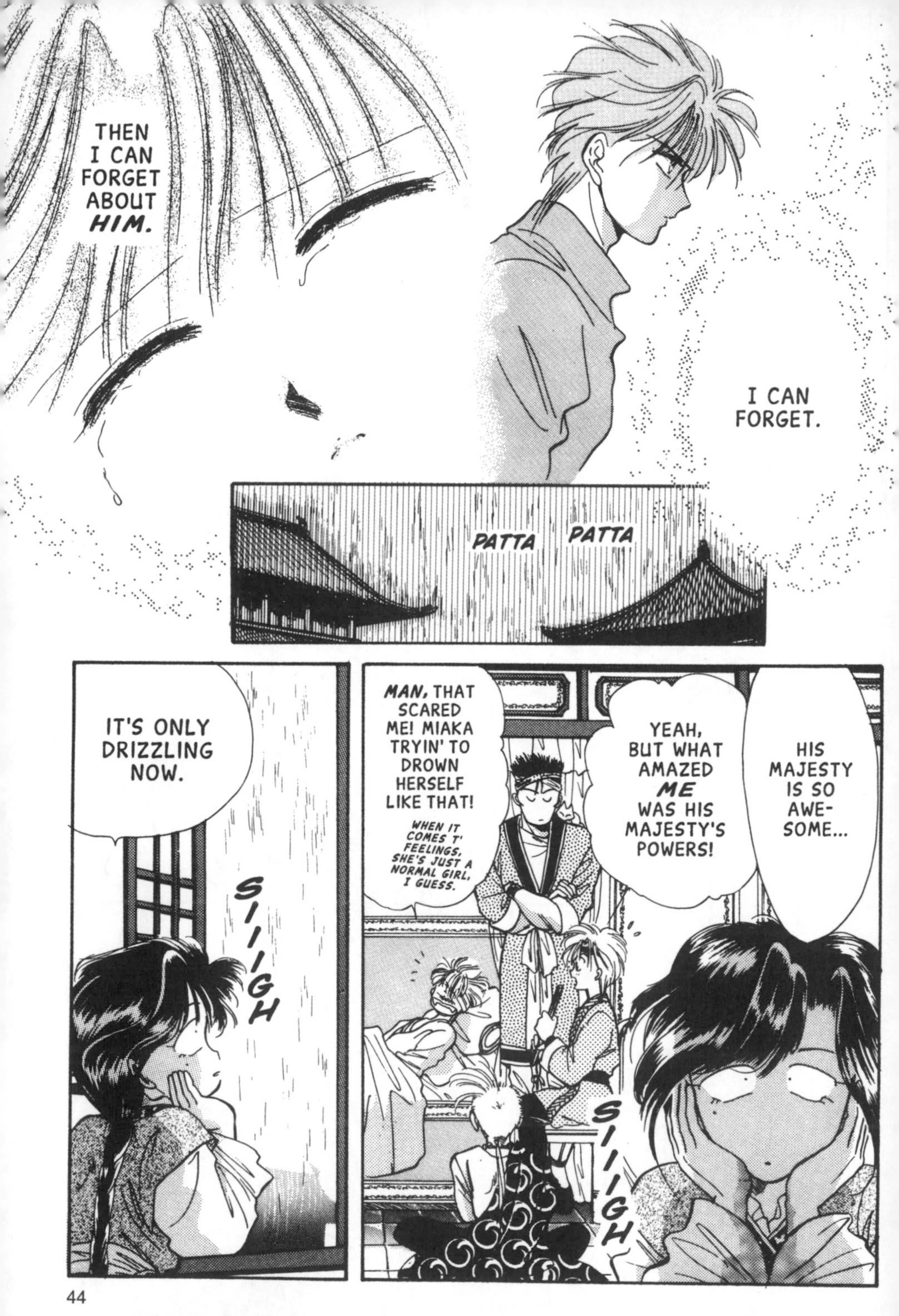
THEN I CAN FORGET ABOUT ***HIM.***
I CAN FORGET.
PATTA PATTA
IT'S ONLY DRIZZLING NOW.
SIIIGH
MAN, THAT SCARED ME! MIAKA TRYIN' TO DROWN HERSELF LIKE THAT!
WHEN IT COMES T' FEELINGS, SHE'S JUST A NORMAL GIRL, I GUESS.
YEAH, BUT WHAT AMAZED ***ME*** WAS HIS MAJESTY'S POWERS!
HIS MAJESTY IS SO AWE-SOME...
SIIIGH

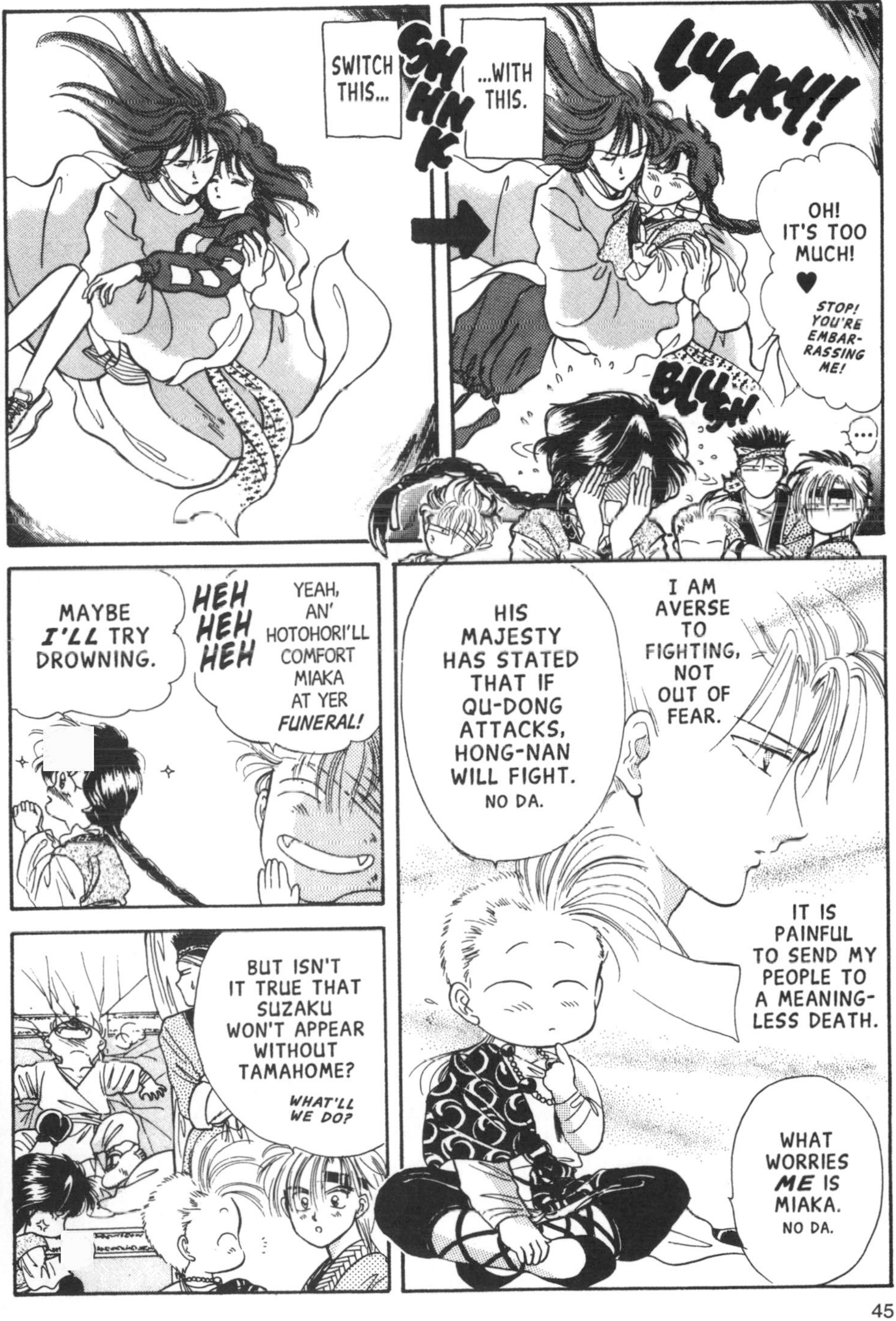
SWITCH THIS...
SHHNK
...WITH THIS.
LUCKY!
OH! IT'S TOO MUCH! ♥
STOP! YOU'RE EMBARRASSING ME!
BLUSH
...
MAYBE I'LL TRY DROWNING.
HEH HEH HEH
YEAH, AN' HOTOHORI'LL COMFORT MIAKA AT YER FUNERAL!
BUT ISN'T IT TRUE THAT SUZAKU WON'T APPEAR WITHOUT TAMAHOME?
WHAT'LL WE DO?
HIS MAJESTY HAS STATED THAT IF QU-DONG ATTACKS, HONG-NAN WILL FIGHT. NO DA.
I AM AVERSE TO FIGHTING, NOT OUT OF FEAR.
IT IS PAINFUL TO SEND MY PEOPLE TO A MEANINGLESS DEATH.
WHAT WORRIES ME IS MIAKA. NO DA.

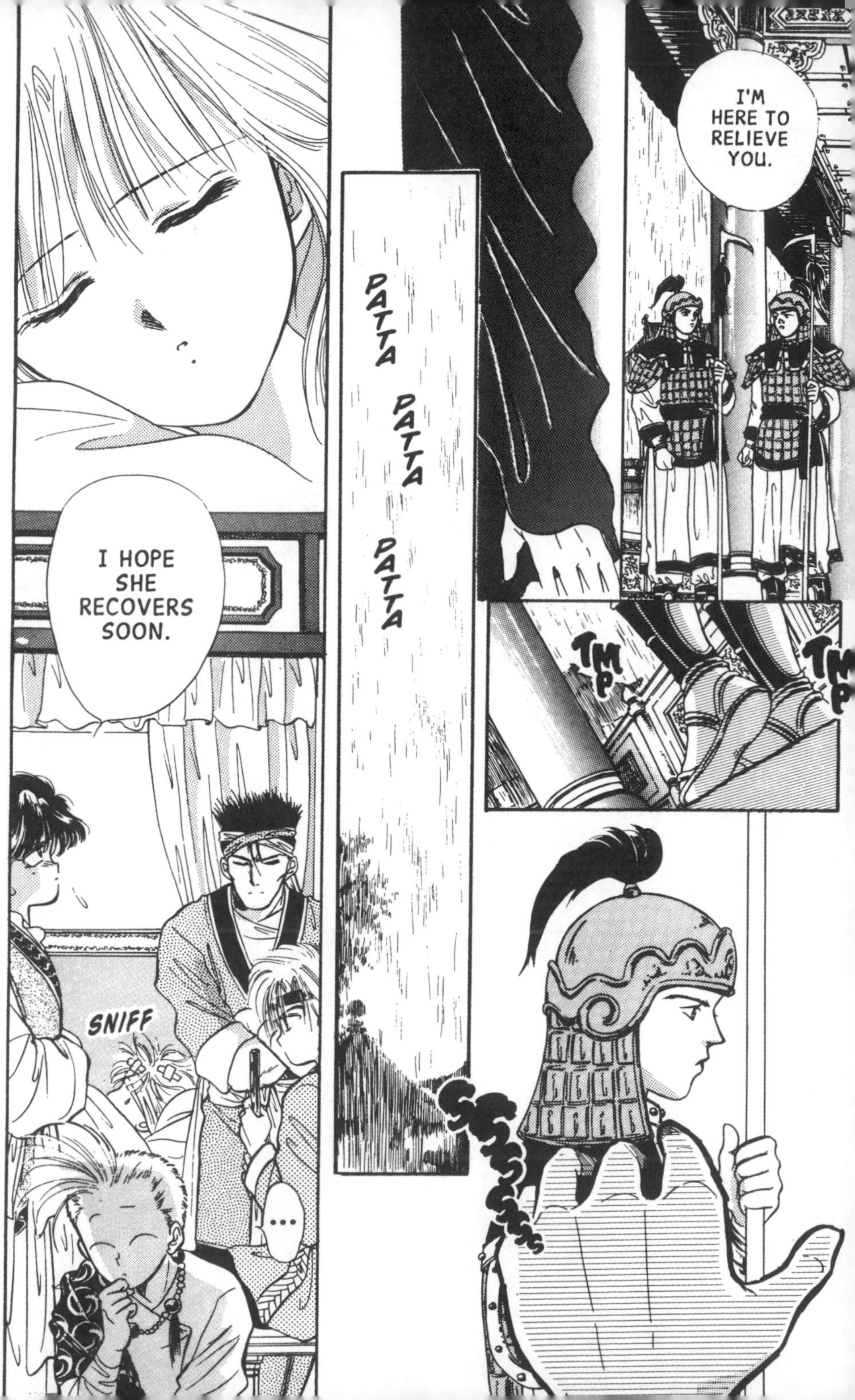
I HOPE SHE RECOVERS SOON.
SNIFF
...
PATTA PATTA PATTA
I'M HERE TO RELIEVE YOU.
TMP
TMP
SSSSSS

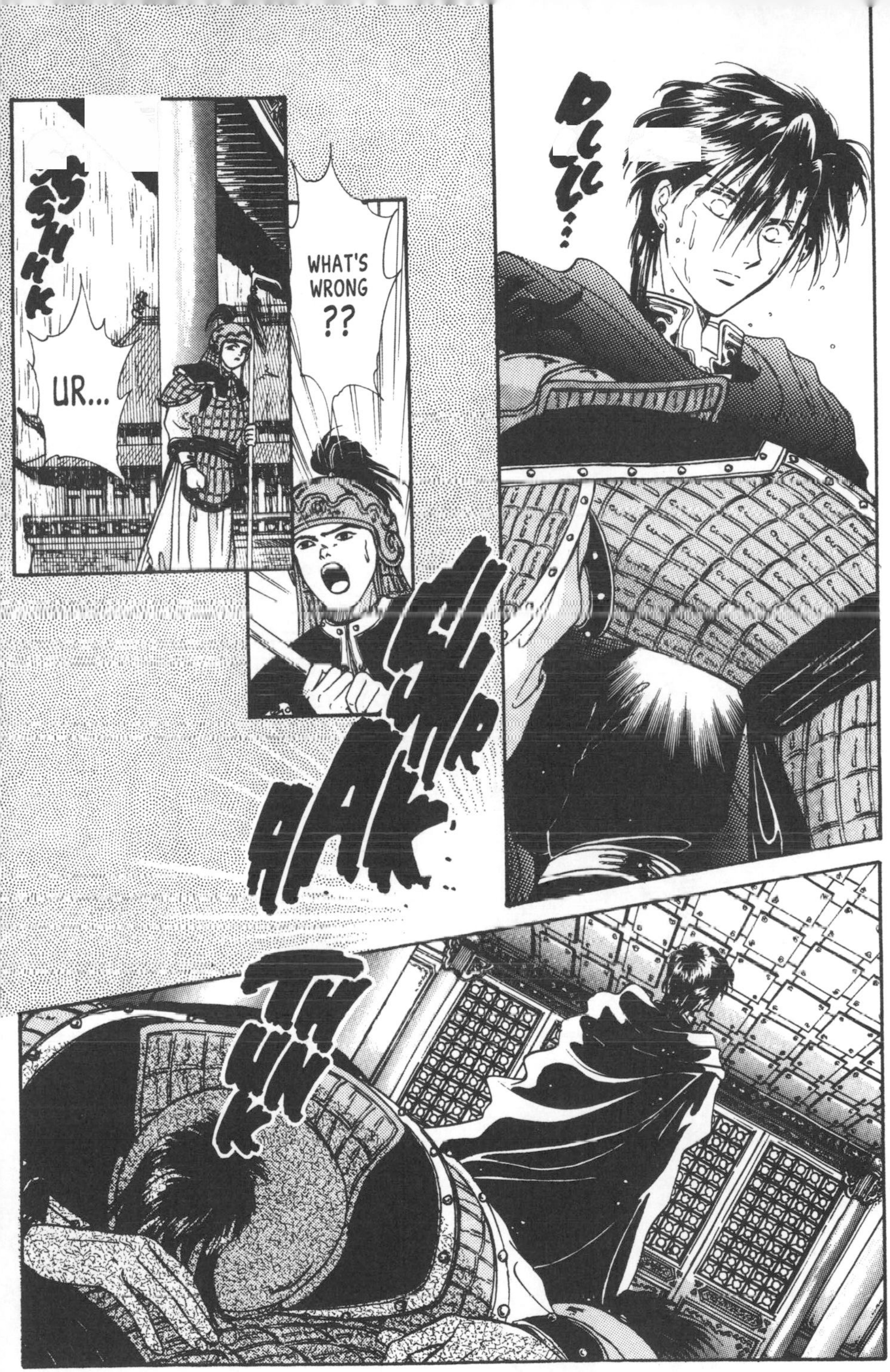
UR...
WHAT'S WRONG ??
THUNK

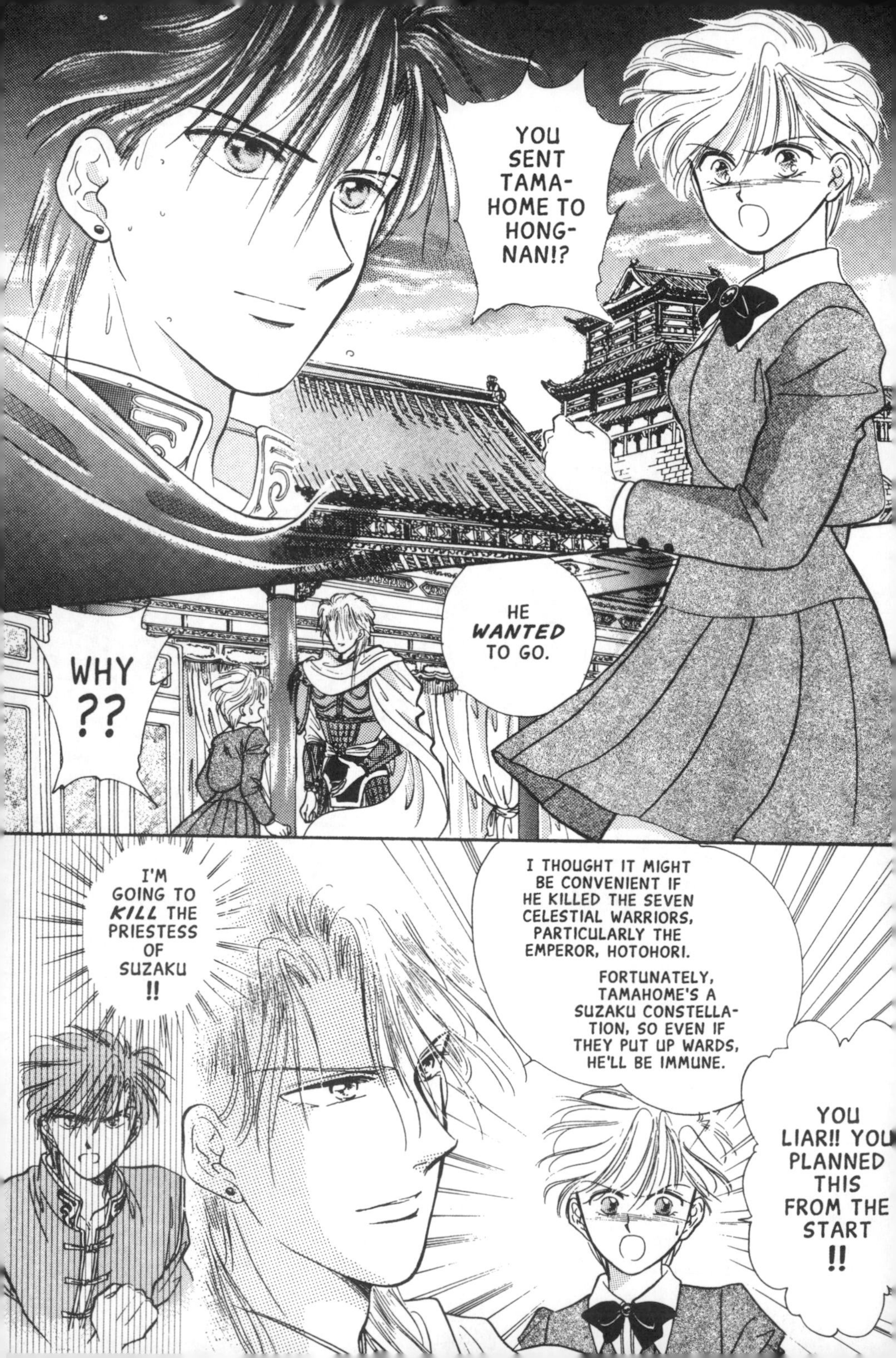
YOU SENT TAMA-HOME TO HONG-NAN!?
WHY ??
HE *WANTED* TO GO.
I'M GOING TO *KILL* THE PRIESTESS OF SUZAKU !!
I THOUGHT IT MIGHT BE CONVENIENT IF HE KILLED THE SEVEN CELESTIAL WARRIORS, PARTICULARLY THE EMPEROR, HOTOHORI.
FORTUNATELY, TAMAHOME'S A SUZAKU CONSTELLA-TION, SO EVEN IF THEY PUT UP WARDS, HE'LL BE IMMUNE.
YOU LIAR!! YOU PLANNED THIS FROM THE START !!

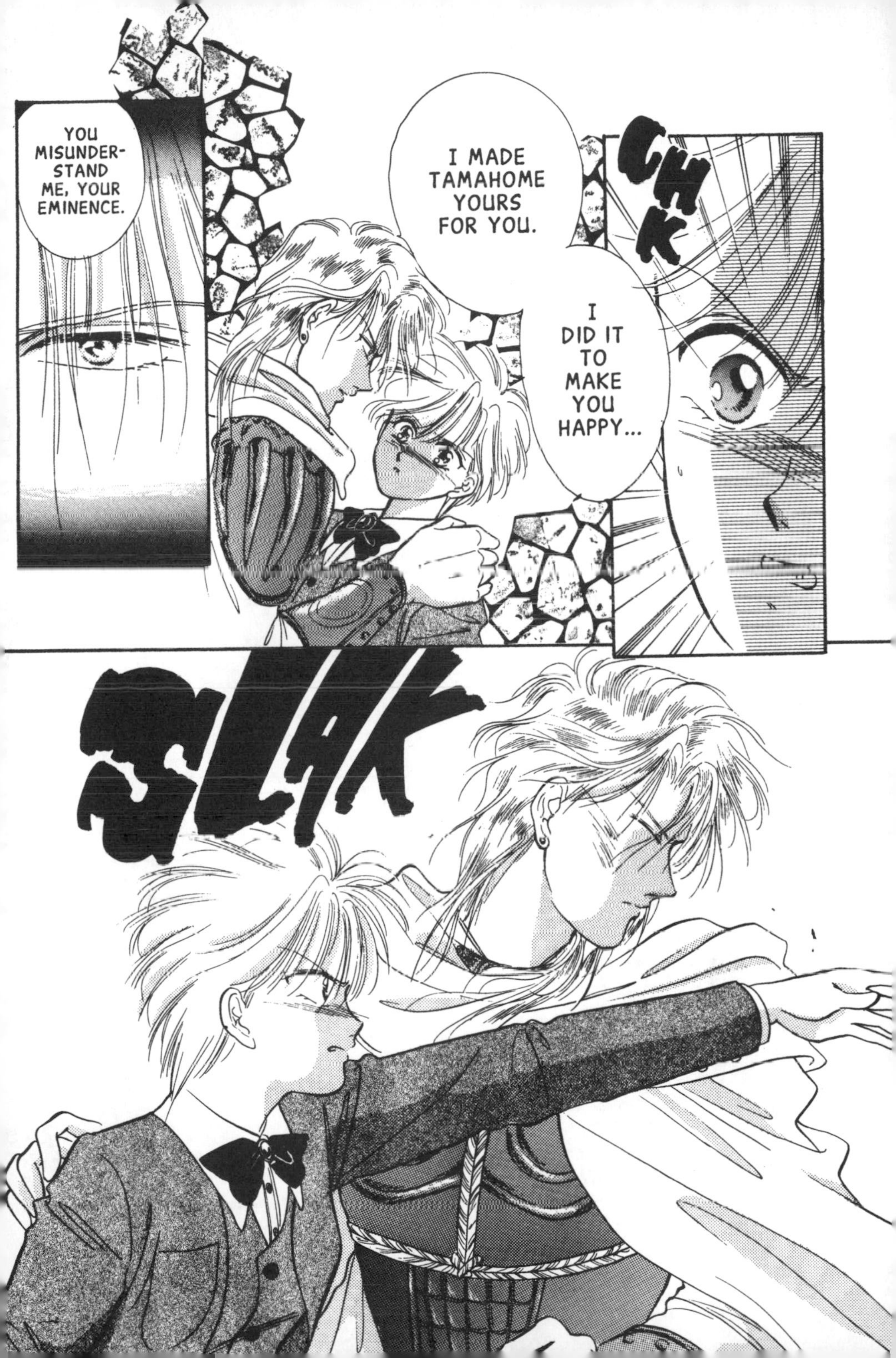
YOU MISUNDER-STAND ME, YOUR EMINENCE.
I MADE TAMAHOME YOURS FOR YOU.
I DID IT TO MAKE YOU HAPPY...
CHK
SLAK

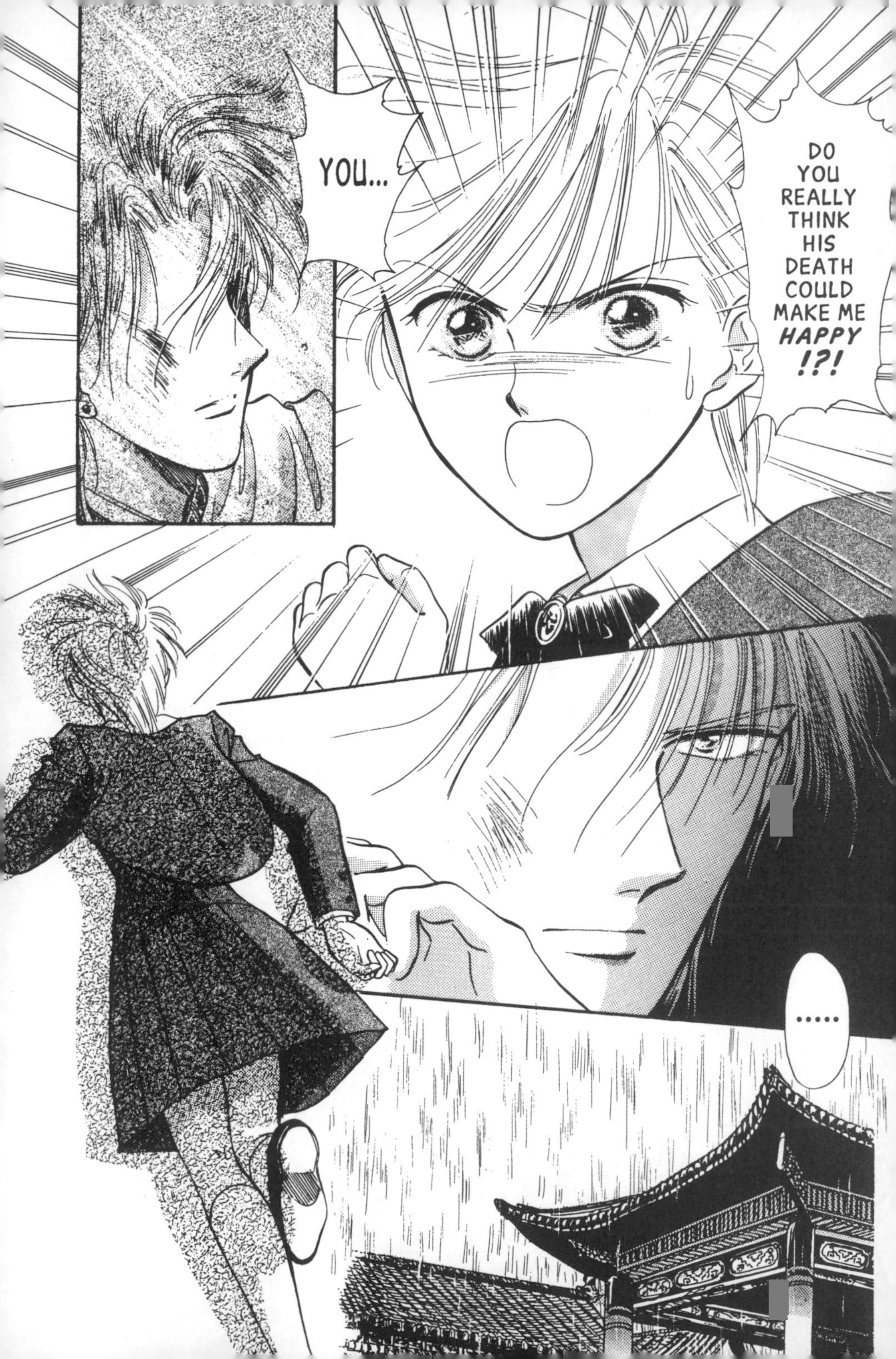
YOU...
DO YOU REALLY THINK HIS DEATH COULD MAKE ME HAPPY !?!
.....

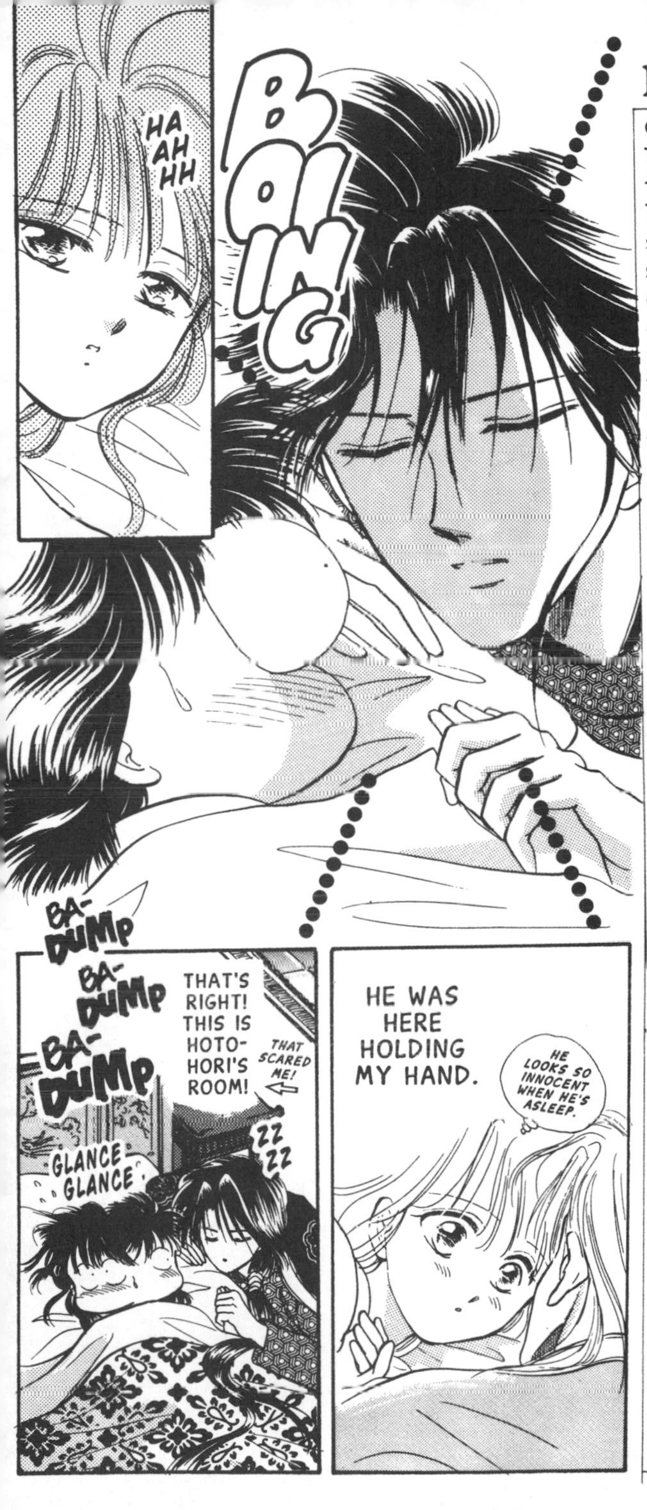
HA AH HH
BOING
BA-DUMP
BA-DUMP
BA-DUMP
THAT'S RIGHT! THIS IS HOTO-HORI'S ROOM!
THAT SCARED ME!
GLANCE GLANCE
ZZ ZZ
HE WAS HERE HOLDING MY HAND.
HE LOOKS SO INNOCENT WHEN HE'S ASLEEP.

Fushigi Yûgi ∾ 6

On with the story.
Three years ago, I moved from Osaka into a house in Tokyo. That's when this strange, and I suppose retrospectively interesting, incident occurred. It started when my assistant (at the time) K was in a deep sleep, but she awoke to find she couldn't move! Of course, our schedule was such that we would work all night and wake up in the afternoon. That could have been playing tricks on our health.

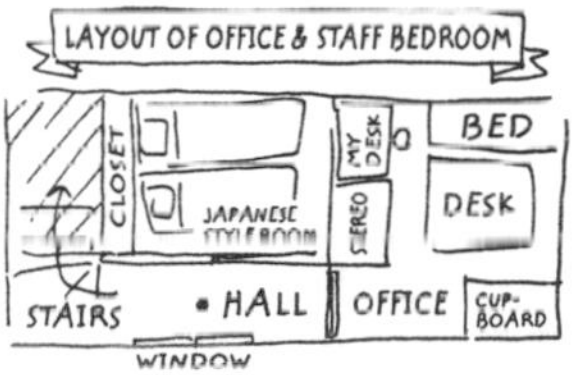
LAYOUT OF OFFICE & STAFF BEDROOM
CLOSET
JAPANESE STYLE ROOM
STEREO
MY DESK
BED
DESK
STAIRS
HALL
OFFICE
CUP-BOARD
WINDOW

The assistants were sleeping in their bedroom, and I was downstairs taking a break with my mom. I went up to wake them up around noon, but before I came upstairs, according to all the assistants, there was a woman who looked into the bedroom. (Was she trying to wake them up?) Then she went downstairs. Apparently, this had been going on for the last six months, and everyone assumed it was my mother. But neither my mother nor my brother ever went upstairs. So the question became, "Who could it possibly be?" Some saw a light shining on her face, others saw her feet, or even heard breathing (it was a dark room), or the rhythmical sound of footsteps ascending or descending the stairs. *(To be continued...)*

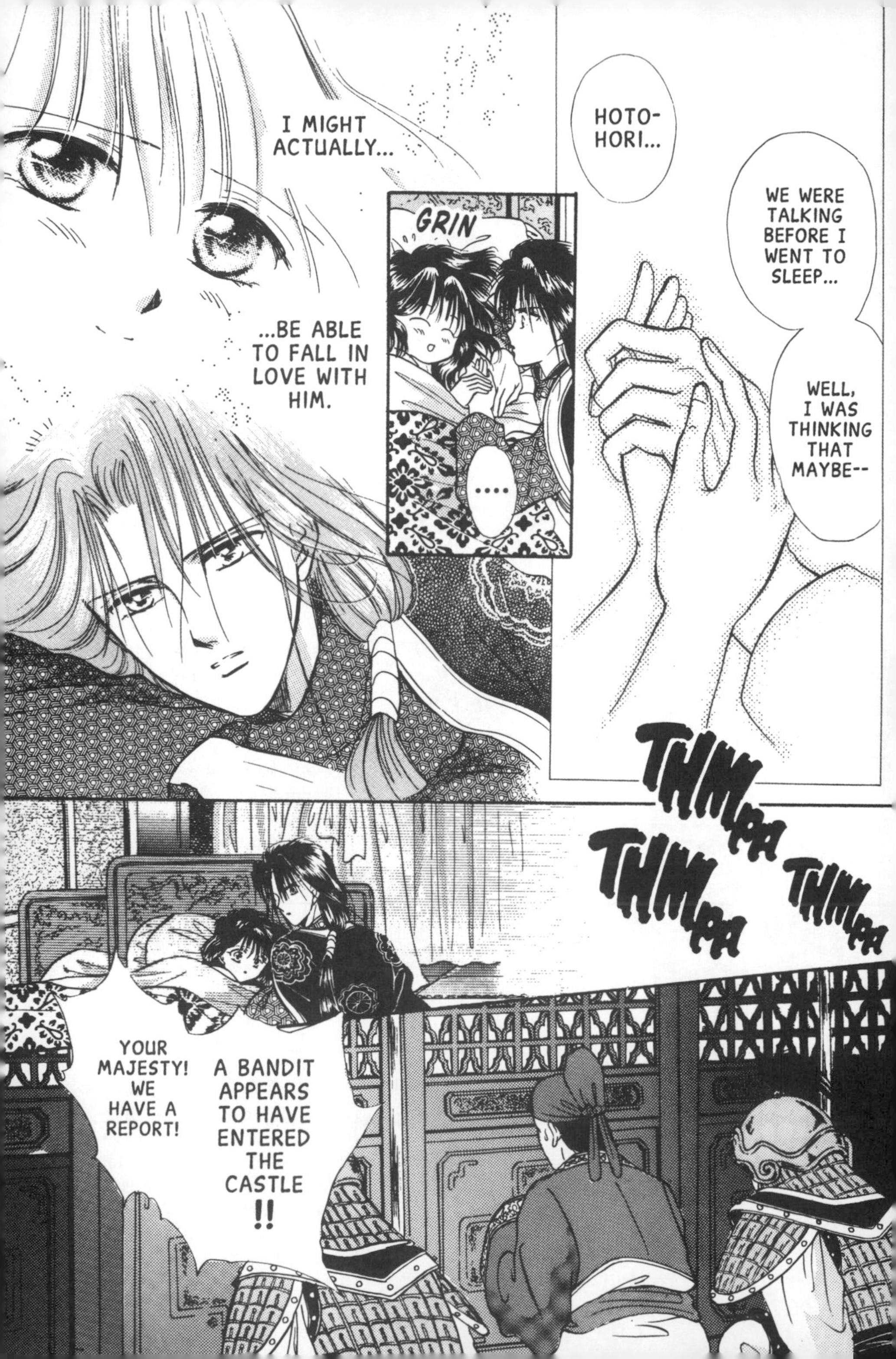
I MIGHT ACTUALLY...
...BE ABLE TO FALL IN LOVE WITH HIM.
GRIN
.....
HOTO-HORI...
WE WERE TALKING BEFORE I WENT TO SLEEP...
WELL, I WAS THINKING THAT MAYBE--
THMPA THMPA THMPA
YOUR MAJESTY! WE HAVE A REPORT!
A BANDIT APPEARS TO HAVE ENTERED THE CASTLE !!

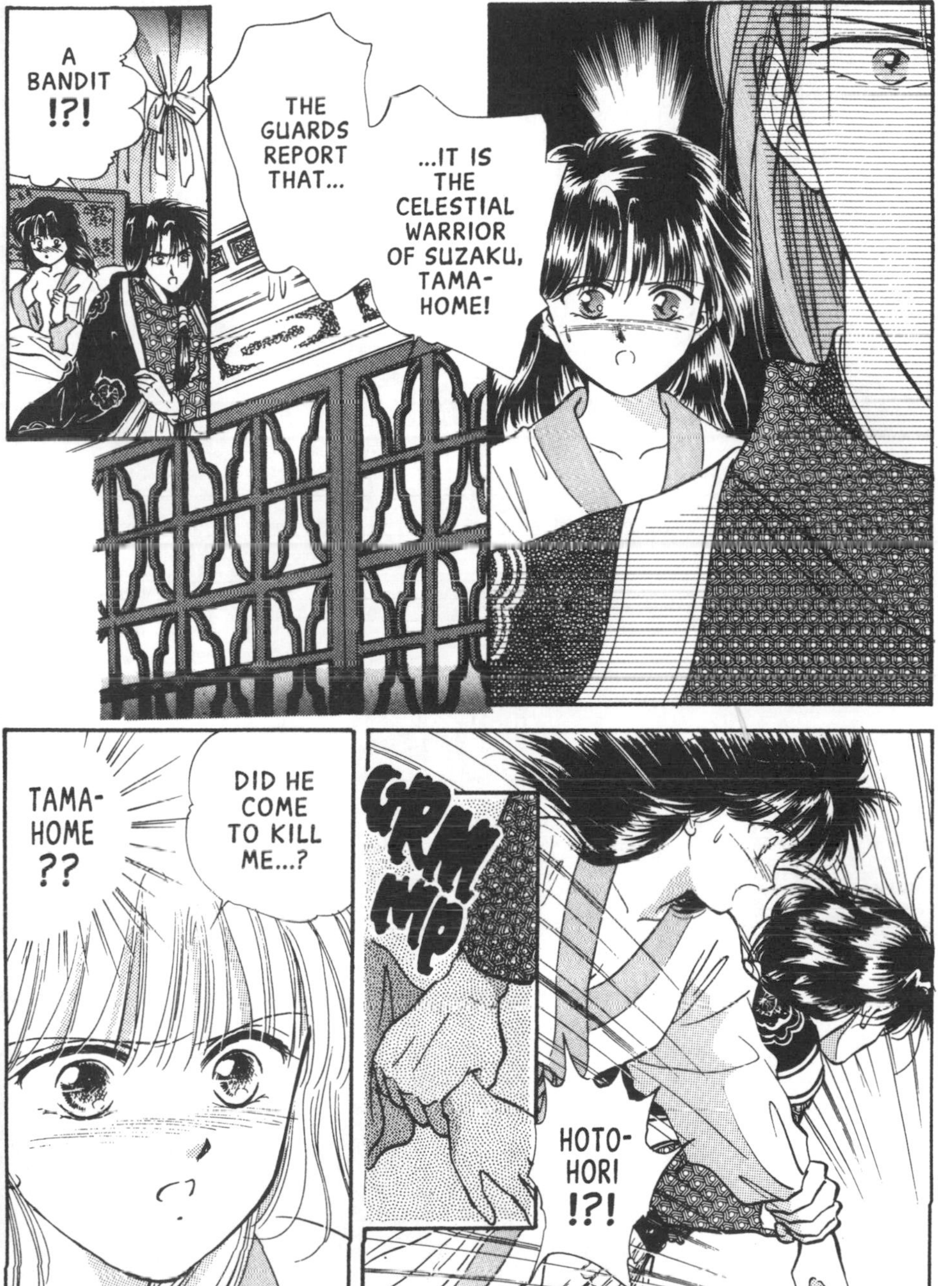
A BANDIT !?!
THE GUARDS REPORT THAT...
...IT IS THE CELESTIAL WARRIOR OF SUZAKU, TAMA-HOME!
TAMA-HOME ??
DID HE COME TO KILL ME...?
GRMMP
HOTO-HORI !?!

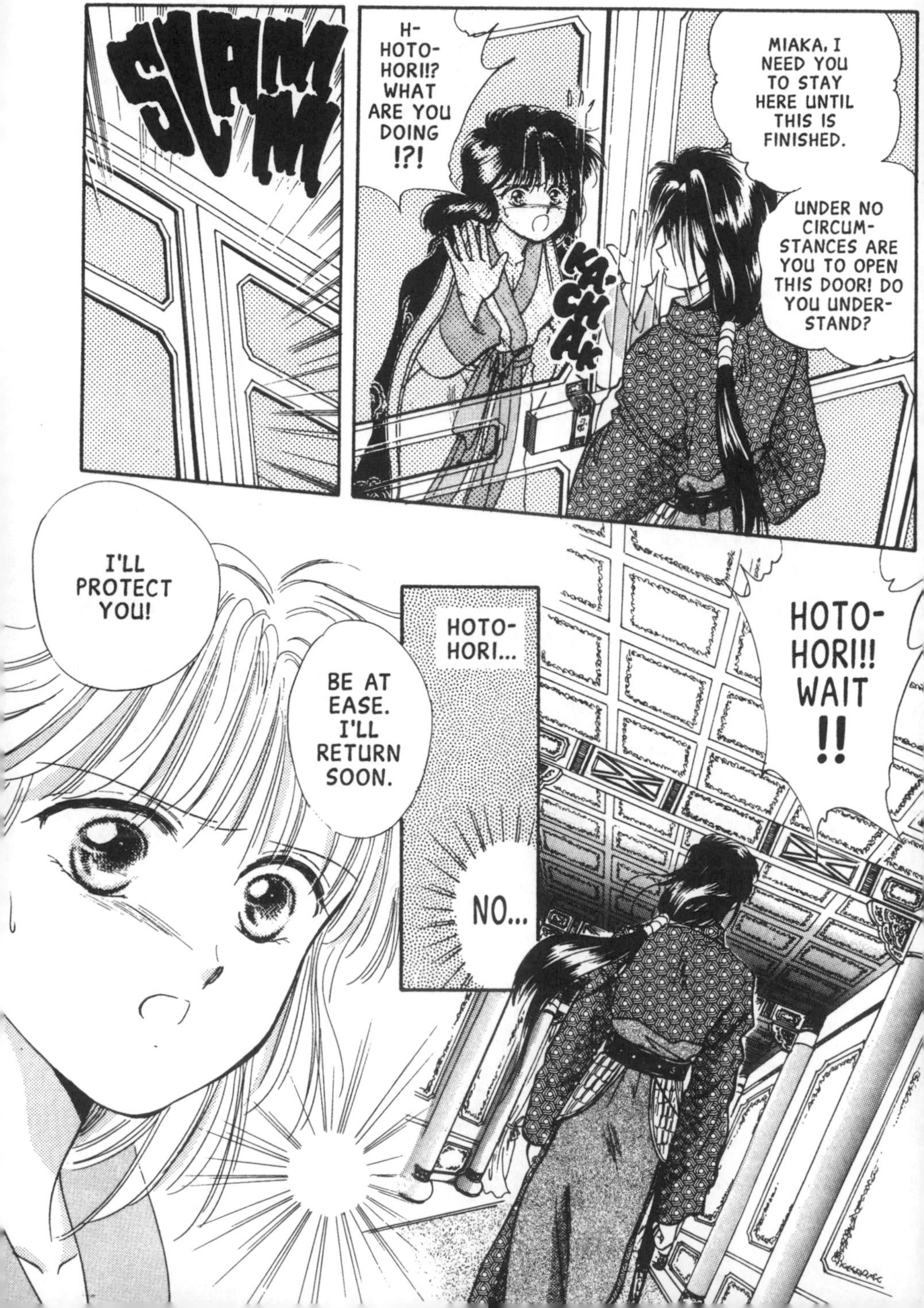

SLAM
H-HOTO-HORI!!? WHAT ARE YOU DOING !?!
KA-CHAK
MIAKA, I NEED YOU TO STAY HERE UNTIL THIS IS FINISHED.
UNDER NO CIRCUM-STANCES ARE YOU TO OPEN THIS DOOR! DO YOU UNDER-STAND?
I'LL PROTECT YOU!
BE AT EASE. I'LL RETURN SOON.
HOTO-HORI...
NO...
HOTO-HORI!! WAIT !!

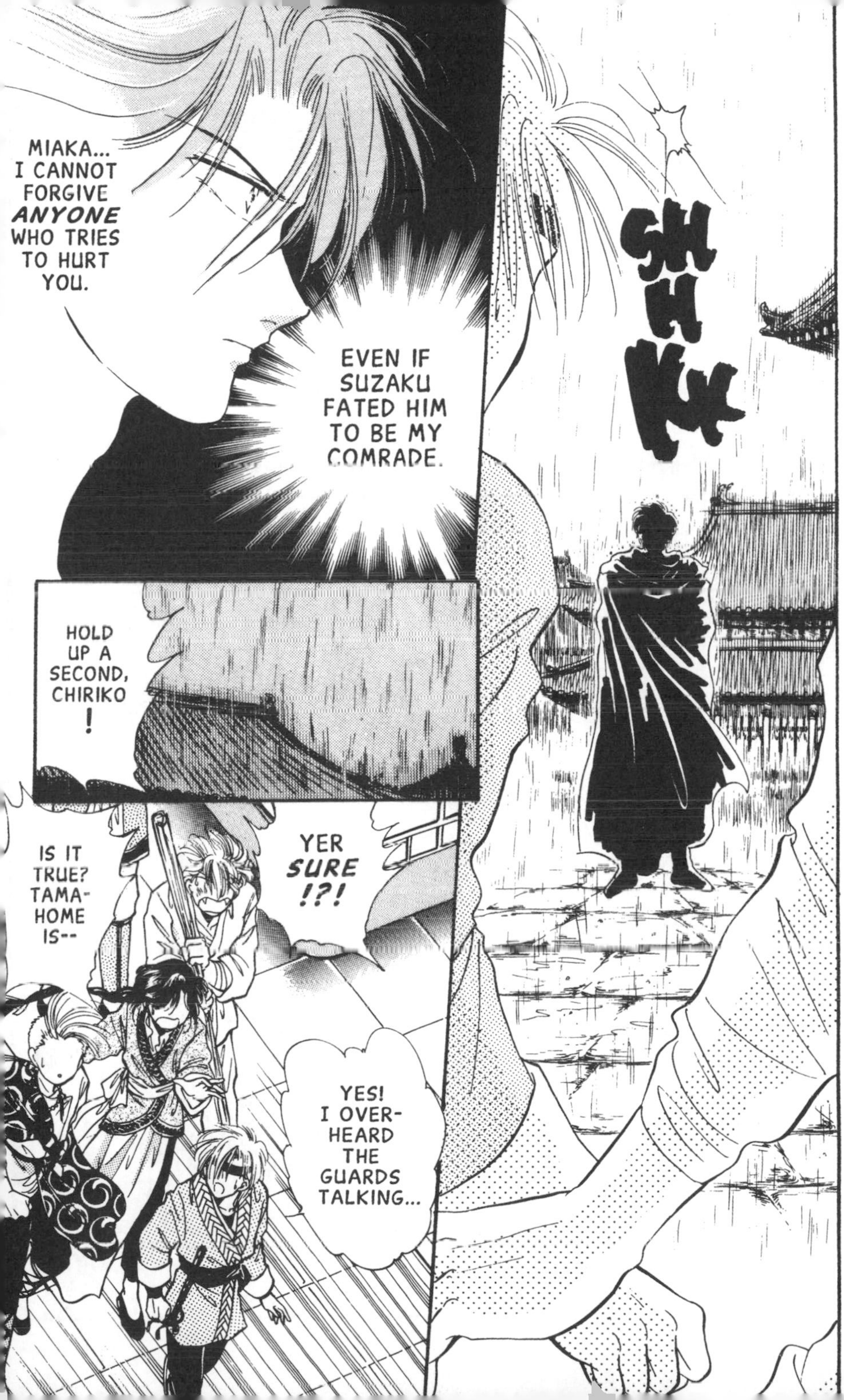
MIAKA... I CANNOT FORGIVE ANYONE WHO TRIES TO HURT YOU.
EVEN IF SUZAKU FATED HIM TO BE MY COMRADE.
HOLD UP A SECOND, CHIRIKO!
IS IT TRUE? TAMA-HOME IS--
YER SURE!?!
YES! I OVER-HEARD THE GUARDS TALKING...
SHHKK

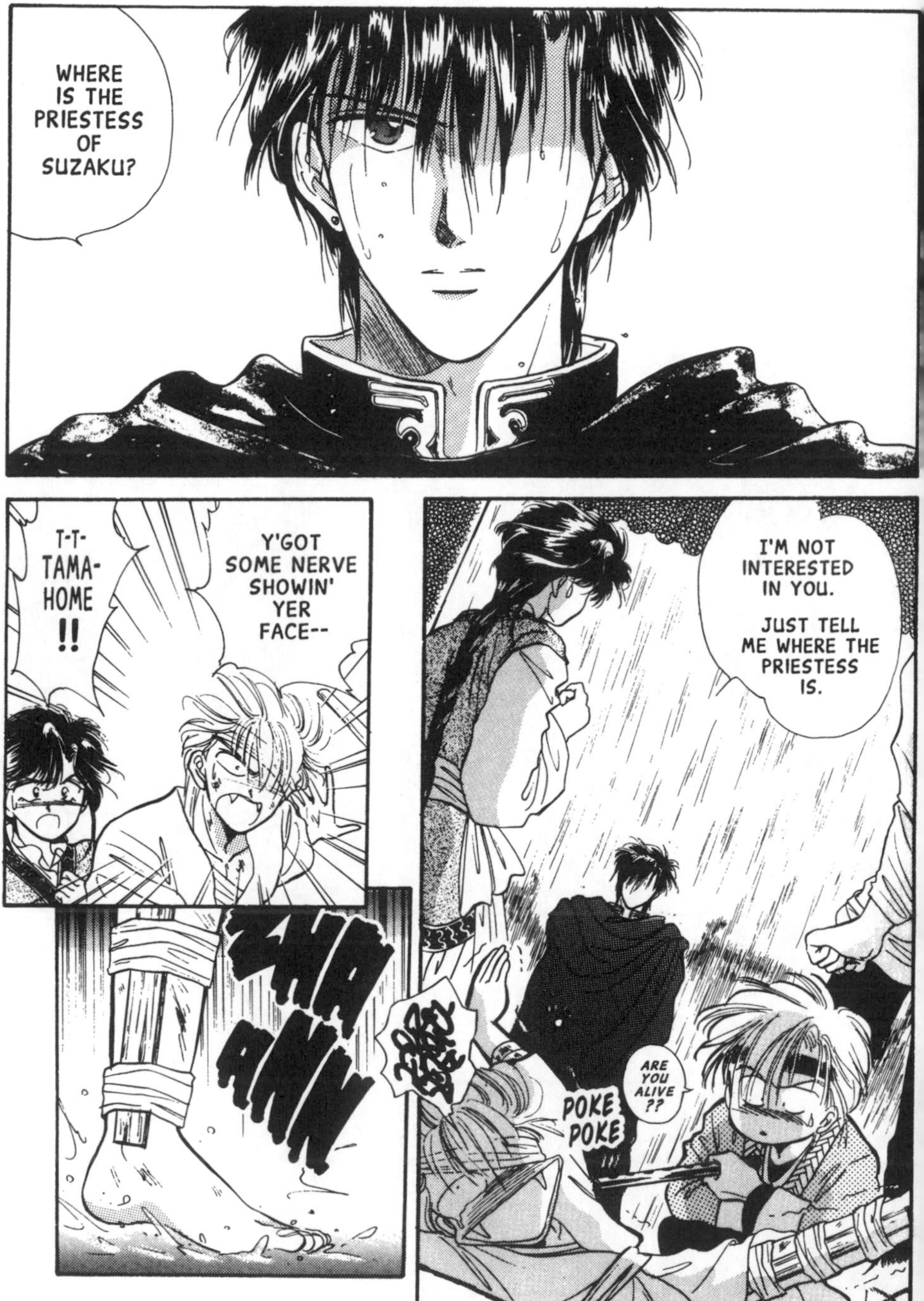

WHERE IS THE PRIESTESS OF SUZAKU?
T-T-TAMA-HOME!!
Y'GOT SOME NERVE SHOWIN' YER FACE--
I'M NOT INTERESTED IN YOU.
JUST TELL ME WHERE THE PRIESTESS IS.
POKE POKE
ARE YOU ALIVE??

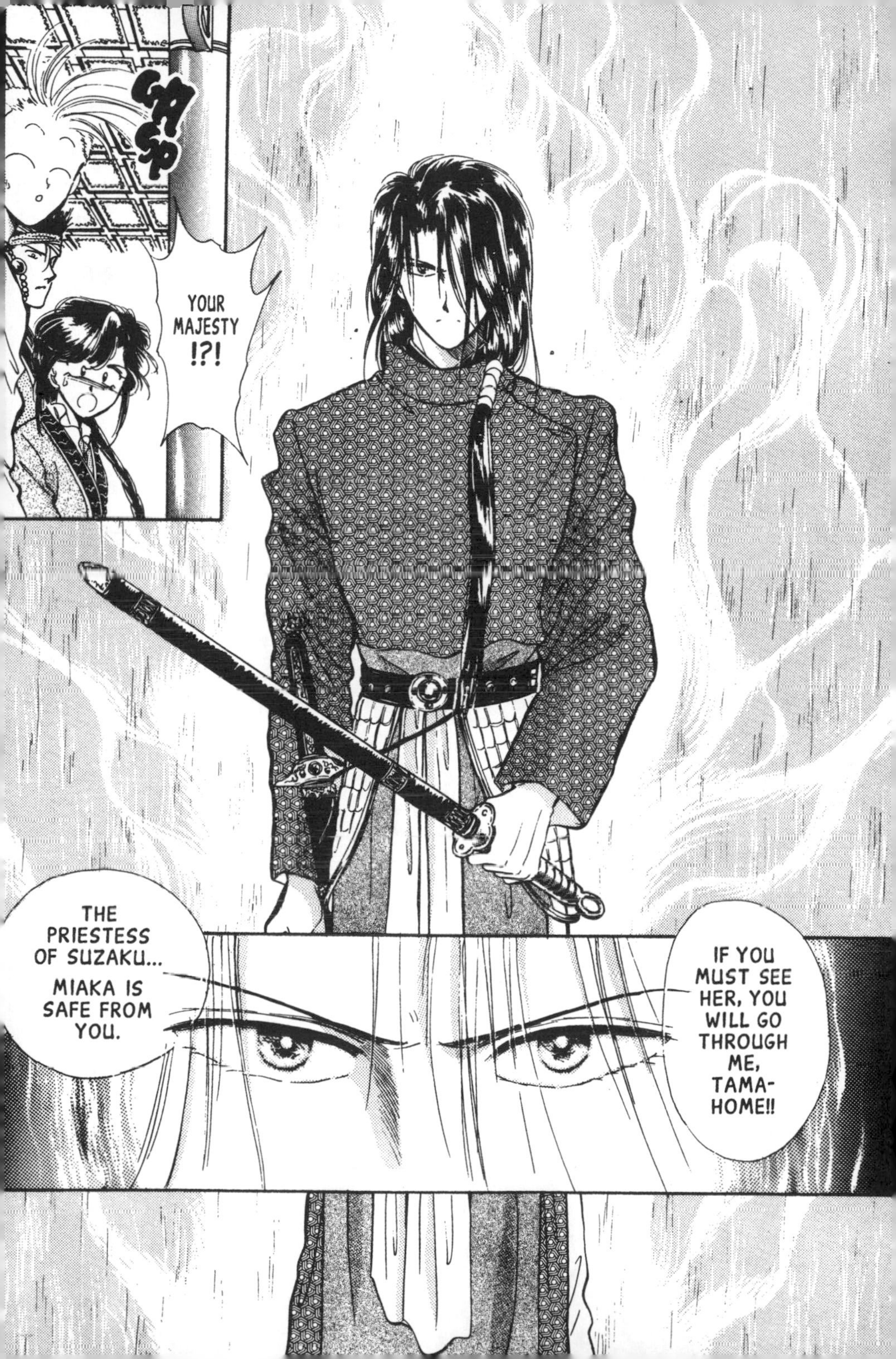
GASP
YOUR MAJESTY !?!
THE PRIESTESS OF SUZAKU... MIAKA IS SAFE FROM YOU.
IF YOU MUST SEE HER, YOU WILL GO THROUGH ME, TAMA-HOME!!

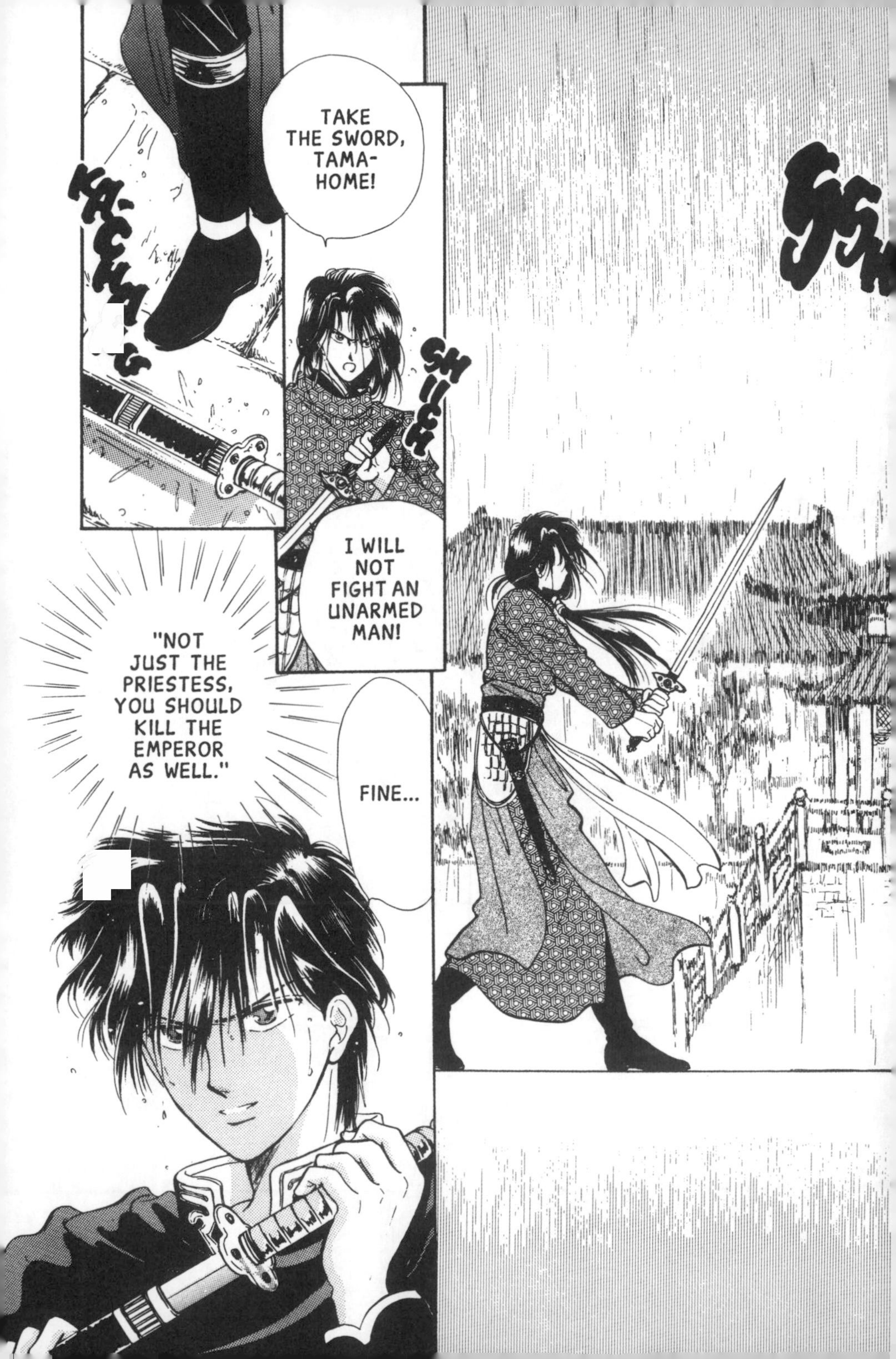
TAKE THE SWORD, TAMA-HOME!
I WILL NOT FIGHT AN UNARMED MAN!
"NOT JUST THE PRIESTESS, YOU SHOULD KILL THE EMPEROR AS WELL."
FINE...

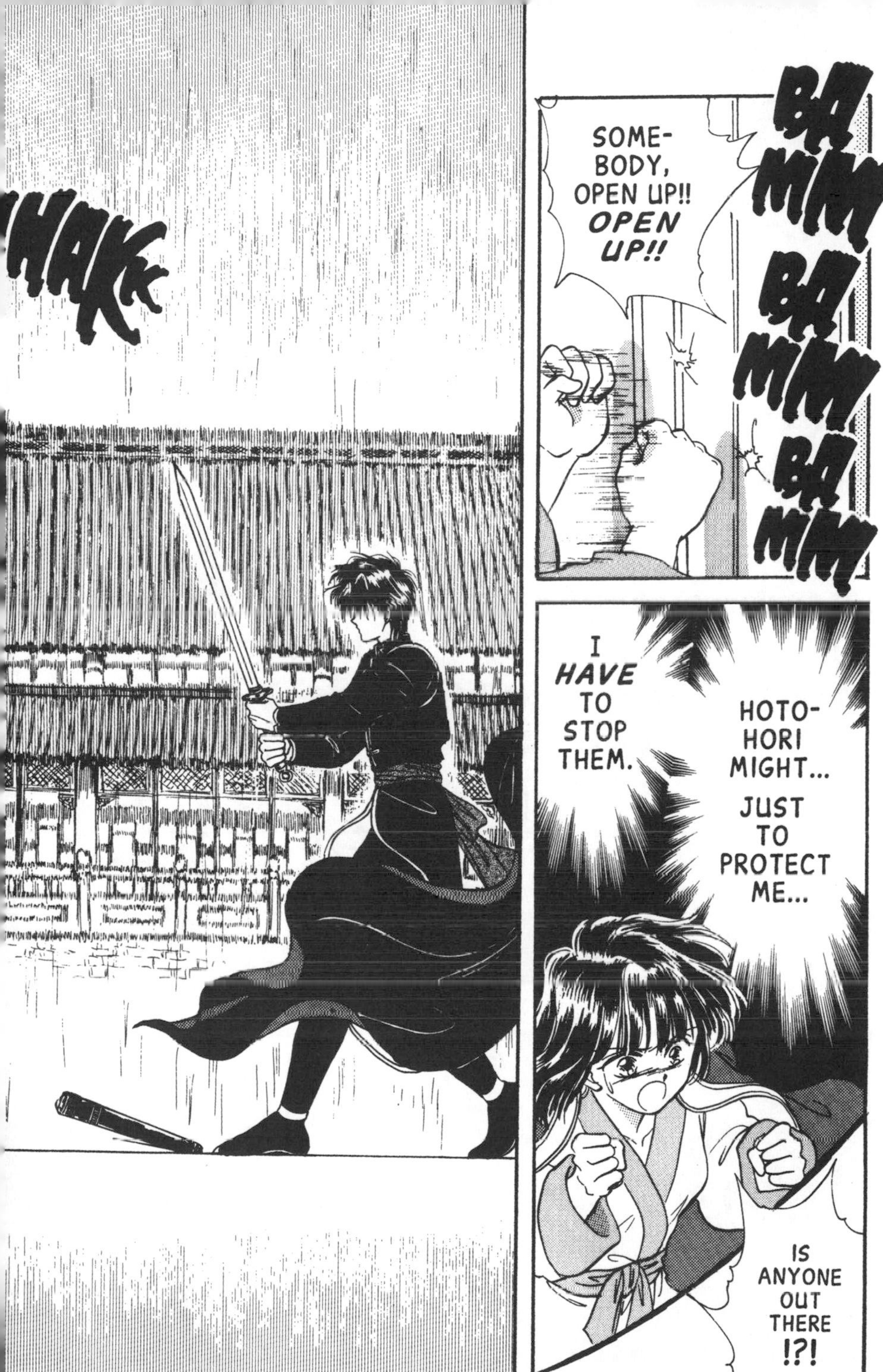
HAKK
SOMEBODY, OPEN UP!! OPEN UP!!
BAMM BAMM BAMM
I HAVE TO STOP THEM.
HOTOHORI MIGHT... JUST TO PROTECT ME...
IS ANYONE OUT THERE !?!

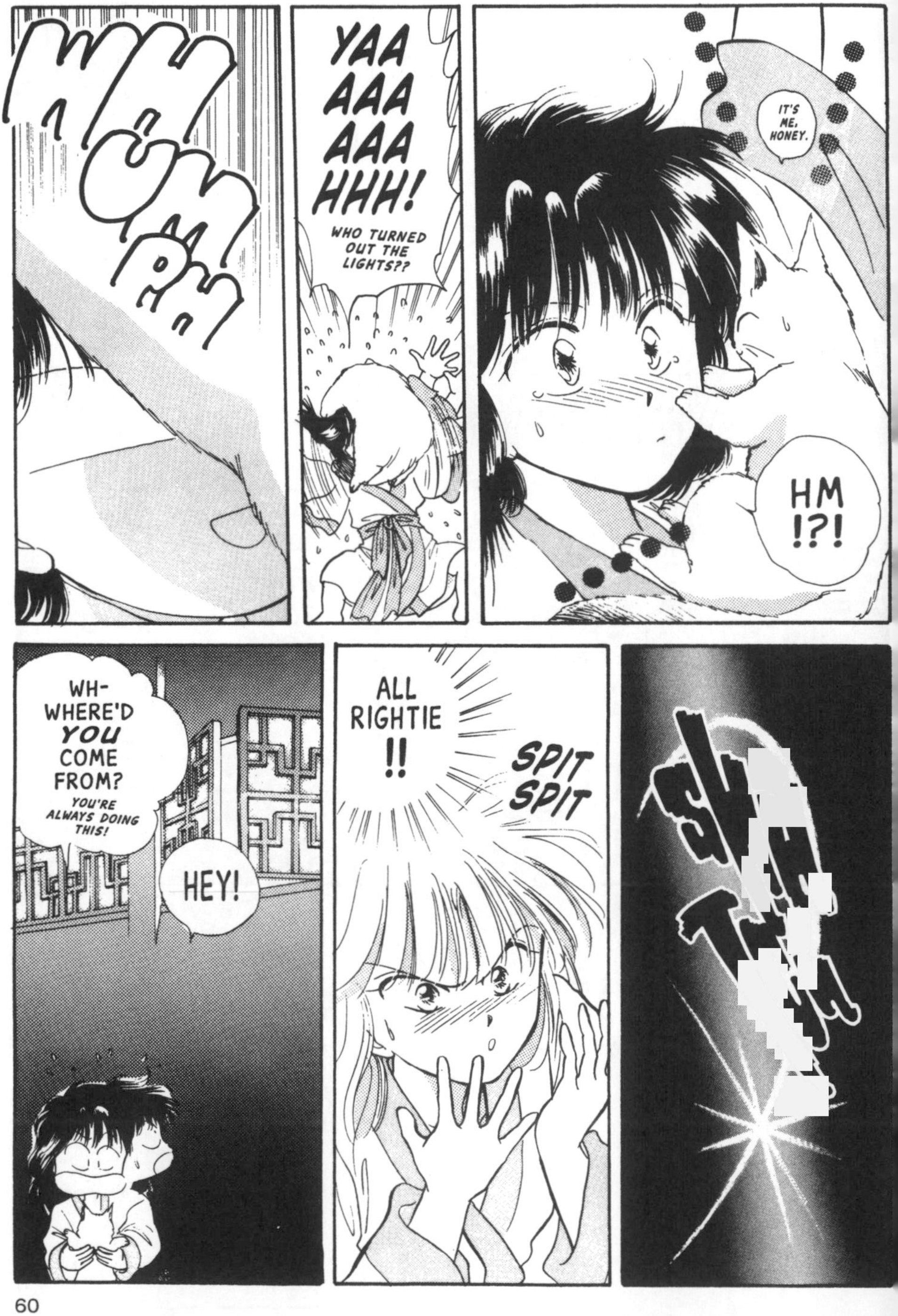
MMMUMMPH
YAAAAAAAAAHHH!
WHO TURNED OUT THE LIGHTS??
IT'S ME, HONEY.
HM !?!
WH- WHERE'D YOU COME FROM?
YOU'RE ALWAYS DOING THIS!
HEY!
ALL RIGHTIE !!
SPIT SPIT

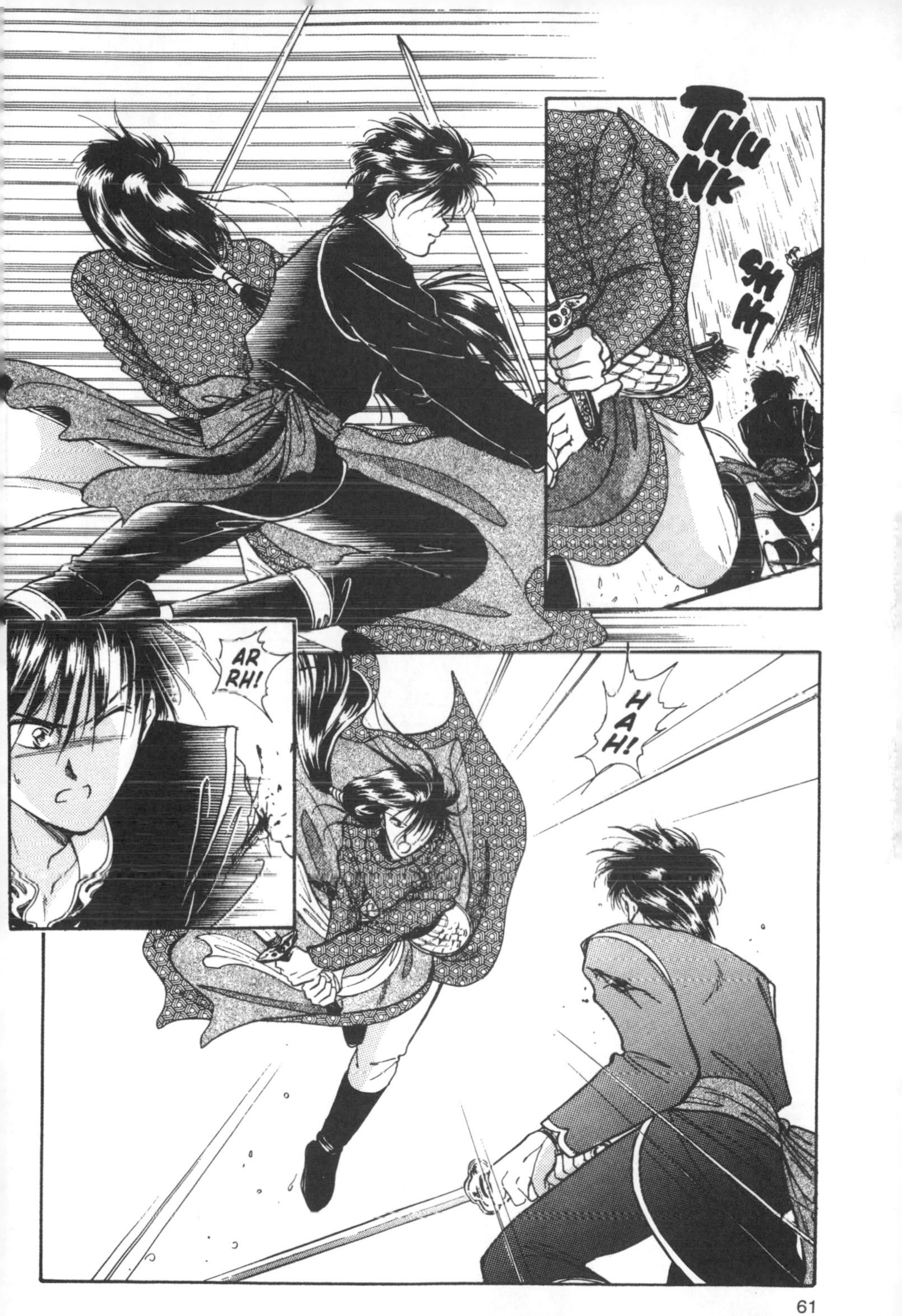
THUNK
SHHT
ARRH!
HAH!

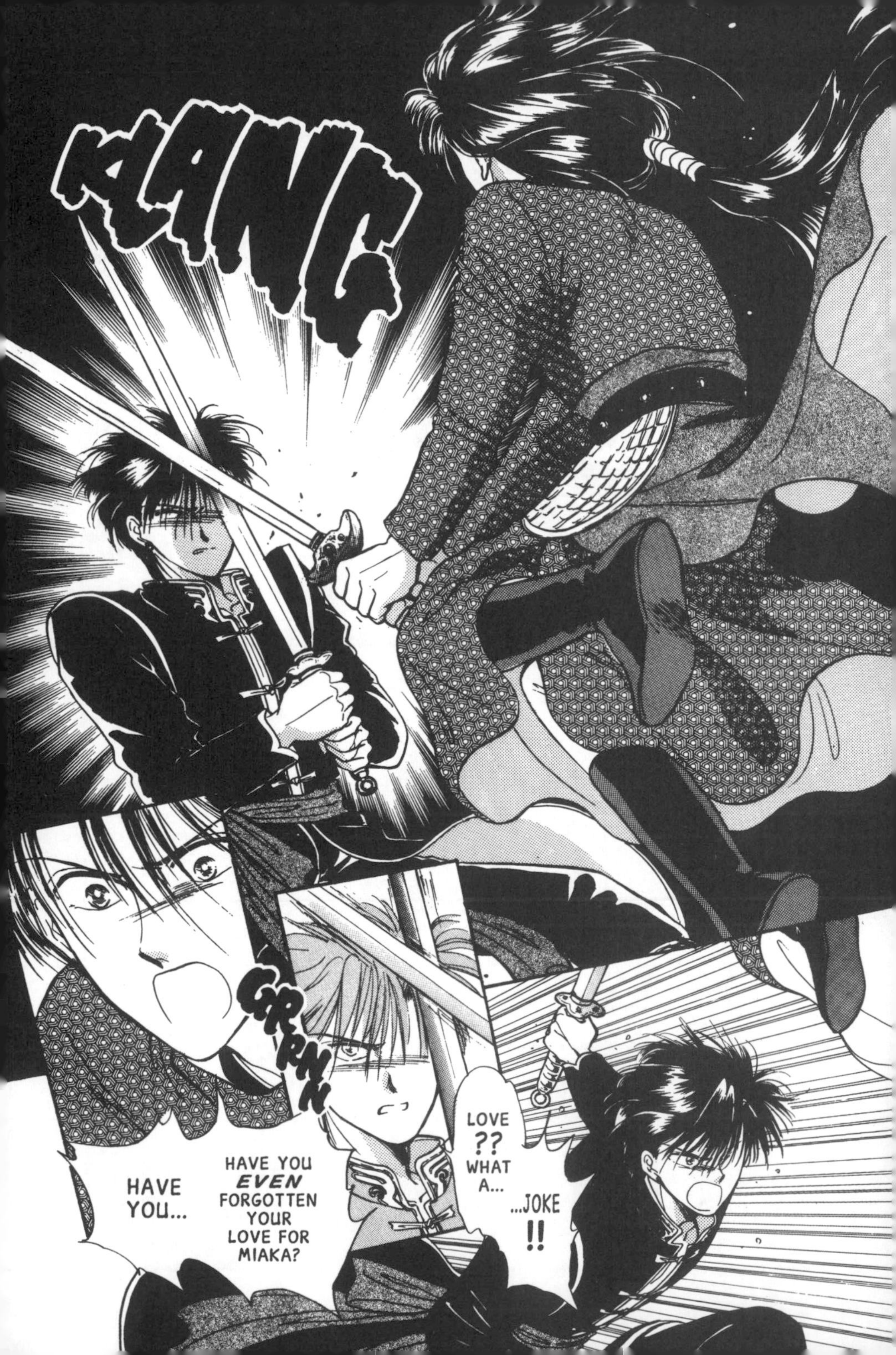
KLANG
GRRNN
HAVE YOU...
HAVE YOU EVEN FORGOTTEN YOUR LOVE FOR MIAKA?
LOVE ?? WHAT A...
...JOKE !!

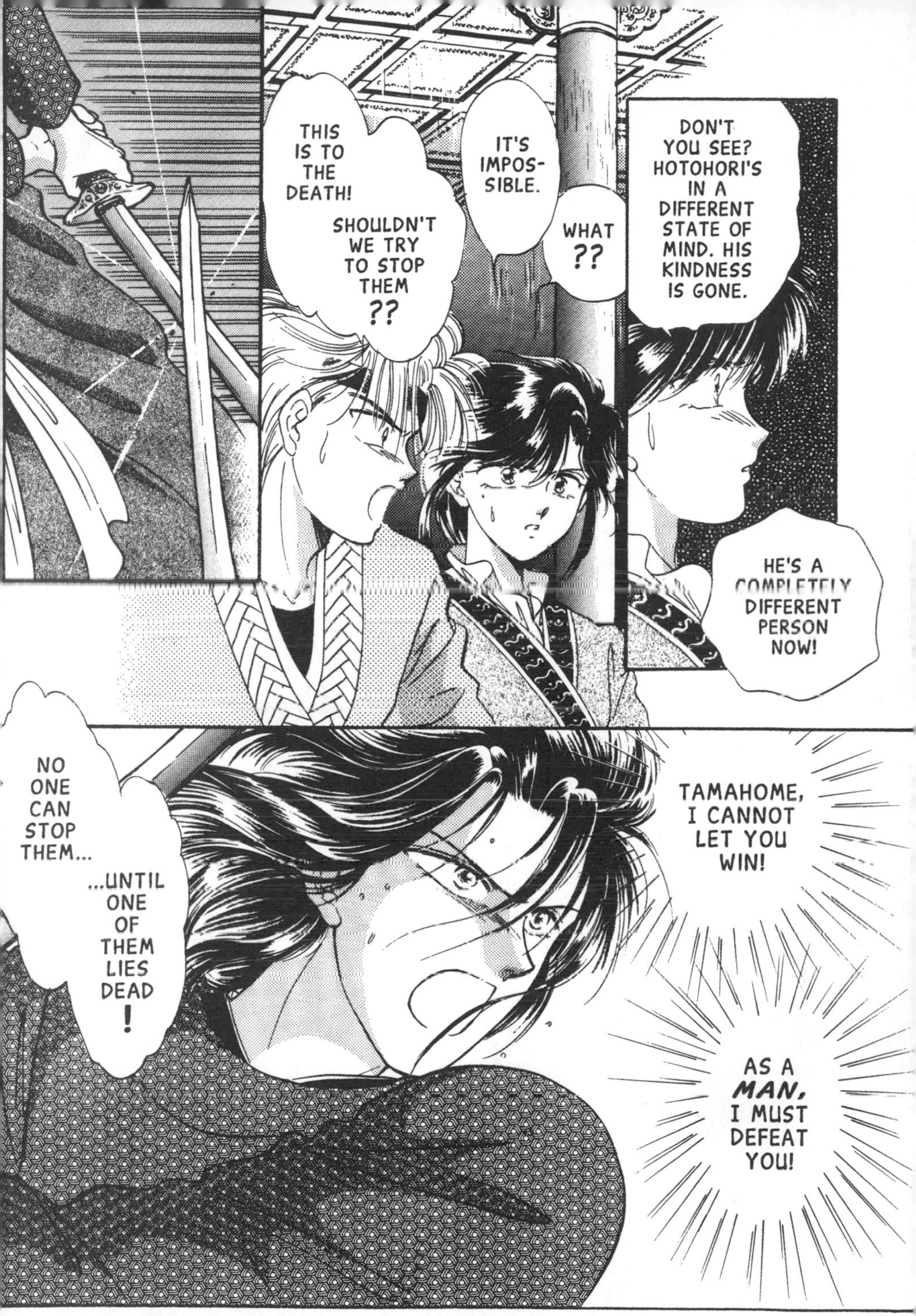

THIS IS TO THE DEATH!
SHOULDN'T WE TRY TO STOP THEM??
IT'S IMPOSSIBLE.
WHAT??
DON'T YOU SEE? HOTOHORI'S IN A DIFFERENT STATE OF MIND. HIS KINDNESS IS GONE.
HE'S A COMPLETELY DIFFERENT PERSON NOW!
NO ONE CAN STOP THEM...
...UNTIL ONE OF THEM LIES DEAD!
TAMAHOME, I CANNOT LET YOU WIN!
AS A *MAN,* I MUST DEFEAT YOU!

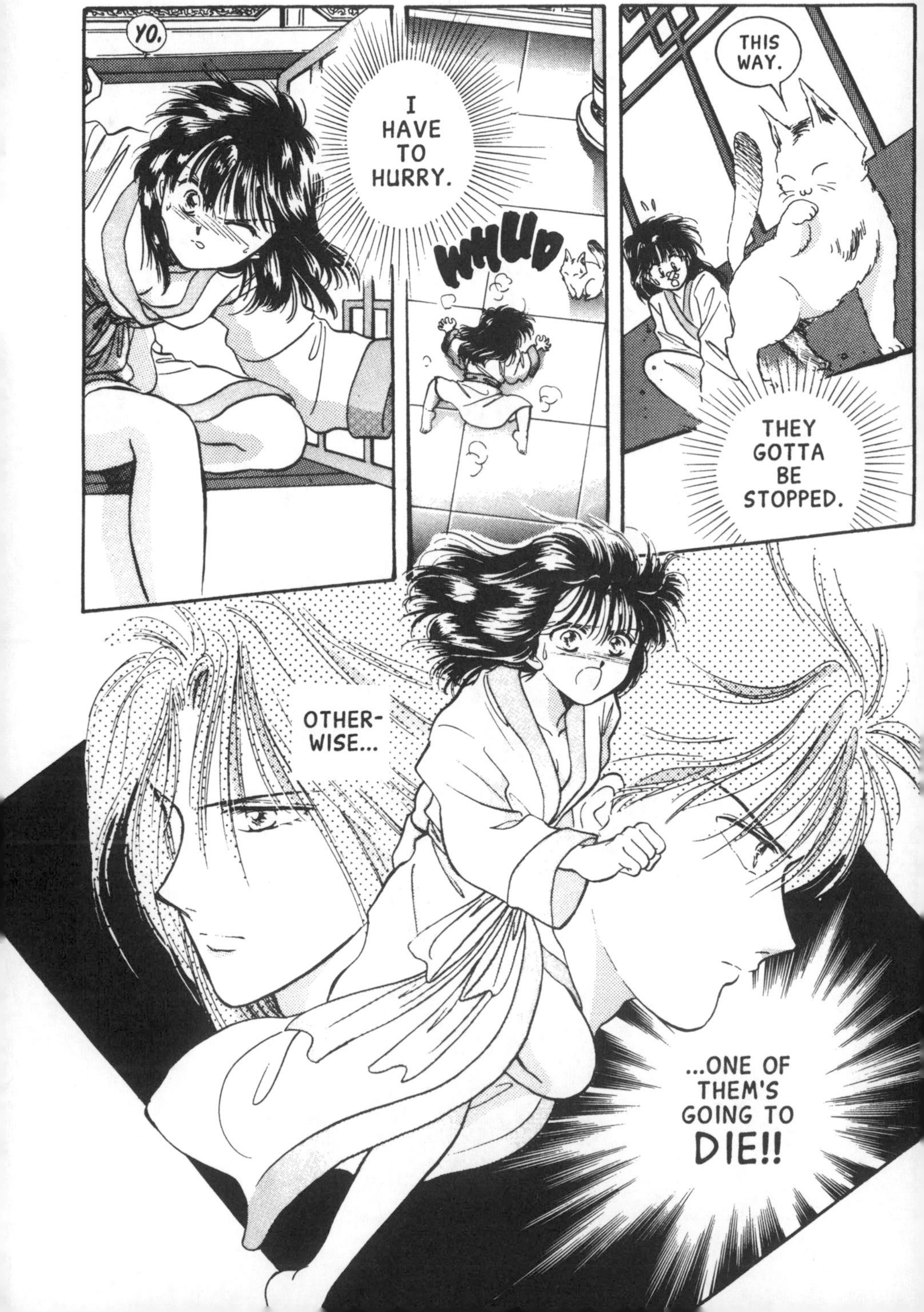
YO.
I HAVE TO HURRY.
WHUD
THIS WAY.
THEY GOTTA BE STOPPED.
OTHER-WISE...
...ONE OF THEM'S GOING TO DIE!!

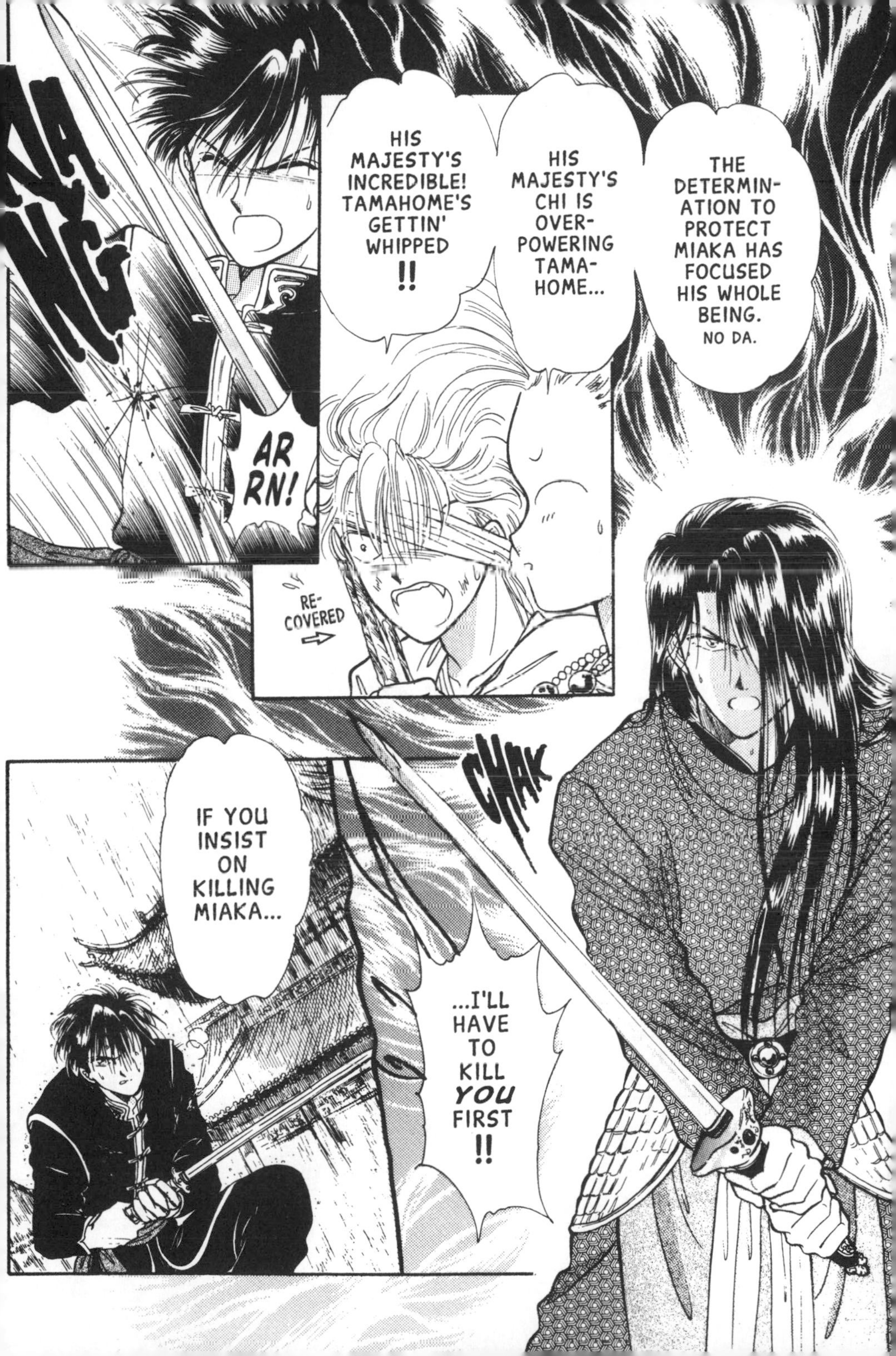
AR RN!
HIS MAJESTY'S INCREDIBLE! TAMAHOME'S GETTIN' WHIPPED !!
HIS MAJESTY'S CHI IS OVER-POWERING TAMA-HOME...
THE DETERMIN-ATION TO PROTECT MIAKA HAS FOCUSED HIS WHOLE BEING. NO DA.
RE-COVERED
IF YOU INSIST ON KILLING MIAKA...
CHAK
...I'LL HAVE TO KILL YOU FIRST !!

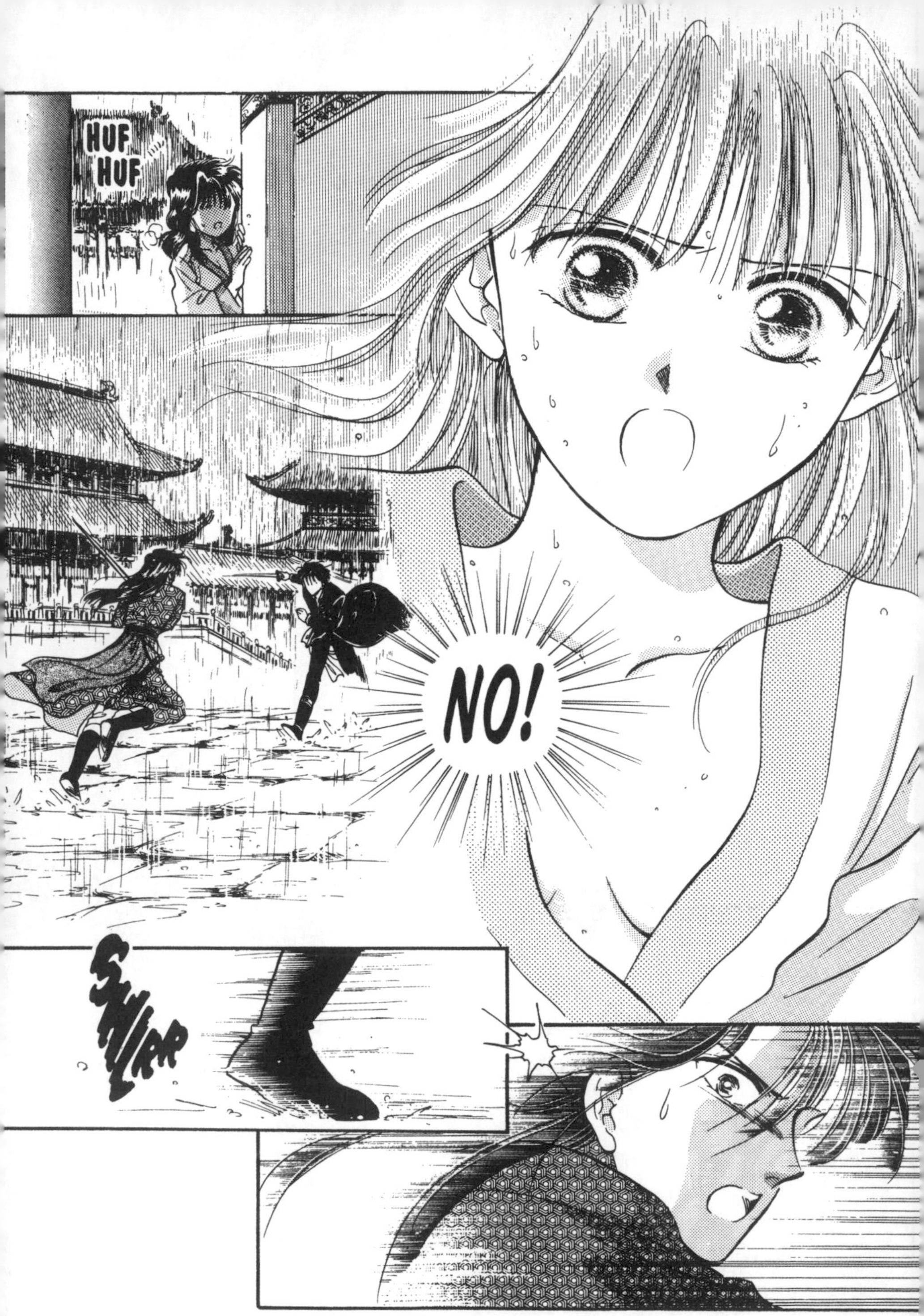
HUF HUF
NO!
SWIRR

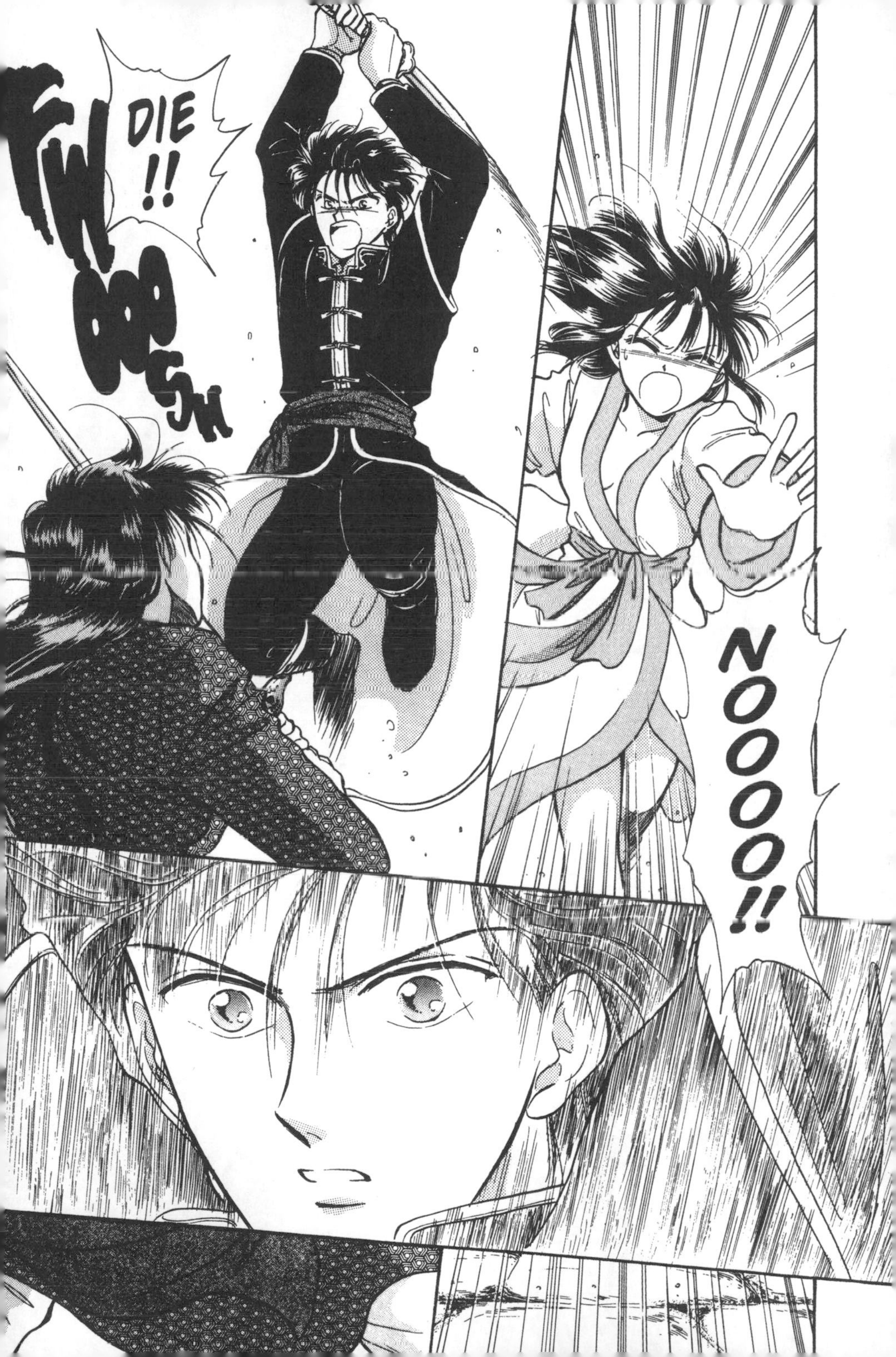
FWOOOSH
DIE !!
NOOOOO!!

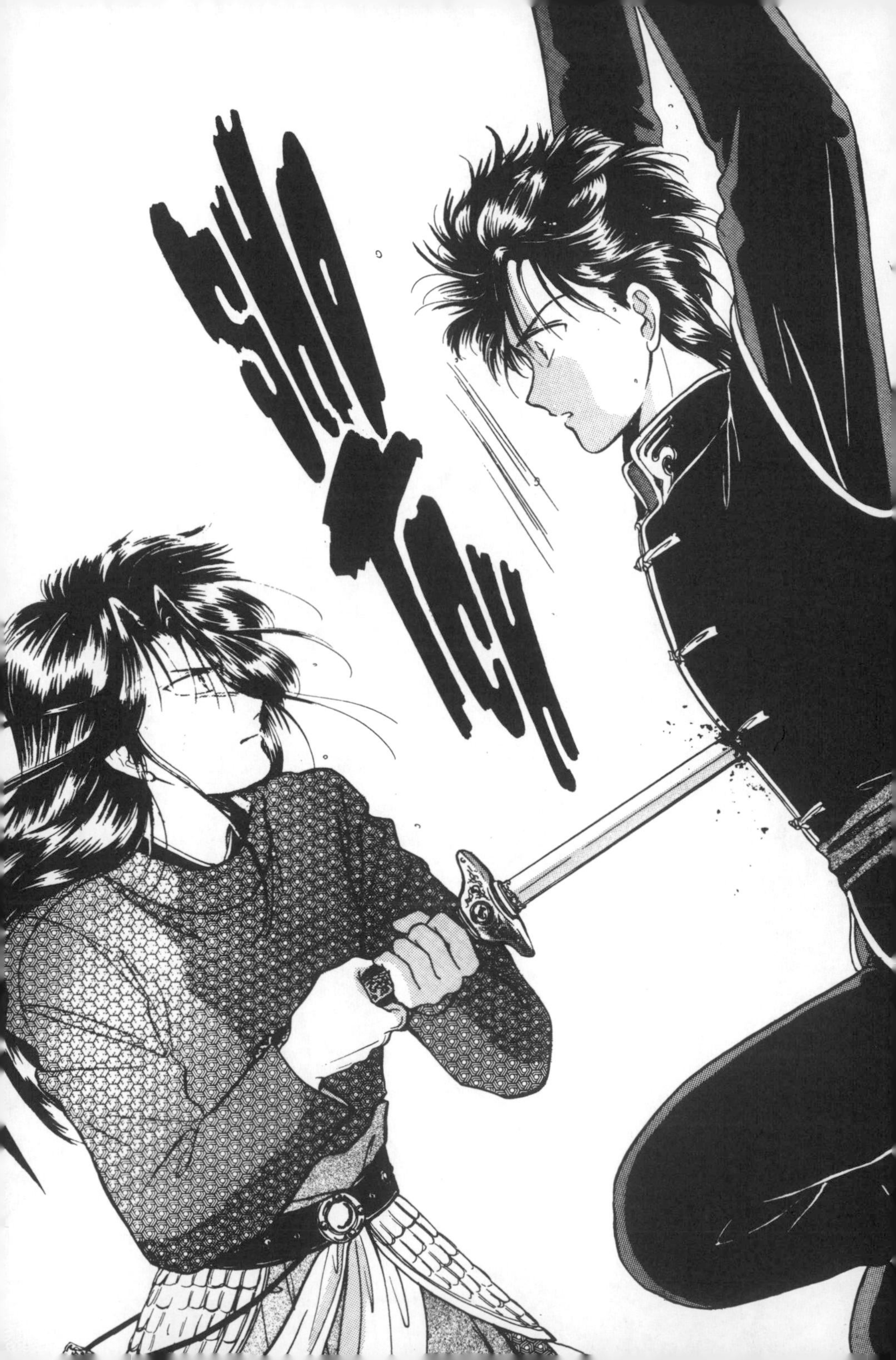

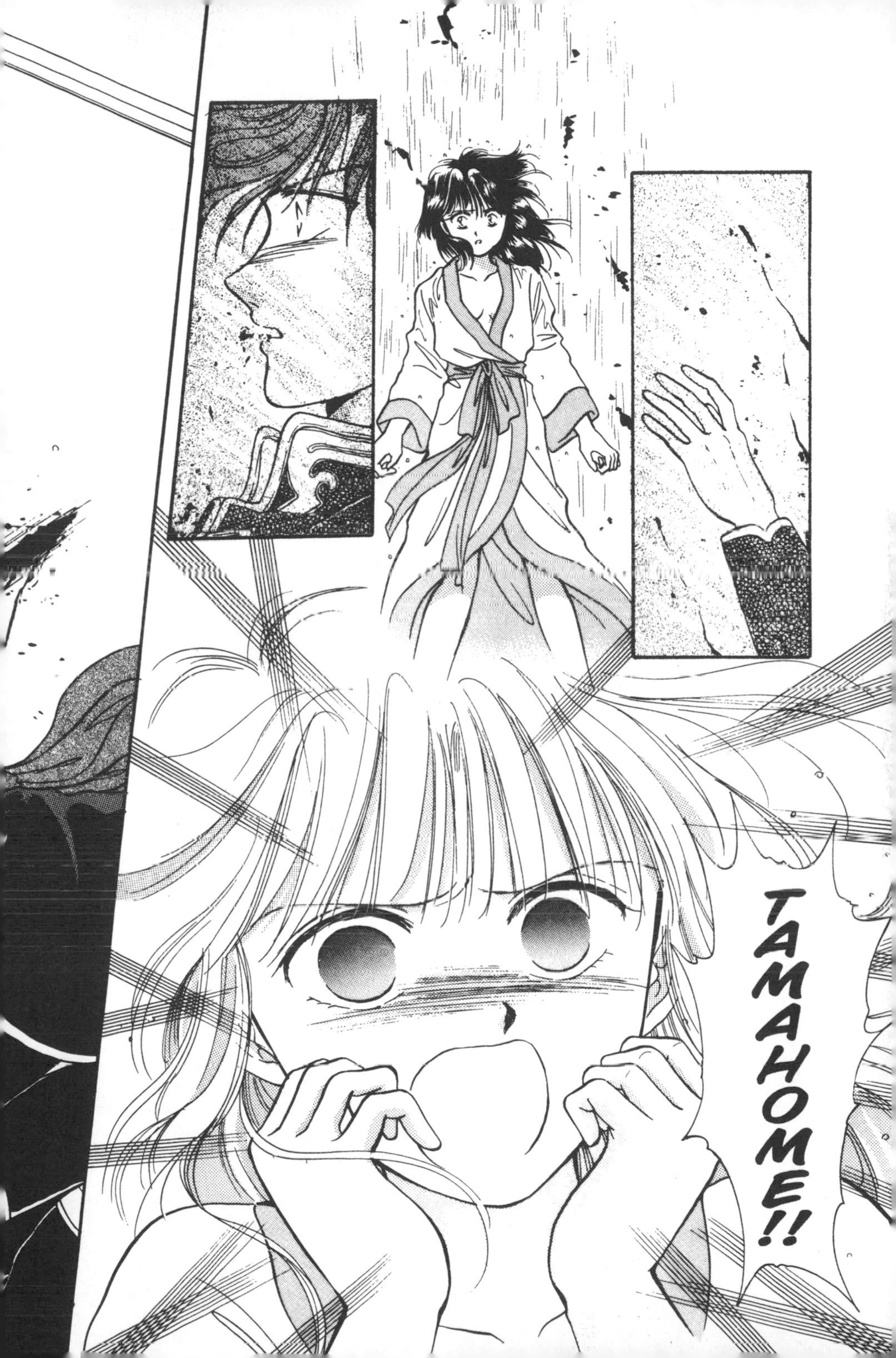
TAMAHOME!!

?

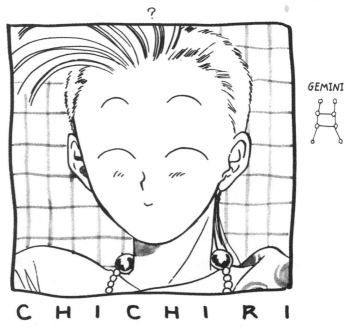

GEMINI

C H I C H I R I

- Born in an unknown location.
  He would call his career "a priest," but he isn't really religious.
- Age: 24. ← Everybody is surprised by his age! But at the very beginning, when
  I asked my assistants, they all were of the opinion that he seemed to
  be in his twenties. So I went along with that. And his confidence isn't
  something that's normal for someone in his teens!
- Family: Unknown. In his teens he had a fiancée, but they broke up.
  (For details, see volume 7.)
- Hobby: Fishing.
- Height: 5' 8". But every now and again, he comes in at under a yard tall.
- Blood Type: Unknown.

An elusive character. A masked man with a seemingly light heart—-Chichiri is a
mystery. He can turn super-deformed, and later be very serious. He's the most
neutral character of the seven celestial warriors of Suzaku. If Tamahome or
Hotohori are the obvious leaders of the warriors, Chichiri is the man manipulating
from the shadows. He's the power behind the throne who always helps out.
(You could also call him the adult who looks after the kids.)
He can use many techniques that Tai Yi-Jun taught him.
He is unconcerned with his own mortality. He has become much like a typical Zen
master with his abandonment of earthly desires.

CHAPTER THIRTY-THREE

NEVER LEAVE YOU

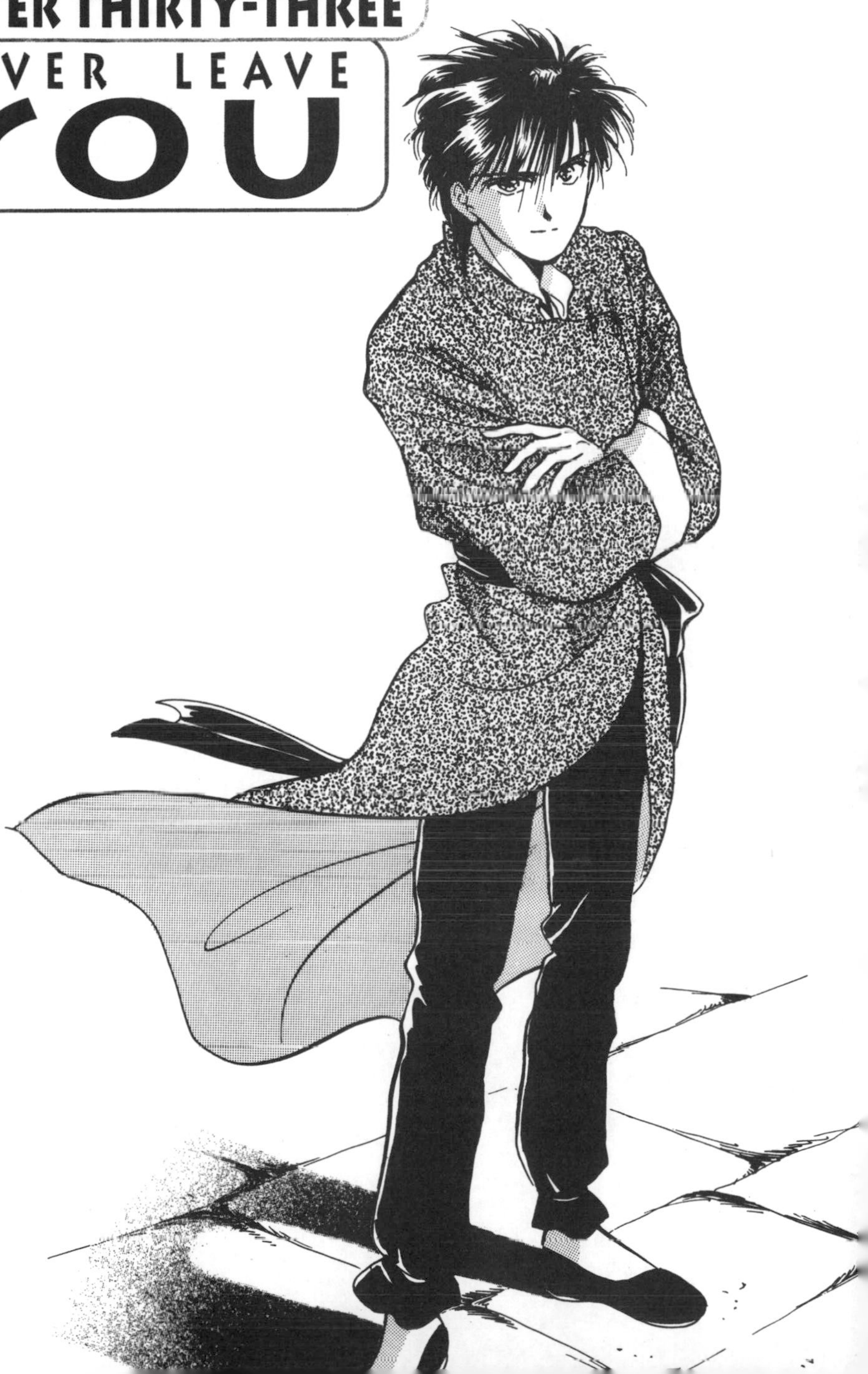

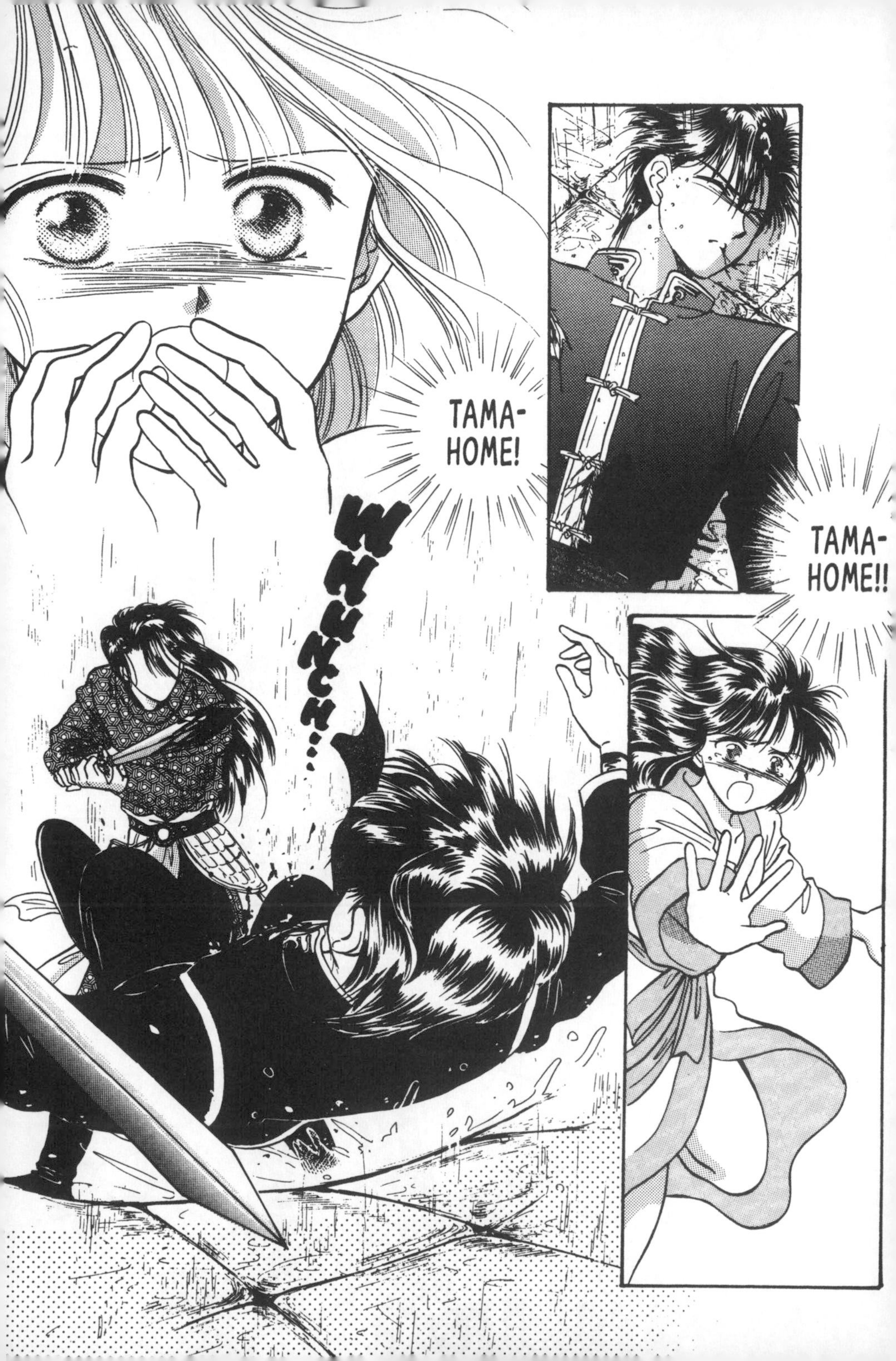
TAMA-
HOME!
TAMA-
HOME!!
WHUNCH...

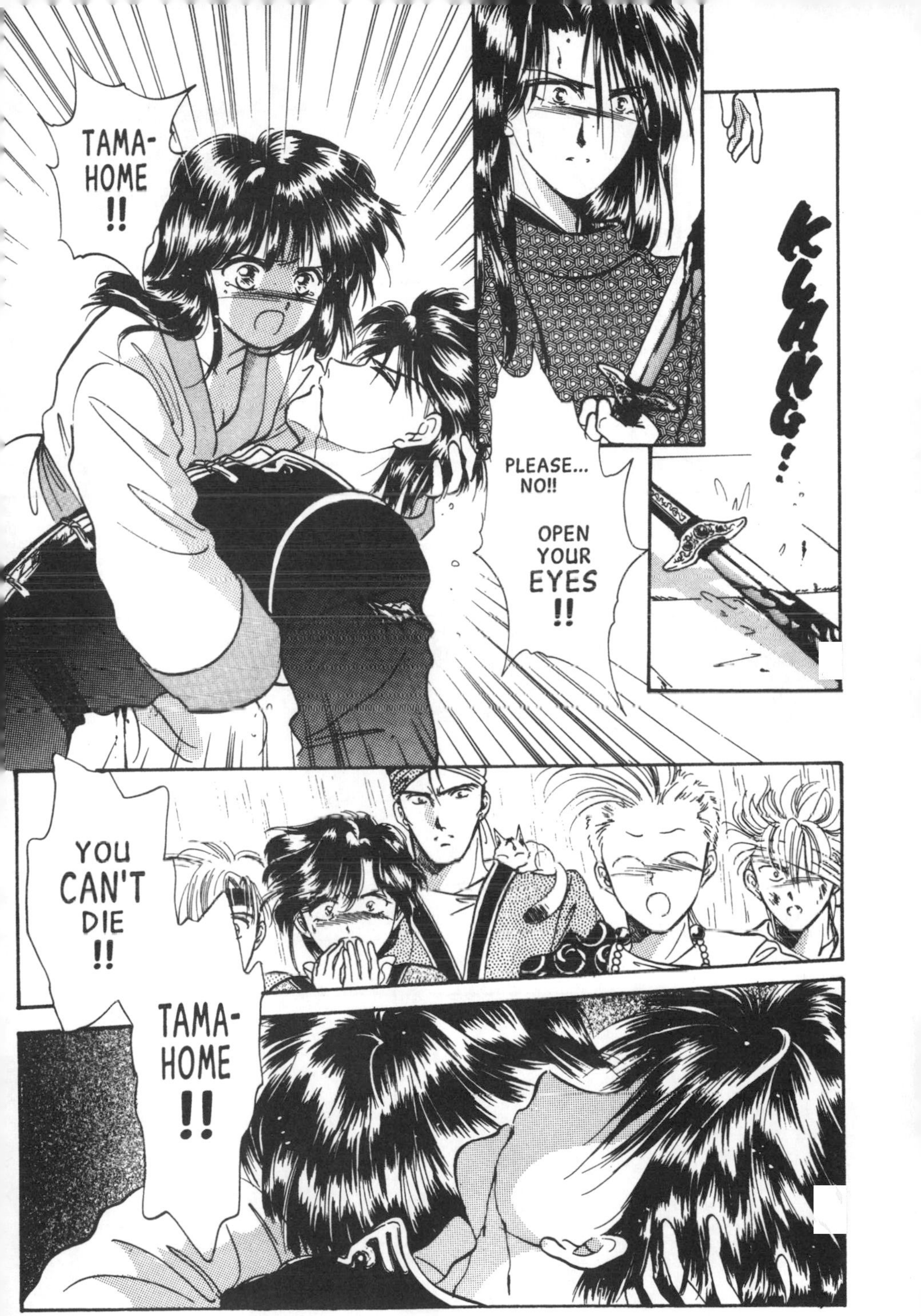
TAMA-HOME !!
KLANG!!
PLEASE... NO!!
OPEN YOUR EYES !!
YOU CAN'T DIE !!
TAMA-HOME !!

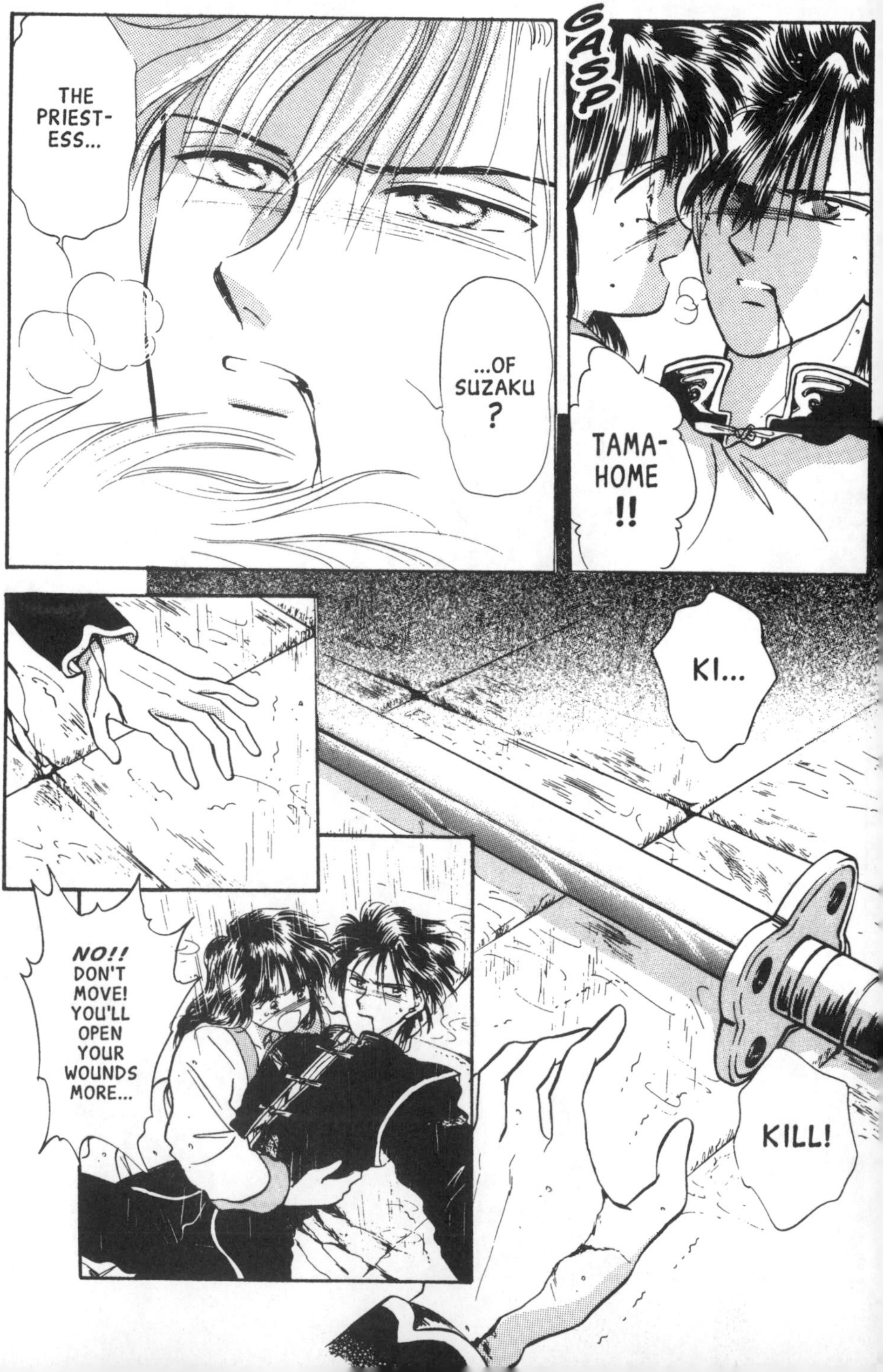
THE PRIEST-ESS...
...OF SUZAKU ?
GASP
TAMA-HOME !!
NO!! DON'T MOVE! YOU'LL OPEN YOUR WOUNDS MORE...
KI...
KILL!

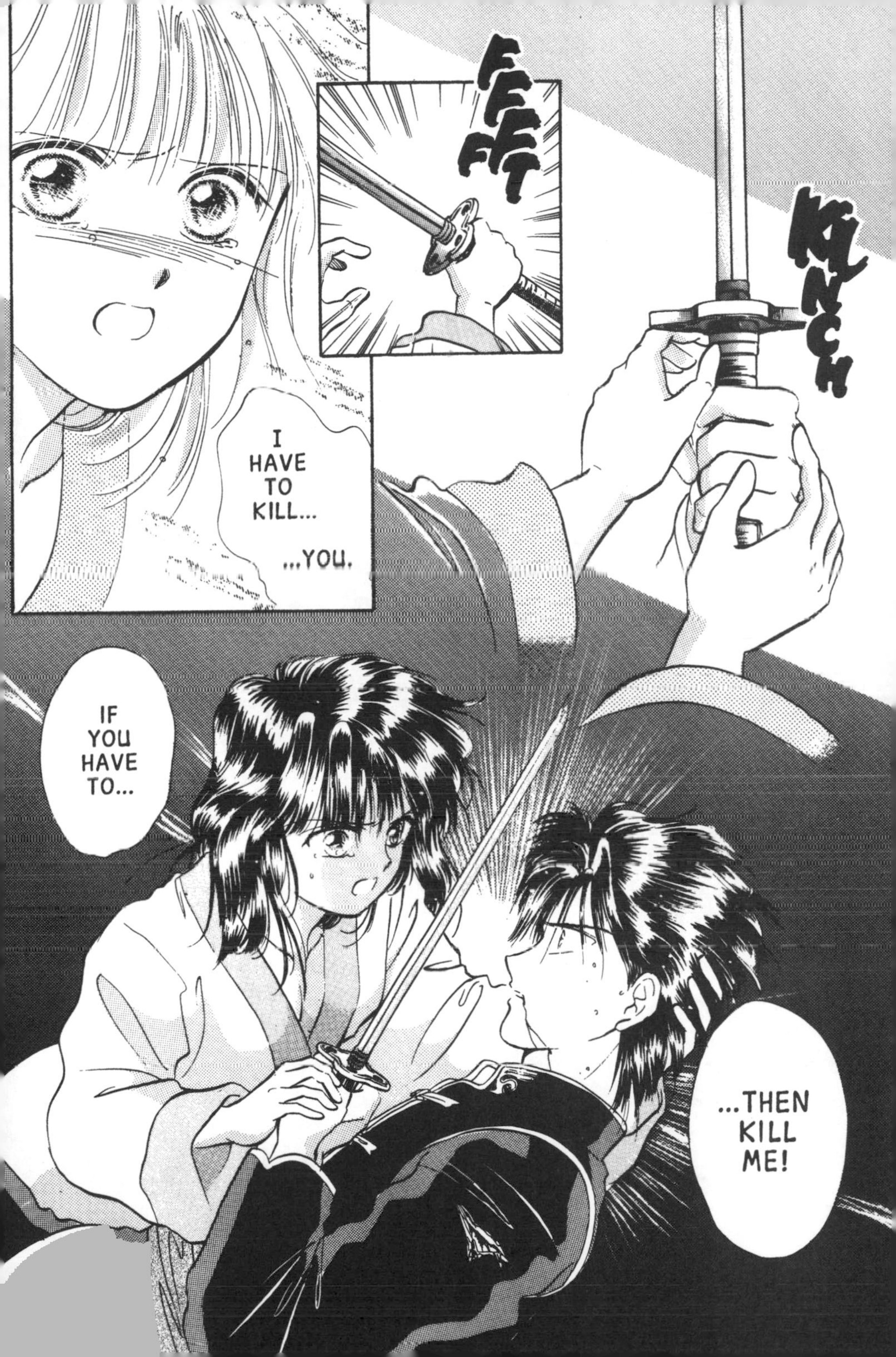
I HAVE TO KILL...
...YOU.
FFFFT
KLINCH
IF YOU HAVE TO...
...THEN KILL ME!

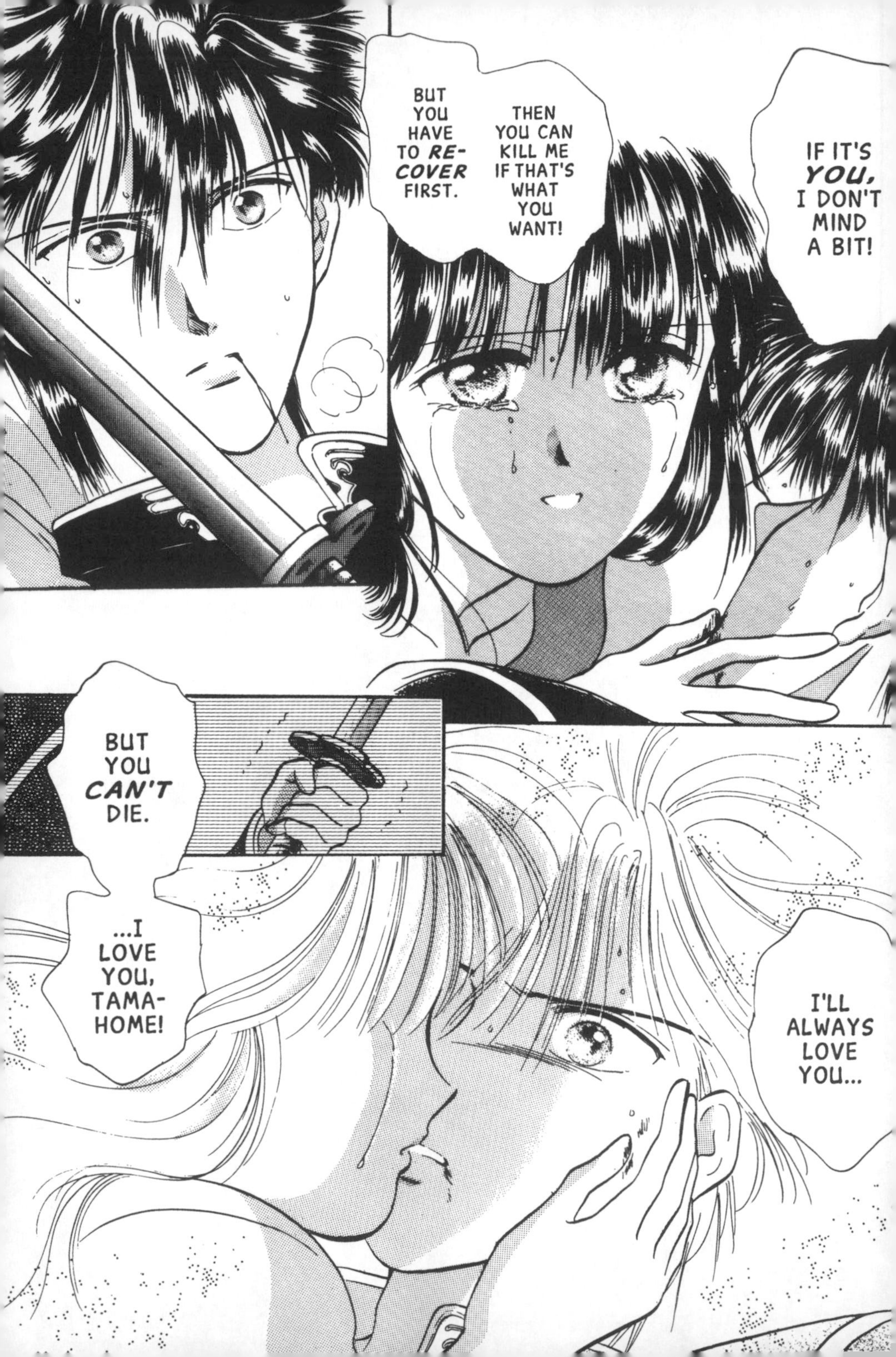
BUT YOU HAVE TO *RE-COVER* FIRST.
THEN YOU CAN KILL ME IF THAT'S WHAT YOU WANT!
IF IT'S *YOU,* I DON'T MIND A BIT!
BUT YOU *CAN'T* DIE.
...I LOVE YOU, TAMA-HOME!
I'LL ALWAYS LOVE YOU...

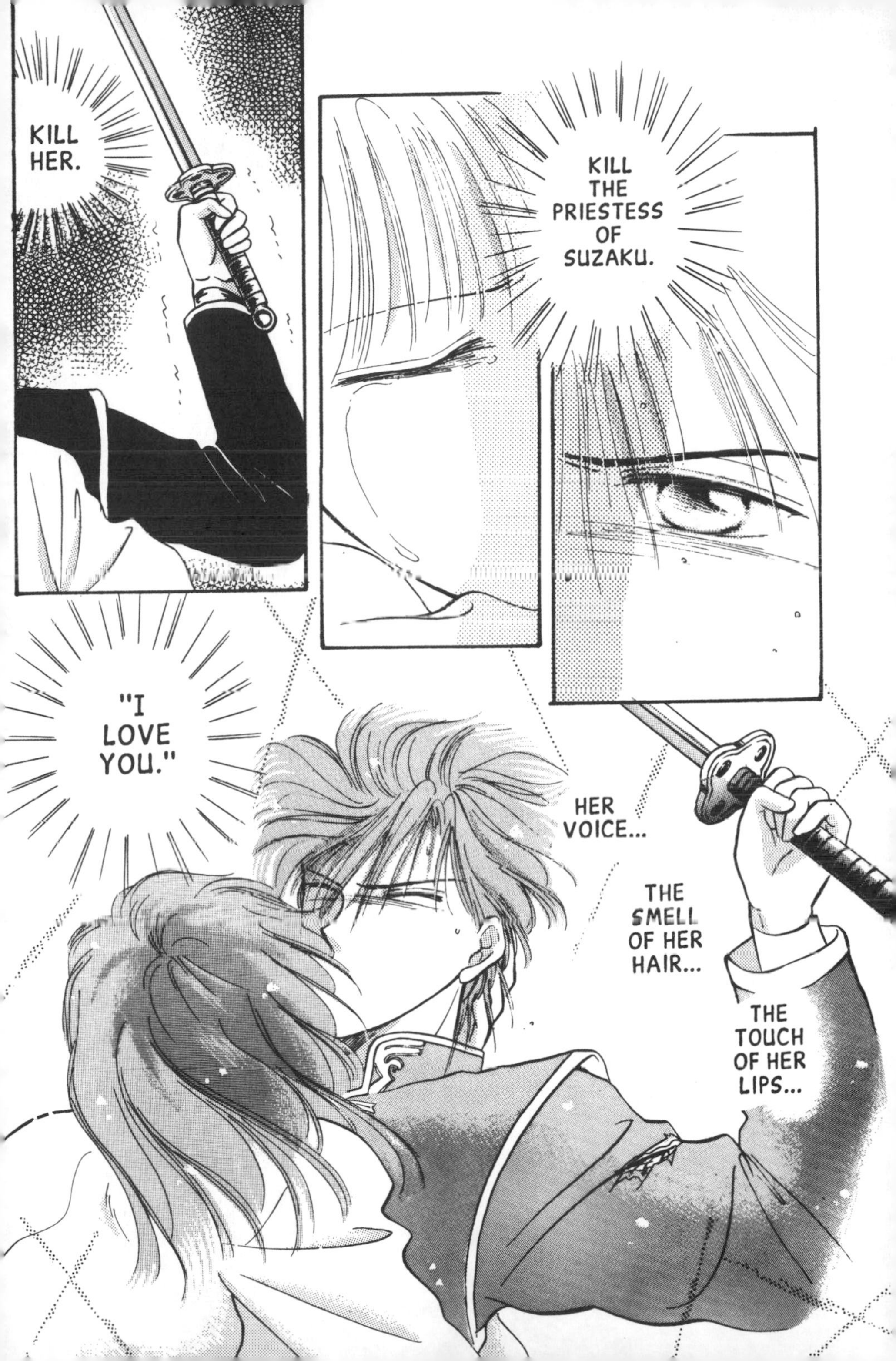
KILL HER.
KILL THE PRIESTESS OF SUZAKU.
"I LOVE YOU."
HER VOICE...
THE SMELL OF HER HAIR...
THE TOUCH OF HER LIPS...

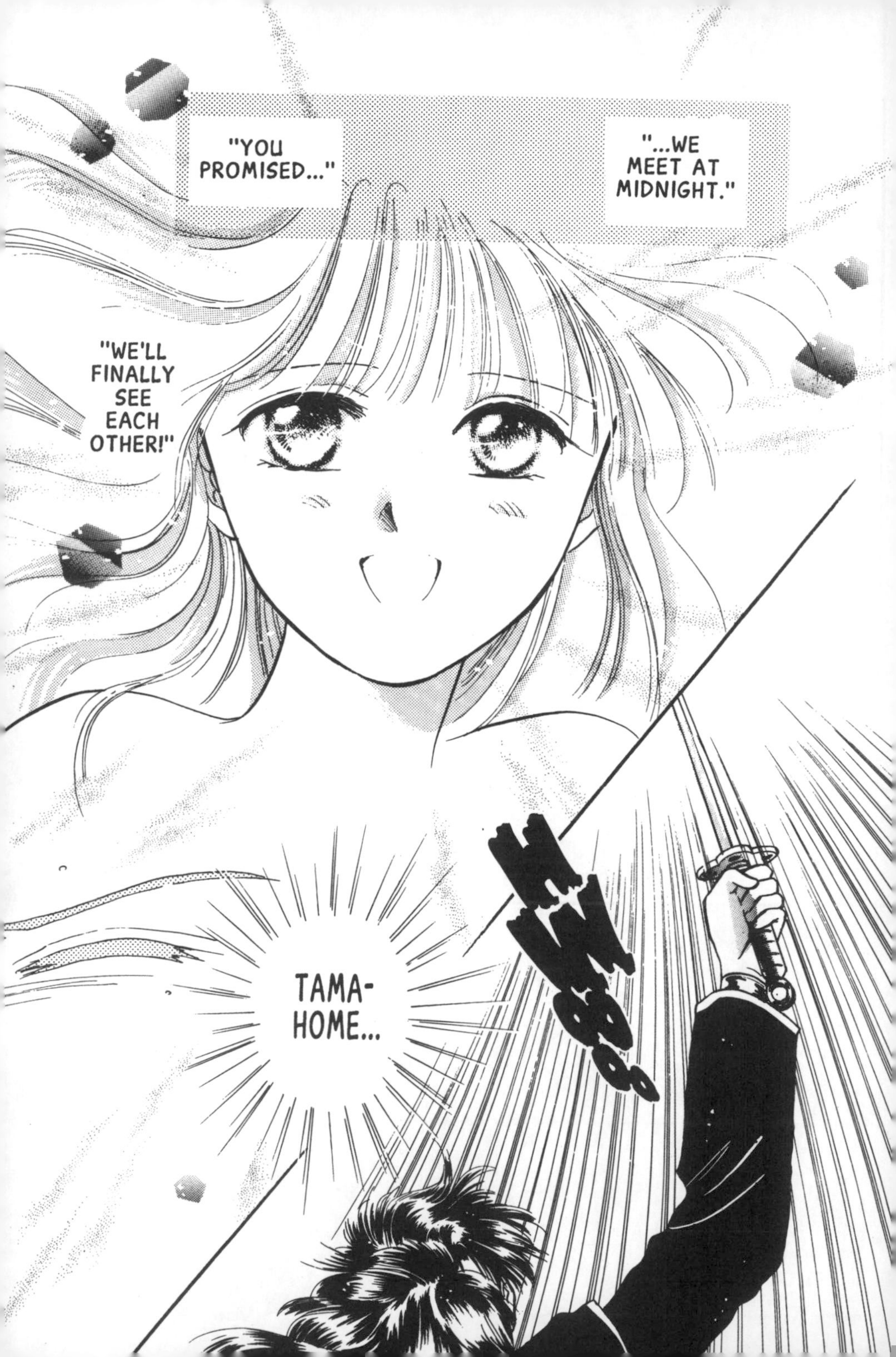
"YOU PROMISED..."
"...WE MEET AT MIDNIGHT."
"WE'LL FINALLY SEE EACH OTHER!"
TAMA-HOME...

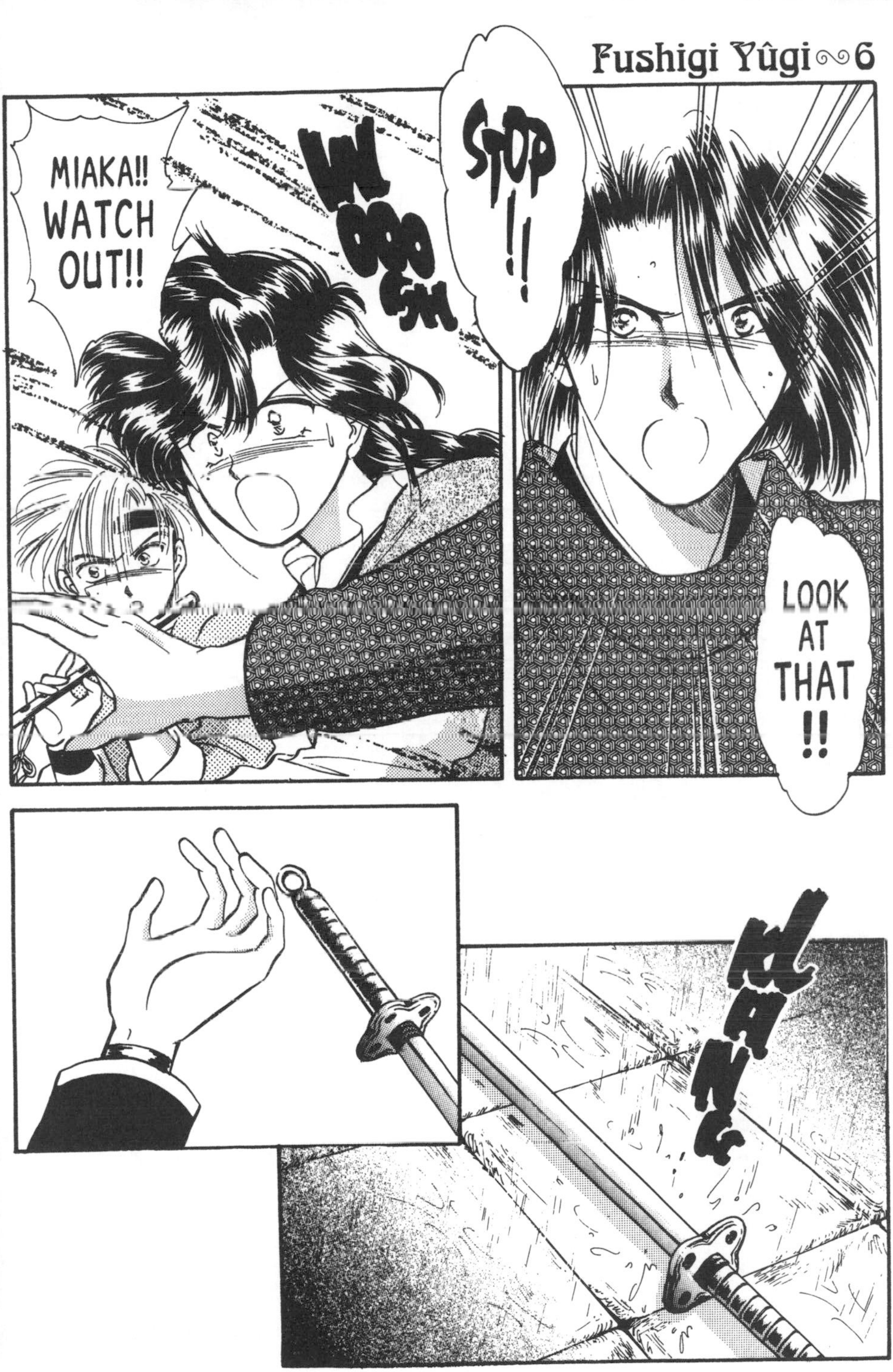
MIAKA!! WATCH OUT!!
WHOOOSH
STOP!!!
LOOK AT THAT!!
KLANG

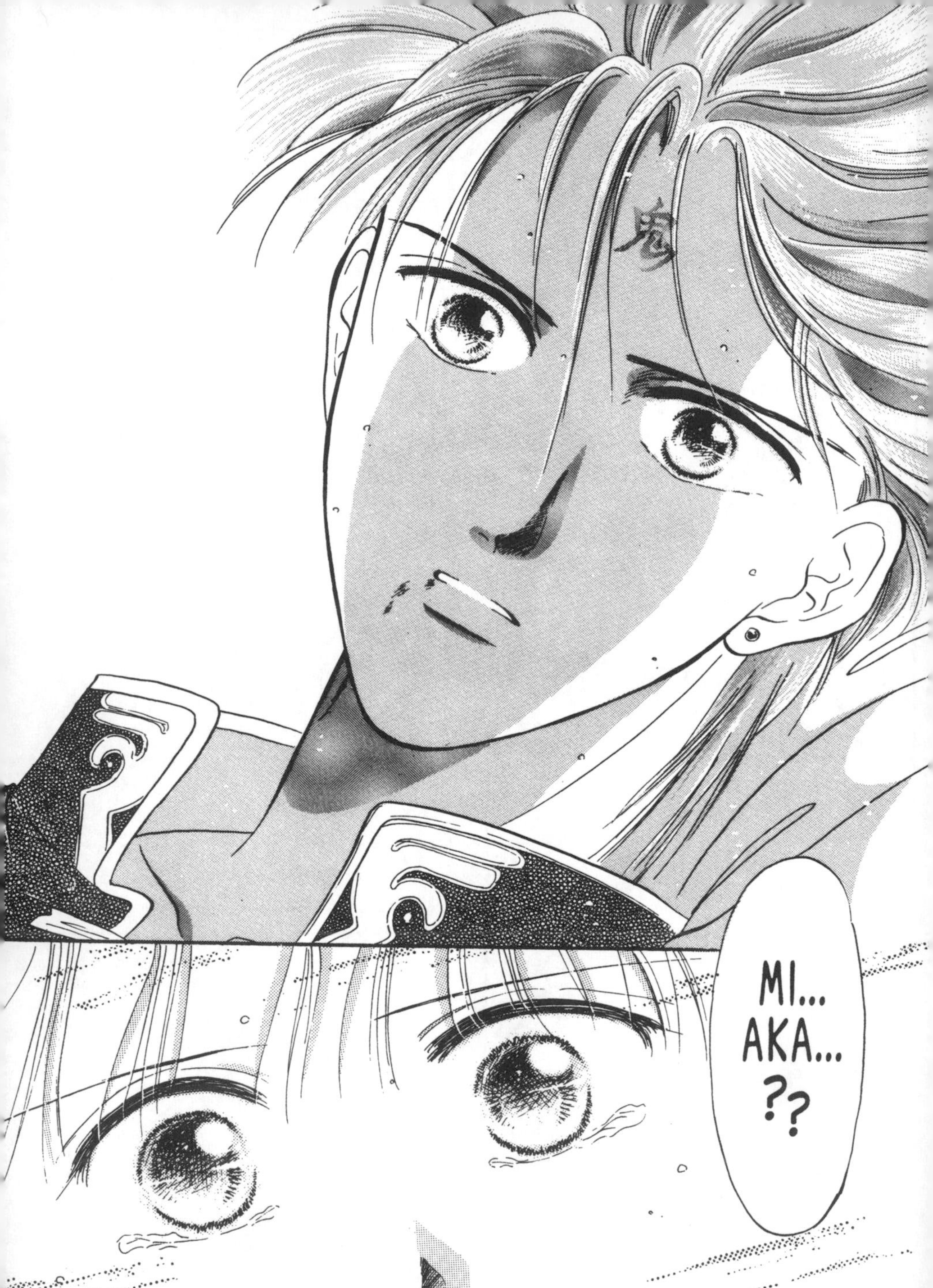
MI... AKA... ??

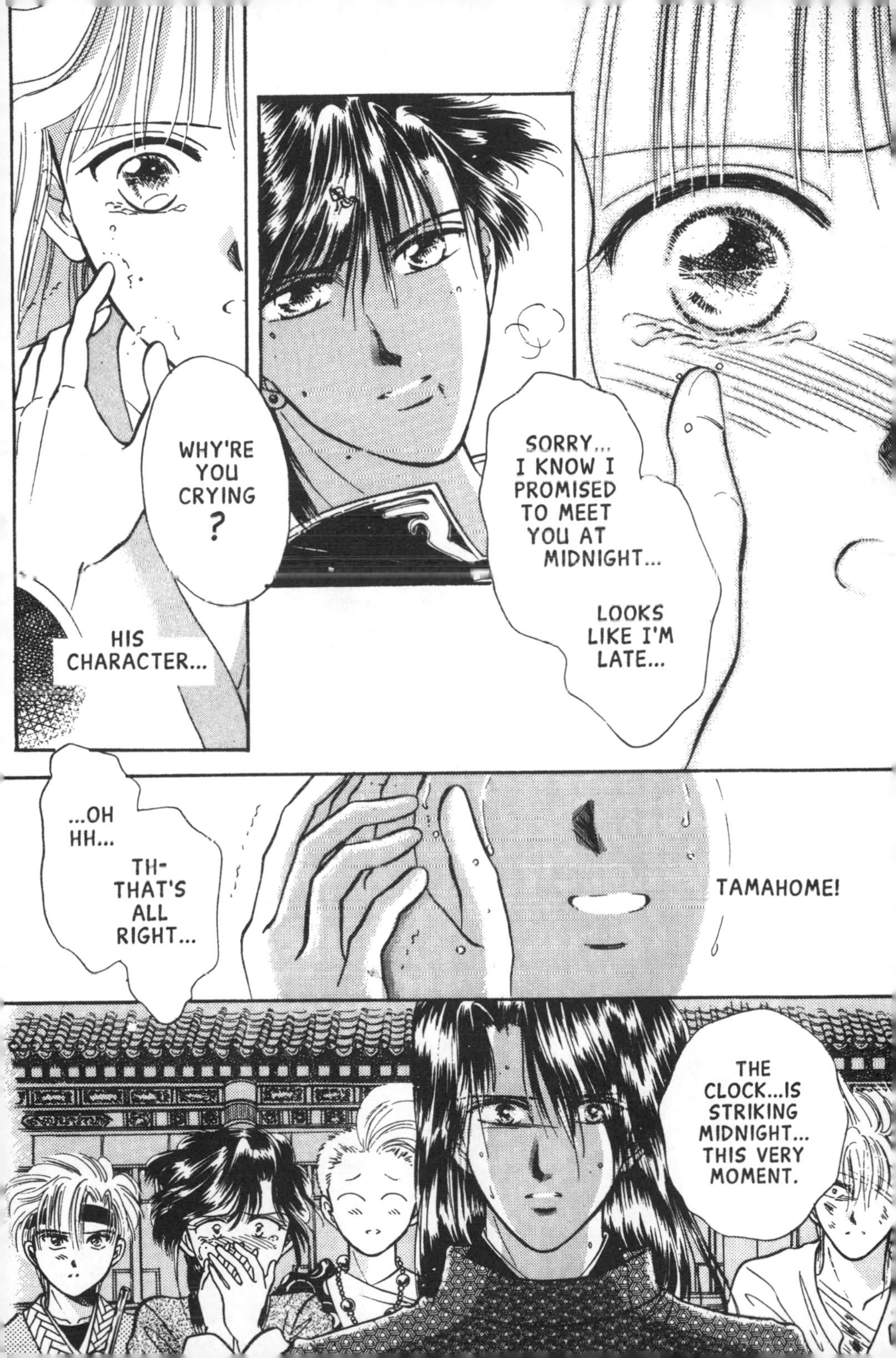
WHY'RE YOU CRYING ?
SORRY... I KNOW I PROMISED TO MEET YOU AT MIDNIGHT...
LOOKS LIKE I'M LATE...
HIS CHARACTER...
...OH HH...
TH-THAT'S ALL RIGHT...
TAMAHOME!
THE CLOCK...IS STRIKING MIDNIGHT... THIS VERY MOMENT.

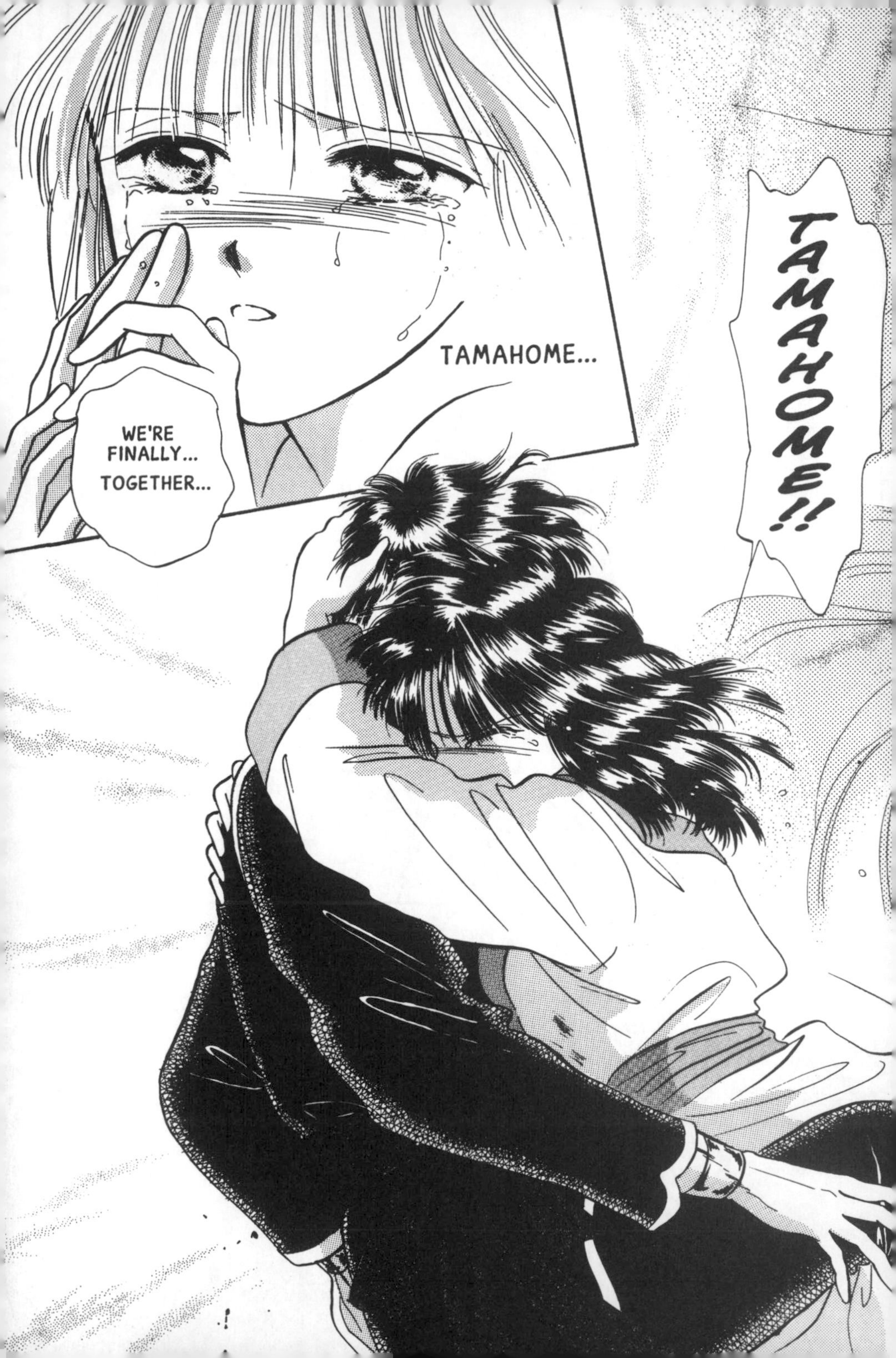
TAMAHOME...
WE'RE FINALLY... TOGETHER...
TAMAHOME!!

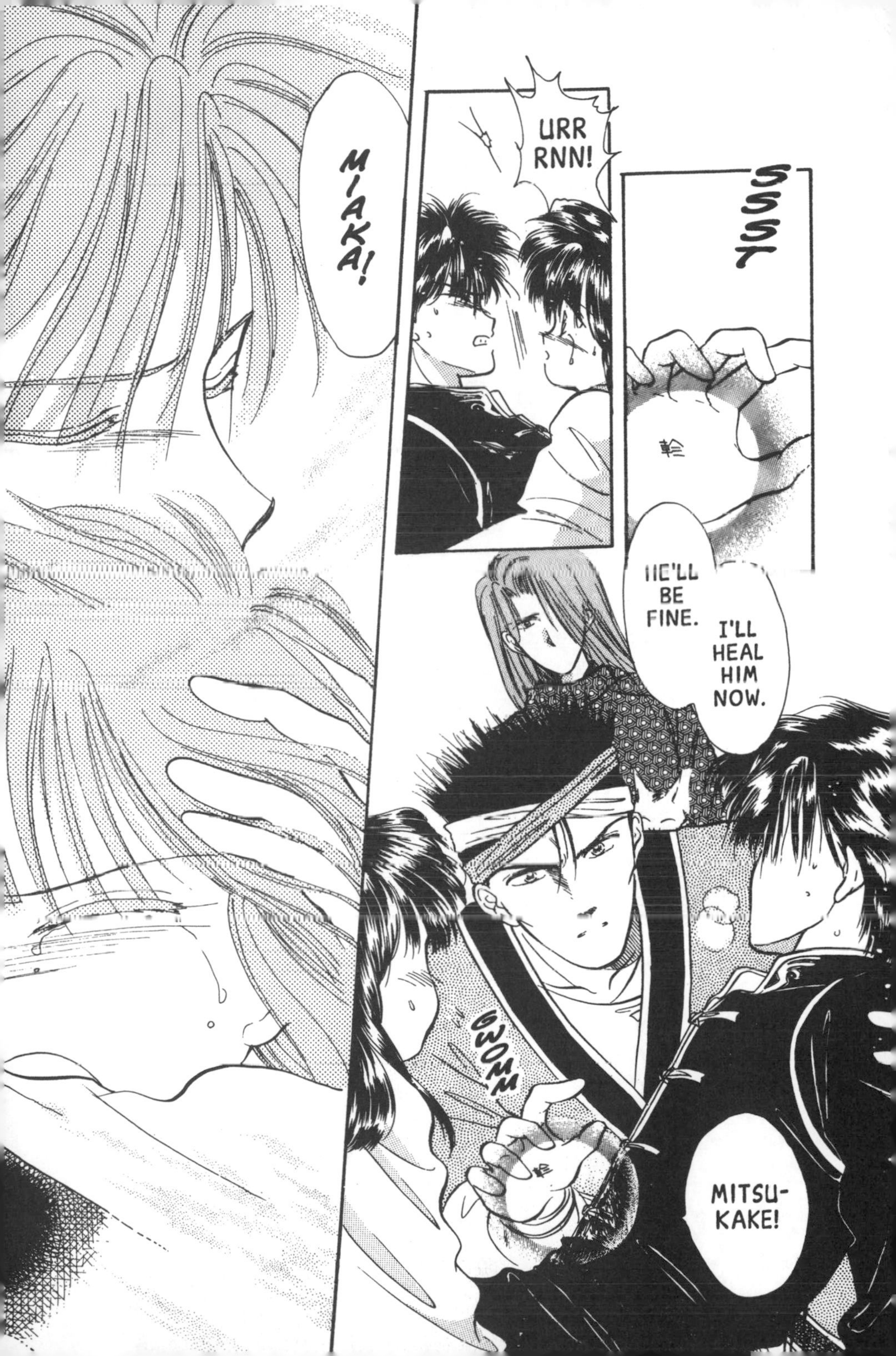
MIAKA!
URR RNN!
SSST
HE'LL BE FINE.
I'LL HEAL HIM NOW.
GWOMM
MITSU-KAKE!

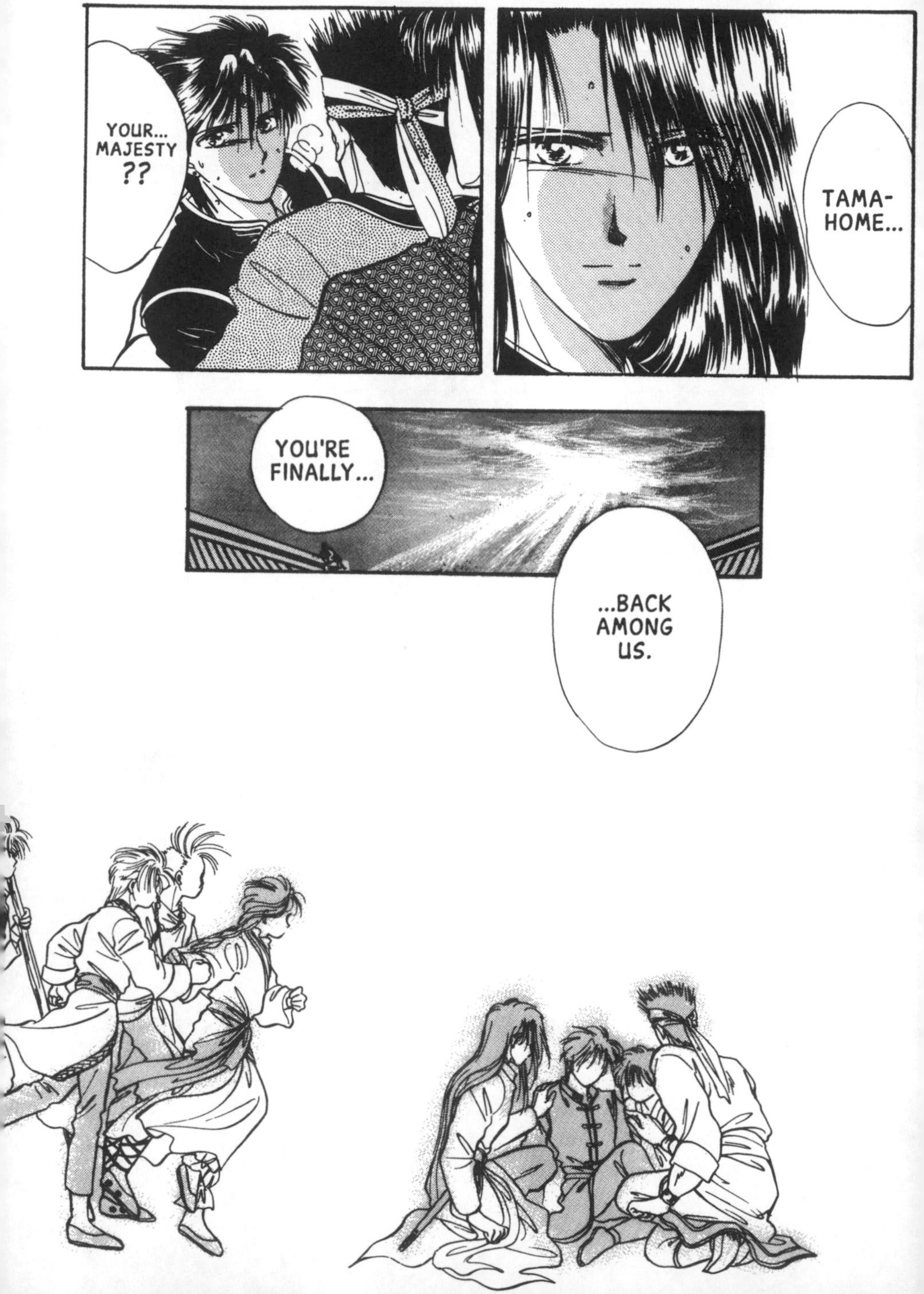
YOUR... MAJESTY ??
TAMA-HOME...
YOU'RE FINALLY...
...BACK AMONG US.

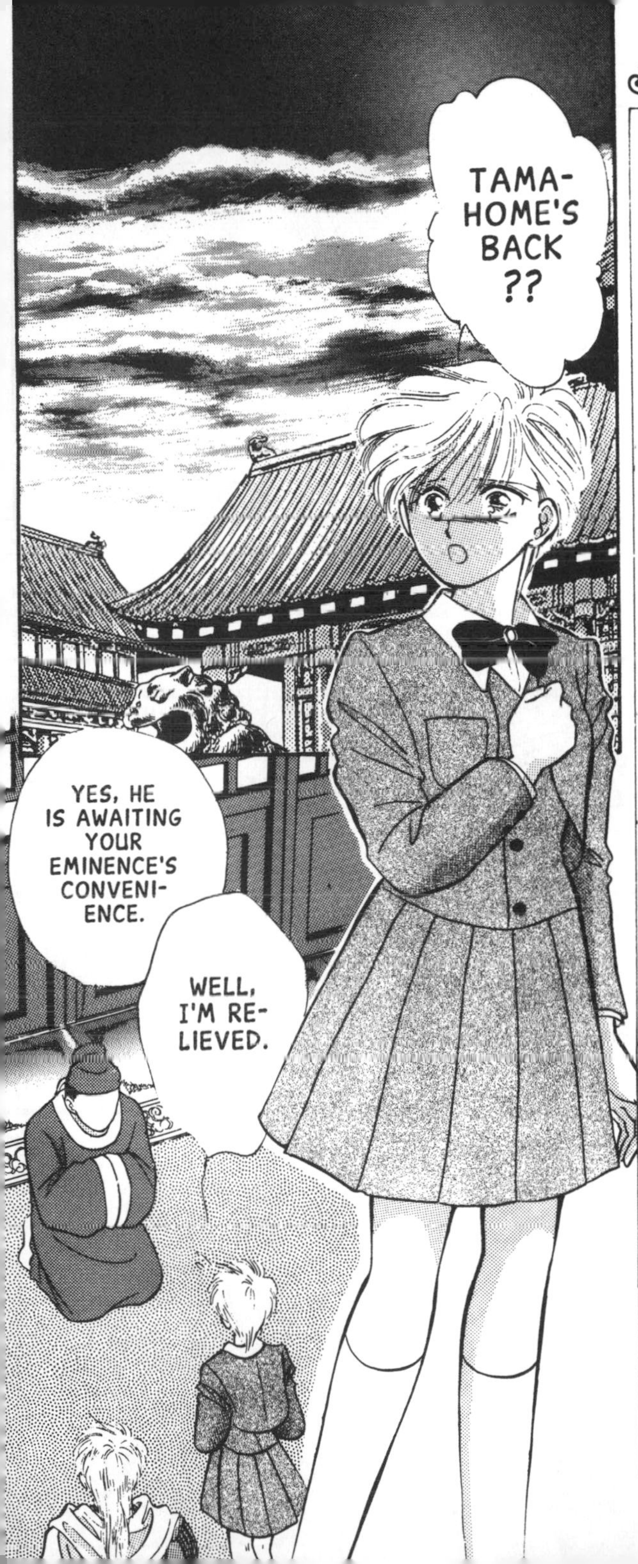
TAMA-HOME'S BACK ??
YES, HE IS AWAITING YOUR EMINENCE'S CONVENI-ENCE.
WELL, I'M RE-LIEVED.

Summoner

Well, no one died in this house. I never heard the footsteps, but I was up late at night working on a color image and the stereo suddenly shut off. It really surprised me. I started dancing in front of the stereo. I apologized, "I'm sorry, this is part of work too!!" Just like a husband making excuses to his wife's complaints! And then I went back to work again. *The stereo turning off really took me by surprise.* I felt like I was being told to go to bed. *The TV turned off while my mom was watching it.* Then the fan in the bathroom would shut off abruptly (it would start working again when I got mad at it), or the door would open on its own downstairs while we'd be sitting in the living room (this hap-pened all the time). Sleeping next to my parents, I could hear one more person breath-ing besides us. Come to think of it, whatever it was, it liked playing pranks. An interesting thing was whenever he (she?) walked up or down the old, creaky stairs, they would only make light thumping sounds. No living human could have made those sounds! The owner came home, so we moved out of the house after two years. Now we're all fine! (?)
I wonder what went on there. There really was something dark and murky about the place. Spider webs would form everywhere. It would get moldy. I hear that houses like that are more "prone"!!
So be careful!!

I wasn't afraid though...

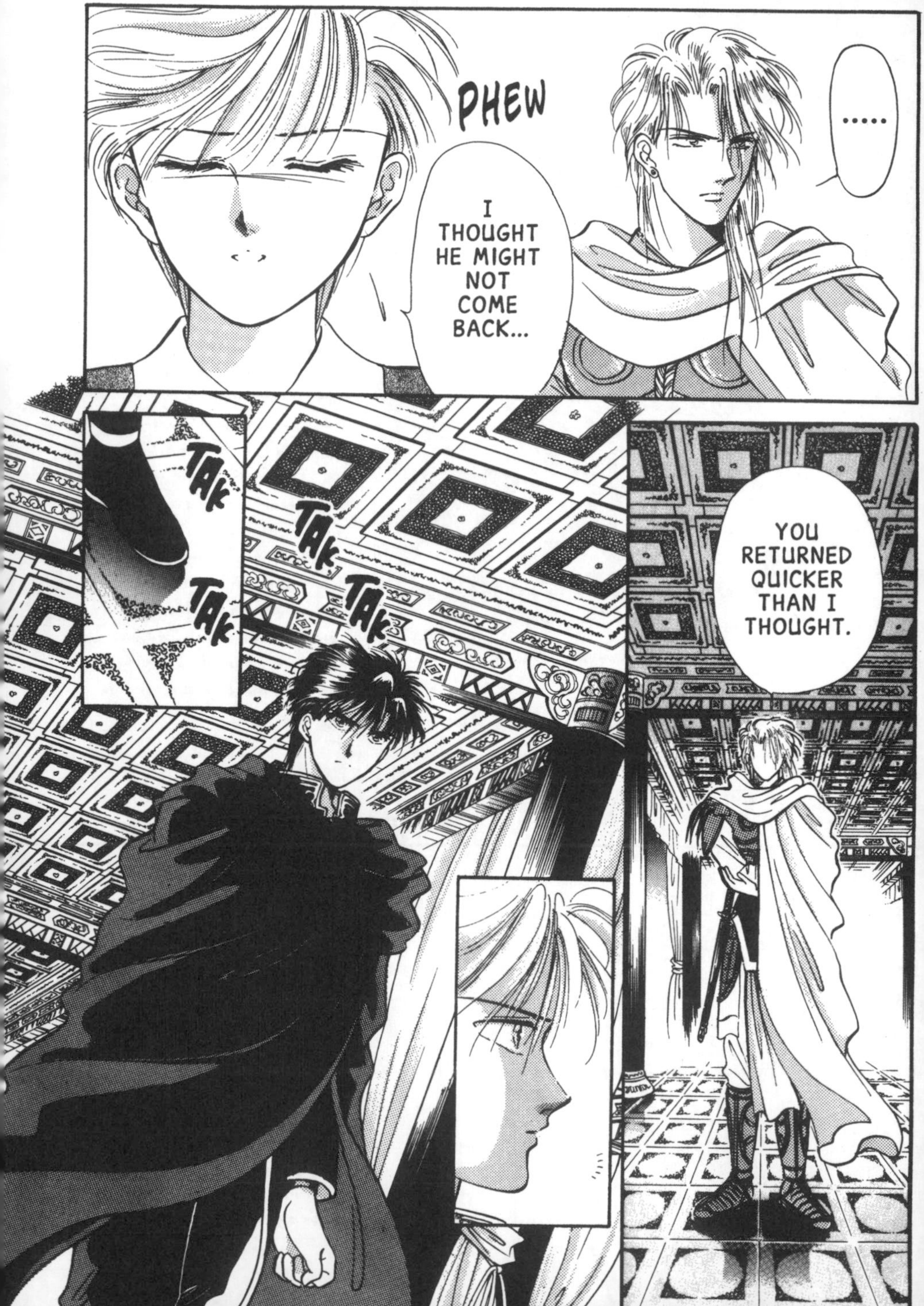
PHEW
I THOUGHT HE MIGHT NOT COME BACK...
......
TAK
TAK
TAK
TAK
YOU RETURNED QUICKER THAN I THOUGHT.

.....
TAK
TAK
SO YOU TOOK CARE OF THE PRIESTESS OF SUZAKU?
YES...
TAK
TAK
TAK
TAK
...TAMA-HOME.

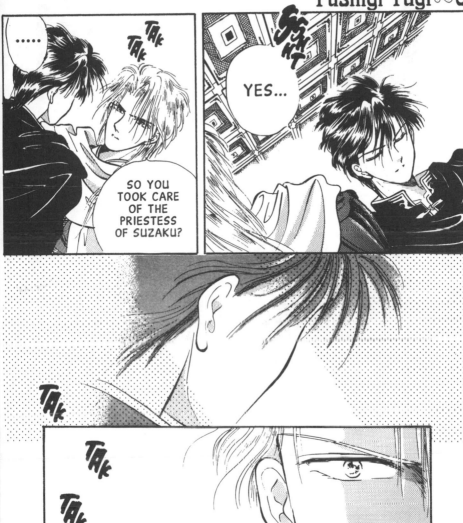

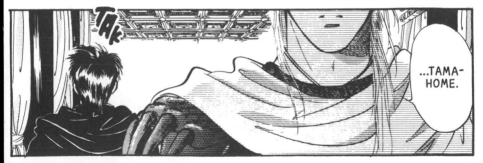

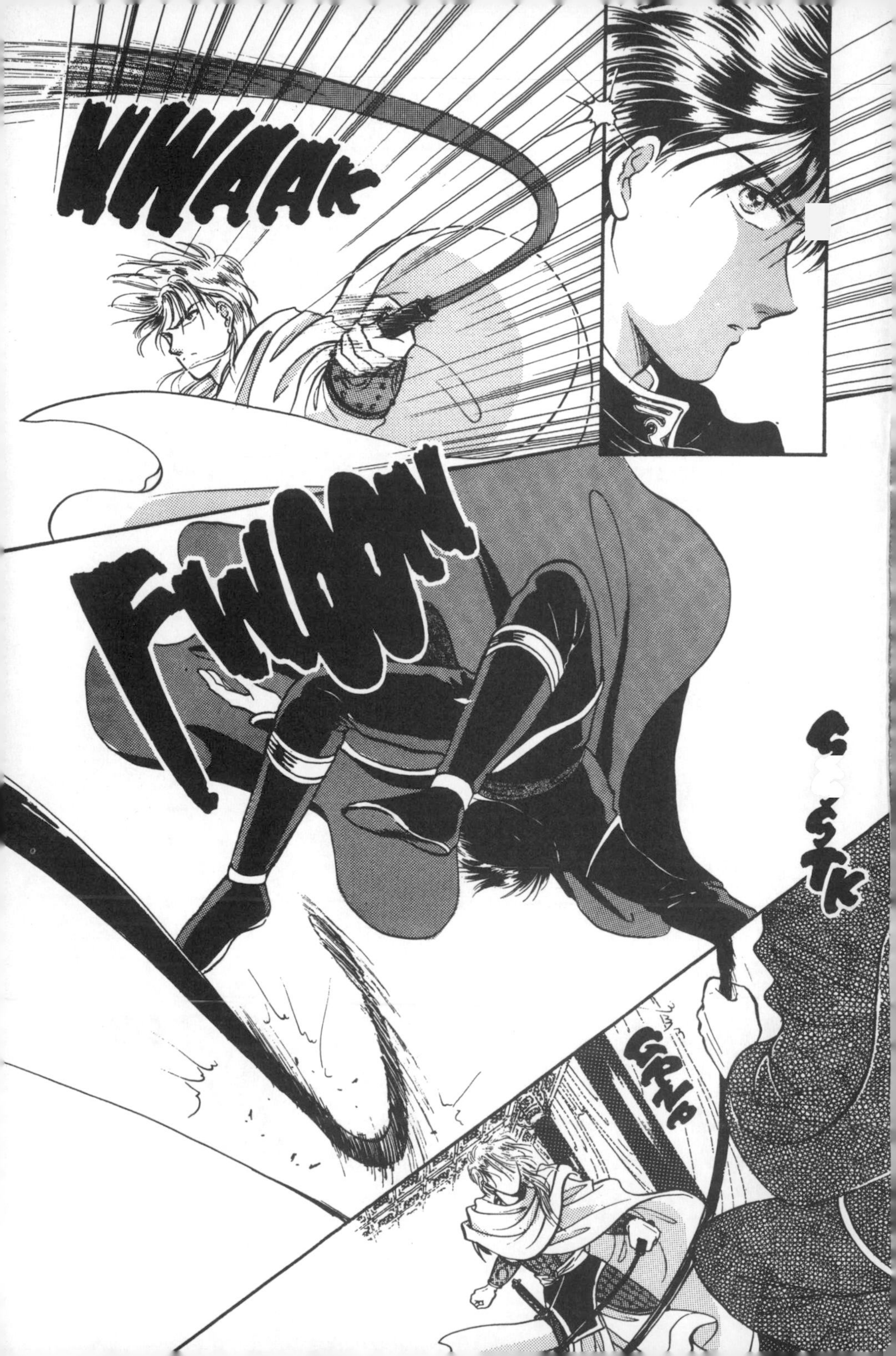
WWAAK
FWOOM
GRIP

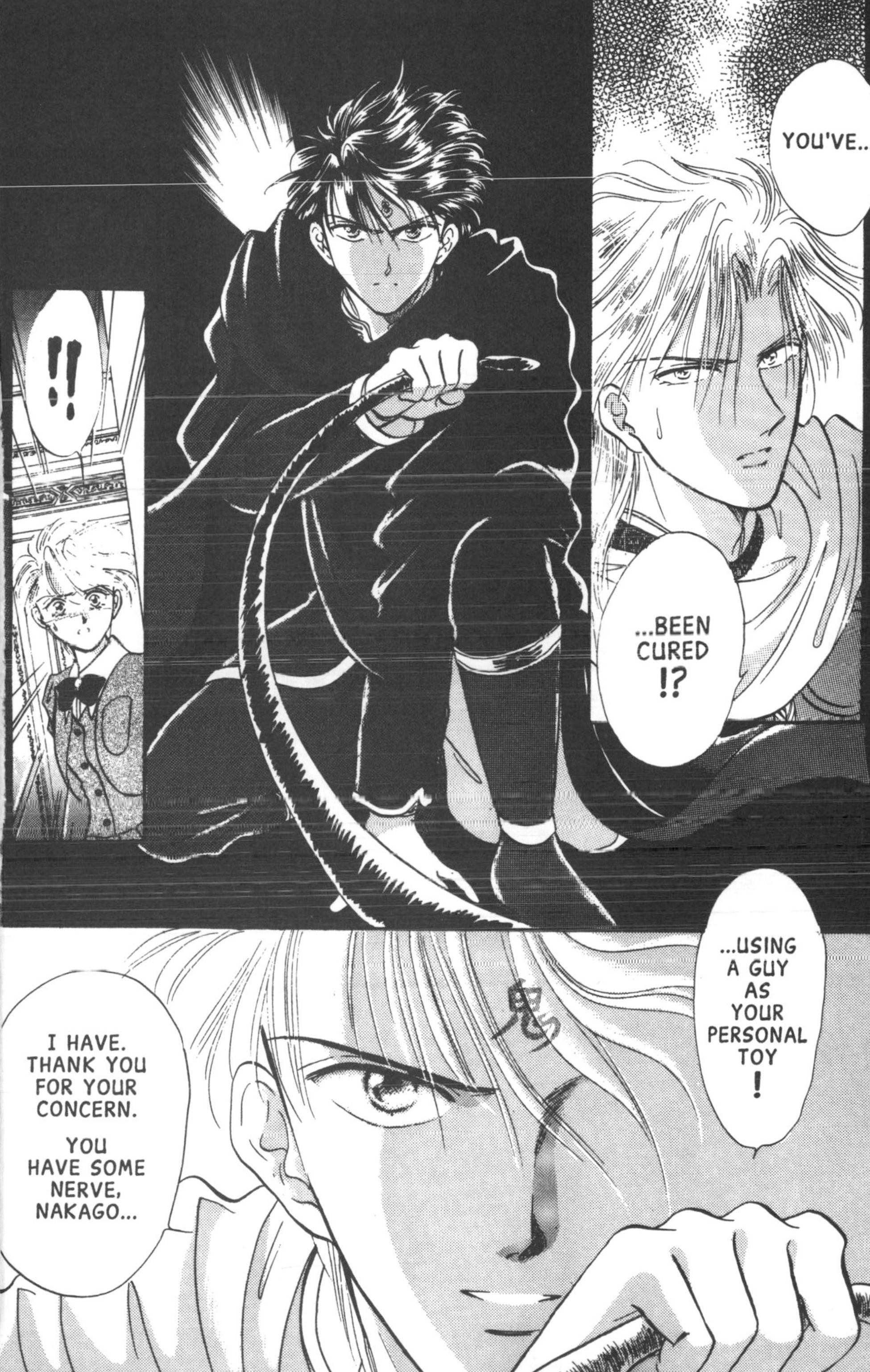
!!
YOU'VE...
...BEEN CURED !?
I HAVE. THANK YOU FOR YOUR CONCERN.
YOU HAVE SOME NERVE, NAKAGO...
...USING A GUY AS YOUR PERSONAL TOY!

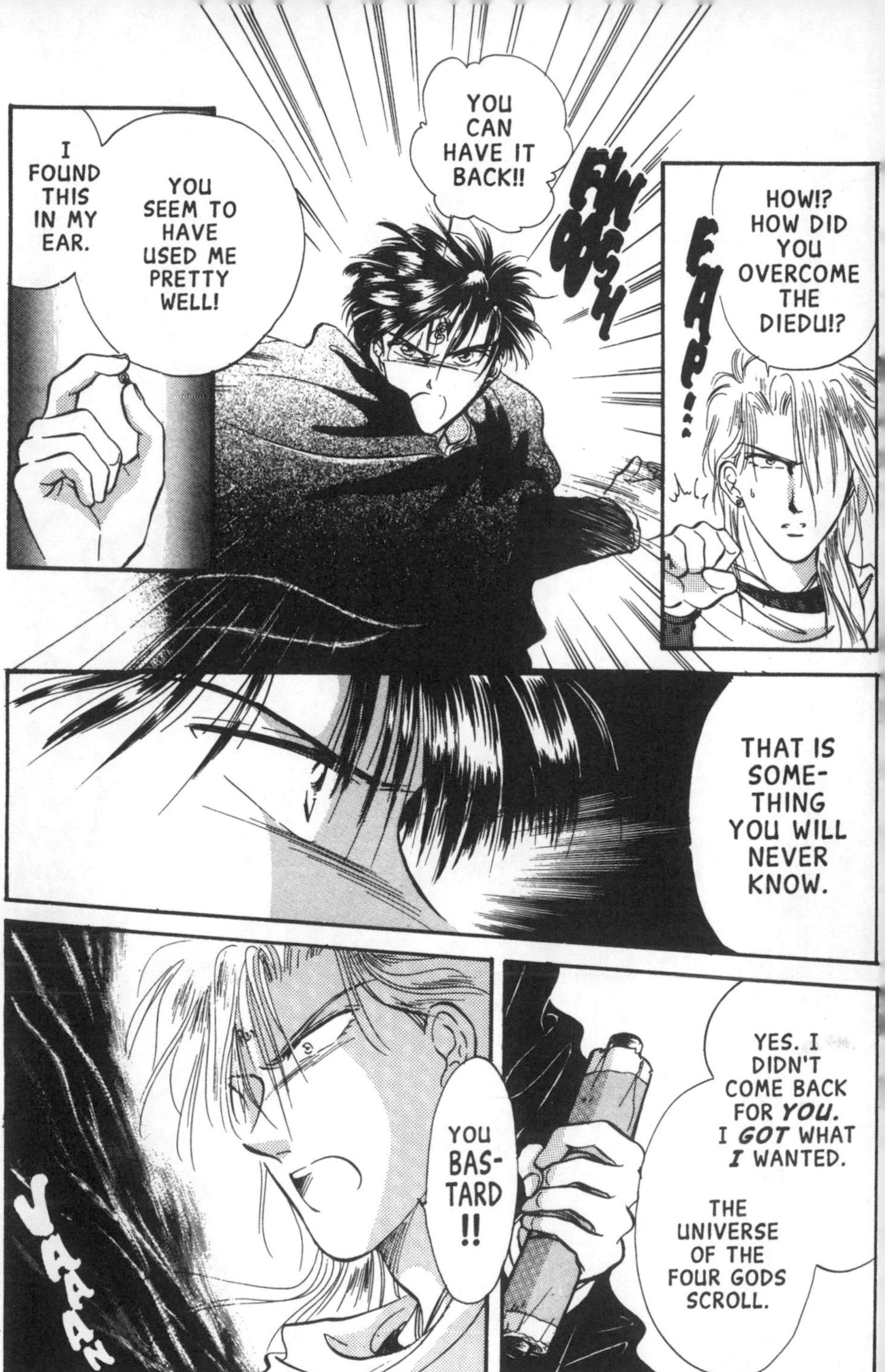
I FOUND THIS IN MY EAR.
YOU SEEM TO HAVE USED ME PRETTY WELL!
YOU CAN HAVE IT BACK!!
FWOOSH
HOW!? HOW DID YOU OVERCOME THE DIEDU!?
THAT IS SOME-THING YOU WILL NEVER KNOW.
VAAAN
YOU BAS-TARD!!
YES. I DIDN'T COME BACK FOR *YOU.* I *GOT* WHAT *I* WANTED.
THE UNIVERSE OF THE FOUR GODS SCROLL.

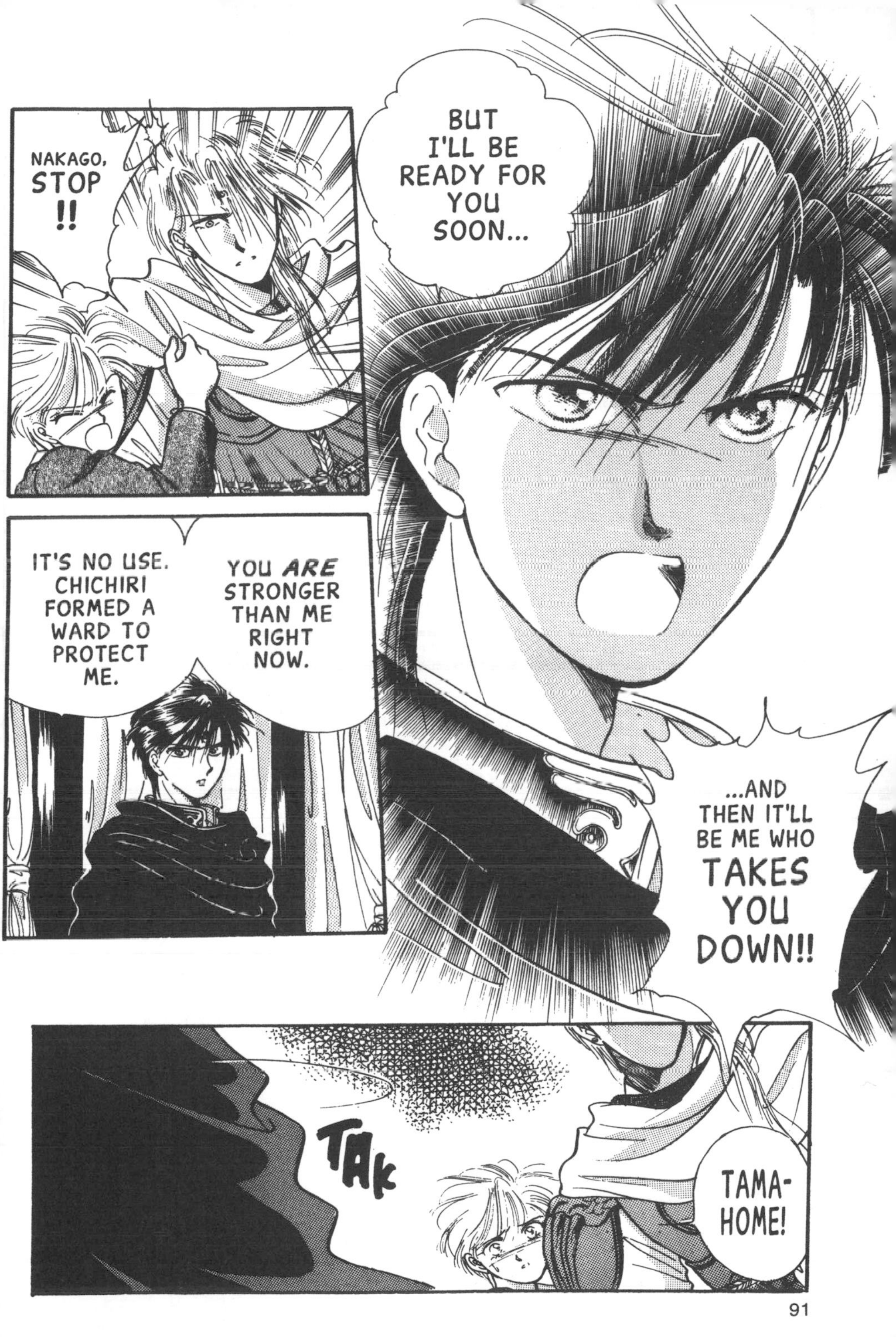
NAKAGO, STOP !!
IT'S NO USE. CHICHIRI FORMED A WARD TO PROTECT ME.
YOU *ARE* STRONGER THAN ME RIGHT NOW.
BUT I'LL BE READY FOR YOU SOON...
...AND THEN IT'LL BE ME WHO TAKES YOU DOWN!!
TAK
TAMA-HOME!

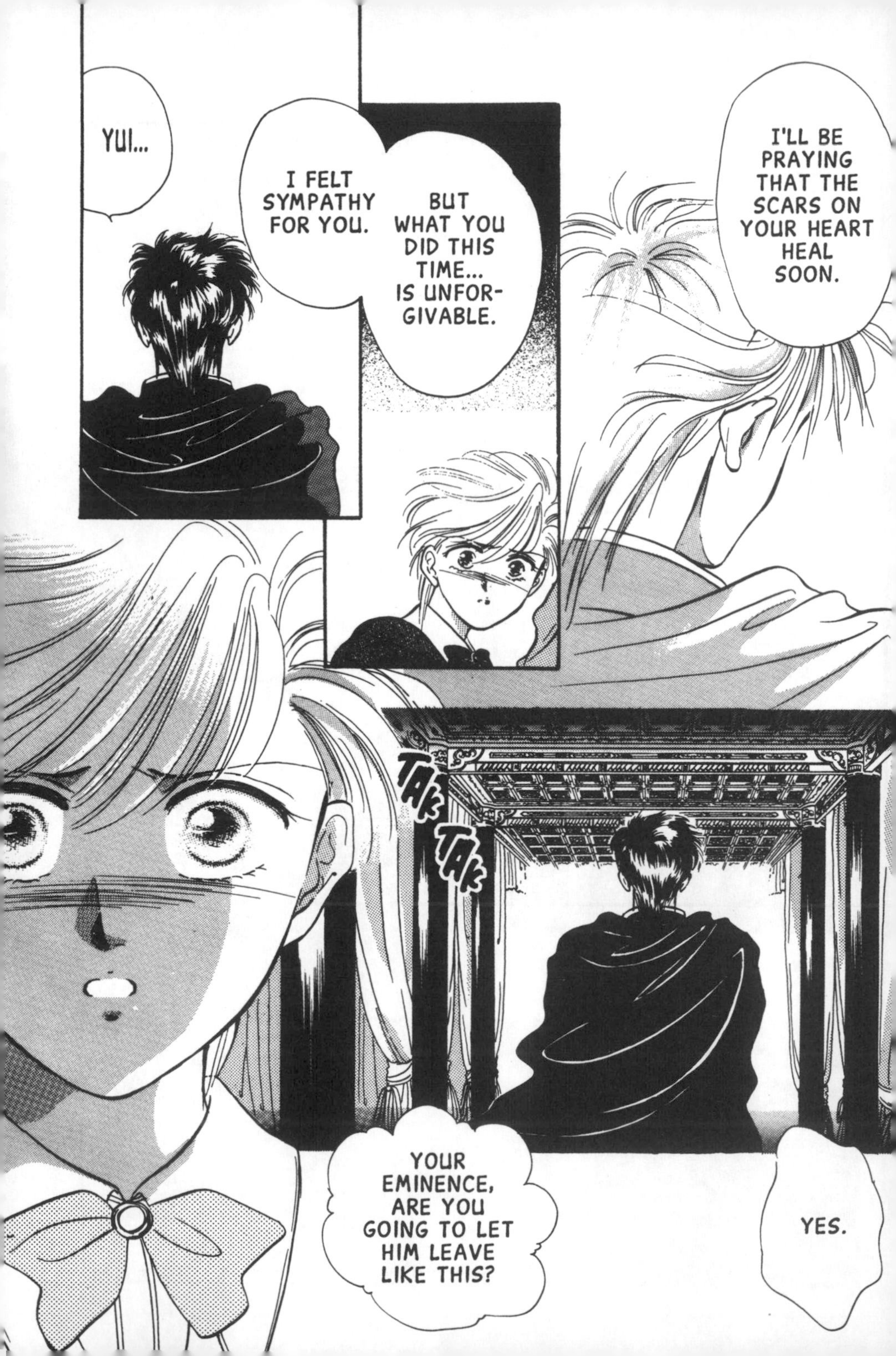
YUI...
I FELT SYMPATHY FOR YOU.
BUT WHAT YOU DID THIS TIME... IS UNFORGIVABLE.
I'LL BE PRAYING THAT THE SCARS ON YOUR HEART HEAL SOON.
TAK TAK
YOUR EMINENCE, ARE YOU GOING TO LET HIM LEAVE LIKE THIS?
YES.

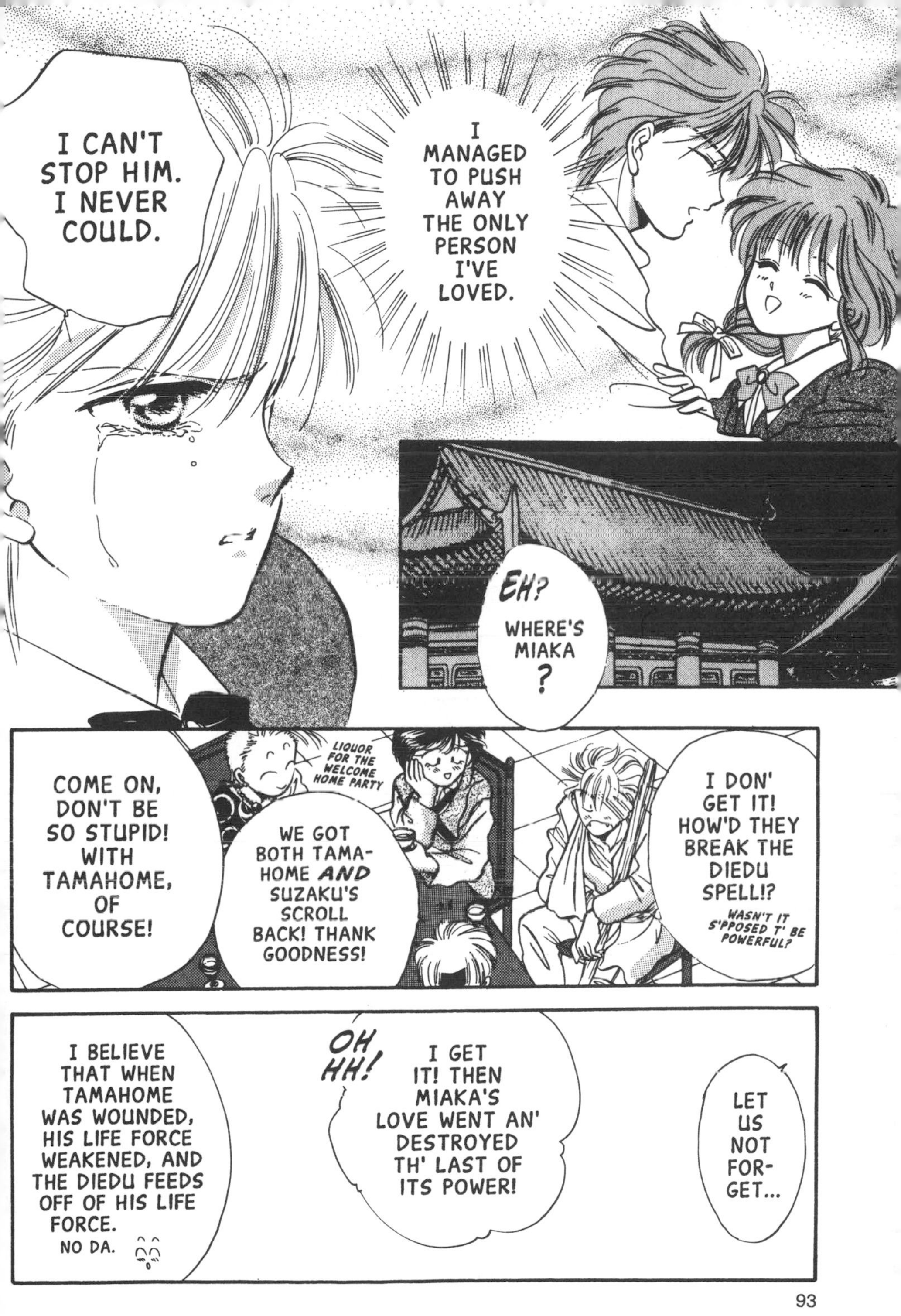

I CAN'T STOP HIM. I NEVER COULD.
I MANAGED TO PUSH AWAY THE ONLY PERSON I'VE LOVED.
EH?
WHERE'S MIAKA ?
COME ON, DON'T BE SO STUPID! WITH TAMAHOME, OF COURSE!
LIQUOR FOR THE WELCOME HOME PARTY
WE GOT BOTH TAMAHOME AND SUZAKU'S SCROLL BACK! THANK GOODNESS!
I DON' GET IT! HOW'D THEY BREAK THE DIEDU SPELL!?
WASN'T IT S'PPOSED T' BE POWERFUL?
I BELIEVE THAT WHEN TAMAHOME WAS WOUNDED, HIS LIFE FORCE WEAKENED, AND THE DIEDU FEEDS OFF OF HIS LIFE FORCE.
NO DA.
OH HH!
I GET IT! THEN MIAKA'S LOVE WENT AN' DESTROYED TH' LAST OF ITS POWER!
LET US NOT FORGET...

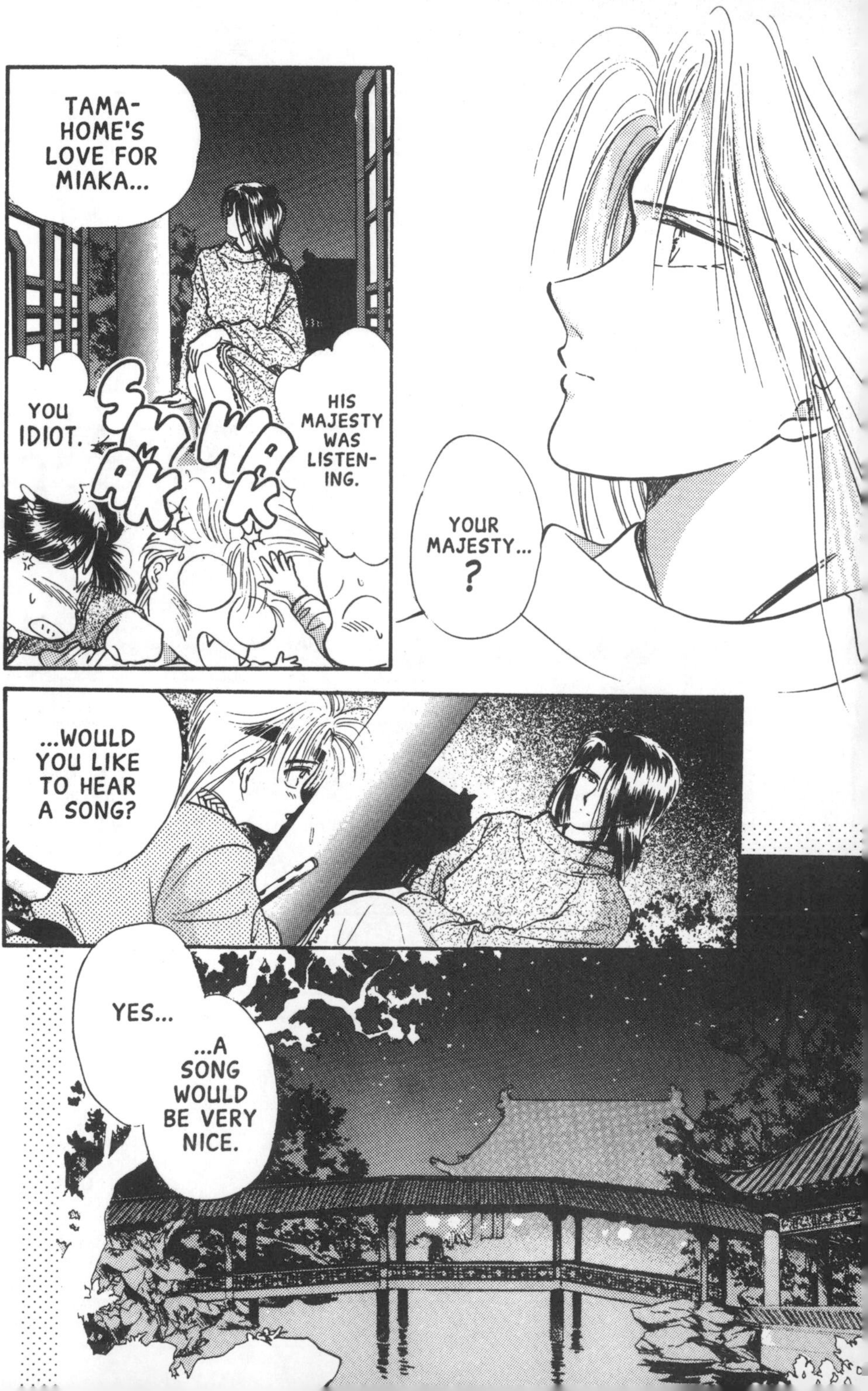
TAMA-HOME'S LOVE FOR MIAKA...
YOU IDIOT.
HIS MAJESTY WAS LISTEN-ING.
YOUR MAJESTY... ?
...WOULD YOU LIKE TO HEAR A SONG?
YES...
...A SONG WOULD BE VERY NICE.

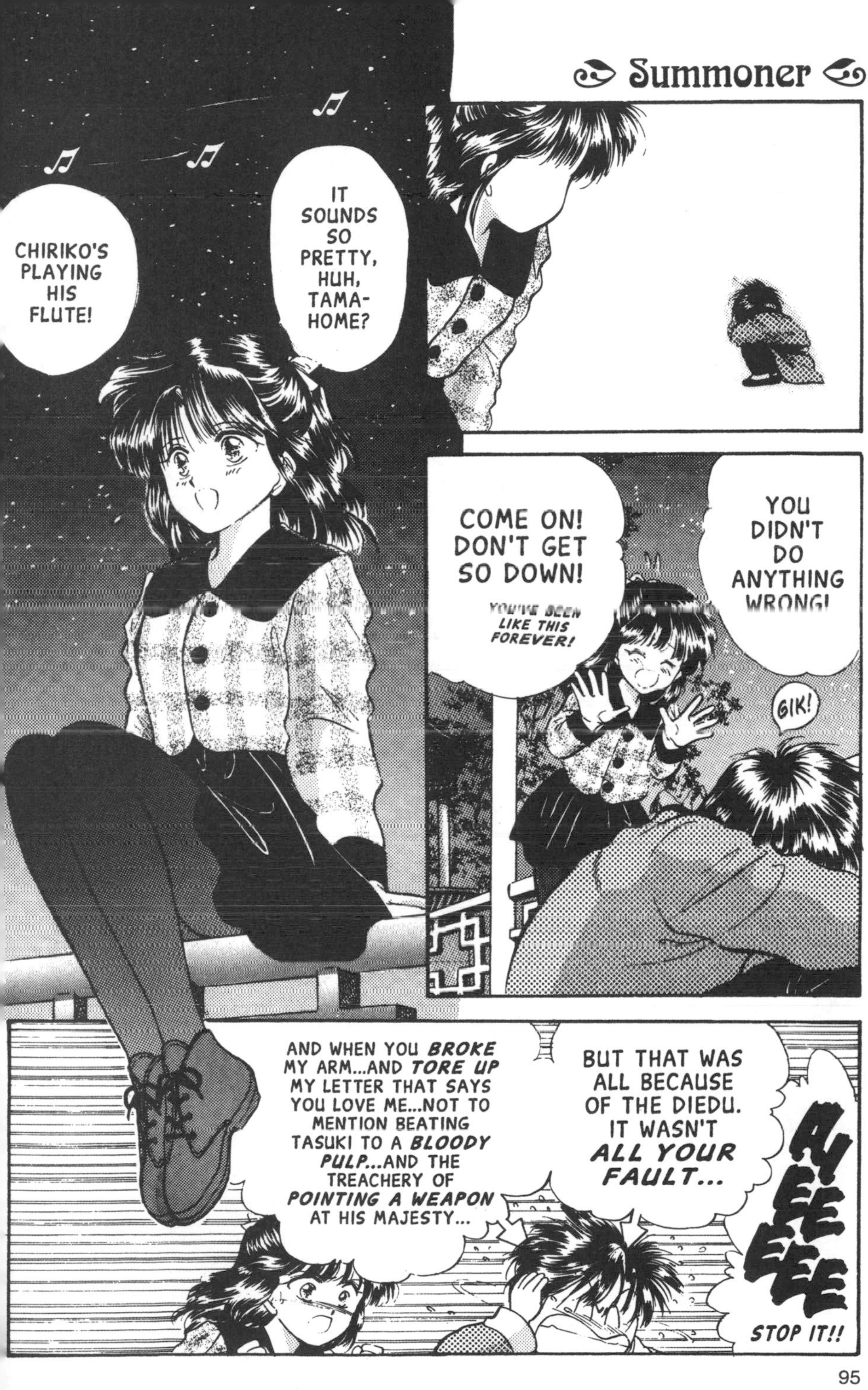

CHIRIKO'S PLAYING HIS FLUTE!
IT SOUNDS SO PRETTY, HUH, TAMA-HOME?
COME ON! DON'T GET SO DOWN!
YOU'VE BEEN LIKE THIS FOREVER!
YOU DIDN'T DO ANYTHING WRONG!
GIK!
AND WHEN YOU BROKE MY ARM...AND TORE UP MY LETTER THAT SAYS YOU LOVE ME...NOT TO MENTION BEATING TASUKI TO A BLOODY PULP...AND THE TREACHERY OF POINTING A WEAPON AT HIS MAJESTY...
BUT THAT WAS ALL BECAUSE OF THE DIEDU. IT WASN'T ALL YOUR FAULT...
AIEEEEEE
STOP IT!!

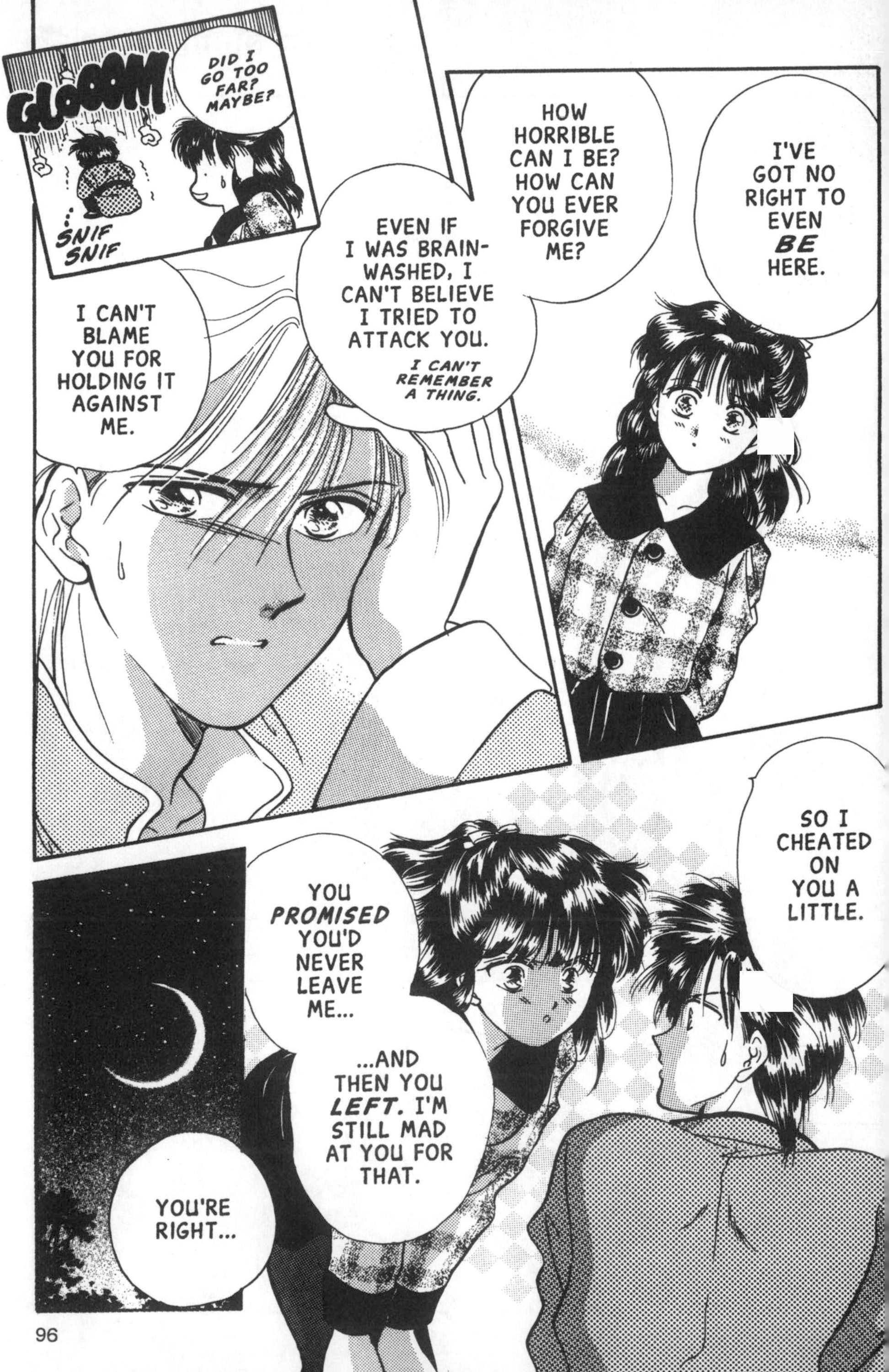
GLOOOM
DID I GO TOO FAR? MAYBE?
SNIF SNIF
I CAN'T BLAME YOU FOR HOLDING IT AGAINST ME.
EVEN IF I WAS BRAIN-WASHED, I CAN'T BELIEVE I TRIED TO ATTACK YOU.
I CAN'T REMEMBER A THING.
HOW HORRIBLE CAN I BE? HOW CAN YOU EVER FORGIVE ME?
I'VE GOT NO RIGHT TO EVEN *BE* HERE.
YOU *PROMISED* YOU'D NEVER LEAVE ME...
...AND THEN YOU *LEFT.* I'M STILL MAD AT YOU FOR THAT.
YOU'RE RIGHT...
SO I CHEATED ON YOU A LITTLE.

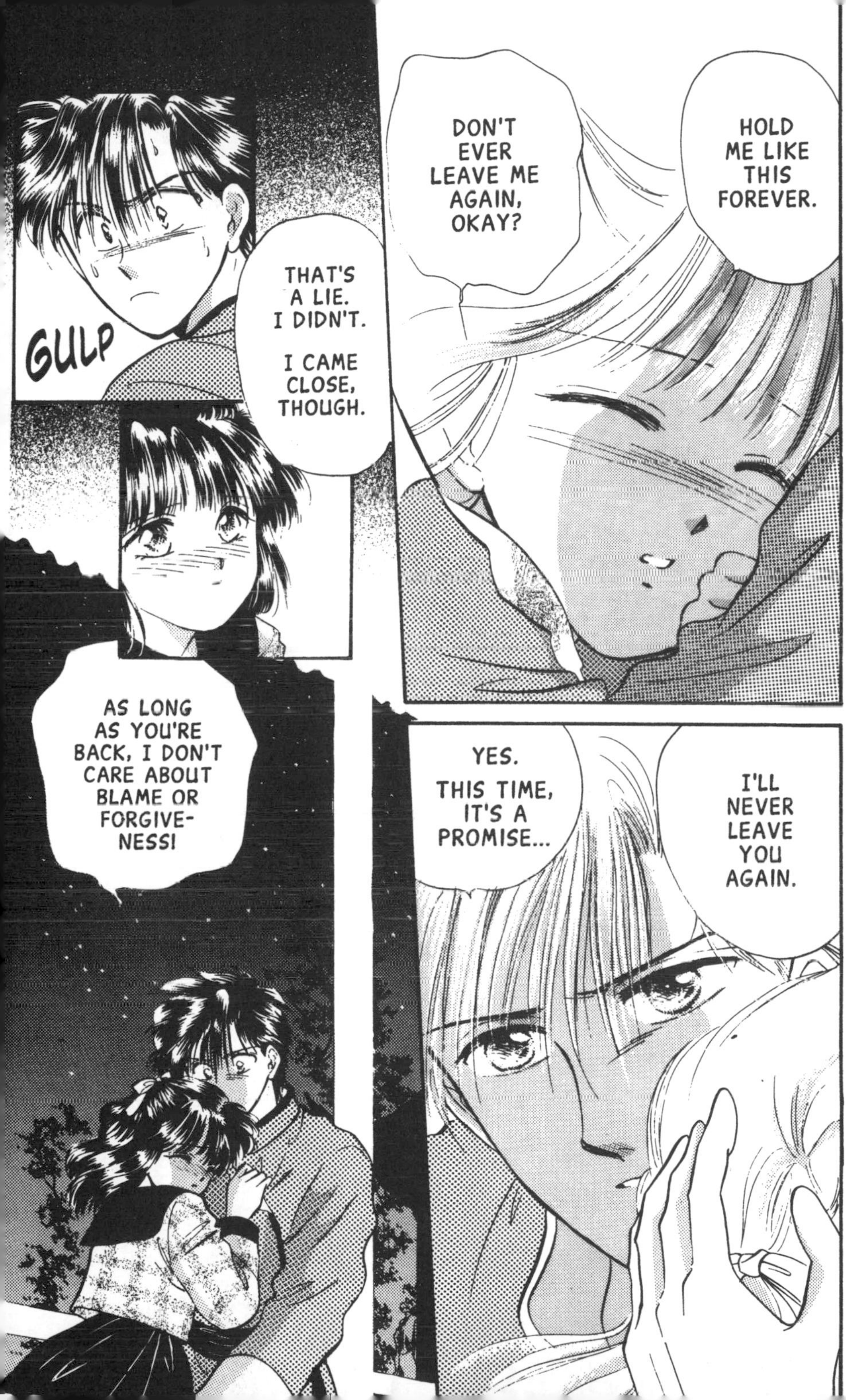
GULP
THAT'S A LIE. I DIDN'T. I CAME CLOSE, THOUGH.
AS LONG AS YOU'RE BACK, I DON'T CARE ABOUT BLAME OR FORGIVE-NESS!
DON'T EVER LEAVE ME AGAIN, OKAY?
HOLD ME LIKE THIS FOREVER.
YES. THIS TIME, IT'S A PROMISE...
I'LL NEVER LEAVE YOU AGAIN.

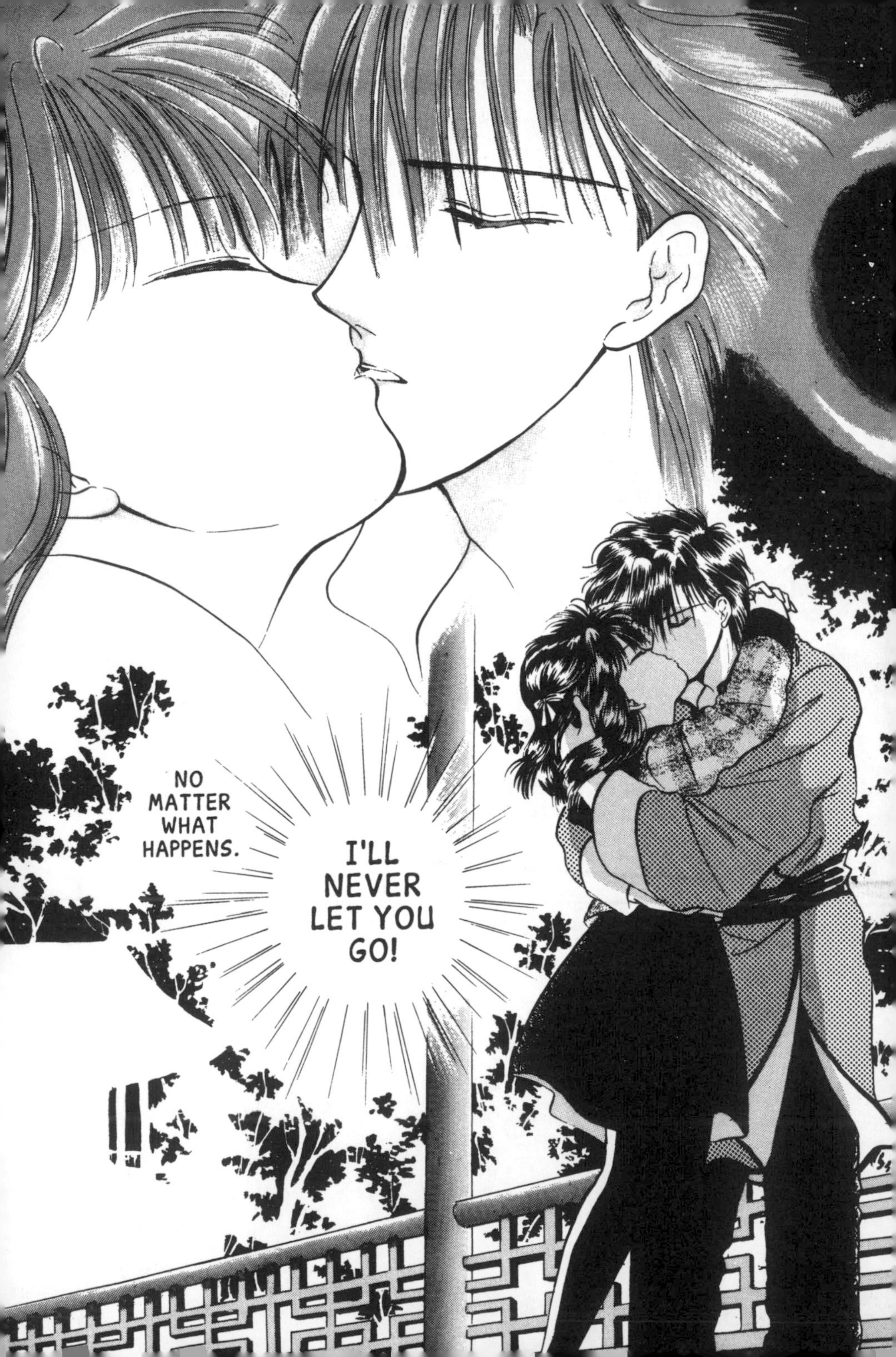
NO MATTER WHAT HAPPENS.
I'LL NEVER LET YOU GO!
!!

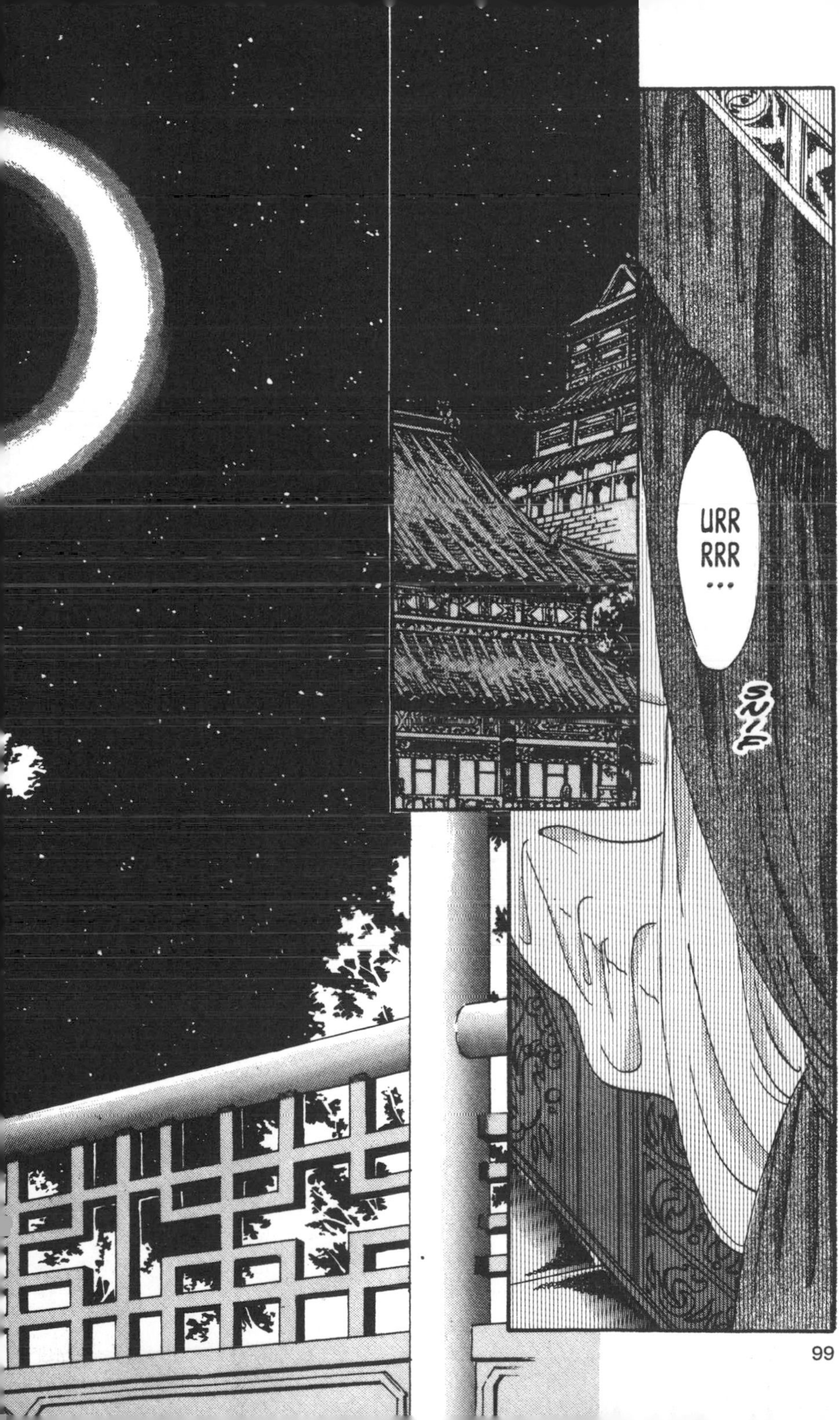
URR RRR ...
SNIF

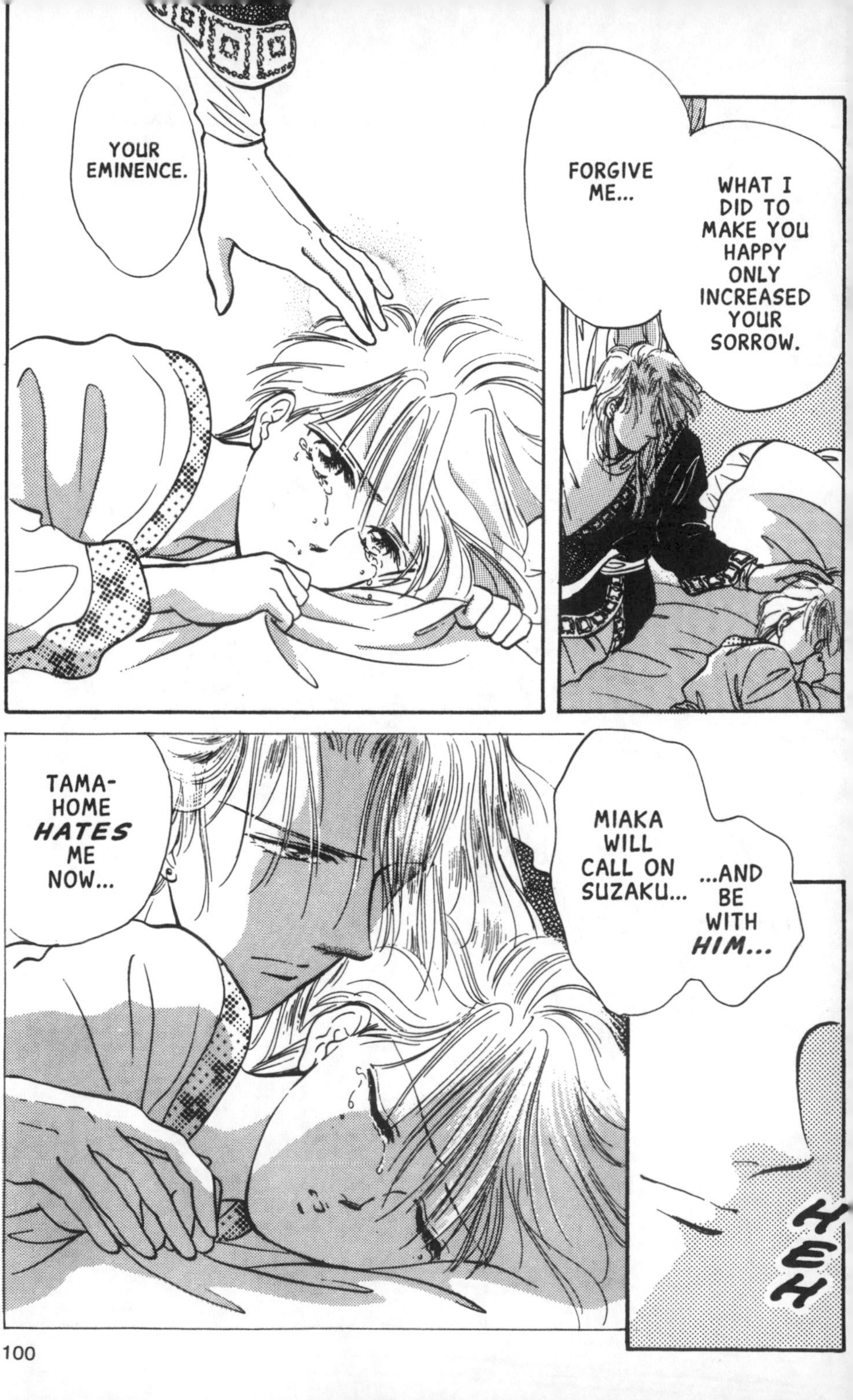
YOUR EMINENCE.
FORGIVE ME...
WHAT I DID TO MAKE YOU HAPPY ONLY INCREASED YOUR SORROW.
TAMA-HOME *HATES* ME NOW...
MIAKA WILL CALL ON SUZAKU...
...AND BE WITH *HIM*...
HEH

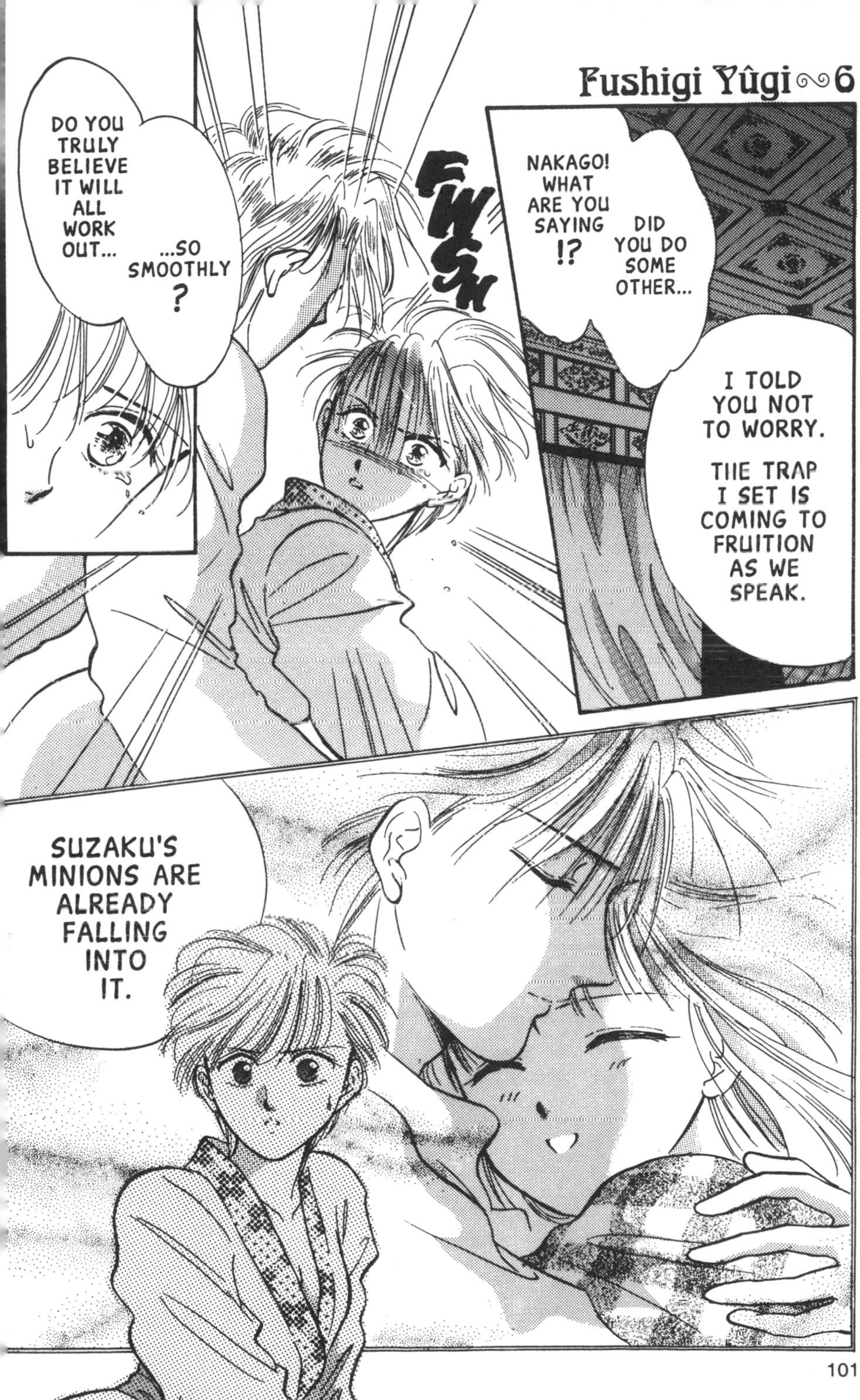
DO YOU TRULY BELIEVE IT WILL ALL WORK OUT...
...SO SMOOTHLY ?
FWSH
NAKAGO! WHAT ARE YOU SAYING !?
DID YOU DO SOME OTHER...
I TOLD YOU NOT TO WORRY.
THE TRAP I SET IS COMING TO FRUITION AS WE SPEAK.
SUZAKU'S MINIONS ARE ALREADY FALLING INTO IT.

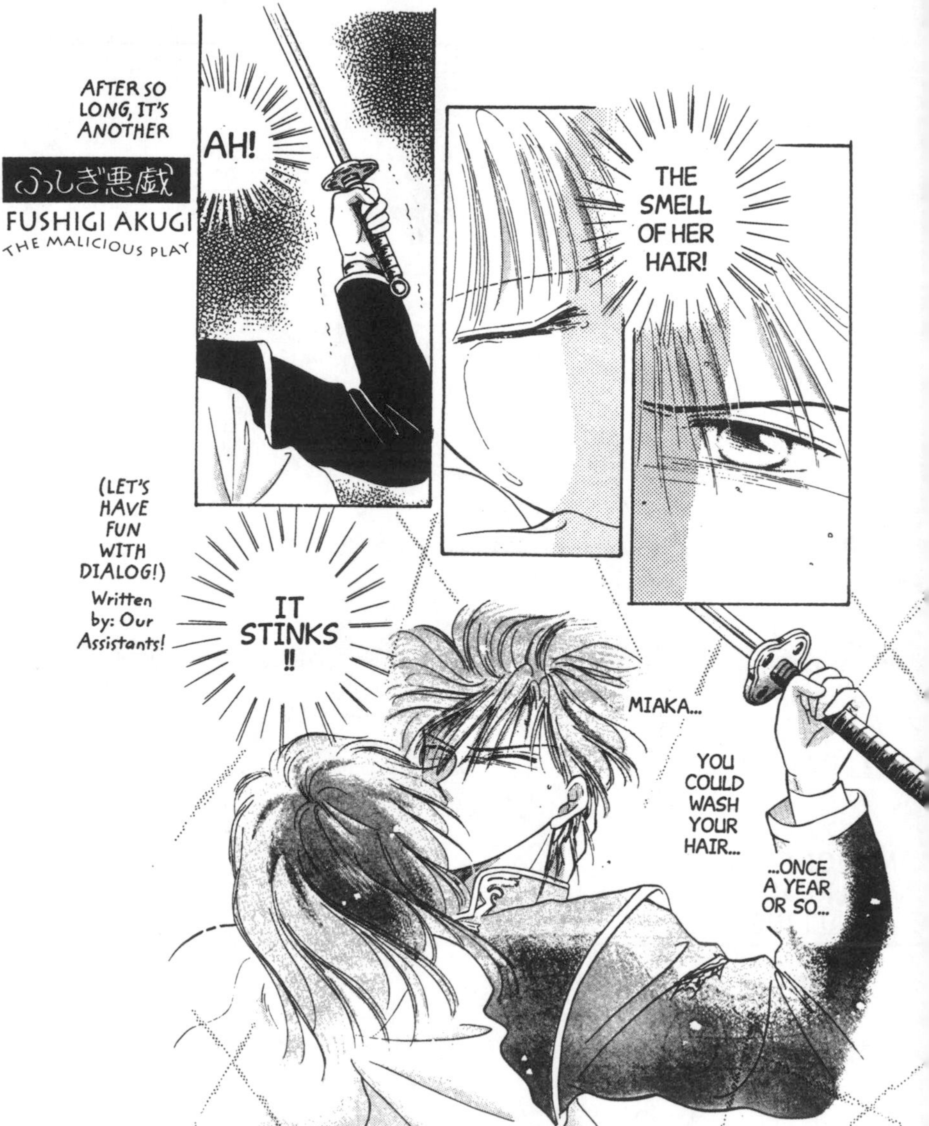
AFTER SO LONG, IT'S ANOTHER
ふしぎ悪戯
FUSHIGI AKUGI
THE MALICIOUS PLAY
(LET'S HAVE FUN WITH DIALOG!)
Written by: Our Assistants!
AH!
THE SMELL OF HER HAIR!
IT STINKS !!
MIAKA...
YOU COULD WASH YOUR HAIR...
...ONCE A YEAR OR SO...

I got a lot of suggestions for this section from the readers. I collected them, put them safely aside, then promptly forgot them! (I'm an idiot!) And *I'LL* do the drawing here, thank you very much.
The scene where the evil Tama goes to hit Miaka with the nunchucks... (by the way, they're actually a weapon called Tasekkon!) *They're NOT nunchucks!* Well, there were loads of suggestions where he hit himself instead.
When I wrote this I patted myself on the back for coming up with an angle nobody else came up with.
What was I trying to do with this corner??

CHAPTER THIRTY-FOUR

THE FINAL EMBRACE

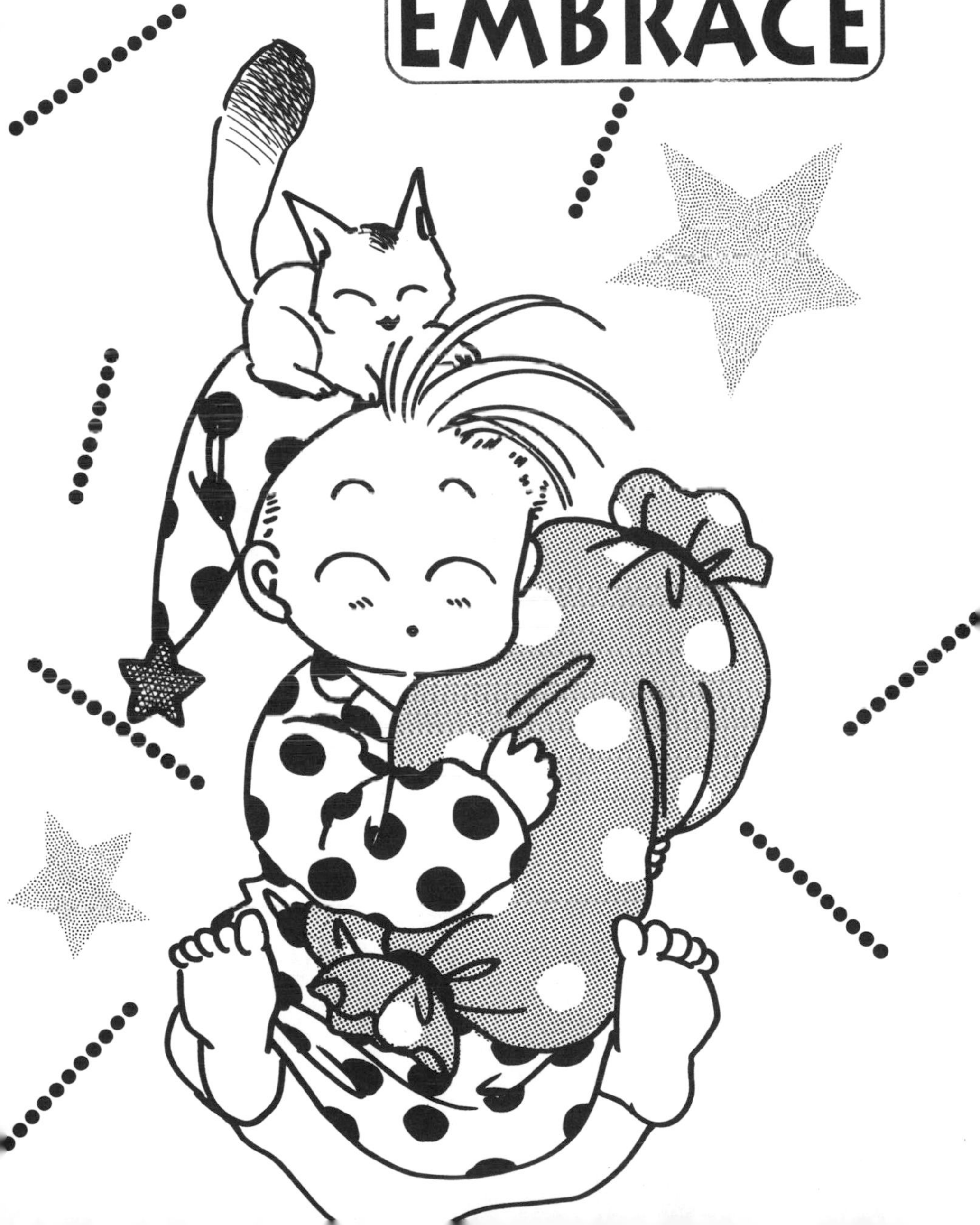

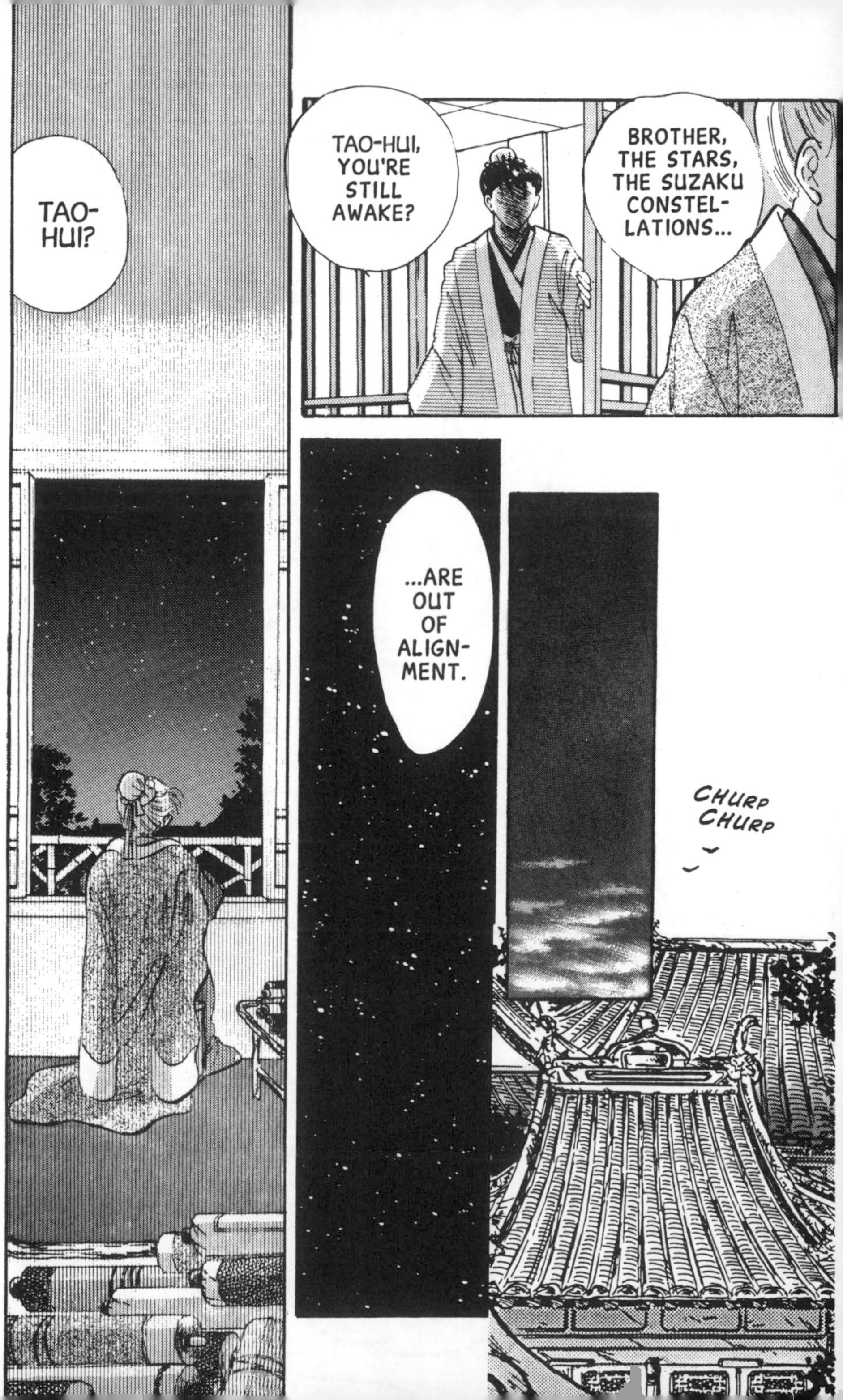
TAO-HUI?
TAO-HUI, YOU'RE STILL AWAKE?
BROTHER, THE STARS, THE SUZAKU CONSTEL-LATIONS...
...ARE OUT OF ALIGN-MENT.
CHURP CHURP

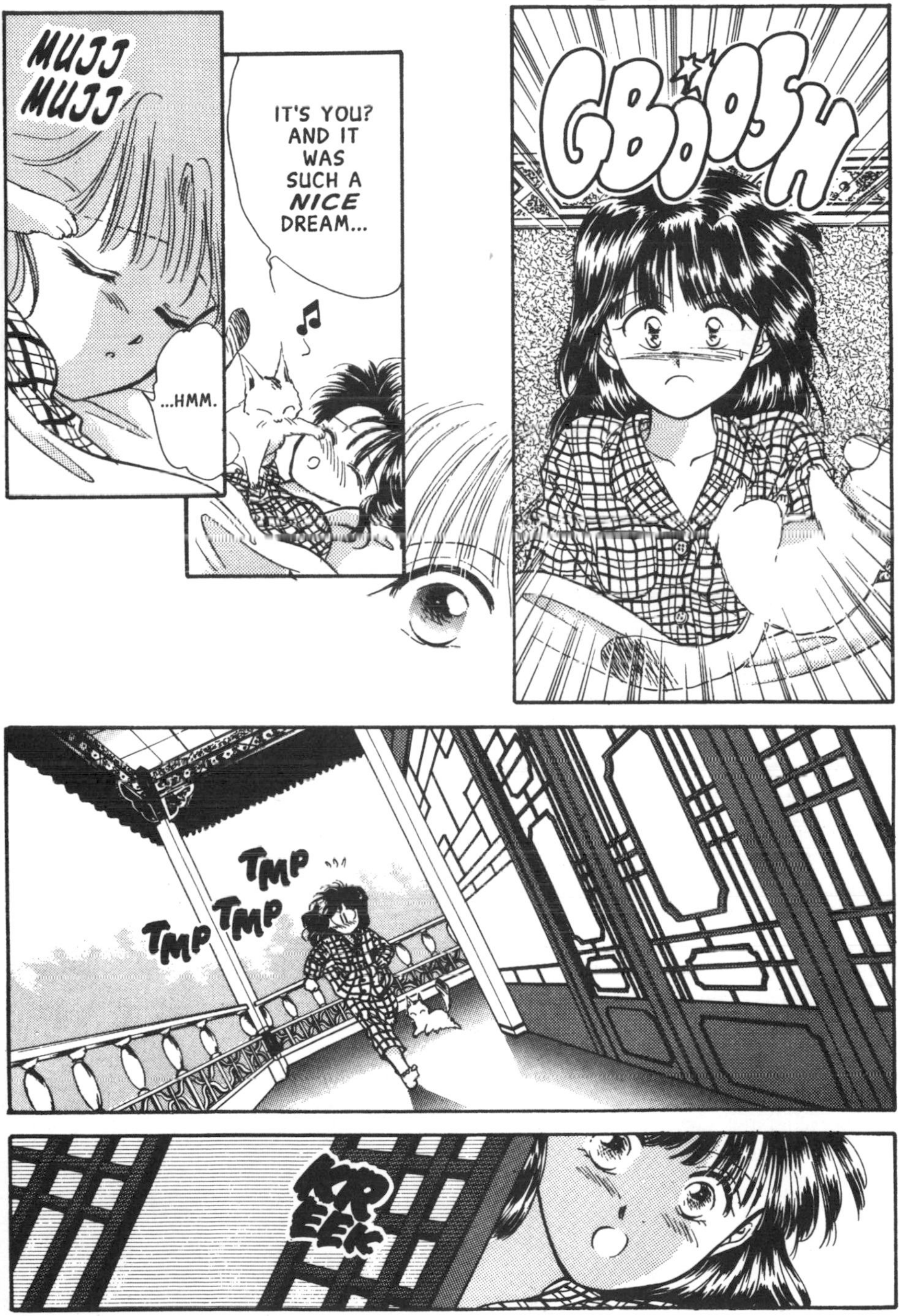
MUJJ MUJJ
...HMM.
IT'S YOU? AND IT WAS SUCH A *NICE* DREAM...
GBOOSH
TMP TMP TMP
KREEK

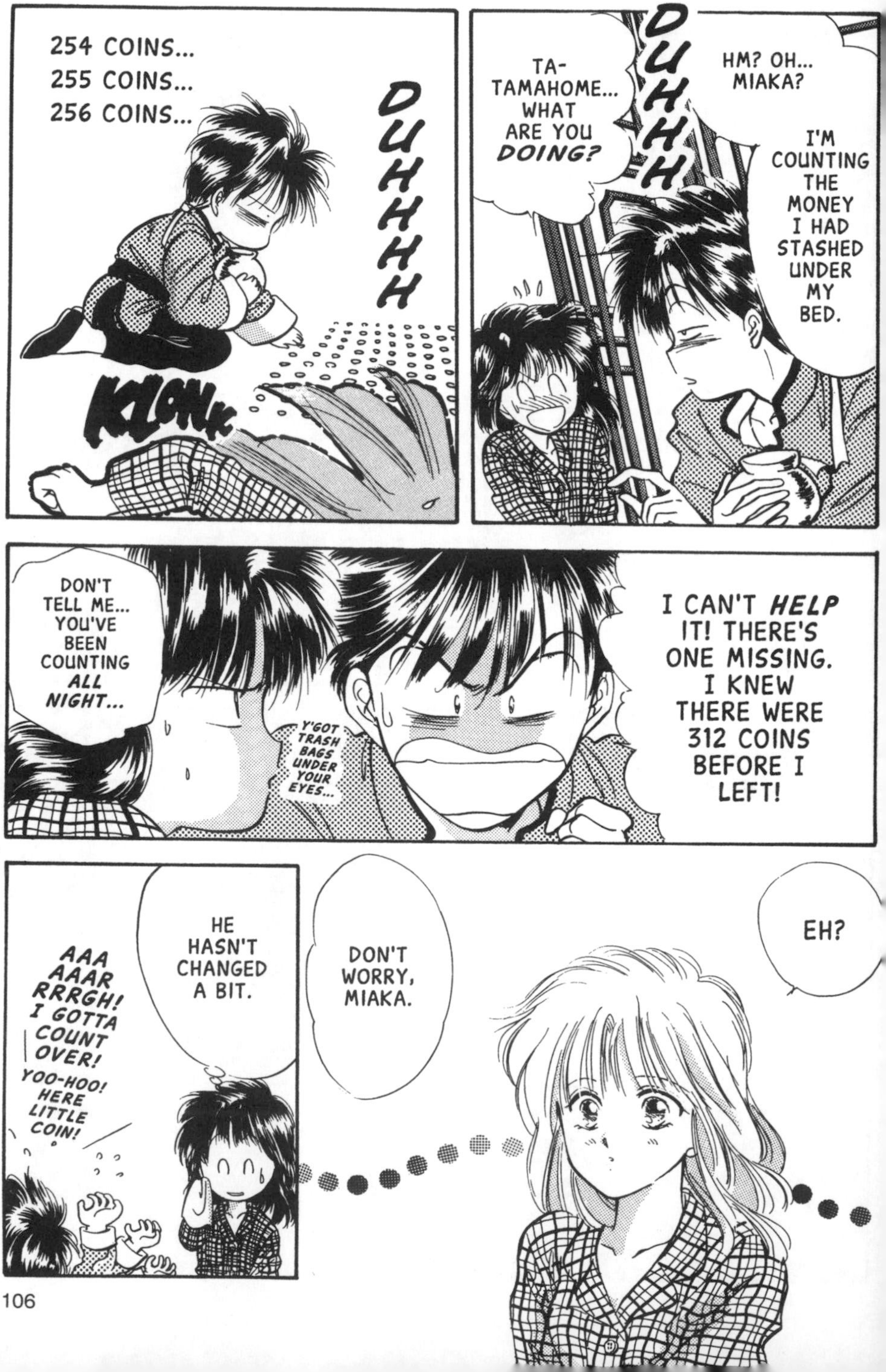
254 COINS... 255 COINS... 256 COINS...
DUHHHHH
KLONK
TA-TAMAHOME... WHAT ARE YOU *DOING?*
DUHHH
HM? OH... MIAKA?
I'M COUNTING THE MONEY I HAD STASHED UNDER MY BED.
DON'T TELL ME... YOU'VE BEEN COUNTING *ALL NIGHT...*
Y'GOT TRASH BAGS UNDER YOUR EYES...
I CAN'T *HELP* IT! THERE'S ONE MISSING. I KNEW THERE WERE 312 COINS BEFORE I LEFT!
AAAAAARRRRGH! I GOTTA COUNT OVER!
YOO-HOO! HERE LITTLE COIN!
HE HASN'T CHANGED A BIT.
DON'T WORRY, MIAKA.
EH?

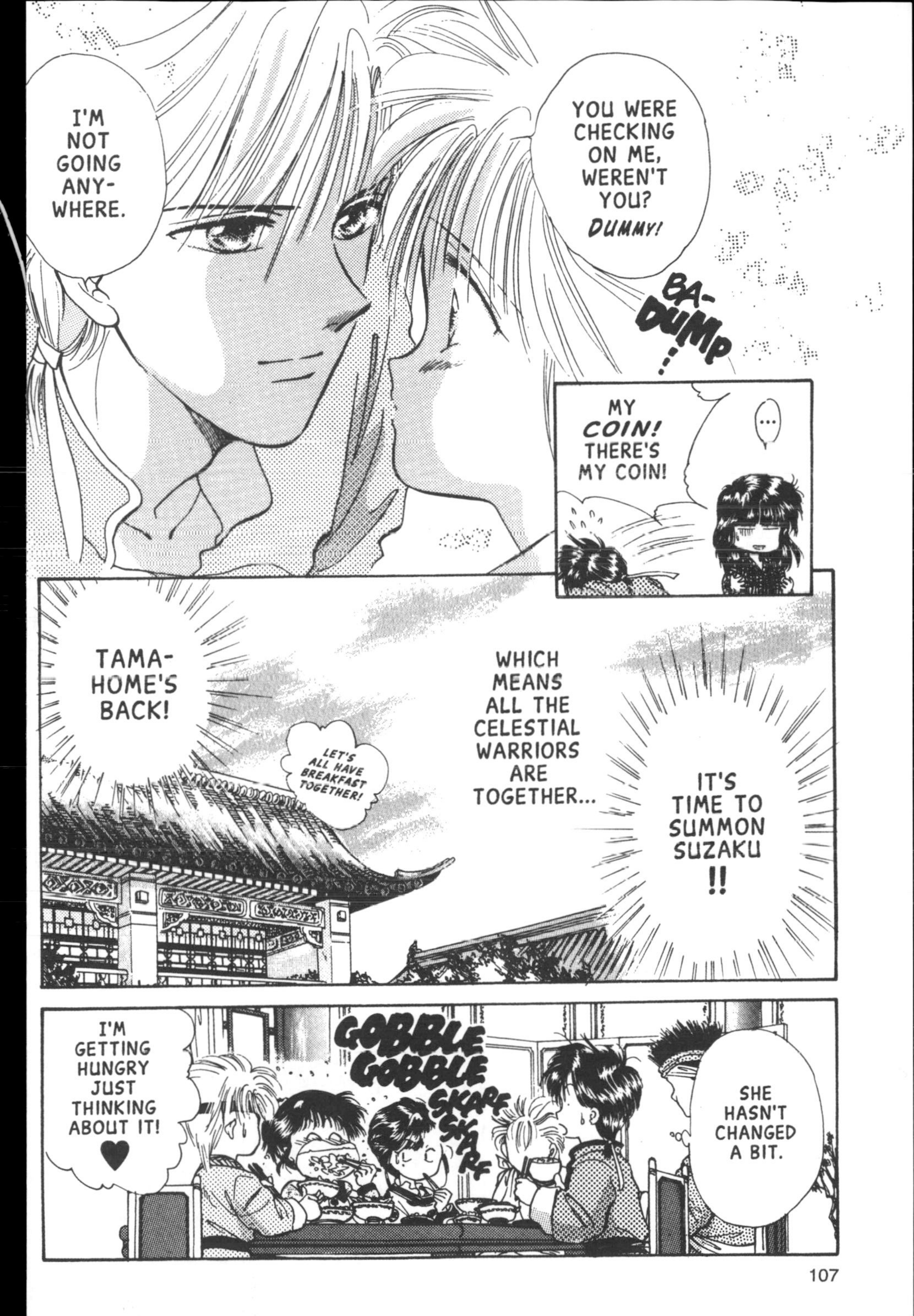
I'M NOT GOING ANY-WHERE.
YOU WERE CHECKING ON ME, WEREN'T YOU? DUMMY!
BA-DUMP...
MY COIN! THERE'S MY COIN!
...
TAMA-HOME'S BACK!
LET'S ALL HAVE BREAKFAST TOGETHER!
WHICH MEANS ALL THE CELESTIAL WARRIORS ARE TOGETHER...
IT'S TIME TO SUMMON SUZAKU !!
I'M GETTING HUNGRY JUST THINKING ABOUT IT! ♥
GOBBLE GOBBLE
SKARF SKARF
SHE HASN'T CHANGED A BIT.

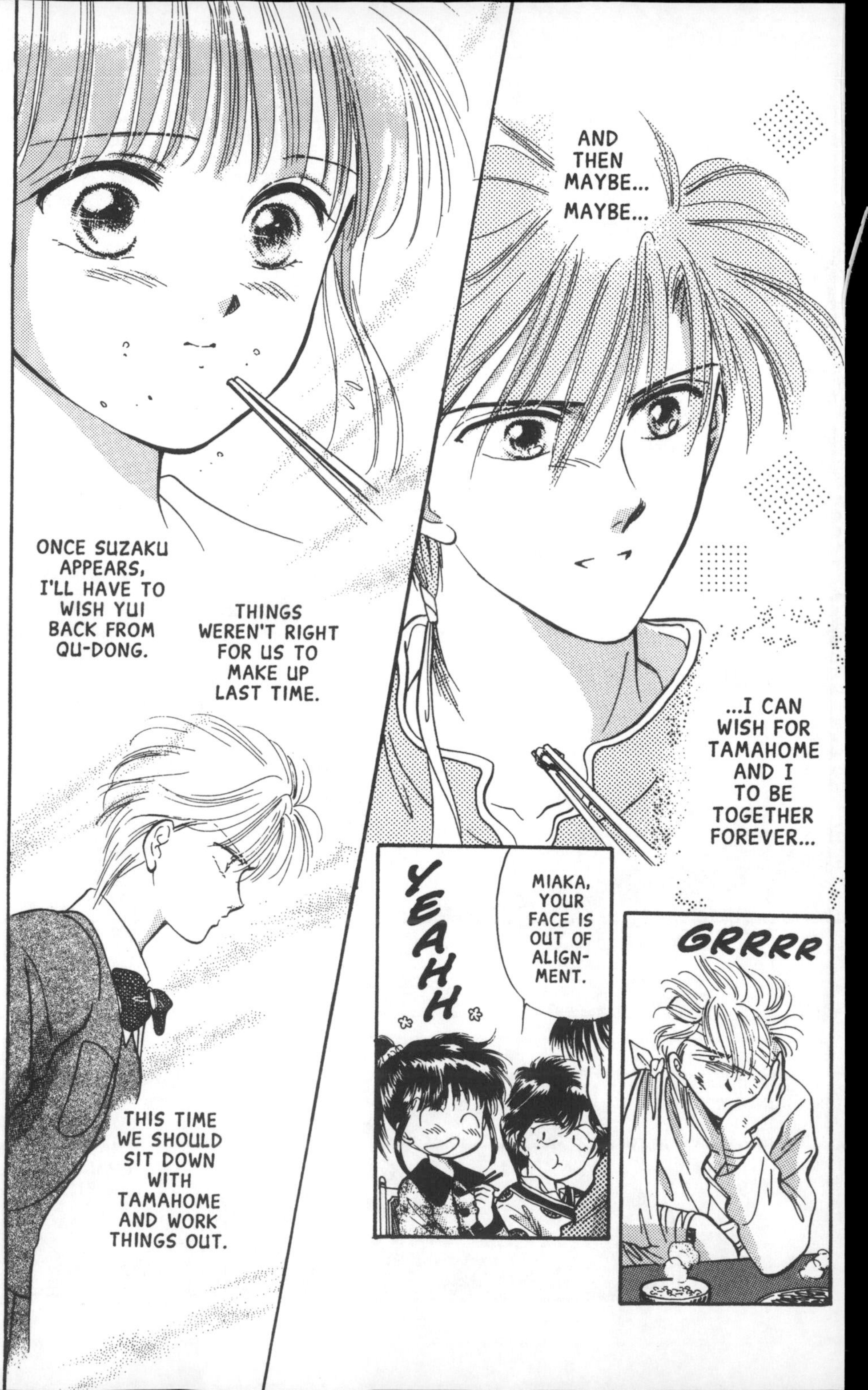

ONCE SUZAKU APPEARS, I'LL HAVE TO WISH YUI BACK FROM QU-DONG.
THINGS WEREN'T RIGHT FOR US TO MAKE UP LAST TIME.
THIS TIME WE SHOULD SIT DOWN WITH TAMAHOME AND WORK THINGS OUT.
AND THEN MAYBE... MAYBE...
...I CAN WISH FOR TAMAHOME AND I TO BE TOGETHER FOREVER...
YEAHH
MIAKA, YOUR FACE IS OUT OF ALIGN-MENT.
GRRRR

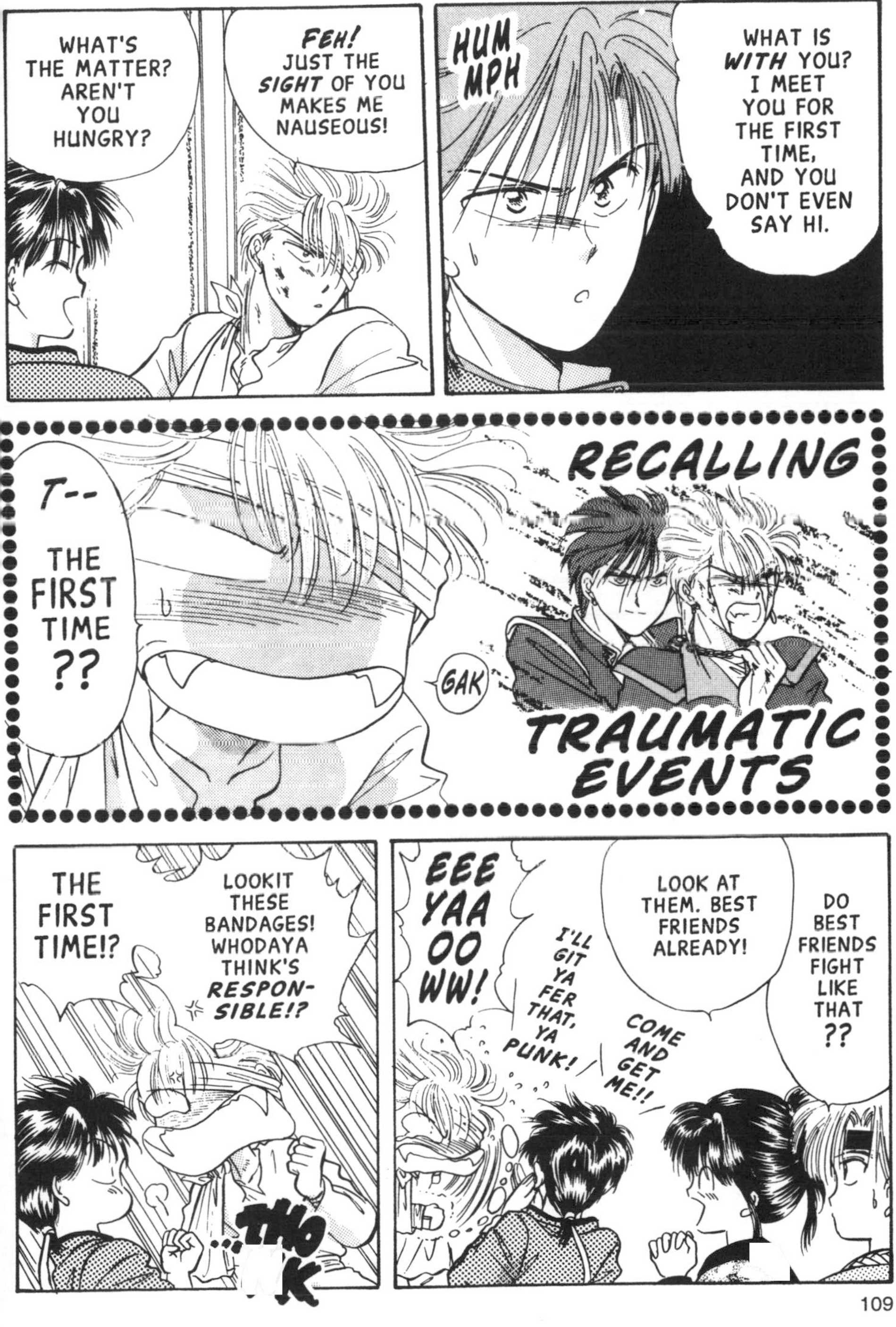
WHAT'S THE MATTER? AREN'T YOU HUNGRY?
FEH! JUST THE SIGHT OF YOU MAKES ME NAUSEOUS!
HUMMPH
WHAT IS WITH YOU? I MEET YOU FOR THE FIRST TIME, AND YOU DON'T EVEN SAY HI.
T-- THE FIRST TIME ??
RECALLING
GAK
TRAUMATIC EVENTS
THE FIRST TIME!?
LOOKIT THESE BANDAGES! WHODAYA THINK'S RESPONSIBLE!?
...THO
K
EEEYAAOOWW!
I'LL GIT YA FER THAT, YA PUNK!
COME AND GET ME!!
LOOK AT THEM. BEST FRIENDS ALREADY!
DO BEST FRIENDS FIGHT LIKE THAT ??

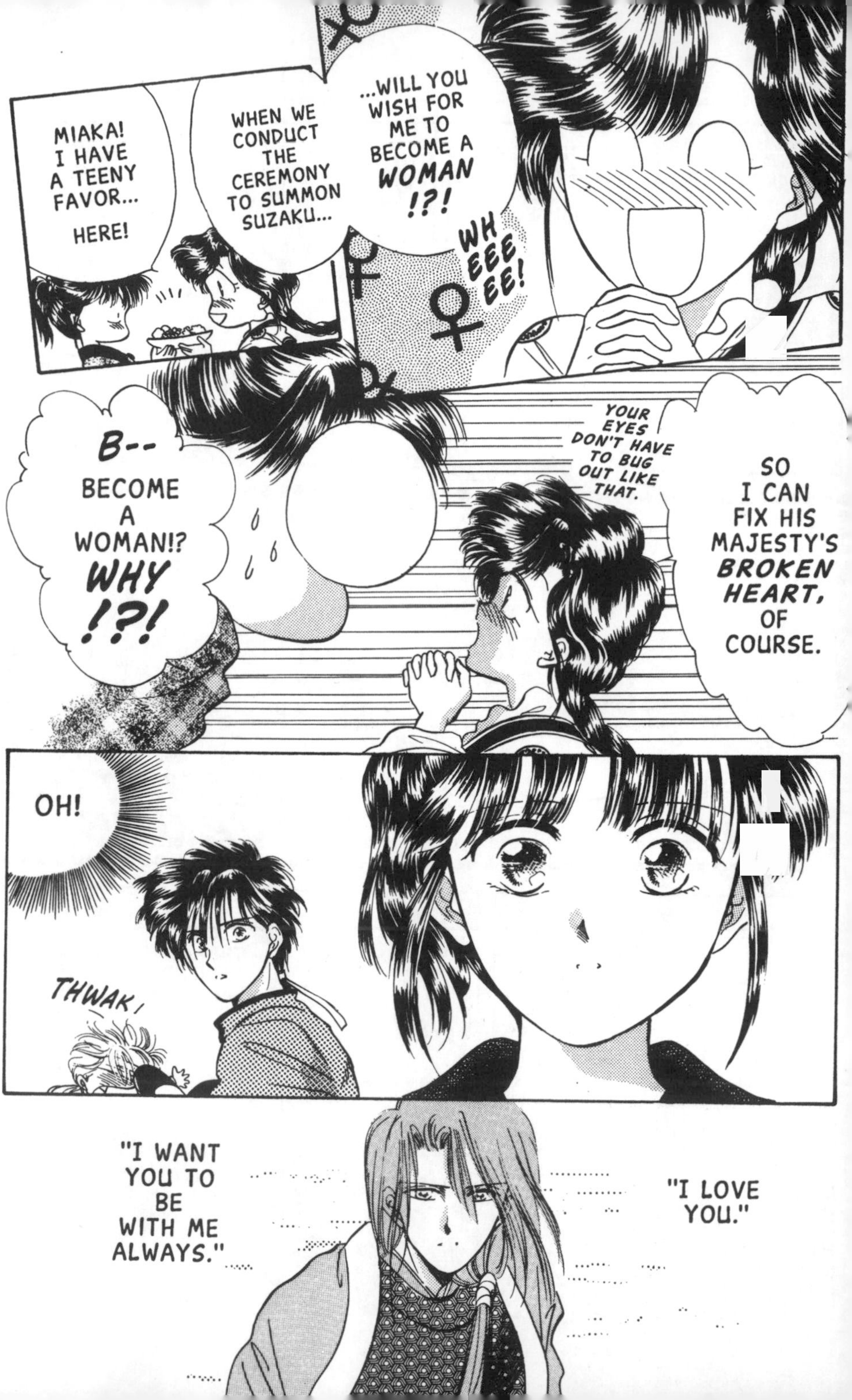
MIAKA! I HAVE A TEENY FAVOR... HERE!
WHEN WE CONDUCT THE CEREMONY TO SUMMON SUZAKU...
...WILL YOU WISH FOR ME TO BECOME A WOMAN !?!
WHEEEEE!
B-- BECOME A WOMAN!? WHY !?!
YOUR EYES DON'T HAVE TO BUG OUT LIKE THAT.
SO I CAN FIX HIS MAJESTY'S BROKEN HEART, OF COURSE.
OH!
THWAK
"I WANT YOU TO BE WITH ME ALWAYS."
"I LOVE YOU."

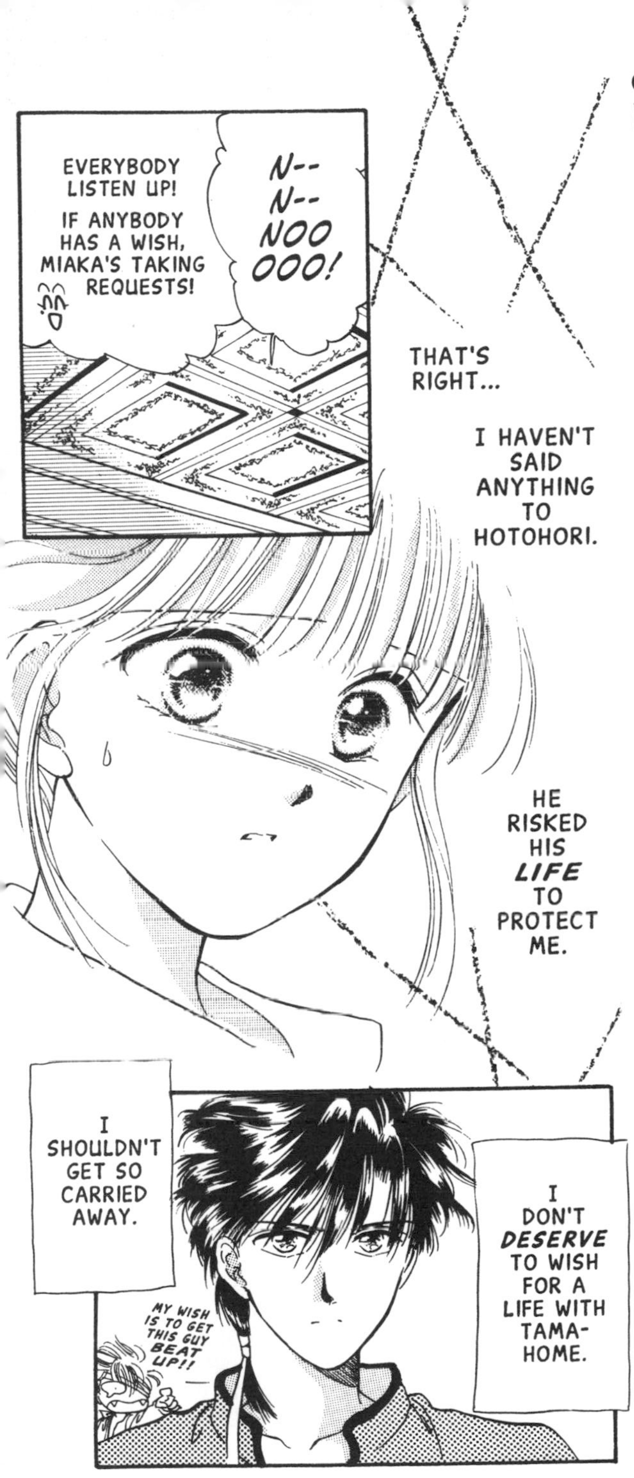
EVERYBODY LISTEN UP!
IF ANYBODY HAS A WISH, MIAKA'S TAKING REQUESTS!
N-- N-- NOO OOO!
THAT'S RIGHT...
I HAVEN'T SAID ANYTHING TO HOTOHORI.
HE RISKED HIS LIFE TO PROTECT ME.
I SHOULDN'T GET SO CARRIED AWAY.
MY WISH IS TO GET THIS GUY BEAT UP!!
I DON'T DESERVE TO WISH FOR A LIFE WITH TAMAHOME.

Summoner

Now, to completely change the subject, we have two new members in my household. One is a Yūsen (cable radio) hookup, and the other is a Yorkshire Terrier five-month-old puppy. I got Yūsen so I can listen to all 440 audio channels at work. *(There must be a lot of homes that have Yūsen now.)* I can pick Japanese pop songs, jazz, classical, or simulcasts ("Disco Tokyo" and other areas), and get "Juliana Tokyo" *Yeaaahhh!* or "Maharaja" *Yeaaahhh!* (At night they have live broadcasts!) They even have karaoke and movie soundtracks, etc. There's so much that it's really fun, but the funniest programs are "Taking Care of Business" (recordings of shopkeepers inviting pedestrians into their shops, store announcements at closing time, etc.), "Battleship March," "Applause" (the neverending sound of applause), "Soroban" (Abacus sounds that go on endlessly), "Alibi" (You can use the noise of pachinko parlors and bars to lie about where you are), "Telephone booth on the street" and many more! *But I'm so serious, I'd NEVER pull a prank like that.* The scary ones are called "spiritual music," "wish fulfillment," "subliminal power enhancement," "spiritual healing." What the heck is this stuff!? There's one called "Hypnosis," and you hear some guy counting sheep endlessly. There's "heart beat" for children. It's a little scary and strange. I mean we're talking about the sound of a heartbeat a fetus hears in the mother's womb. A baby might feel secure, but for an adult like me it's kinda creepy.

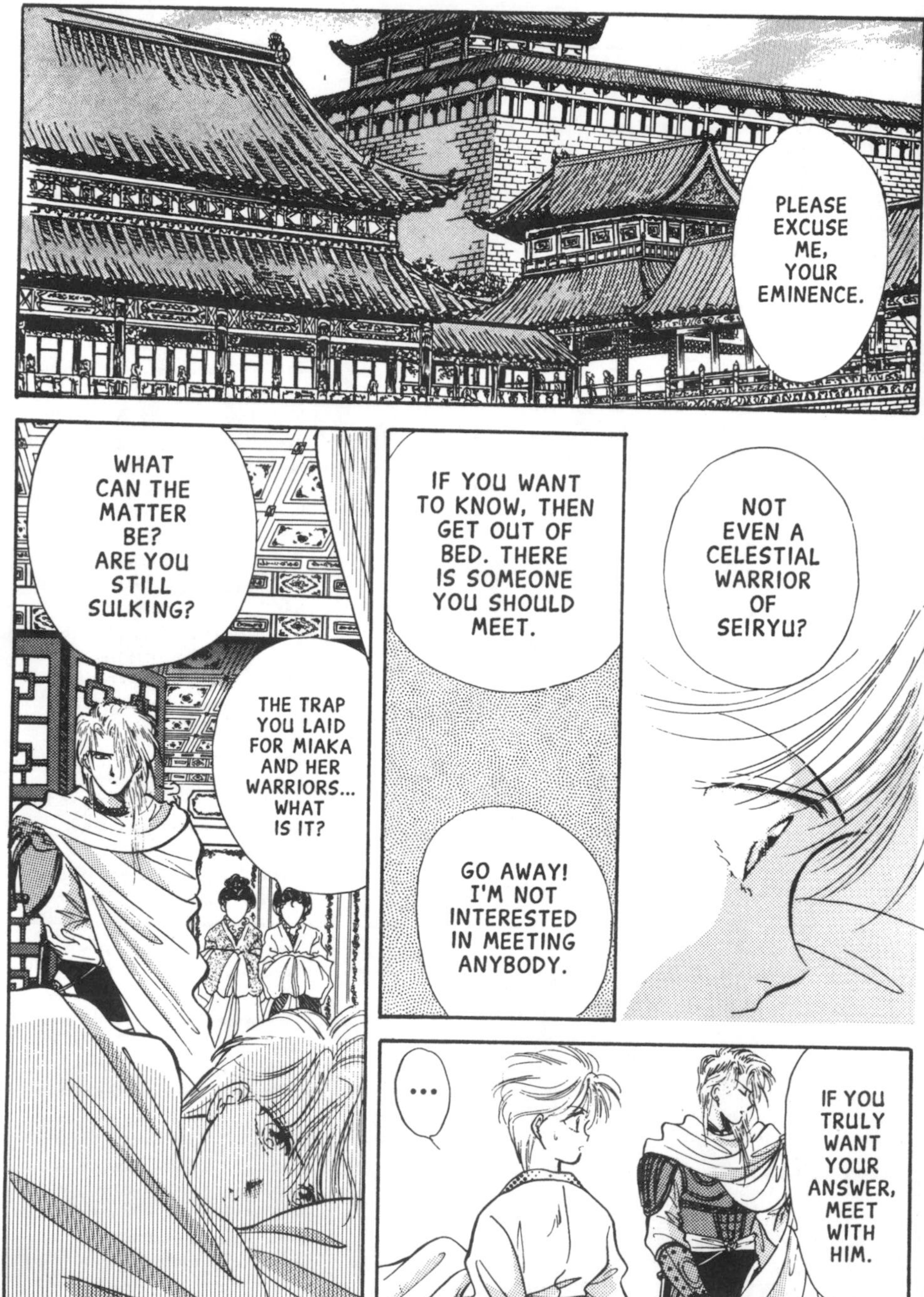
PLEASE EXCUSE ME, YOUR EMINENCE.
WHAT CAN THE MATTER BE? ARE YOU STILL SULKING?
THE TRAP YOU LAID FOR MIAKA AND HER WARRIORS... WHAT IS IT?
IF YOU WANT TO KNOW, THEN GET OUT OF BED. THERE IS SOMEONE YOU SHOULD MEET.
GO AWAY! I'M NOT INTERESTED IN MEETING ANYBODY.
NOT EVEN A CELESTIAL WARRIOR OF SEIRYU?
...
IF YOU TRULY WANT YOUR ANSWER, MEET WITH HIM.

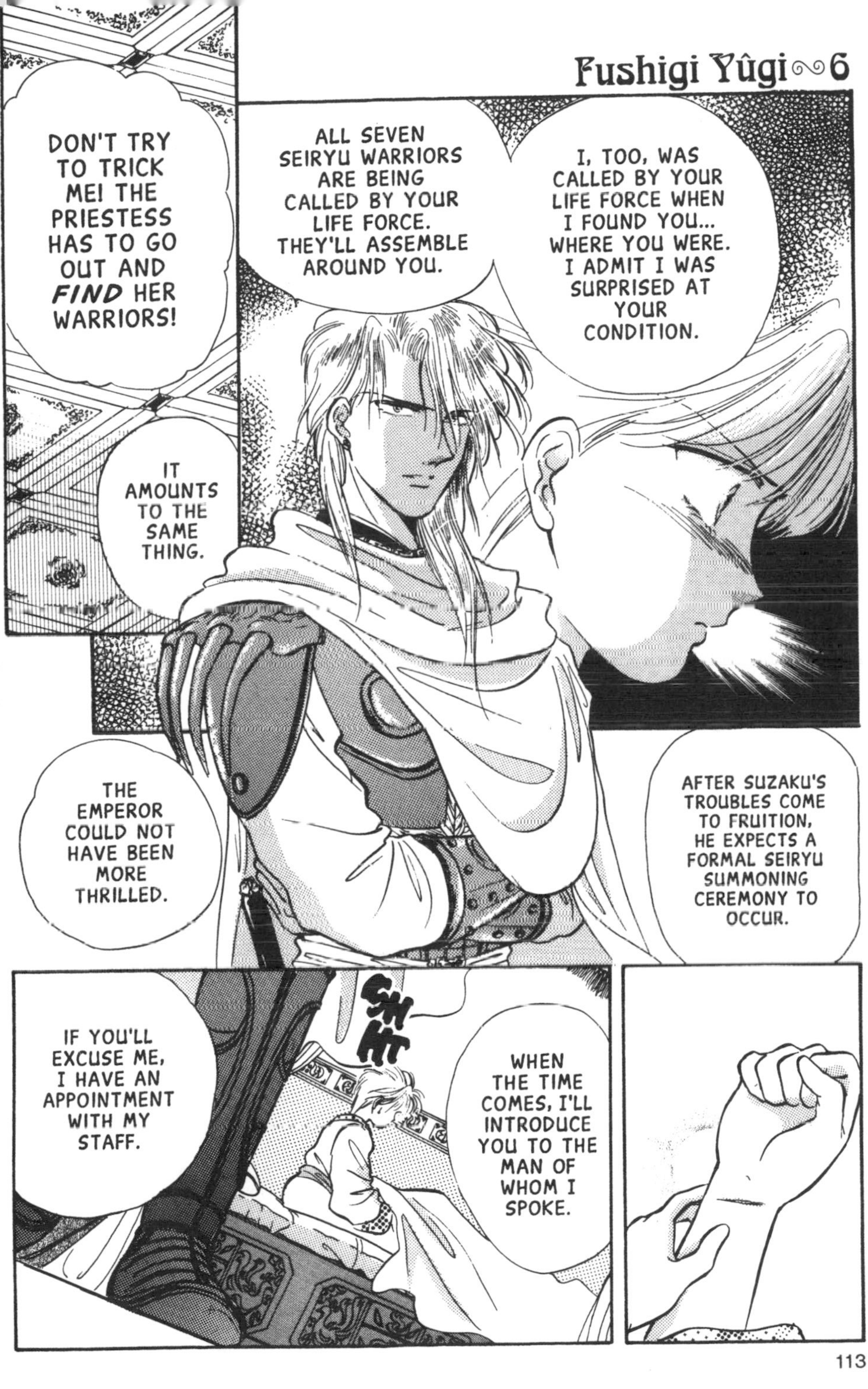
DON'T TRY TO TRICK ME! THE PRIESTESS HAS TO GO OUT AND *FIND* HER WARRIORS!
IT AMOUNTS TO THE SAME THING.
ALL SEVEN SEIRYU WARRIORS ARE BEING CALLED BY YOUR LIFE FORCE. THEY'LL ASSEMBLE AROUND YOU.
I, TOO, WAS CALLED BY YOUR LIFE FORCE WHEN I FOUND YOU... WHERE YOU WERE. I ADMIT I WAS SURPRISED AT YOUR CONDITION.
THE EMPEROR COULD NOT HAVE BEEN MORE THRILLED.
AFTER SUZAKU'S TROUBLES COME TO FRUITION, HE EXPECTS A FORMAL SEIRYU SUMMONING CEREMONY TO OCCUR.
IF YOU'LL EXCUSE ME, I HAVE AN APPOINTMENT WITH MY STAFF.
SHHT
WHEN THE TIME COMES, I'LL INTRODUCE YOU TO THE MAN OF WHOM I SPOKE.

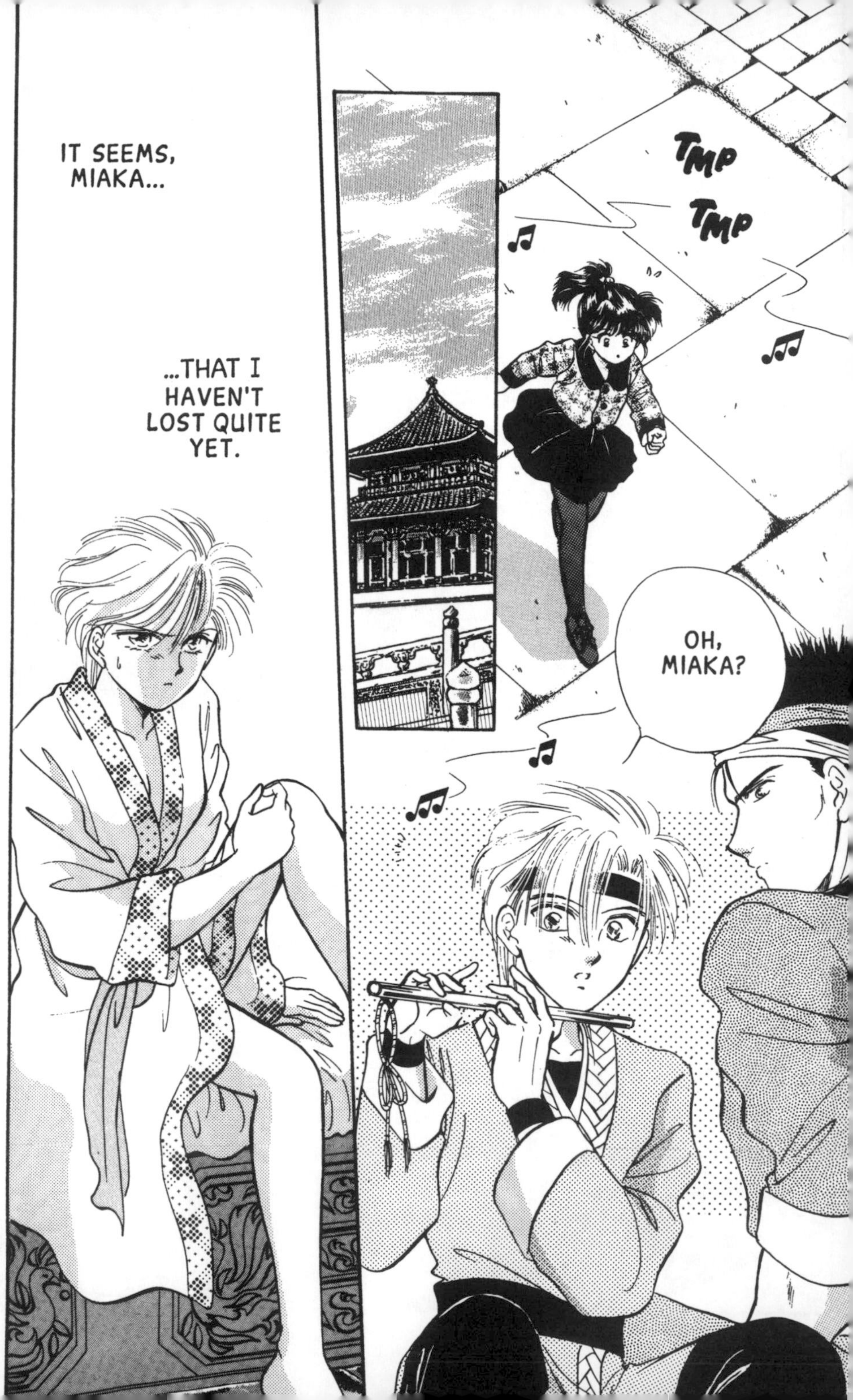
IT SEEMS, MIAKA...
...THAT I HAVEN'T LOST QUITE YET.
TMP
TMP
OH, MIAKA?

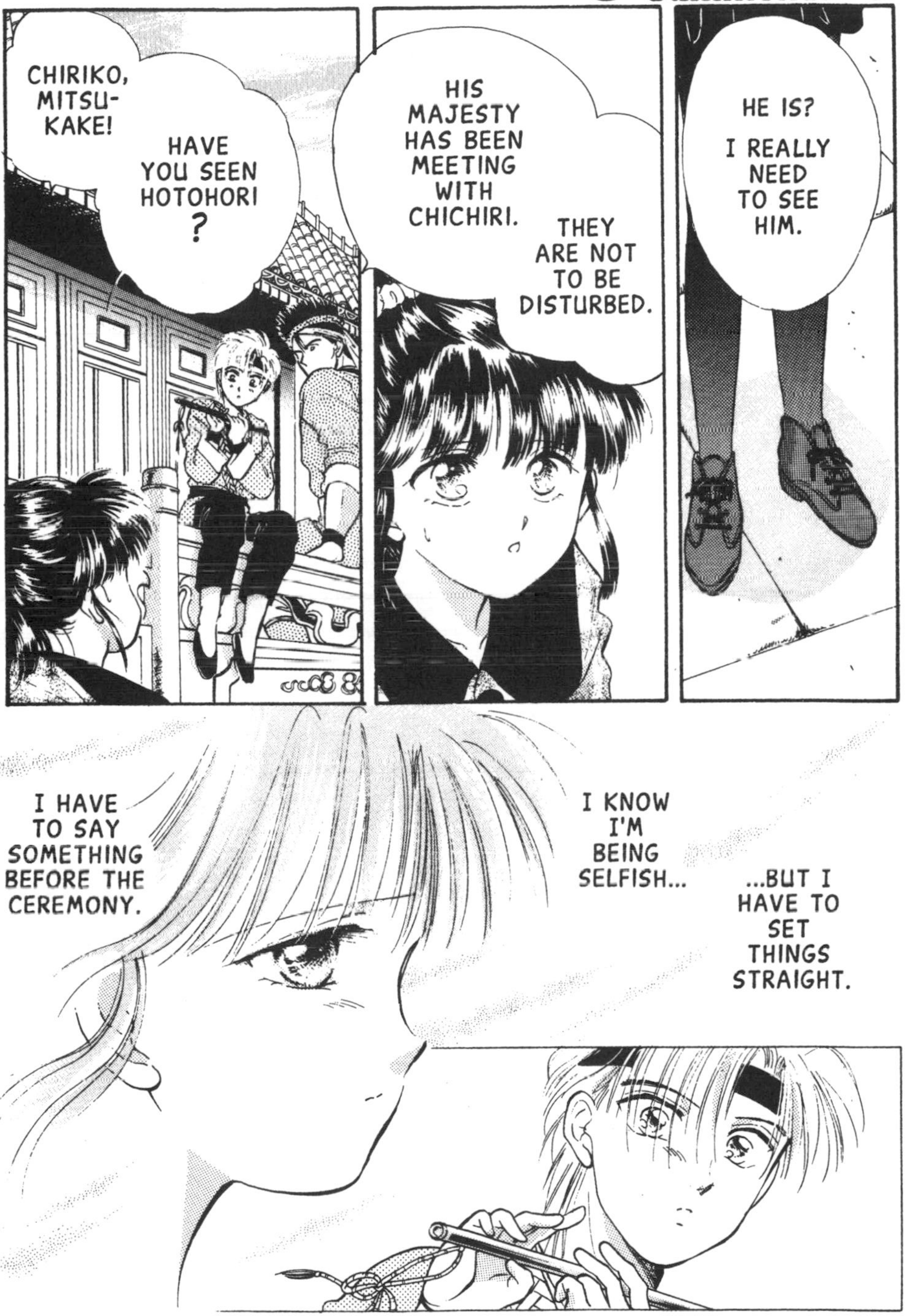
CHIRIKO, MITSU-KAKE!
HAVE YOU SEEN HOTOHORI?
HIS MAJESTY HAS BEEN MEETING WITH CHICHIRI.
THEY ARE NOT TO BE DISTURBED.
HE IS?
I REALLY NEED TO SEE HIM.
I HAVE TO SAY SOMETHING BEFORE THE CEREMONY.
I KNOW I'M BEING SELFISH...
...BUT I HAVE TO SET THINGS STRAIGHT.

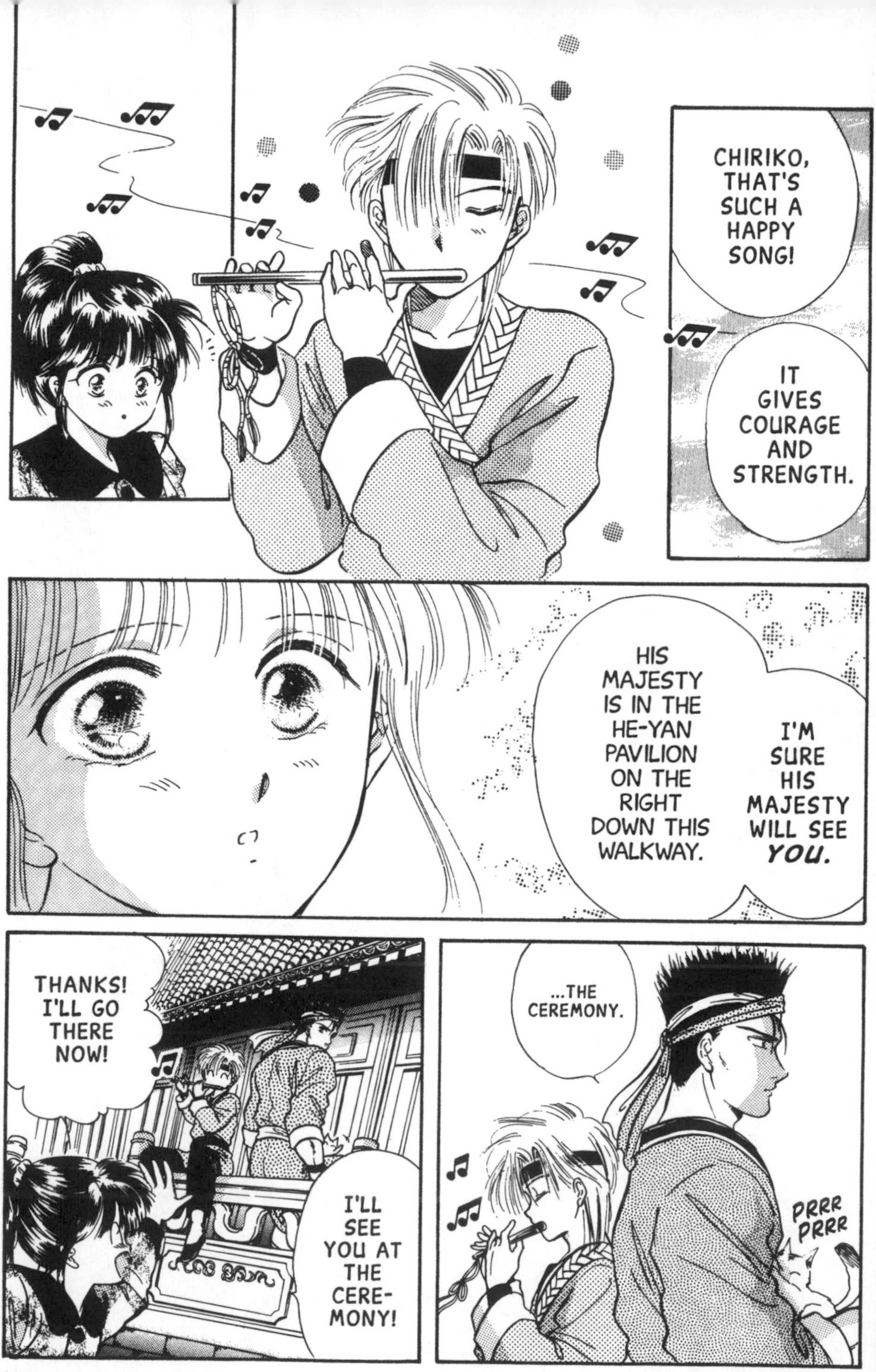
CHIRIKO, THAT'S SUCH A HAPPY SONG!
IT GIVES COURAGE AND STRENGTH.
HIS MAJESTY IS IN THE HE-YAN PAVILION ON THE RIGHT DOWN THIS WALKWAY.
I'M SURE HIS MAJESTY WILL SEE *YOU.*
THANKS! I'LL GO THERE NOW!
I'LL SEE YOU AT THE CERE-MONY!
...THE CEREMONY.
PRRR PRRR

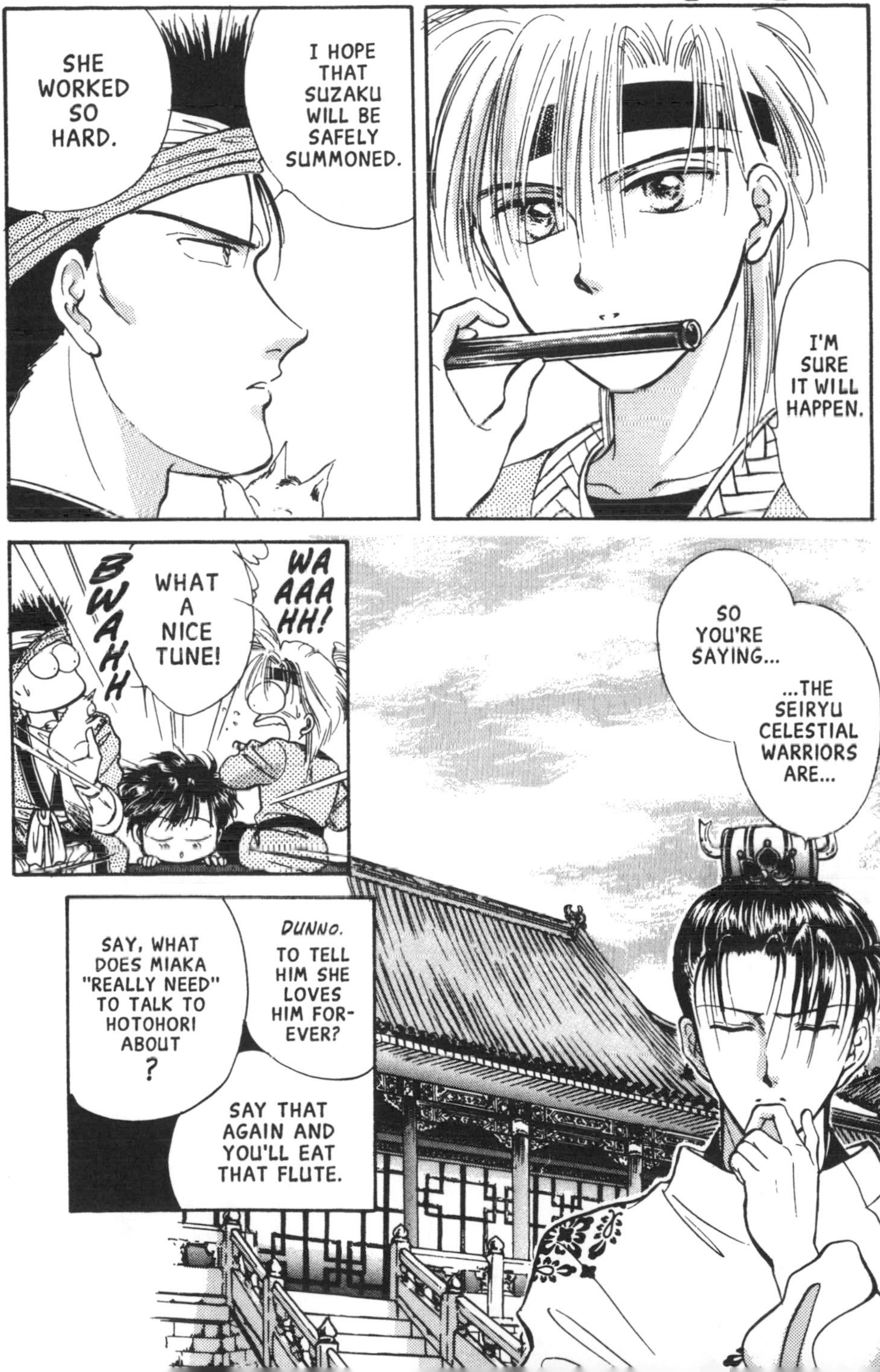
SHE WORKED SO HARD.
I HOPE THAT SUZAKU WILL BE SAFELY SUMMONED.
I'M SURE IT WILL HAPPEN.
BWAHH
WHAT A NICE TUNE!
WAAAAHH!
SO YOU'RE SAYING...
...THE SEIRYU CELESTIAL WARRIORS ARE...
SAY, WHAT DOES MIAKA "REALLY NEED" TO TALK TO HOTOHORI ABOUT ?
DUNNO.
TO TELL HIM SHE LOVES HIM FOR-EVER?
SAY THAT AGAIN AND YOU'LL EAT THAT FLUTE.

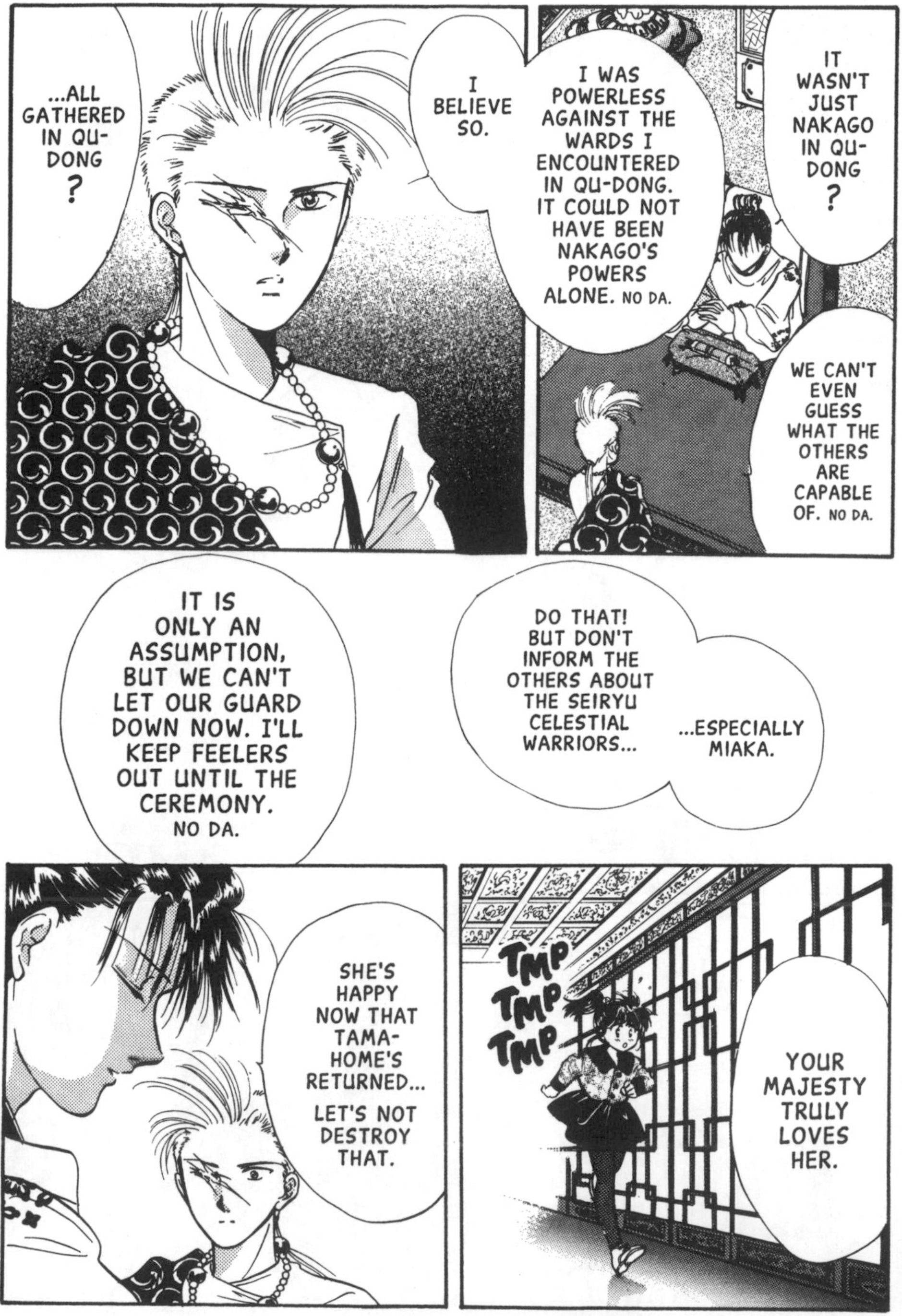
...ALL GATHERED IN QU-DONG?
I BELIEVE SO.
I WAS POWERLESS AGAINST THE WARDS I ENCOUNTERED IN QU-DONG. IT COULD NOT HAVE BEEN NAKAGO'S POWERS ALONE. NO DA.
IT WASN'T JUST NAKAGO IN QU-DONG?
WE CAN'T EVEN GUESS WHAT THE OTHERS ARE CAPABLE OF. NO DA.
IT IS ONLY AN ASSUMPTION, BUT WE CAN'T LET OUR GUARD DOWN NOW. I'LL KEEP FEELERS OUT UNTIL THE CEREMONY. NO DA.
DO THAT! BUT DON'T INFORM THE OTHERS ABOUT THE SEIRYU CELESTIAL WARRIORS...
...ESPECIALLY MIAKA.
SHE'S HAPPY NOW THAT TAMA-HOME'S RETURNED...
LET'S NOT DESTROY THAT.
TMP TMP TMP
YOUR MAJESTY TRULY LOVES HER.

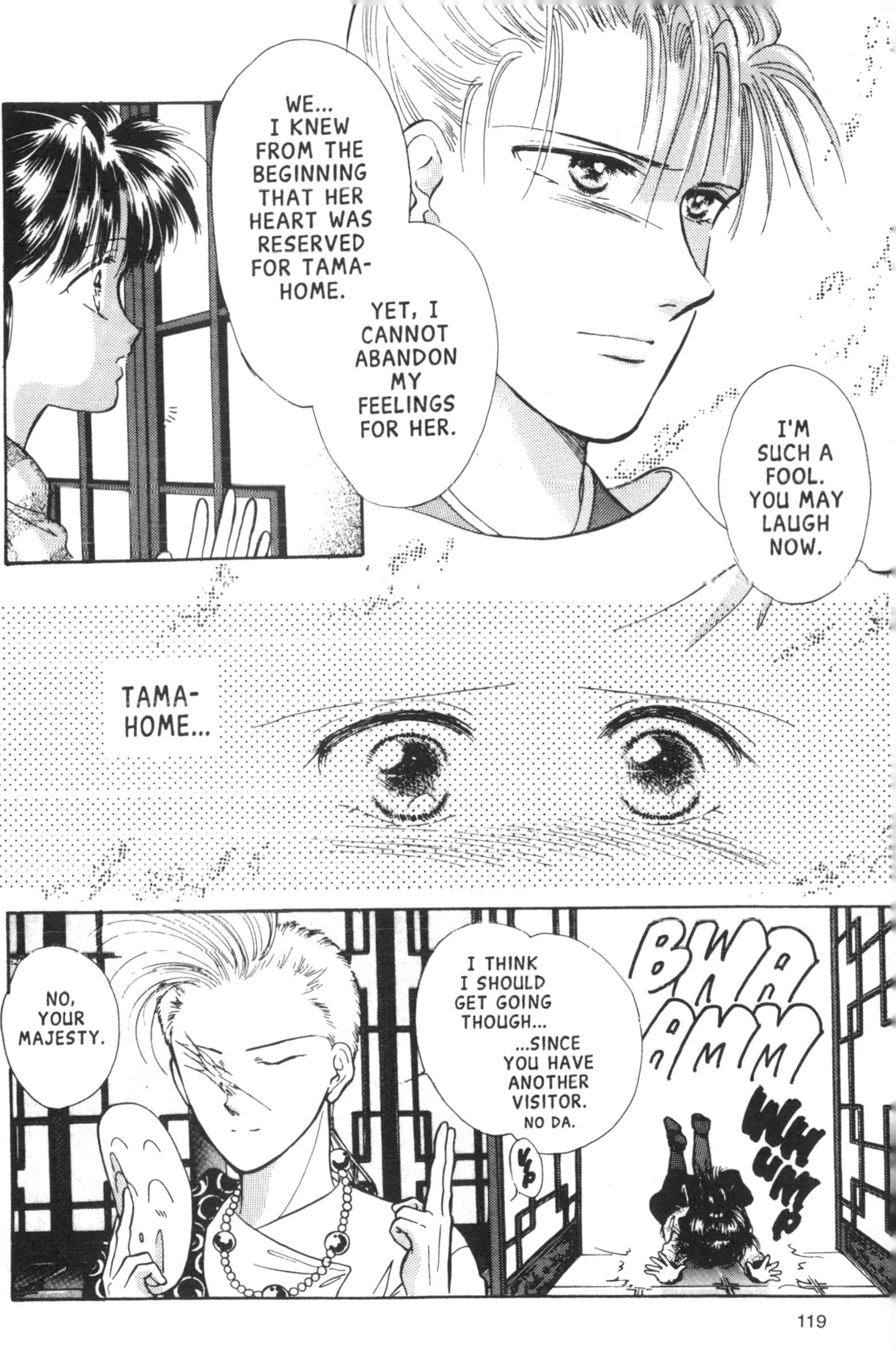
WE... I KNEW FROM THE BEGINNING THAT HER HEART WAS RESERVED FOR TAMA-HOME.
YET, I CANNOT ABANDON MY FEELINGS FOR HER.
I'M SUCH A FOOL. YOU MAY LAUGH NOW.
TAMA-HOME...
NO, YOUR MAJESTY.
I THINK I SHOULD GET GOING THOUGH... ...SINCE YOU HAVE ANOTHER VISITOR. NO DA.
YIP
BWAAMMM
WHUMP

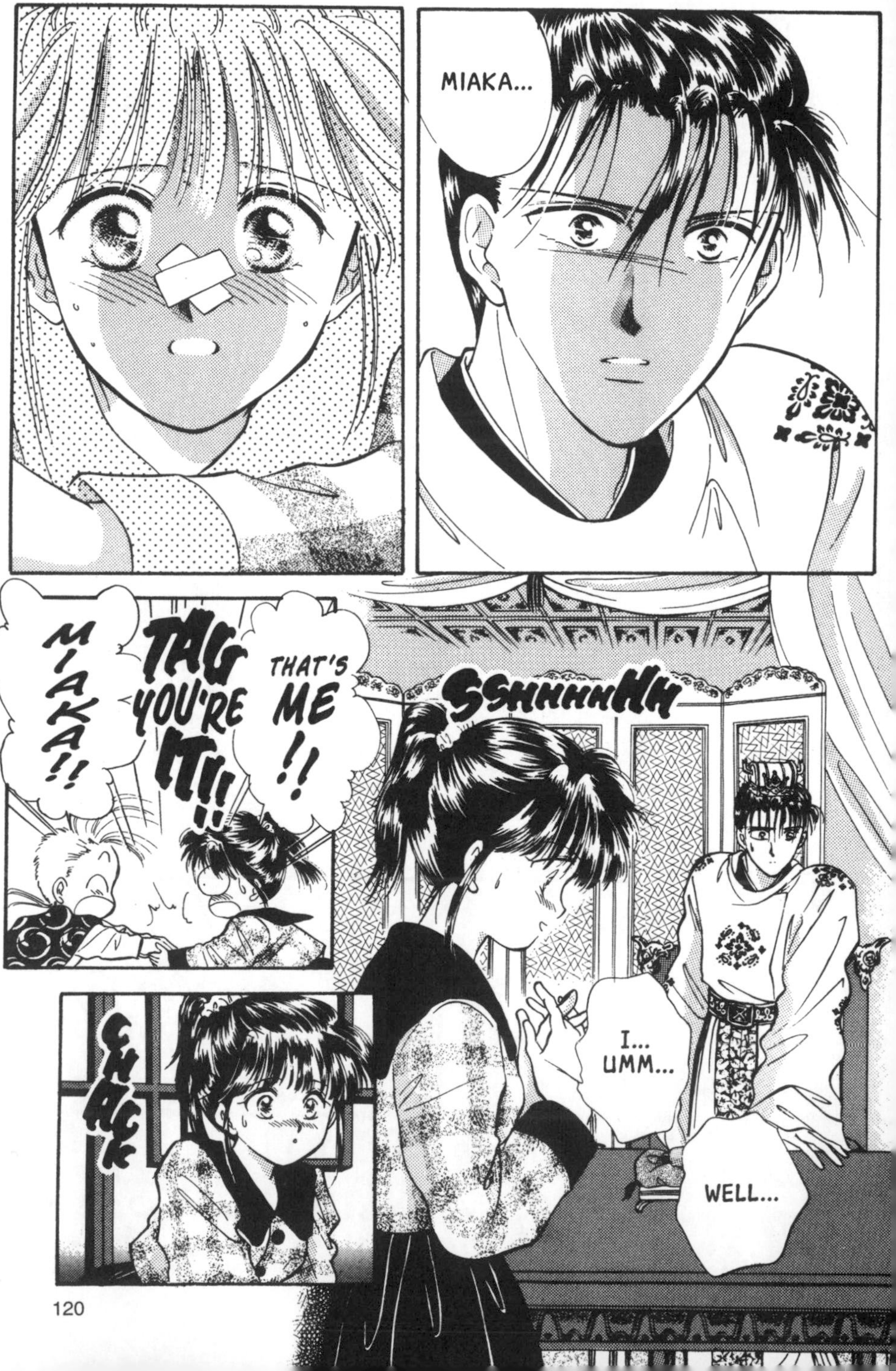

MIAKA...
MIAKA!!
TAG YOU'RE IT!!
THAT'S ME!!
CHACK
SSHHHHHH
I... UMM...
WELL...

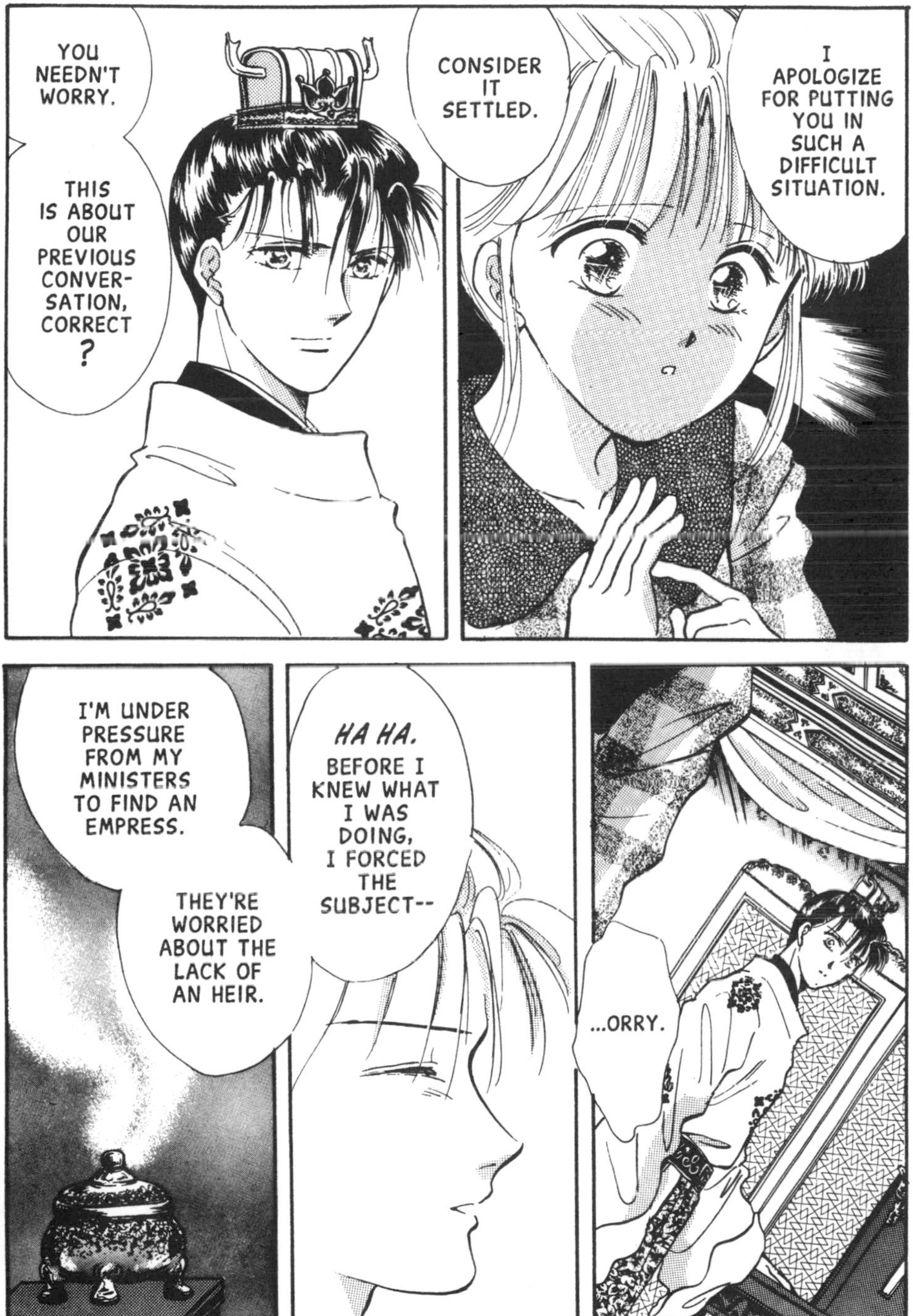
YOU NEEDN'T WORRY.
THIS IS ABOUT OUR PREVIOUS CONVER-SATION, CORRECT ?
CONSIDER IT SETTLED.
I APOLOGIZE FOR PUTTING YOU IN SUCH A DIFFICULT SITUATION.
I'M UNDER PRESSURE FROM MY MINISTERS TO FIND AN EMPRESS.
THEY'RE WORRIED ABOUT THE LACK OF AN HEIR.
HA HA.
BEFORE I KNEW WHAT I WAS DOING, I FORCED THE SUBJECT--
...ORRY.

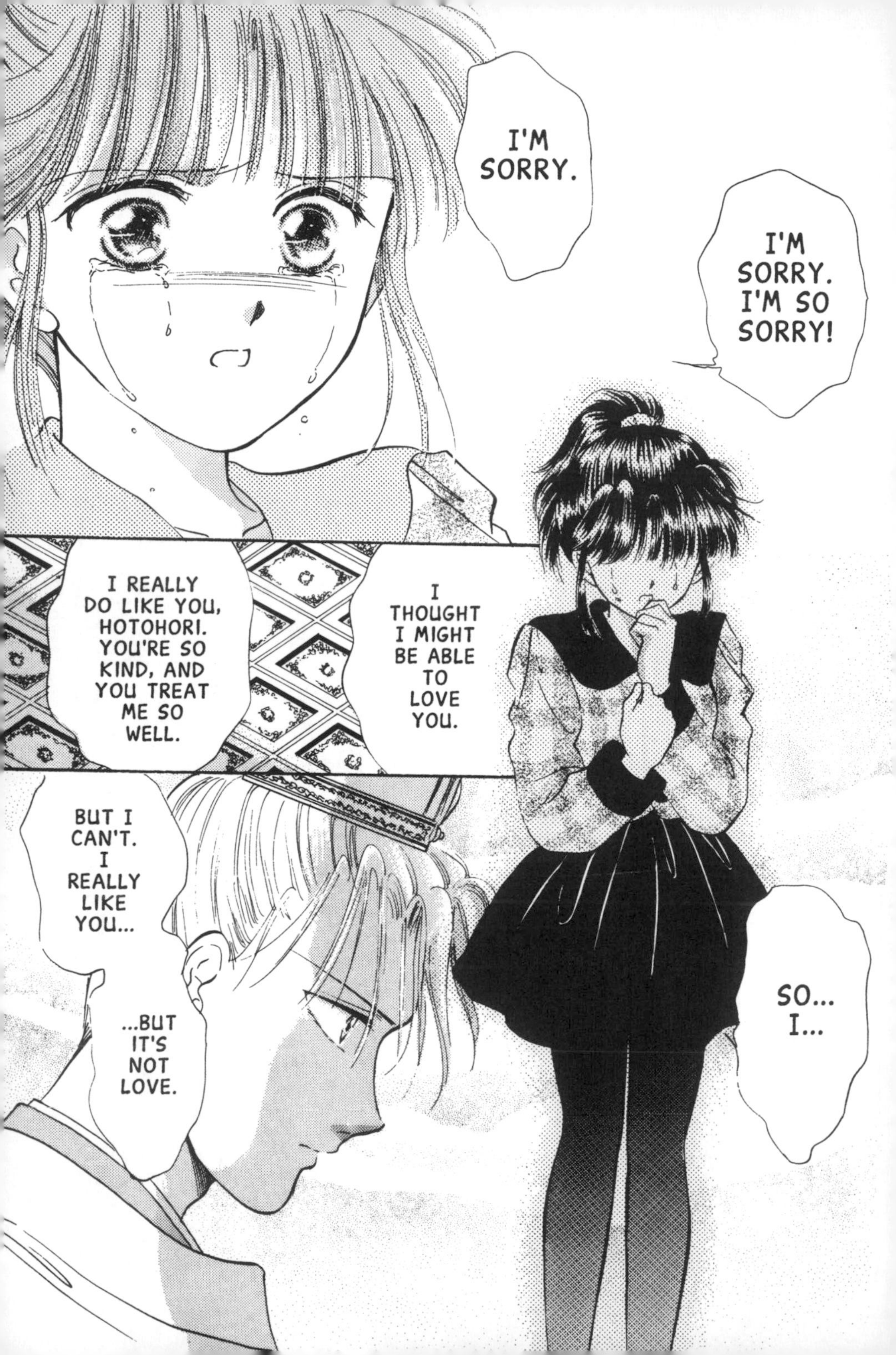
I'M SORRY.
I'M SORRY. I'M SO SORRY!
I REALLY DO LIKE YOU, HOTOHORI. YOU'RE SO KIND, AND YOU TREAT ME SO WELL.
I THOUGHT I MIGHT BE ABLE TO LOVE YOU.
BUT I CAN'T. I REALLY LIKE YOU...
...BUT IT'S NOT LOVE.
SO... I...

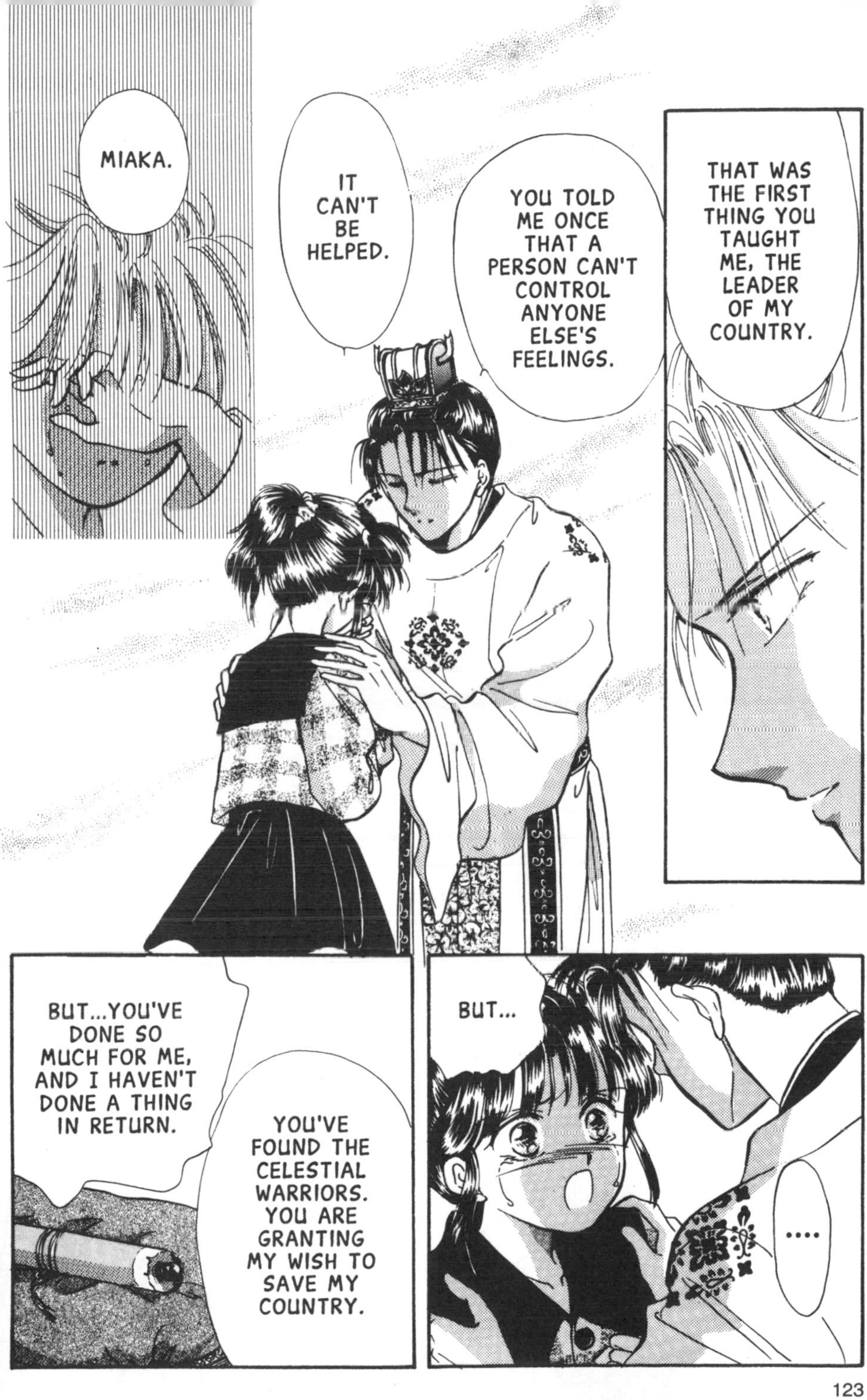
MIAKA.
IT CAN'T BE HELPED.
YOU TOLD ME ONCE THAT A PERSON CAN'T CONTROL ANYONE ELSE'S FEELINGS.
THAT WAS THE FIRST THING YOU TAUGHT ME, THE LEADER OF MY COUNTRY.
BUT...YOU'VE DONE SO MUCH FOR ME, AND I HAVEN'T DONE A THING IN RETURN.
YOU'VE FOUND THE CELESTIAL WARRIORS. YOU ARE GRANTING MY WISH TO SAVE MY COUNTRY.
BUT...
....

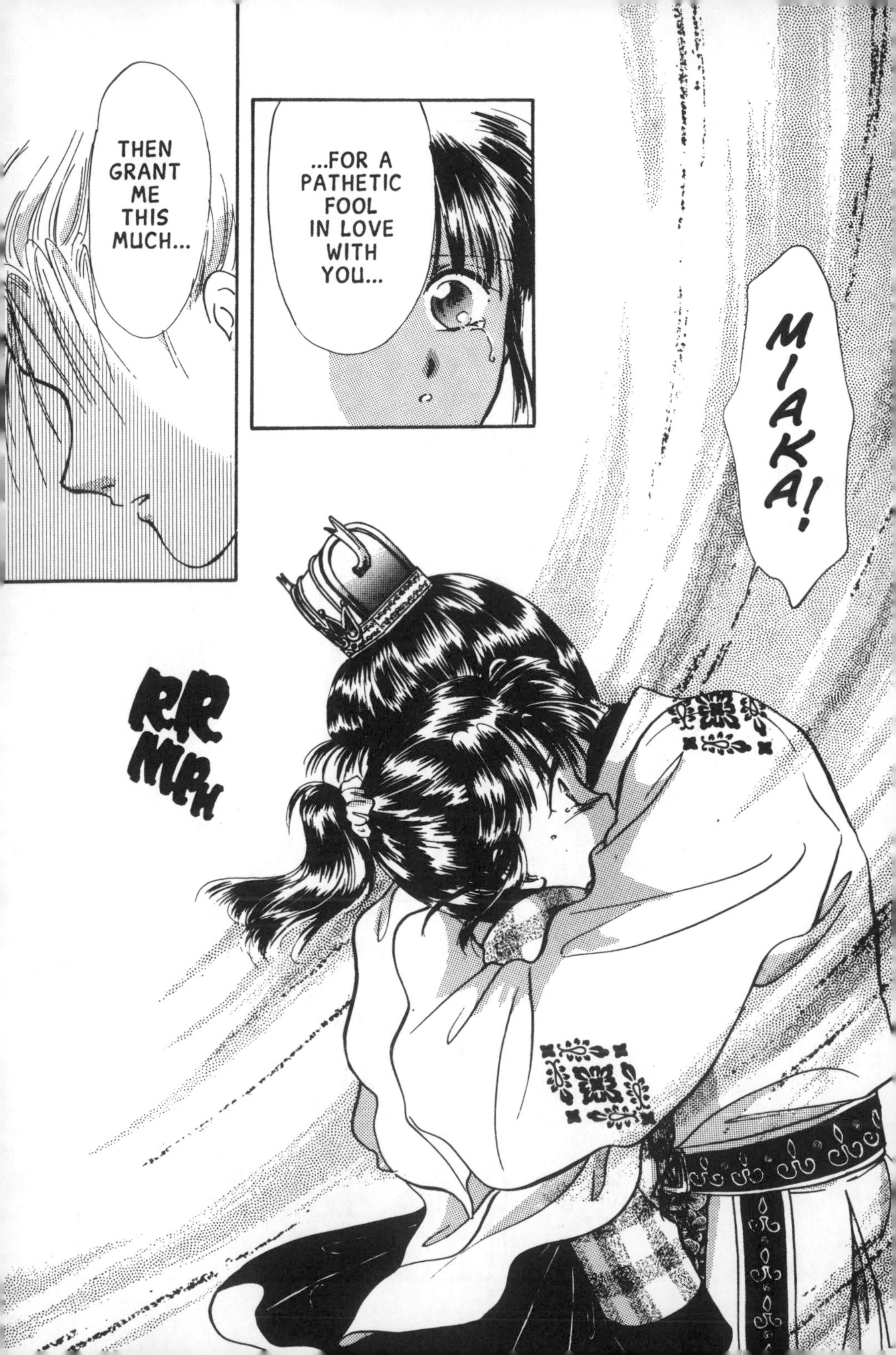
THEN GRANT ME THIS MUCH...
...FOR A PATHETIC FOOL IN LOVE WITH YOU...
MIAKA!
RR MPH

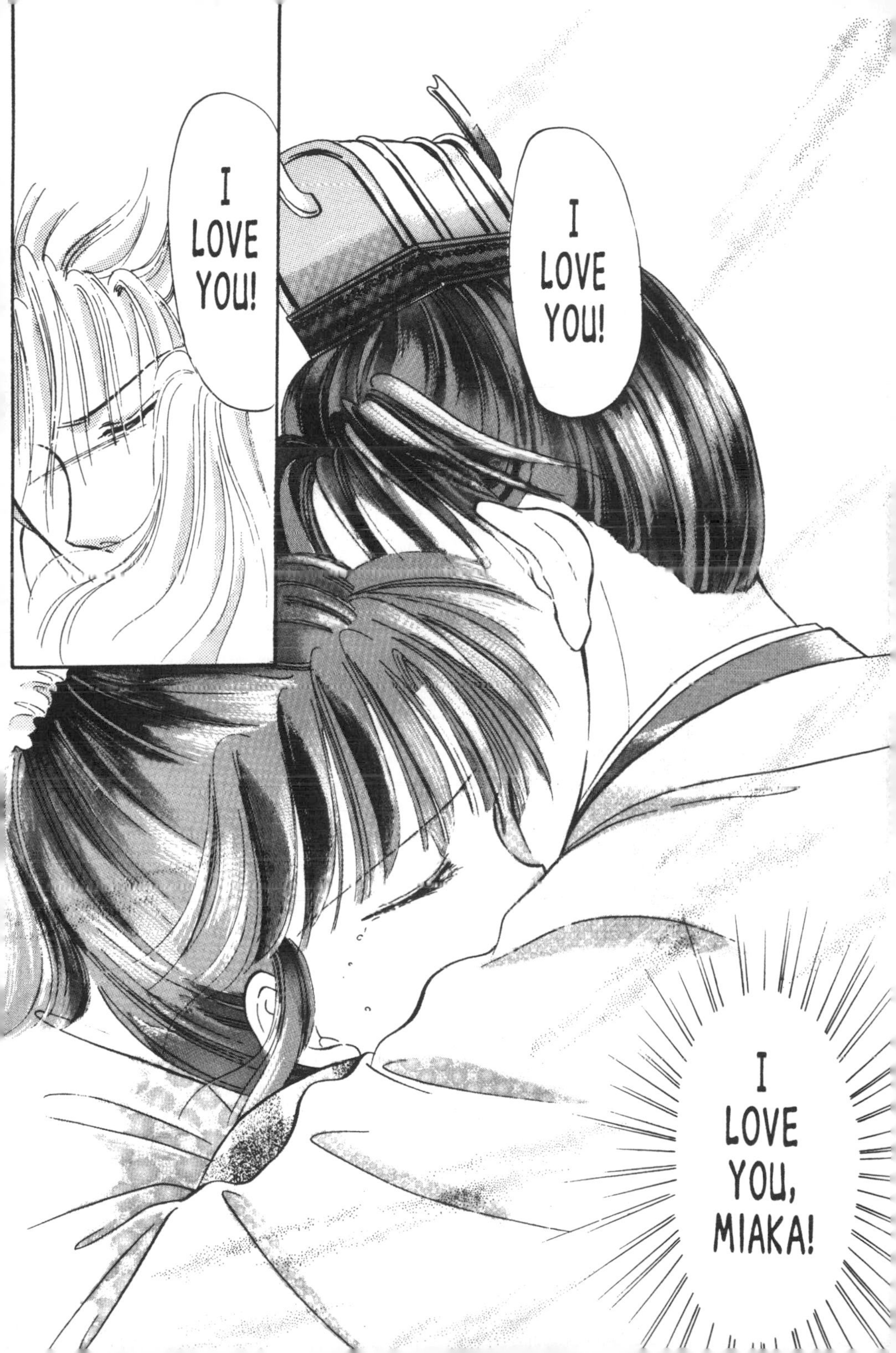

I LOVE YOU!
I LOVE YOU!
I LOVE YOU, MIAKA!

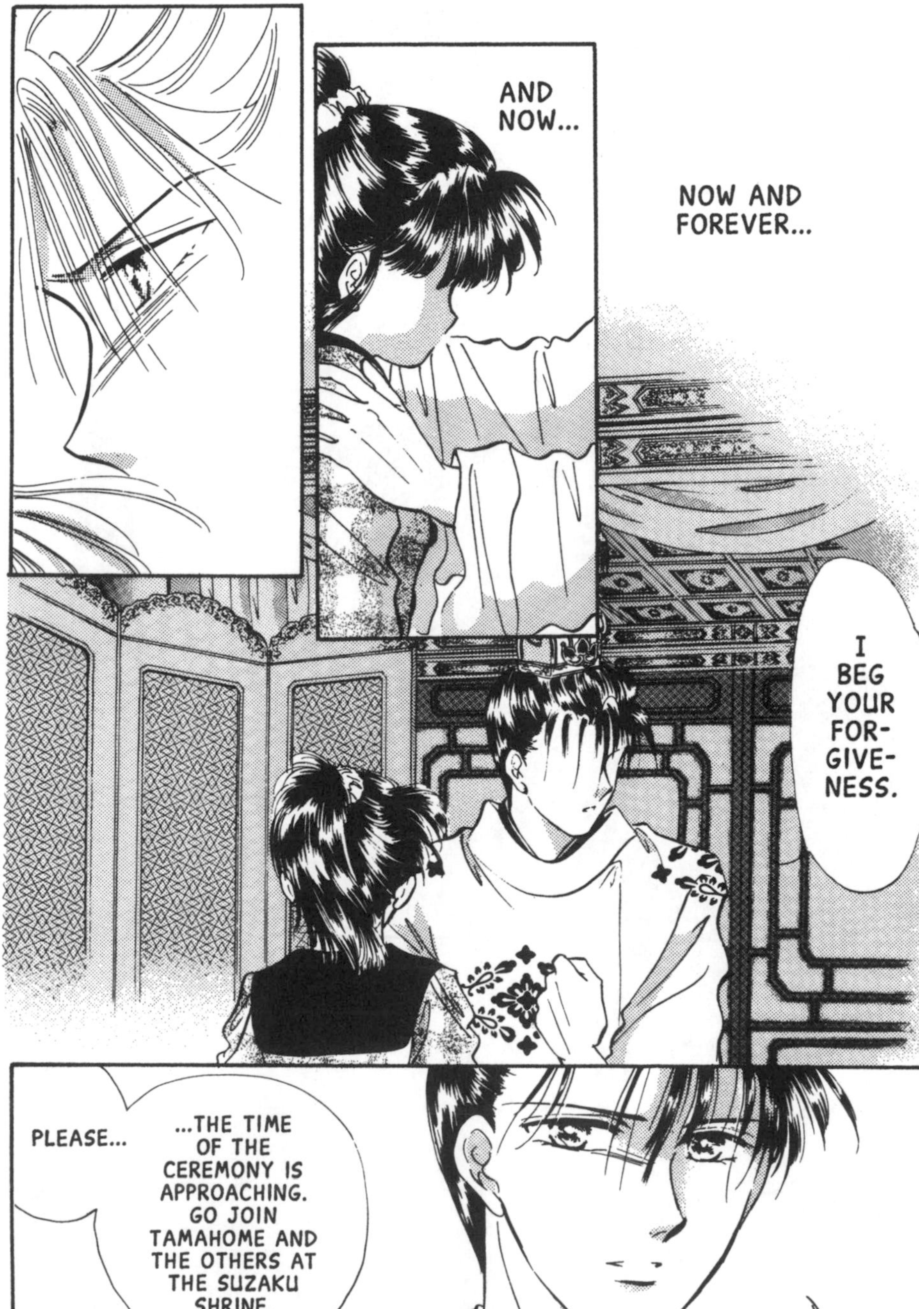
AND NOW...
NOW AND FOREVER...
I BEG YOUR FOR-GIVE-NESS.
PLEASE...
...THE TIME OF THE CEREMONY IS APPROACHING. GO JOIN TAMAHOME AND THE OTHERS AT THE SUZAKU SHRINE.

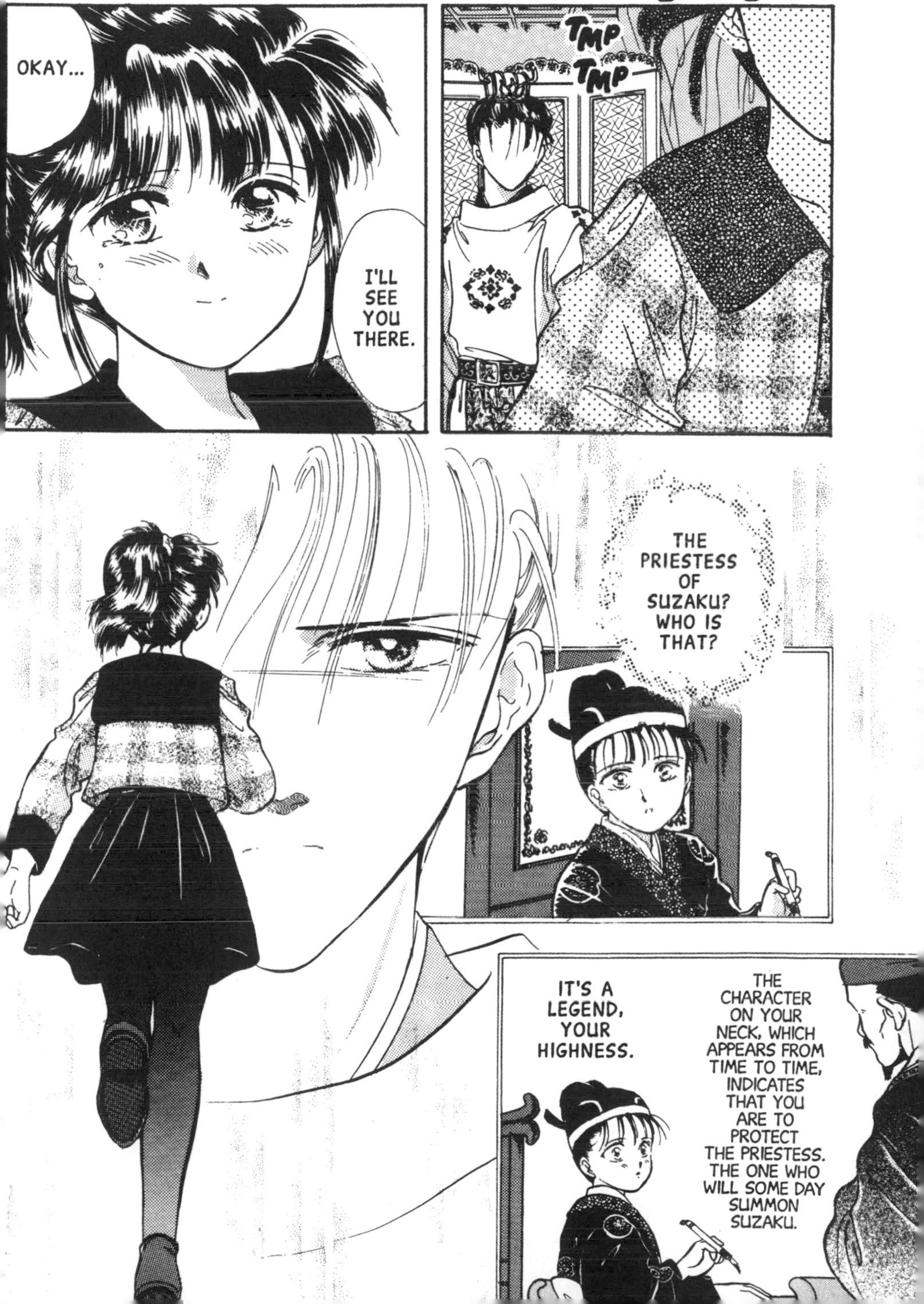
OKAY...
I'LL SEE YOU THERE.
TMP TMP
THE PRIESTESS OF SUZAKU? WHO IS THAT?
IT'S A LEGEND, YOUR HIGHNESS.
THE CHARACTER ON YOUR NECK, WHICH APPEARS FROM TIME TO TIME, INDICATES THAT YOU ARE TO PROTECT THE PRIESTESS. THE ONE WHO WILL SOME DAY SUMMON SUZAKU.

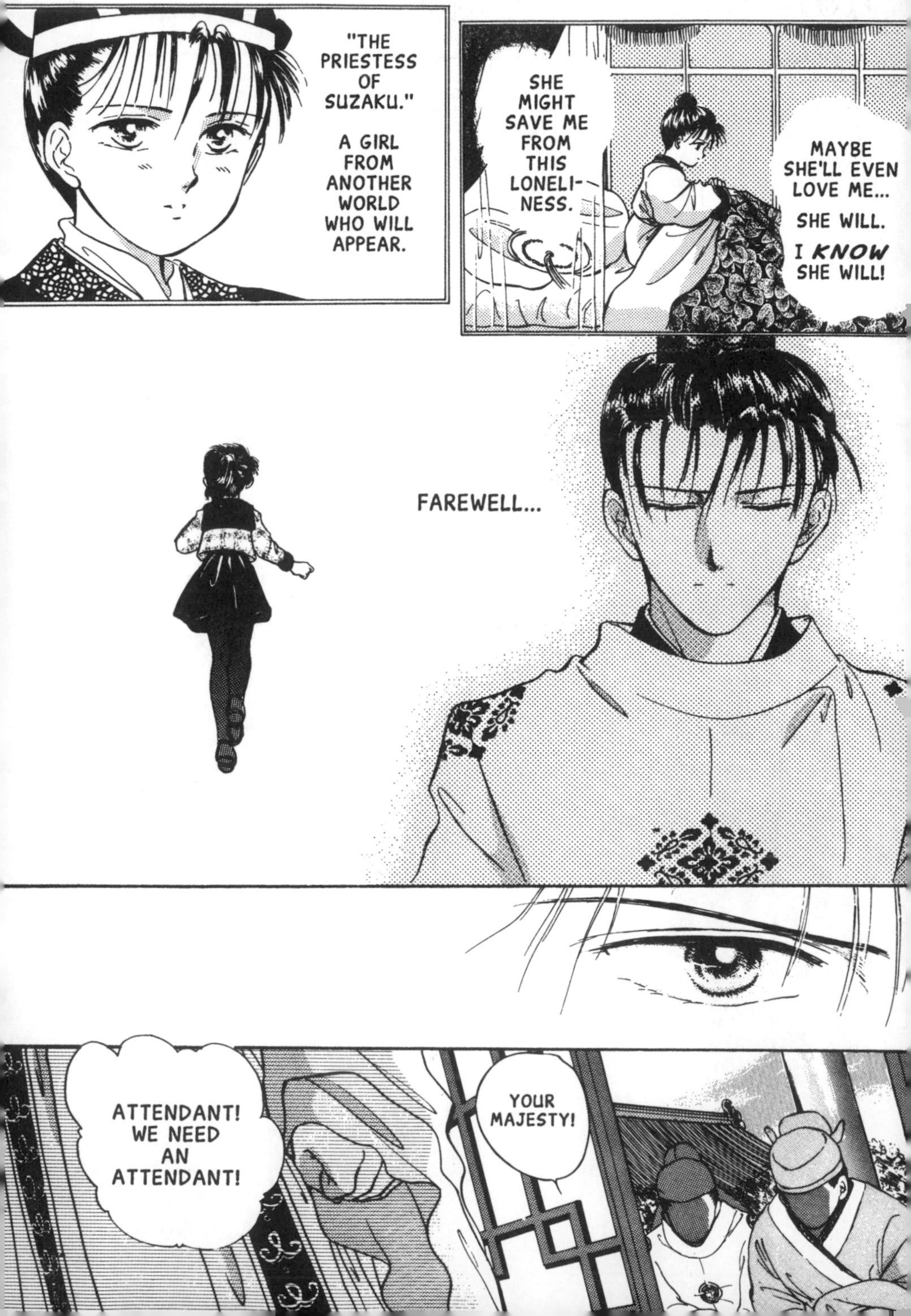
"THE PRIESTESS OF SUZAKU."
A GIRL FROM ANOTHER WORLD WHO WILL APPEAR.
SHE MIGHT SAVE ME FROM THIS LONELI-NESS.
MAYBE SHE'LL EVEN LOVE ME...
SHE WILL.
I *KNOW* SHE WILL!
FAREWELL...
ATTENDANT! WE NEED AN ATTENDANT!
YOUR MAJESTY!

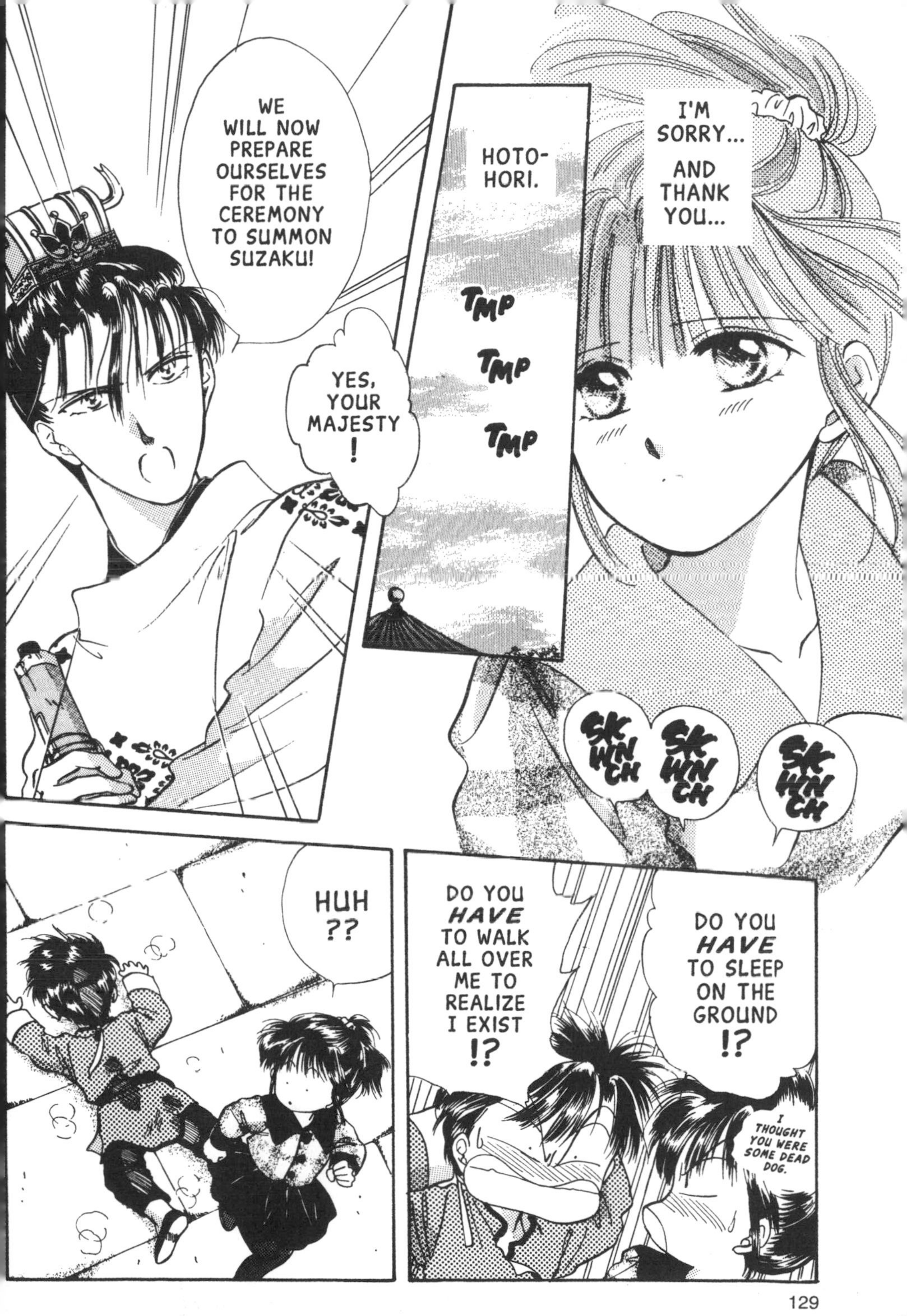
WE WILL NOW PREPARE OURSELVES FOR THE CEREMONY TO SUMMON SUZAKU!
YES, YOUR MAJESTY!
HOTO-HORI.
TMP
TMP
TMP
I'M SORRY...
AND THANK YOU...
SKWNCH
SKWNCH
SKWNCH
HUH ??
DO YOU *HAVE* TO WALK ALL OVER ME TO REALIZE I EXIST !?
DO YOU *HAVE* TO SLEEP ON THE GROUND !?
I THOUGHT YOU WERE SOME DEAD DOG.

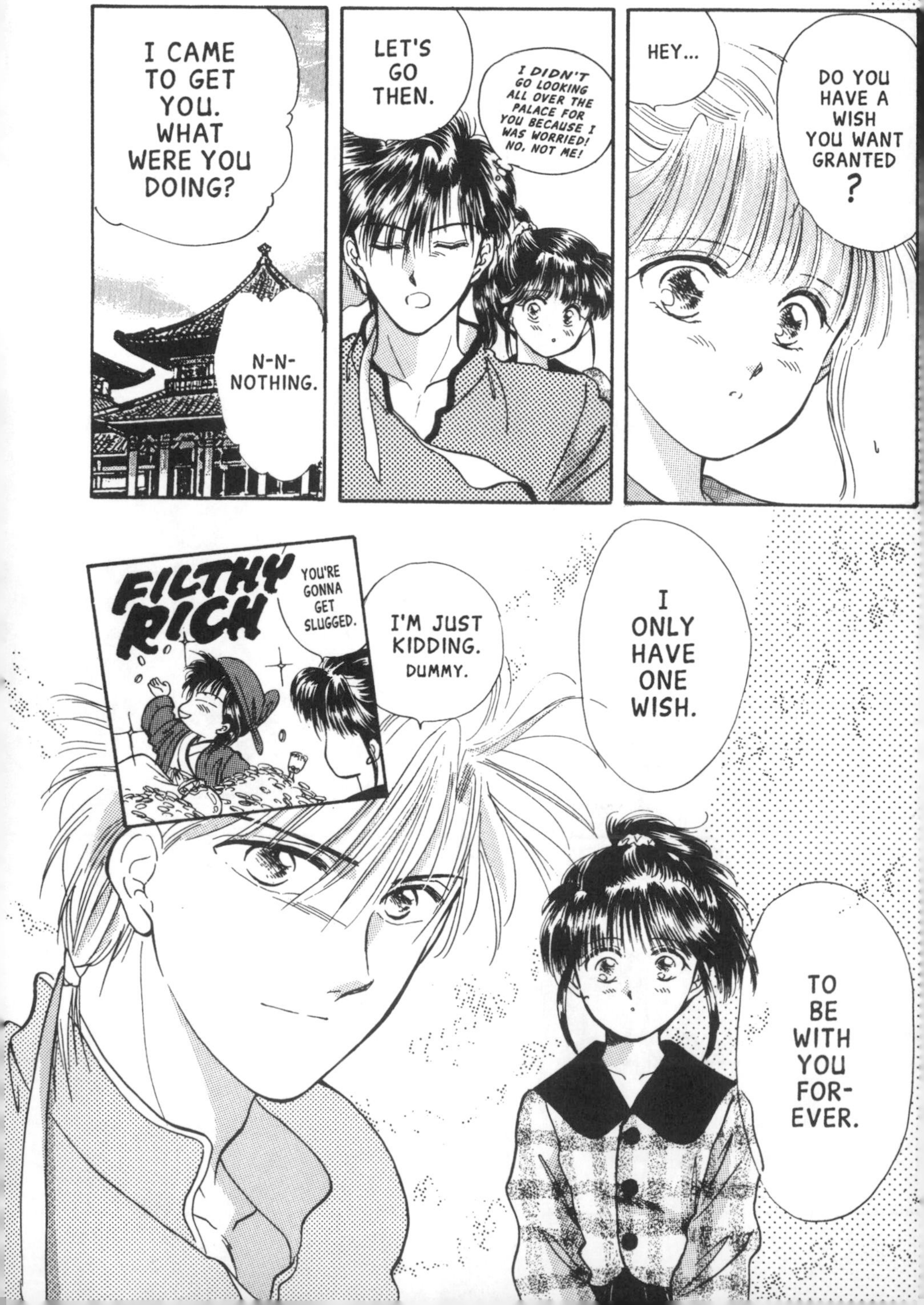
I CAME TO GET YOU. WHAT WERE YOU DOING?
N-N-NOTHING.
LET'S GO THEN.
I DIDN'T GO LOOKING ALL OVER THE PALACE FOR YOU BECAUSE I WAS WORRIED! NO, NOT ME!
HEY...
DO YOU HAVE A WISH YOU WANT GRANTED?
FILTHY RICH
YOU'RE GONNA GET SLUGGED.
I'M JUST KIDDING. DUMMY.
I ONLY HAVE ONE WISH.
TO BE WITH YOU FOR-EVER.

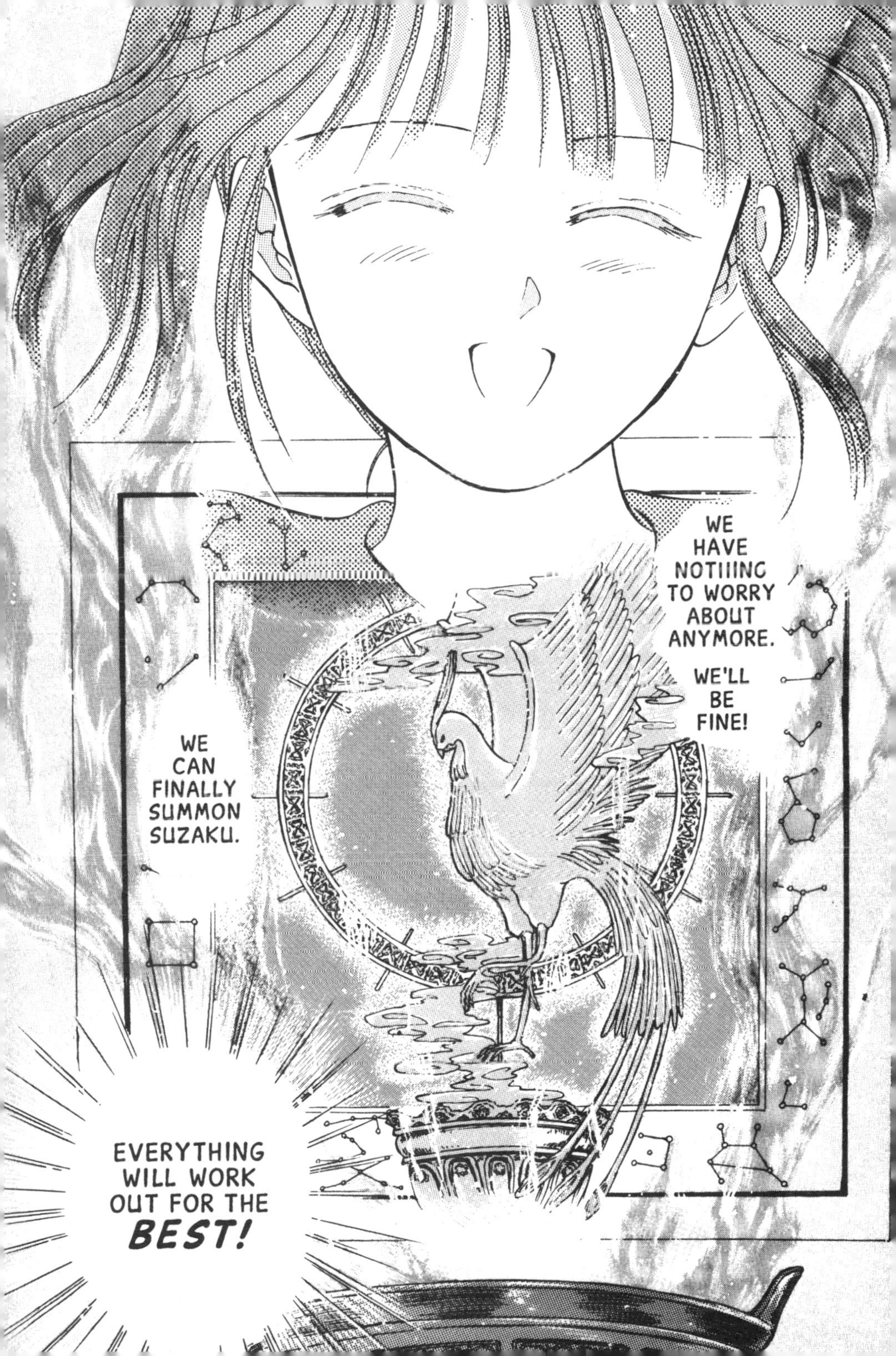
WE CAN FINALLY SUMMON SUZAKU.
WE HAVE NOTHING TO WORRY ABOUT ANYMORE.
WE'LL BE FINE!
EVERYTHING WILL WORK OUT FOR THE ***BEST!***

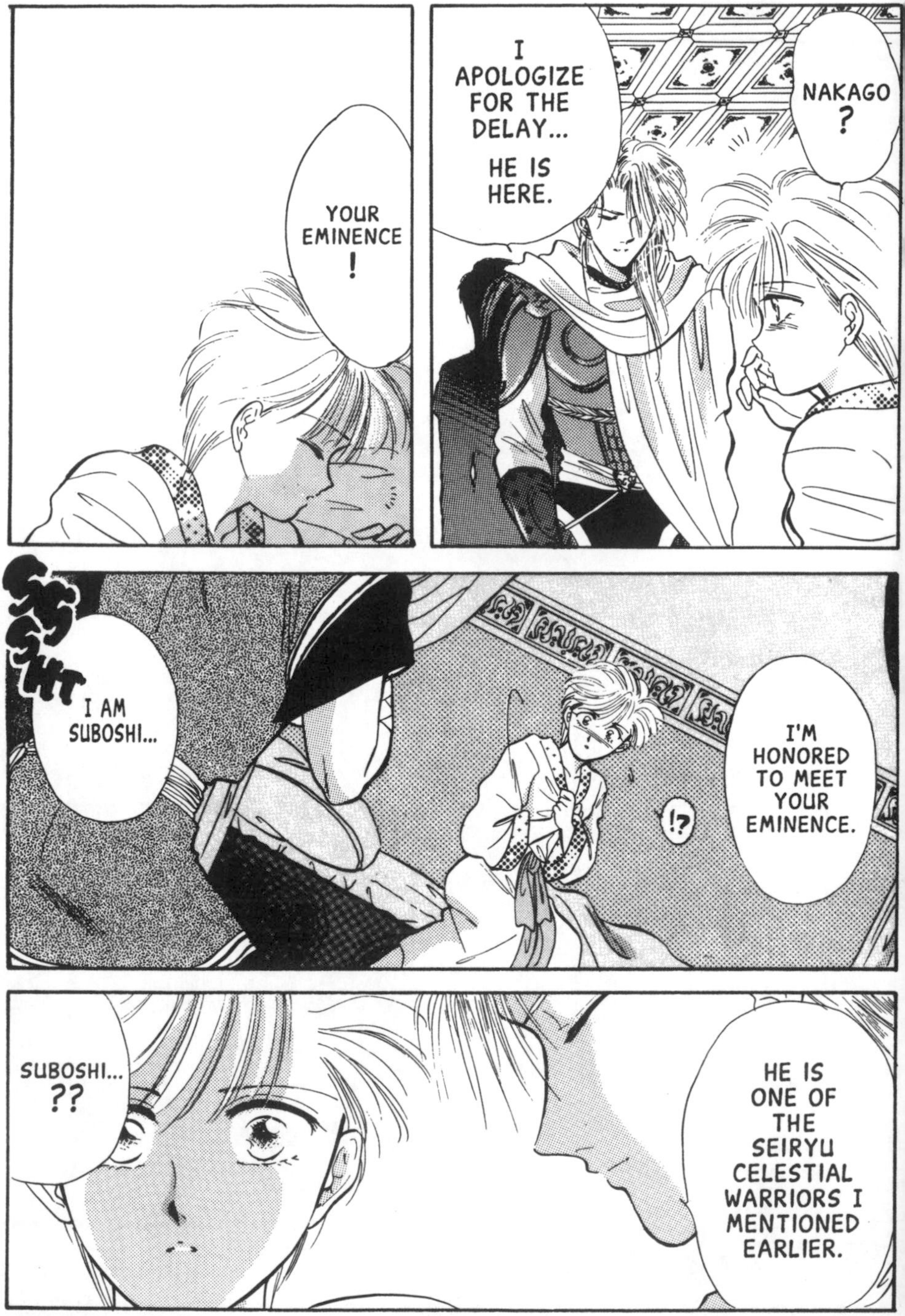
YOUR EMINENCE !
I APOLOGIZE FOR THE DELAY... HE IS HERE.
NAKAGO ?
SSSHT
I AM SUBOSHI...
!?
I'M HONORED TO MEET YOUR EMINENCE.
SUBOSHI... ??
HE IS ONE OF THE SEIRYU CELESTIAL WARRIORS I MENTIONED EARLIER.

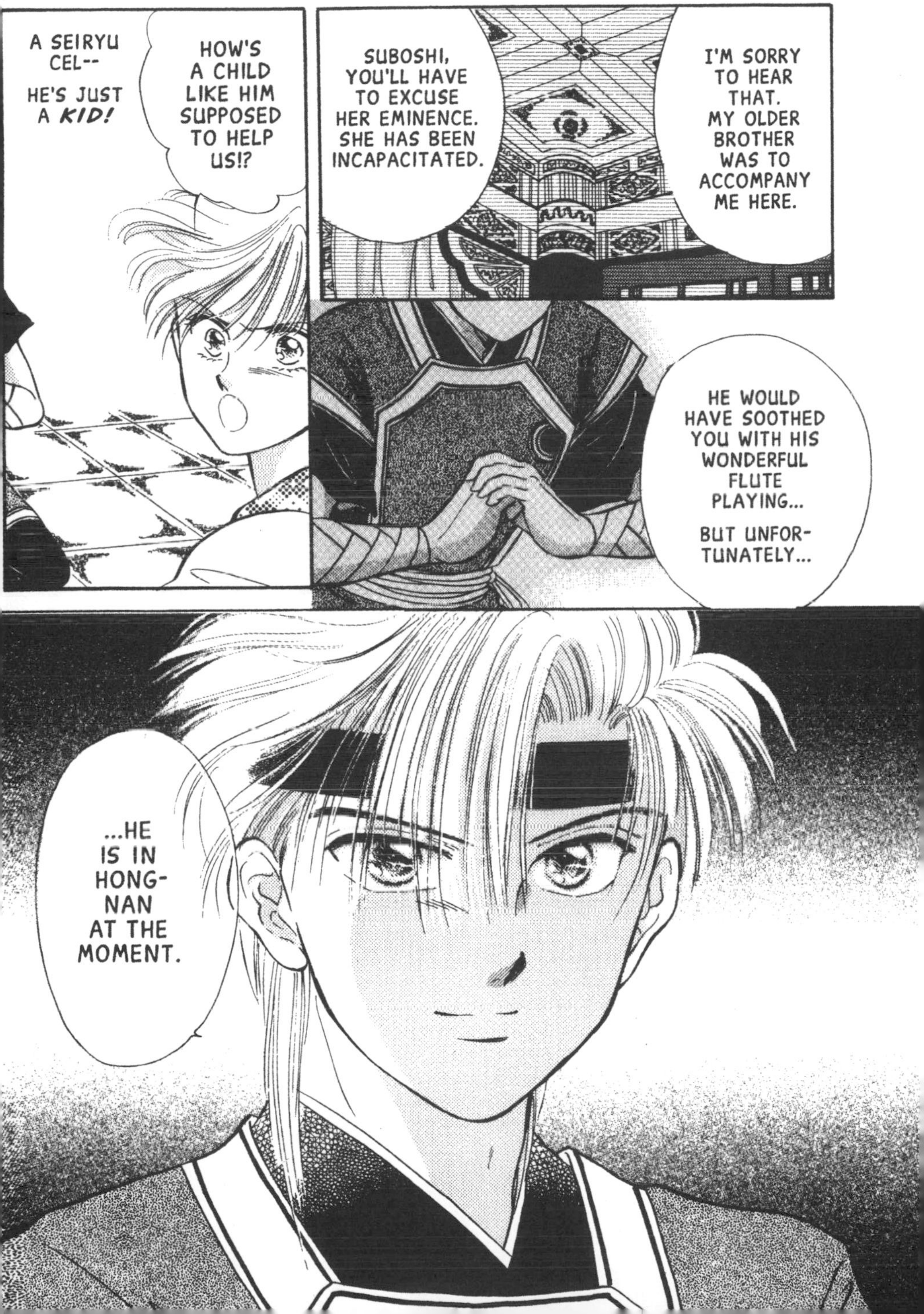
A SEIRYU CEL--
HE'S JUST A *KID!*
HOW'S A CHILD LIKE HIM SUPPOSED TO HELP US!?
SUBOSHI, YOU'LL HAVE TO EXCUSE HER EMINENCE. SHE HAS BEEN INCAPACITATED.
I'M SORRY TO HEAR THAT. MY OLDER BROTHER WAS TO ACCOMPANY ME HERE.
HE WOULD HAVE SOOTHED YOU WITH HIS WONDERFUL FLUTE PLAYING...
BUT UNFORTUNATELY...
...HE IS IN HONG-NAN AT THE MOMENT.

HOU CHUN YU 侯俊宇 (HUAN LANG 幻狼)

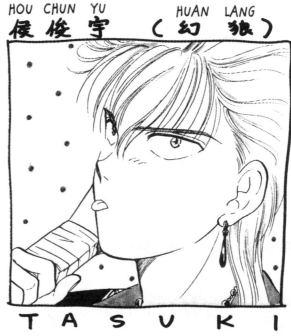

Whoops!→ I drew the kanji in bold! Awwww, who'll ever notice?

CRATER ← Something of a mystery.

TASUKI

- Born in the town of Tai-Tou at the foot of Ligé-San Mountain in the prefecture of Ko.
- Age: 17.
- Family: Parents and five sisters--a house dominated by women. (It's thought that this is where his woman-hating tendencies started.)
- Hobby: Picking fights.
- Height: 5' 10" ● Blood Type: B (naturally!)

He's like a little boy who got bigger but no more mature. As a child he wasn't very brave. But when the chief bandit of Ligé-San Mountain took Tasuki under his wing, Tasuki found his calling. He started to improve his martial skills in order to be like--and carry on after--his mentor as the bandit leader. He also learned the use of the iron harisen. Now that he's left his close friend Knei-Gong as the bandit leader, Tasuki's gone off to help Miaka in her quests. Tasuki is too straight-forward, simple-minded, and quick to pick a fight. Despite that, he is bound by chivalry, gets emotional easily, and is surprisingly shy. He puts on an overly macho act and will beat up on people, but he's probably the most "manly" of the group.

KNEI-GONG (19 years old) Knei-Gong took Tasuki's place as the bandit leader. In a way, he's something of a Tasuki hero-worshiper.

WANT TO KNOW ANY OF HUAN-LANG'S SECRETS? JUST ASK ME!

Ummm... Rui-Ni hid in the shadows and listened while Tasuki learned the use of the iron harisen, and that's why he was able to use it. But nowadays, Tasuki is the only person in the world that can use it. It's so heavy!!

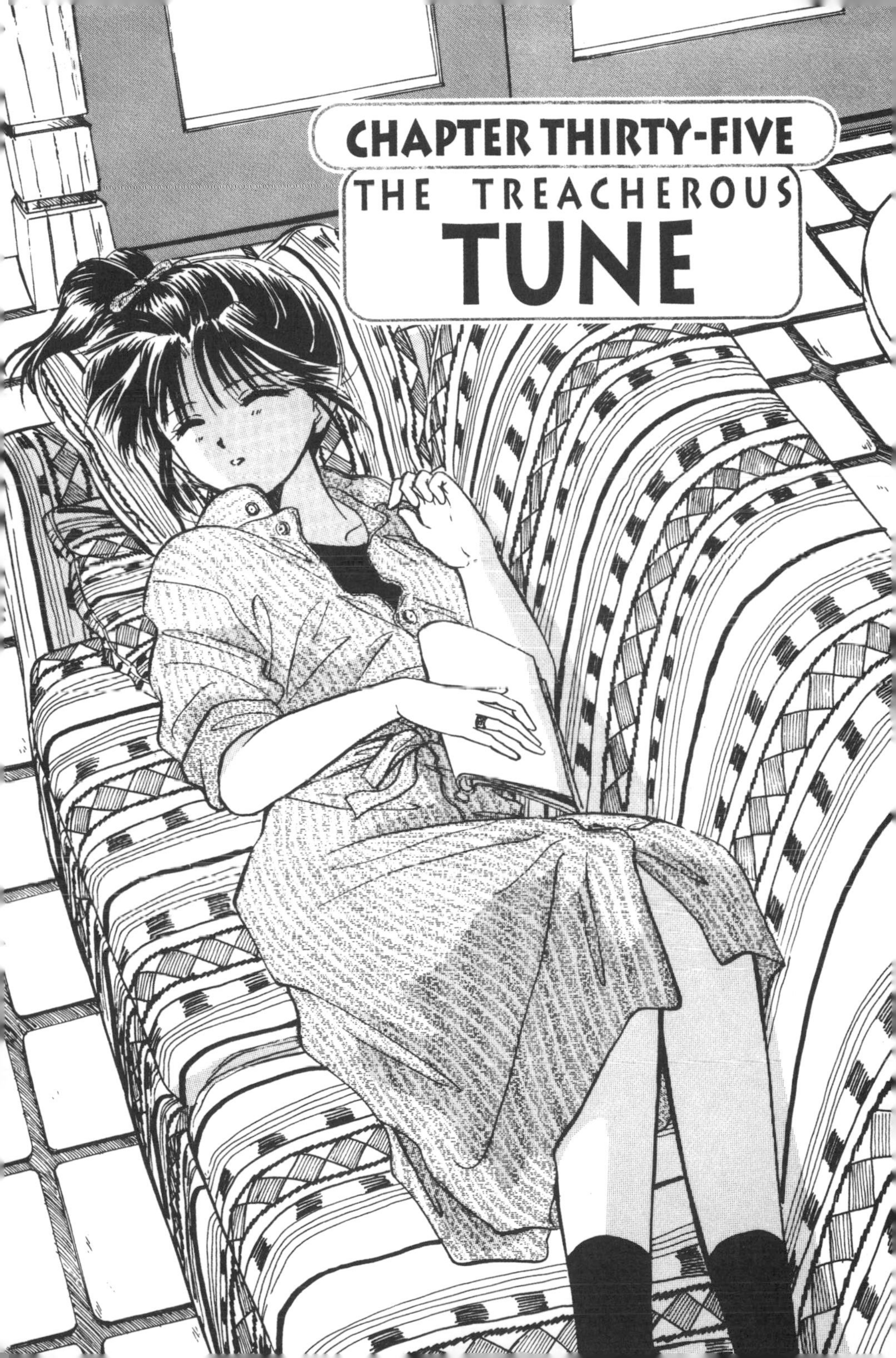
CHAPTER THIRTY-FIVE
THE TREACHEROUS
TUNE

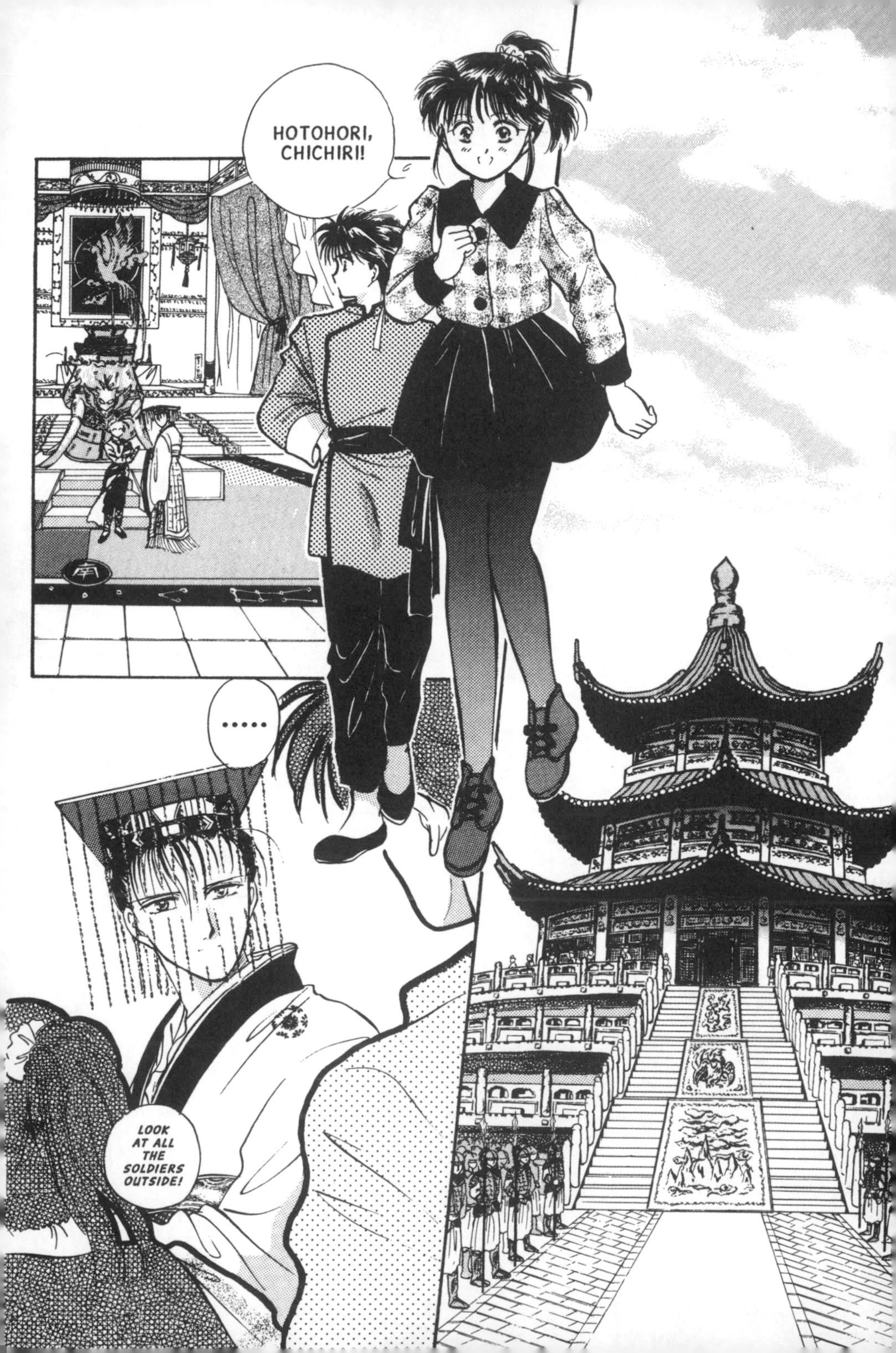
HOTOHORI, CHICHIRI!
......
LOOK AT ALL THE SOLDIERS OUTSIDE!

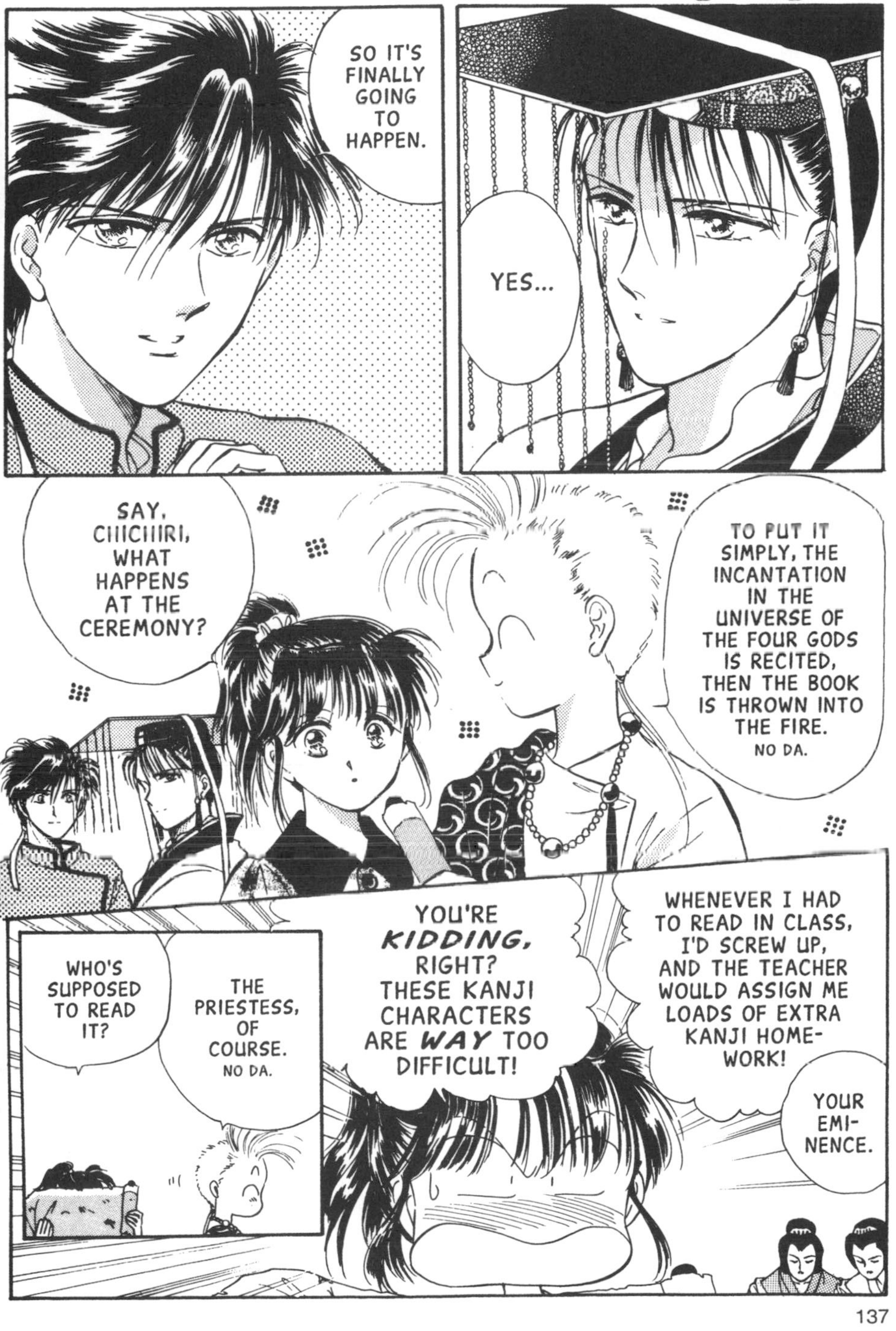
SO IT'S FINALLY GOING TO HAPPEN.
YES...
SAY, CHICHIRI, WHAT HAPPENS AT THE CEREMONY?
TO PUT IT SIMPLY, THE INCANTATION IN THE UNIVERSE OF THE FOUR GODS IS RECITED, THEN THE BOOK IS THROWN INTO THE FIRE.
NO DA.
WHO'S SUPPOSED TO READ IT?
THE PRIESTESS, OF COURSE.
NO DA.
YOU'RE *KIDDING,* RIGHT? THESE KANJI CHARACTERS ARE *WAY* TOO DIFFICULT!
WHENEVER I HAD TO READ IN CLASS, I'D SCREW UP, AND THE TEACHER WOULD ASSIGN ME LOADS OF EXTRA KANJI HOME-WORK!
YOUR EMI-NENCE.

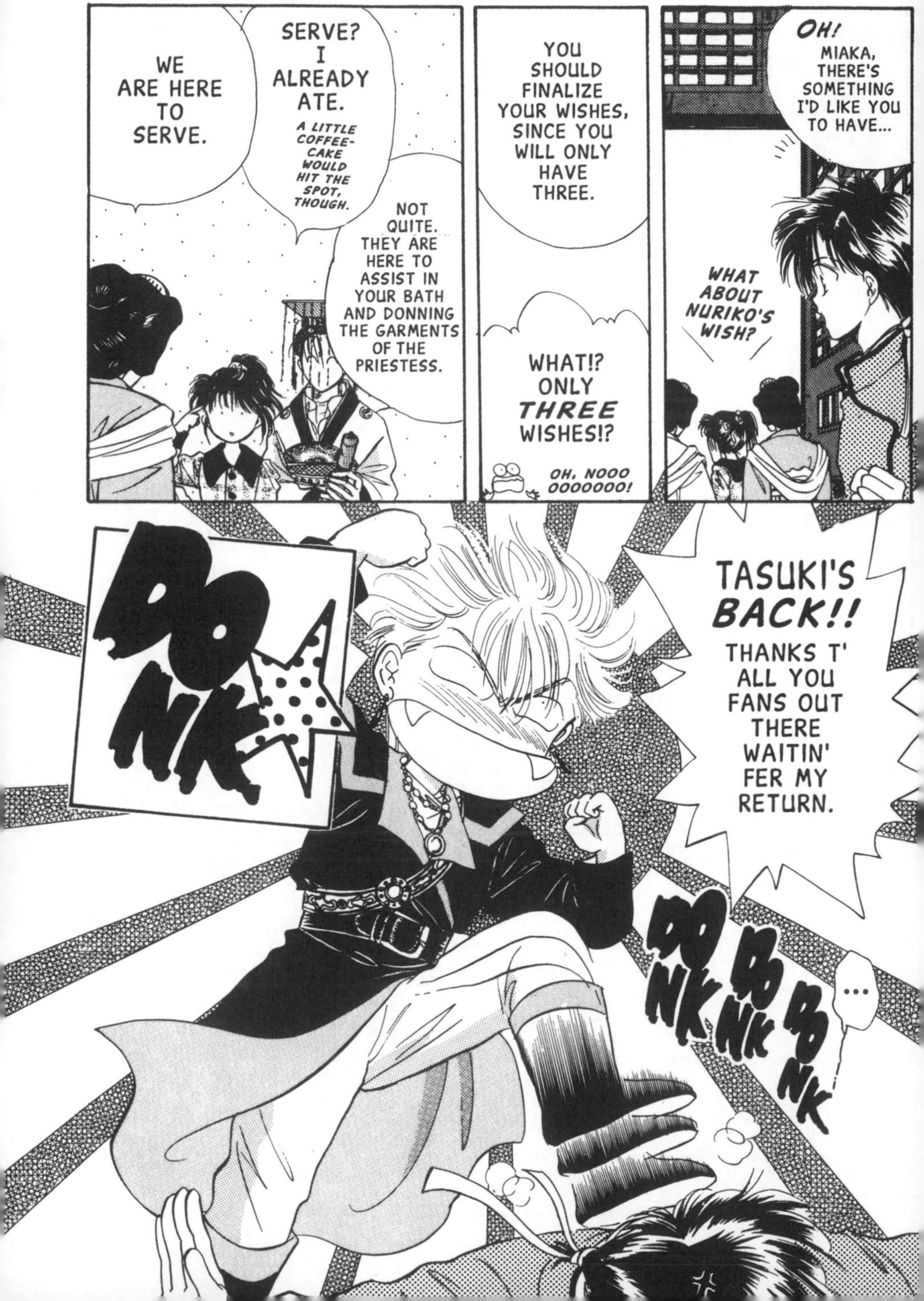
WE ARE HERE TO SERVE.
SERVE? I ALREADY ATE.
A LITTLE COFFEE-CAKE WOULD HIT THE SPOT, THOUGH.
NOT QUITE. THEY ARE HERE TO ASSIST IN YOUR BATH AND DONNING THE GARMENTS OF THE PRIESTESS.
YOU SHOULD FINALIZE YOUR WISHES, SINCE YOU WILL ONLY HAVE THREE.
WHAT!? ONLY THREE WISHES!?
OH, NOOO OOOOOOO!
OH! MIAKA, THERE'S SOMETHING I'D LIKE YOU TO HAVE...
WHAT ABOUT NURIKO'S WISH?
DONK
TASUKI'S BACK!! THANKS T' ALL YOU FANS OUT THERE WAITIN' FER MY RETURN.
DONK DONK DONK
...

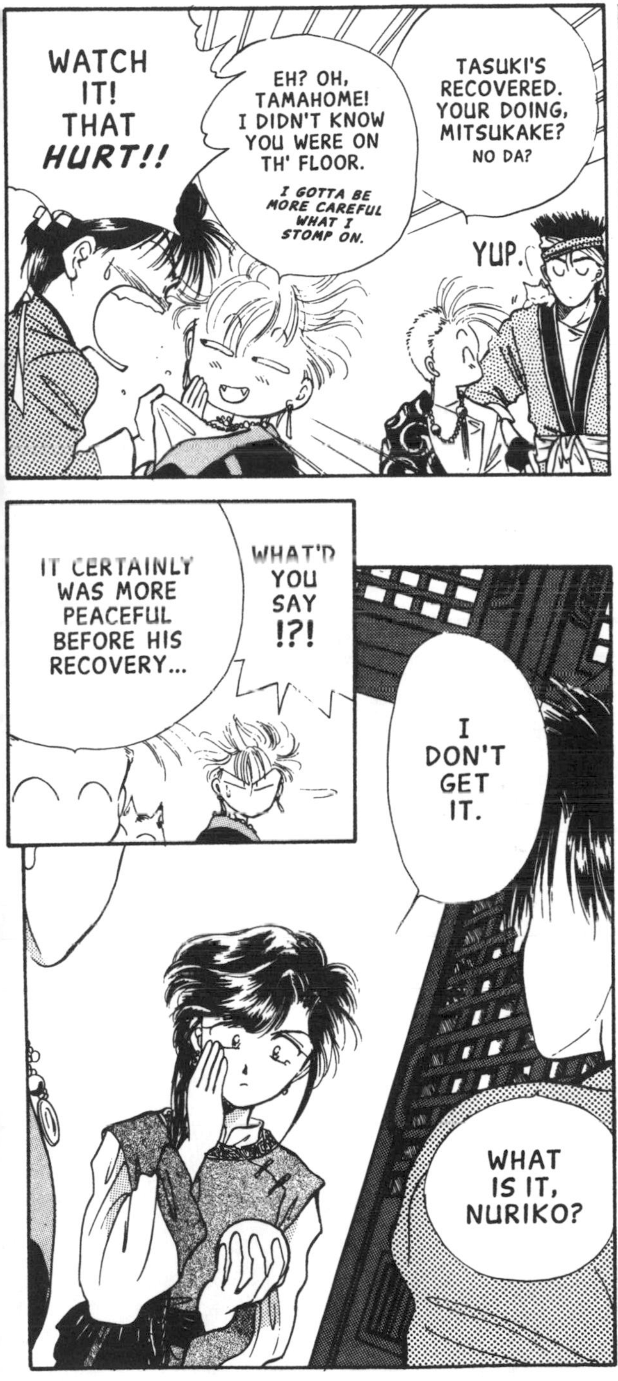
WATCH IT! THAT HURT!!
EH? OH, TAMAHOME! I DIDN'T KNOW YOU WERE ON TH' FLOOR.
I GOTTA BE MORE CAREFUL WHAT I STOMP ON.
TASUKI'S RECOVERED. YOUR DOING, MITSUKAKE? NO DA?
YUP.
IT CERTAINLY WAS MORE PEACEFUL BEFORE HIS RECOVERY...
WHAT'D YOU SAY !?!
I DON'T GET IT.
WHAT IS IT, NURIKO?

Summoner

So what have I been listening to on the Yūsen cable radio? "Music of Fear." It's the kind of music you'd hear in a horror movie, one tune right after the next. Oh, no! Some girl's crying! It's too creepy, so I'll change the channel. And just to create a mood for the manga, I changed it to the "Traditional Chinese Music Channel." LA LA LA!
I'd like to talk about my Yorkshire terrier, but I don't have enough space to describe how immensely cute he is! So I'll save it for later.

He's soooooo cute!

It's been a while since I answered my fan mail. I thought I'd get this question when the serial began, but I didn't, and so finally now someone asks, "How can Miaka and Tamahome speak to each other?" It's simple. This Universe of the Four Gods is a Japanese translation! Some of the store signs and such haven't been translated. So Tamahome and the others are all speaking Japanese. *Let's just leave it at that.* Also, this world might be based on China, but it's not really China. However, I had to use "Wo ai ni" because I just loved the sound of the expression. I'll also answer the question, "In Chapter 10, Tamahome and Hotohori give blood to Miaka, but how could they all have the same blood type?" That wasn't real blood but blood energy. Also, "Why is it that Miaka can communicate with Yui, but she can't with her brother?" Hmmm. Very perceptive.

To be continued...

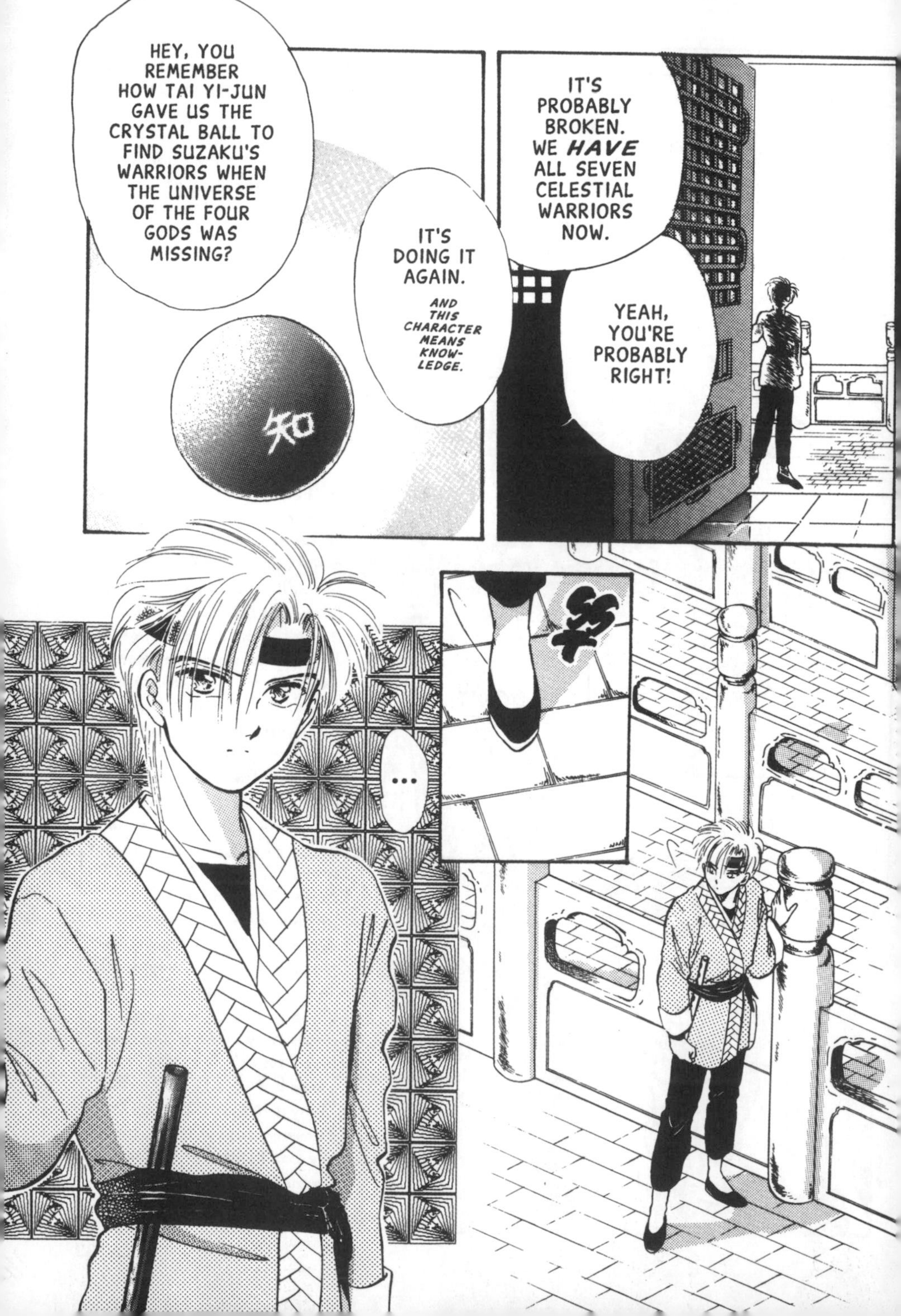
HEY, YOU REMEMBER HOW TAI YI-JUN GAVE US THE CRYSTAL BALL TO FIND SUZAKU'S WARRIORS WHEN THE UNIVERSE OF THE FOUR GODS WAS MISSING?
IT'S DOING IT AGAIN.
AND THIS CHARACTER MEANS KNOW-LEDGE.
IT'S PROBABLY BROKEN. WE ***HAVE*** ALL SEVEN CELESTIAL WARRIORS NOW.
YEAH, YOU'RE PROBABLY RIGHT!
...

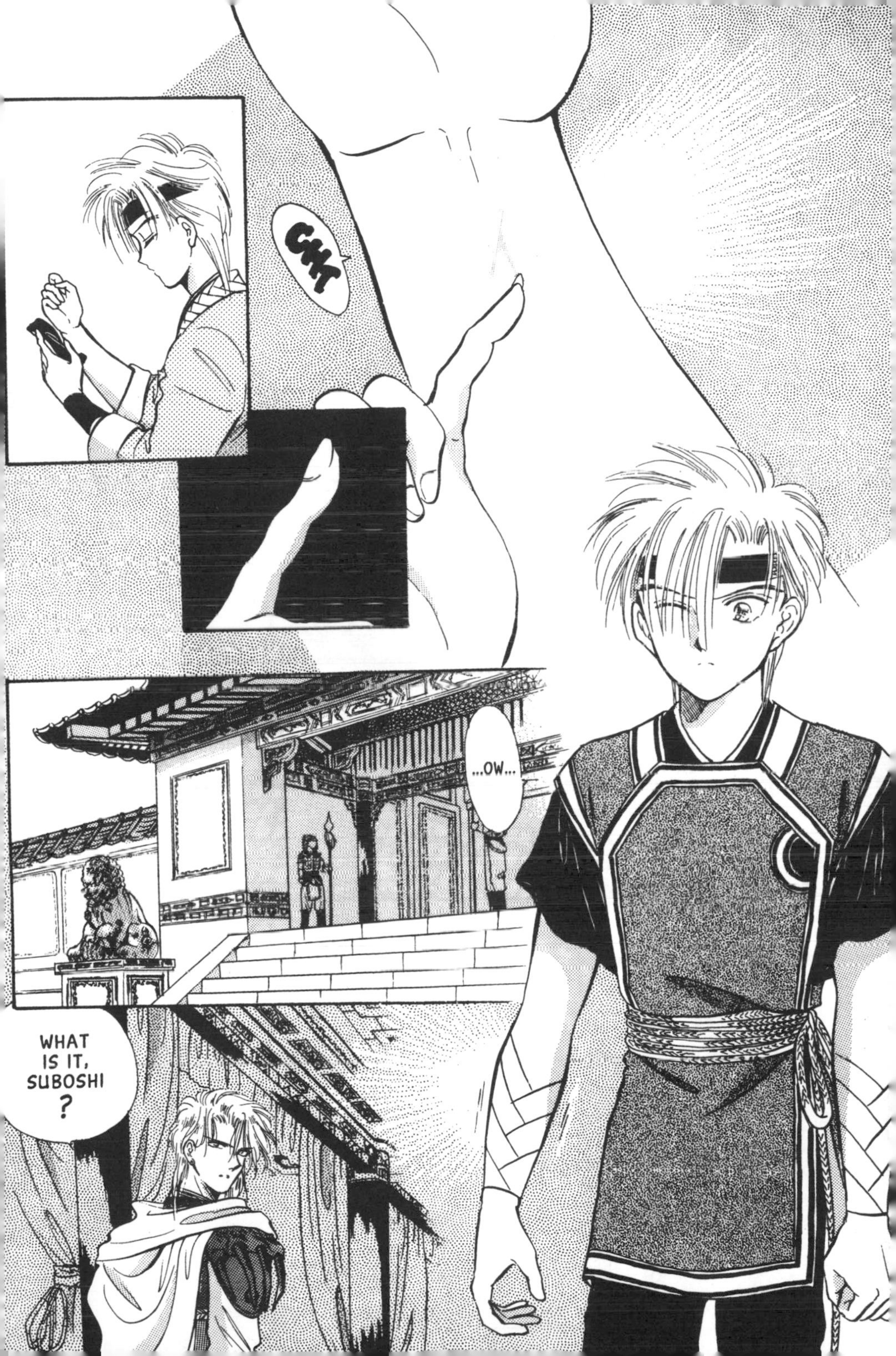
GKK
...OW...
WHAT IS IT, SUBOSHI?

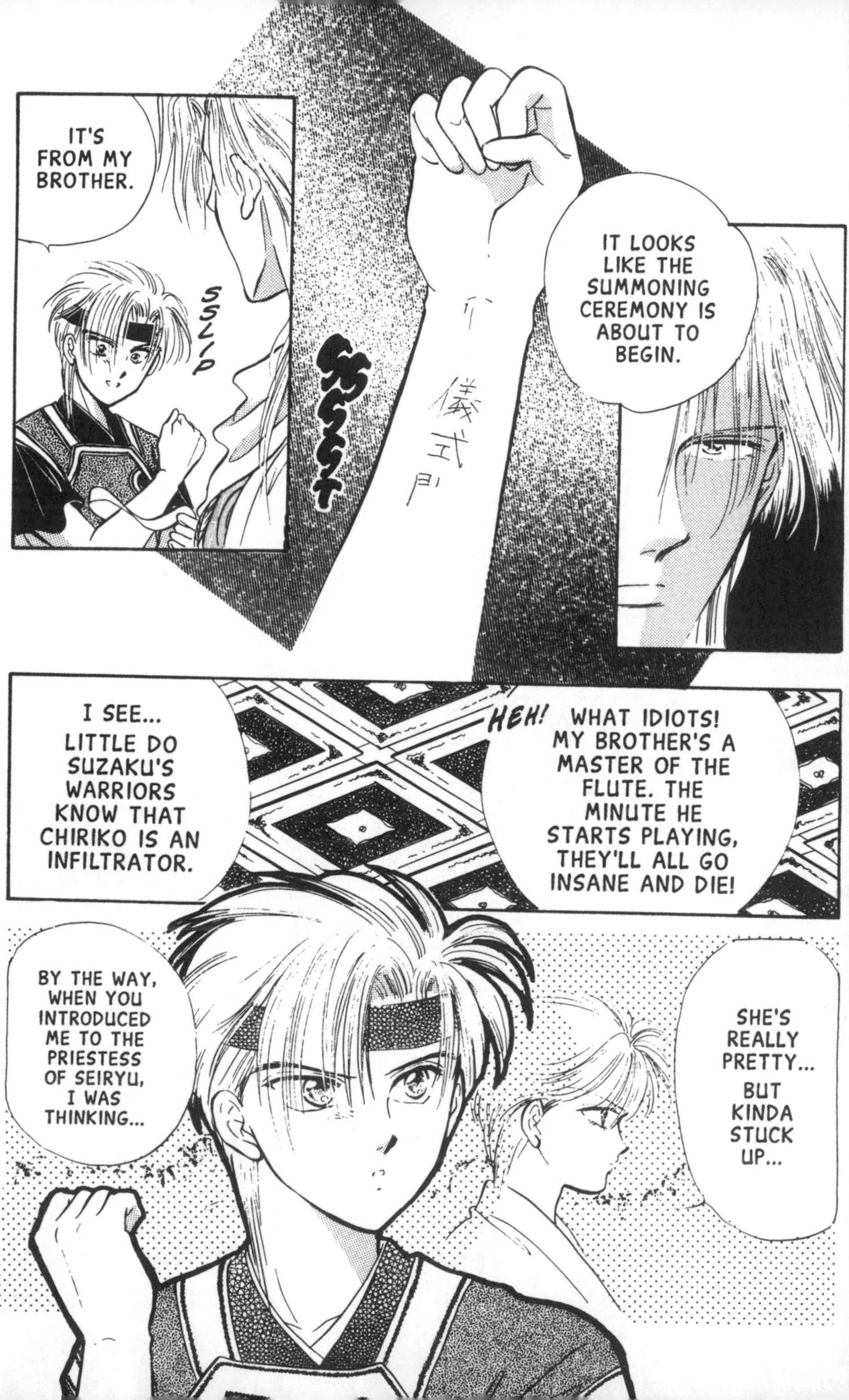
IT'S FROM MY BROTHER.
SSLIP
IT LOOKS LIKE THE SUMMONING CEREMONY IS ABOUT TO BEGIN.
I SEE... LITTLE DO SUZAKU'S WARRIORS KNOW THAT CHIRIKO IS AN INFILTRATOR.
HEH!
WHAT IDIOTS! MY BROTHER'S A MASTER OF THE FLUTE. THE MINUTE HE STARTS PLAYING, THEY'LL ALL GO INSANE AND DIE!
BY THE WAY, WHEN YOU INTRODUCED ME TO THE PRIESTESS OF SEIRYU, I WAS THINKING...
SHE'S REALLY PRETTY... BUT KINDA STUCK UP...

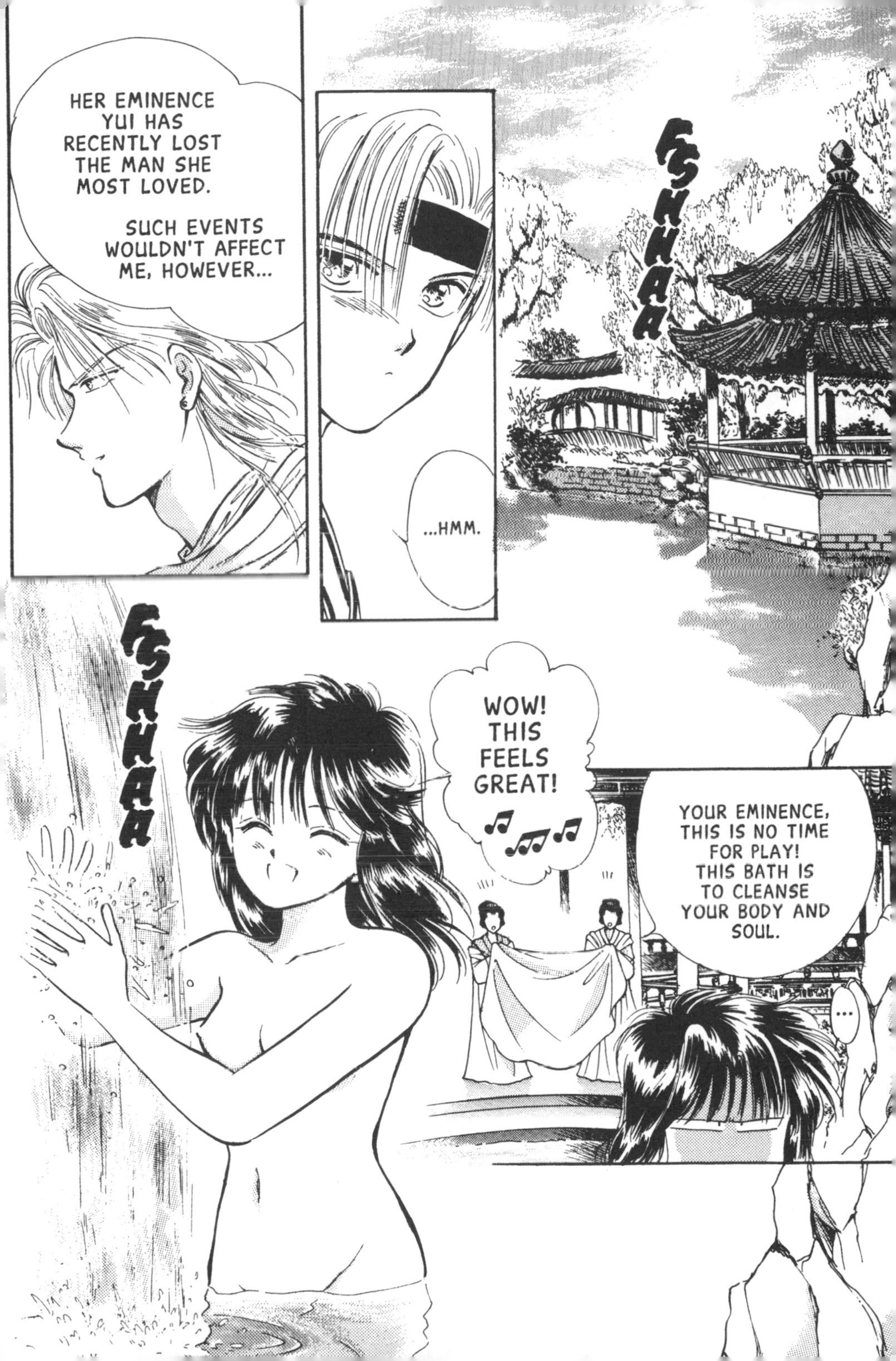
HER EMINENCE YUI HAS RECENTLY LOST THE MAN SHE MOST LOVED.
SUCH EVENTS WOULDN'T AFFECT ME, HOWEVER...
...HMM.
FSHHAA
FSHHAA
WOW! THIS FEELS GREAT! ♫ ♫♫ ♫
YOUR EMINENCE, THIS IS NO TIME FOR PLAY! THIS BATH IS TO CLEANSE YOUR BODY AND SOUL.
...

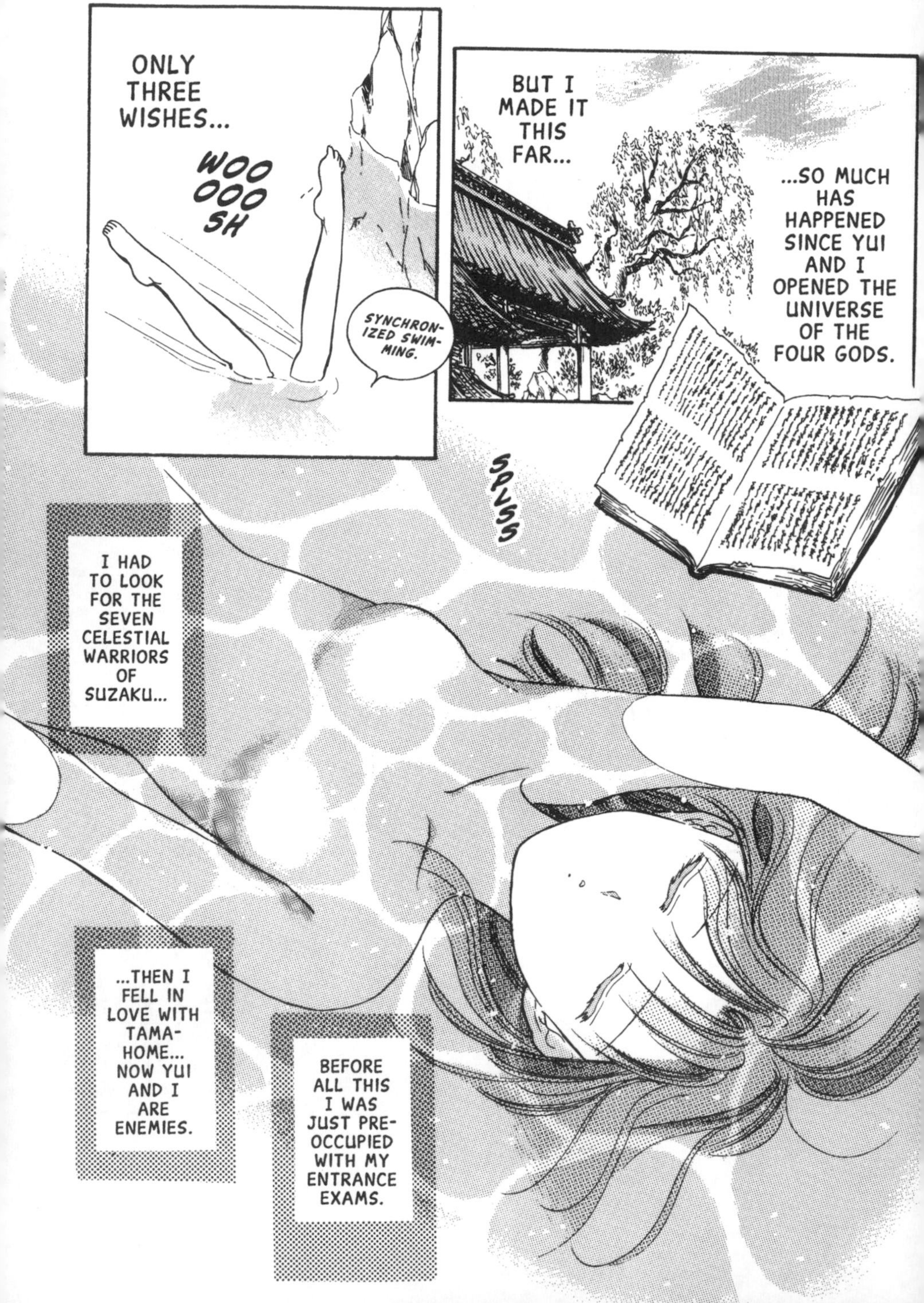
ONLY THREE WISHES...
WOOOOOOSH
SYNCHRONIZED SWIMMING.
BUT I MADE IT THIS FAR...
...SO MUCH HAS HAPPENED SINCE YUI AND I OPENED THE UNIVERSE OF THE FOUR GODS.
SPLSS
I HAD TO LOOK FOR THE SEVEN CELESTIAL WARRIORS OF SUZAKU...
...THEN I FELL IN LOVE WITH TAMAHOME... NOW YUI AND I ARE ENEMIES.
BEFORE ALL THIS I WAS JUST PREOCCUPIED WITH MY ENTRANCE EXAMS.

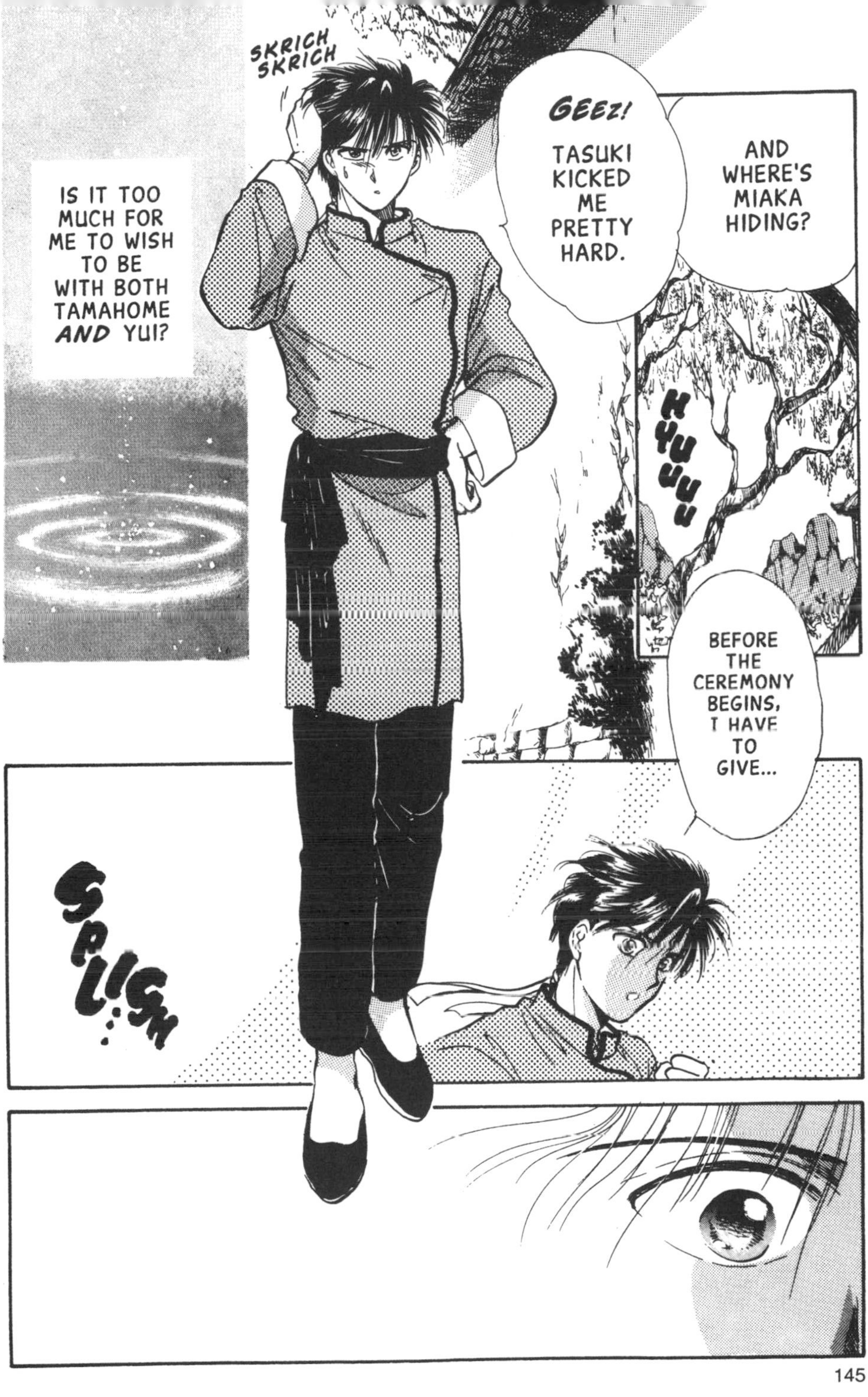
IS IT TOO MUCH FOR ME TO WISH TO BE WITH BOTH TAMAHOME AND YUI?
SKRICH SKRICH
GEEZ! TASUKI KICKED ME PRETTY HARD.
AND WHERE'S MIAKA HIDING?
HYUUUU
BEFORE THE CEREMONY BEGINS, I HAVE TO GIVE...
SPLISH

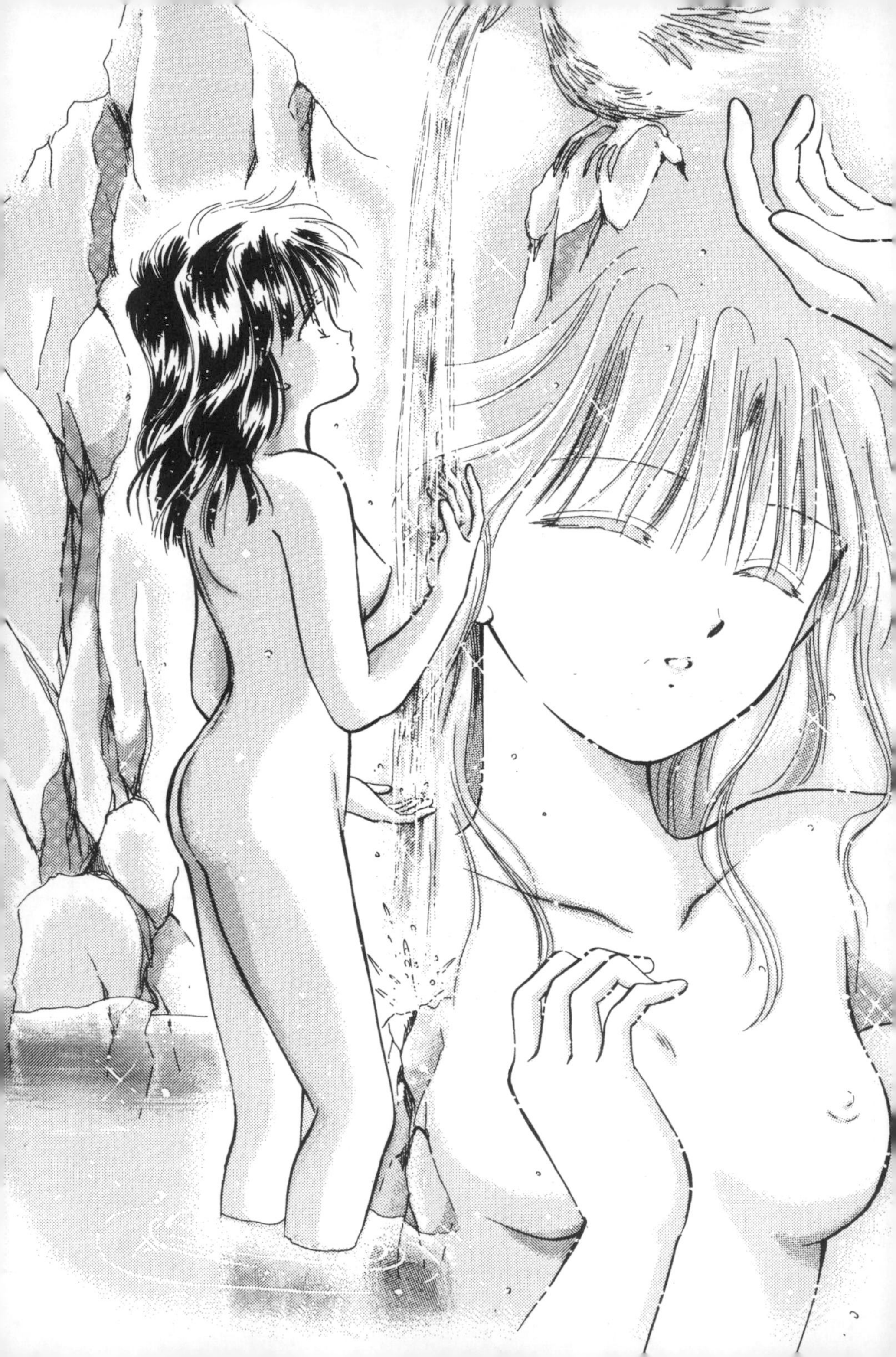

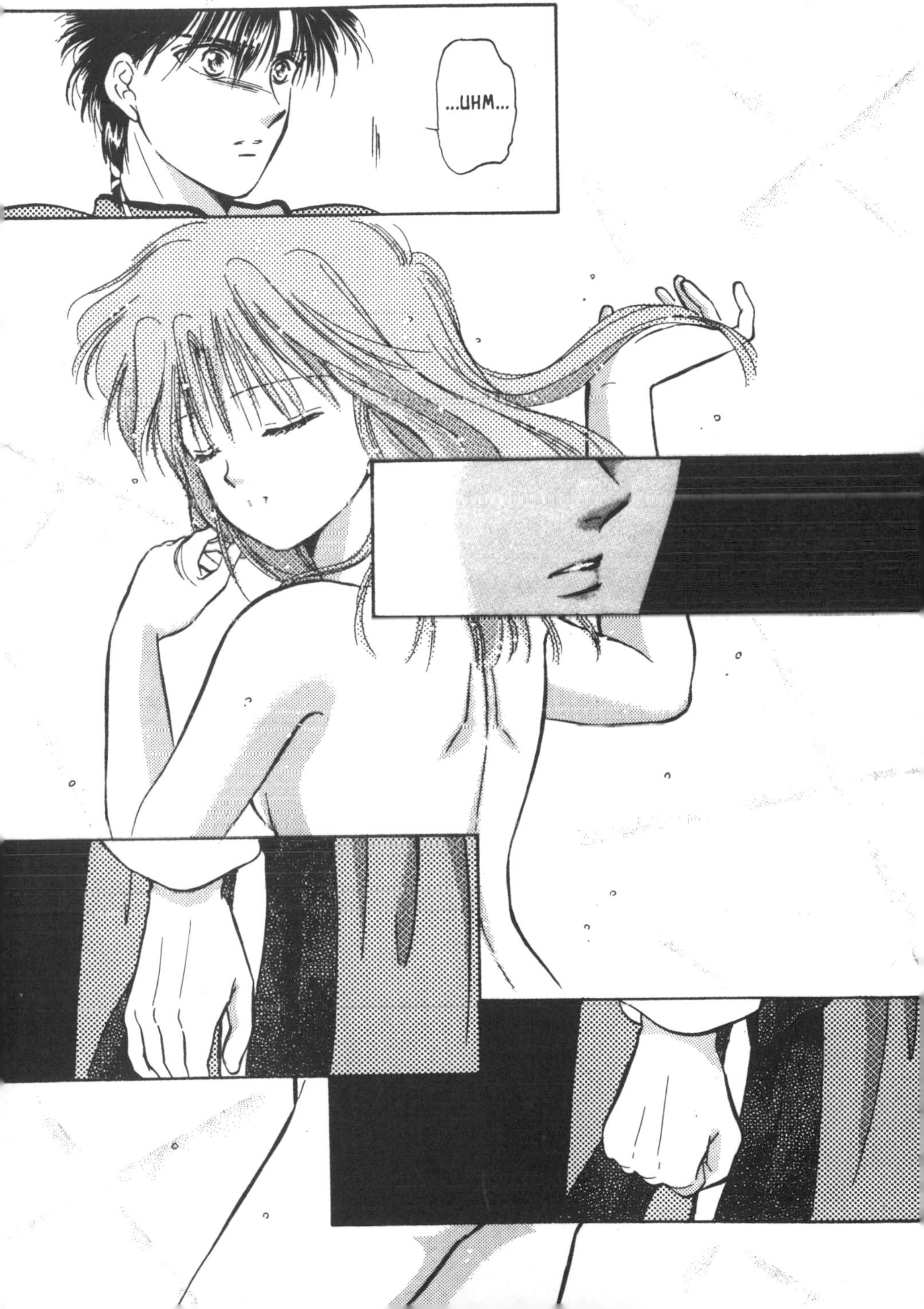
...UHM...

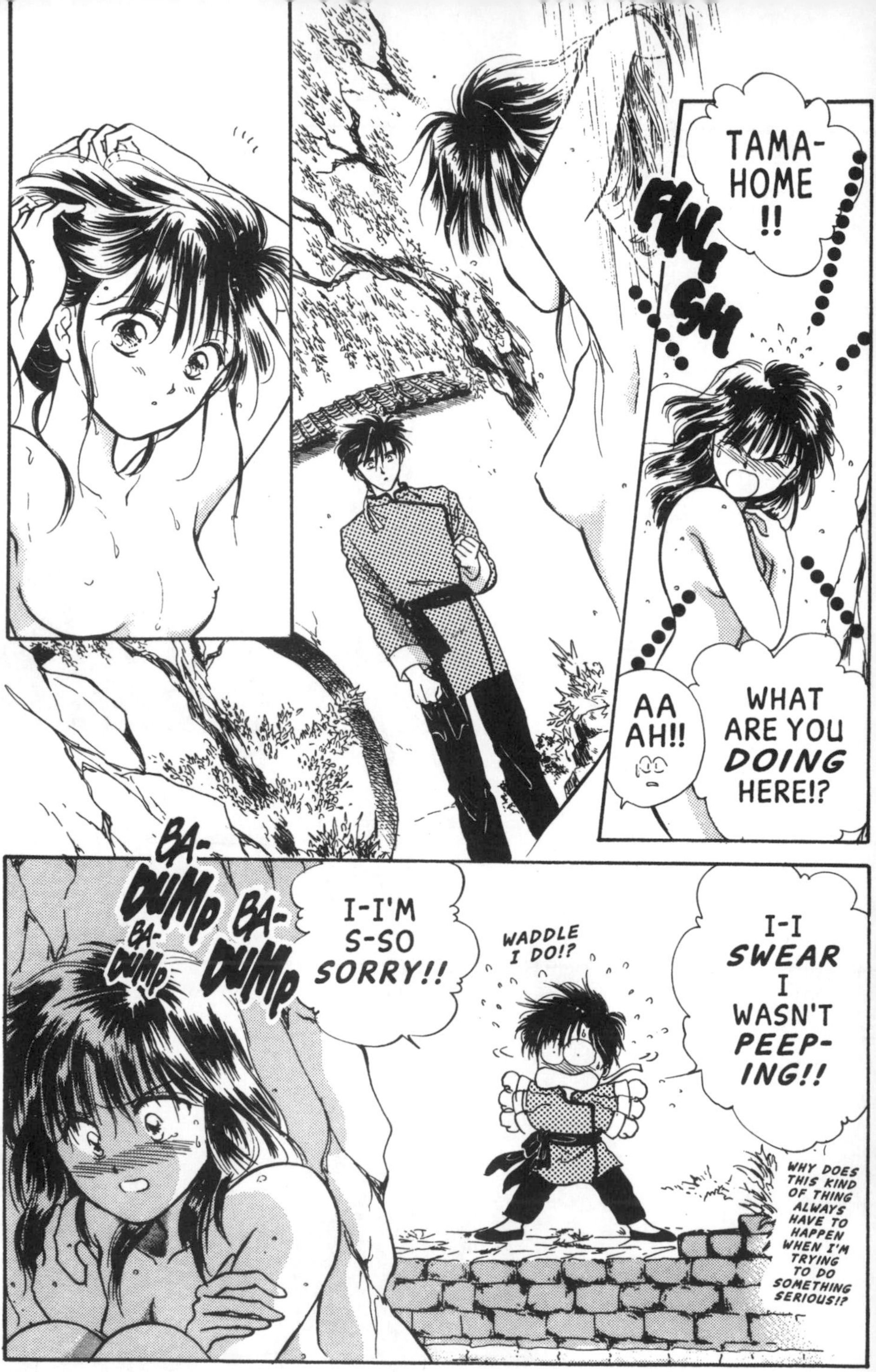
TAMA-HOME!!
FWASH
AA AH!!
WHAT ARE YOU DOING HERE!?
BA-DUMP
BA-DUMP
BA-DUMP
I-I'M S-SO SORRY!!
WADDLE I DO!?
I-I SWEAR I WASN'T PEEP-ING!!
WHY DOES THIS KIND OF THING ALWAYS HAVE TO HAPPEN WHEN I'M TRYING TO DO SOMETHING SERIOUS!?

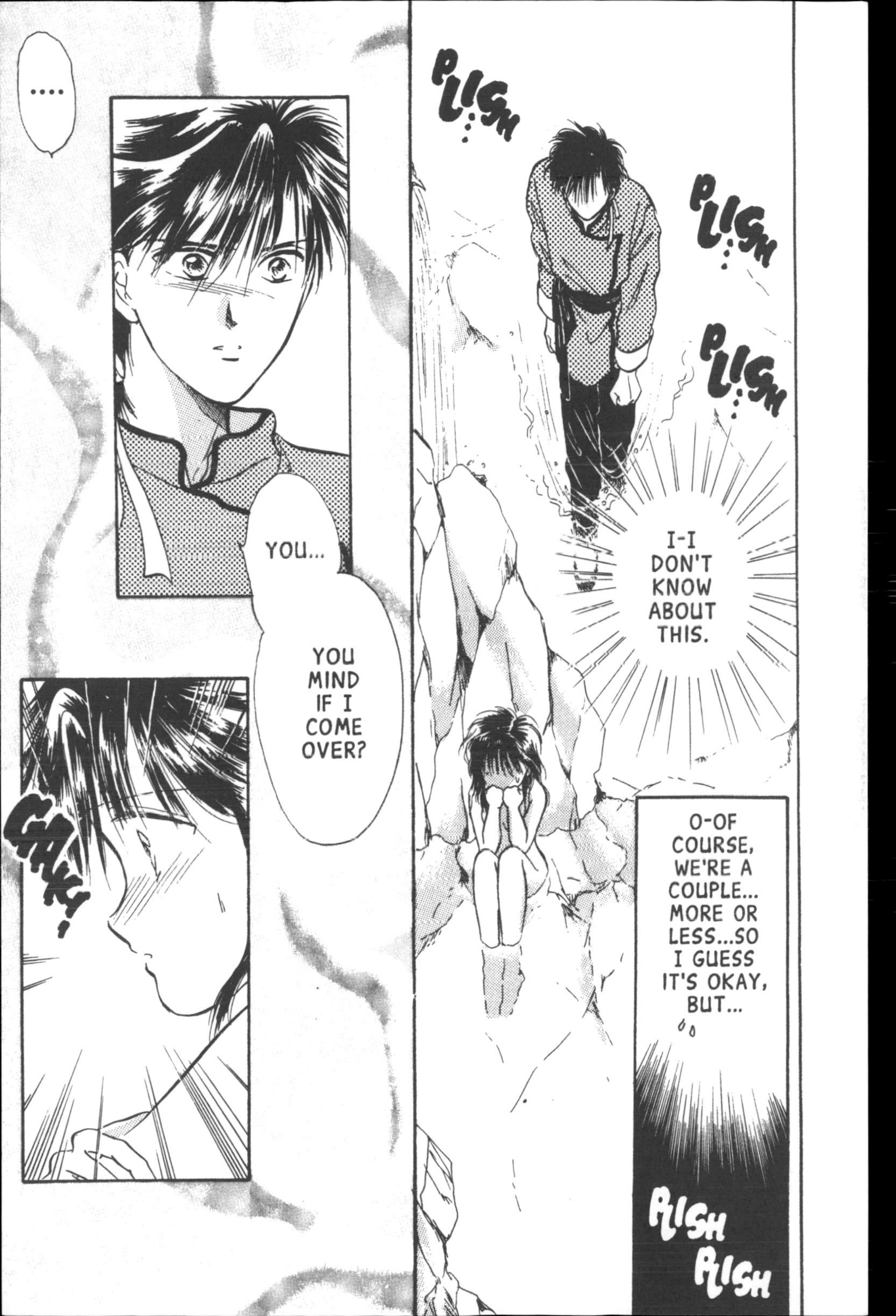
....
YOU...
YOU MIND IF I COME OVER?
PLISH
PLISH
PLISH
I-I DON'T KNOW ABOUT THIS.
O-OF COURSE, WE'RE A COUPLE... MORE OR LESS...SO I GUESS IT'S OKAY, BUT...
PLISH PLISH

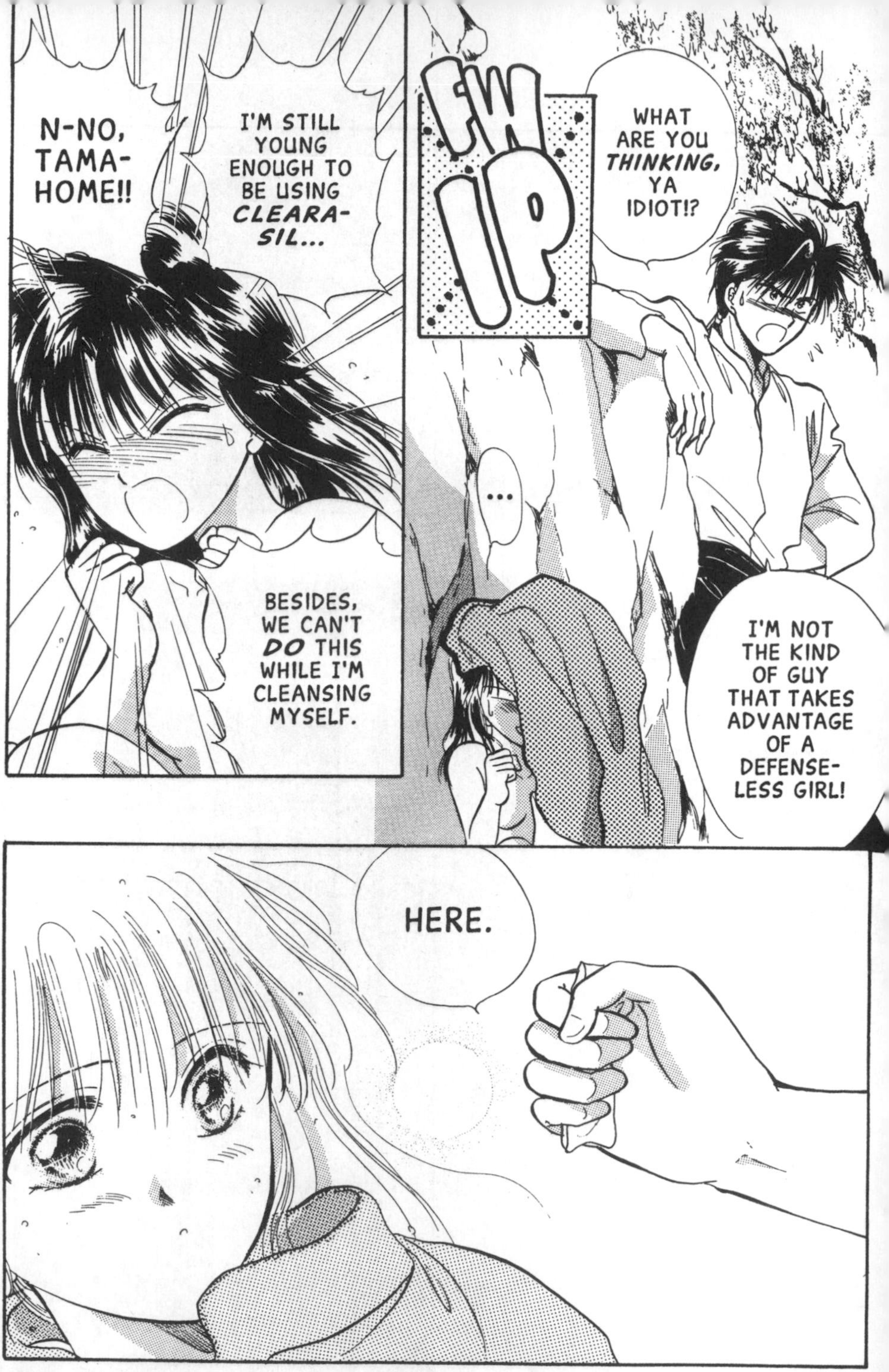
N-NO, TAMA-HOME!!
I'M STILL YOUNG ENOUGH TO BE USING CLEARA-SIL...
BESIDES, WE CAN'T DO THIS WHILE I'M CLEANSING MYSELF.
FWIP
WHAT ARE YOU THINKING, YA IDIOT!?
...
I'M NOT THE KIND OF GUY THAT TAKES ADVANTAGE OF A DEFENSE-LESS GIRL!
HERE.

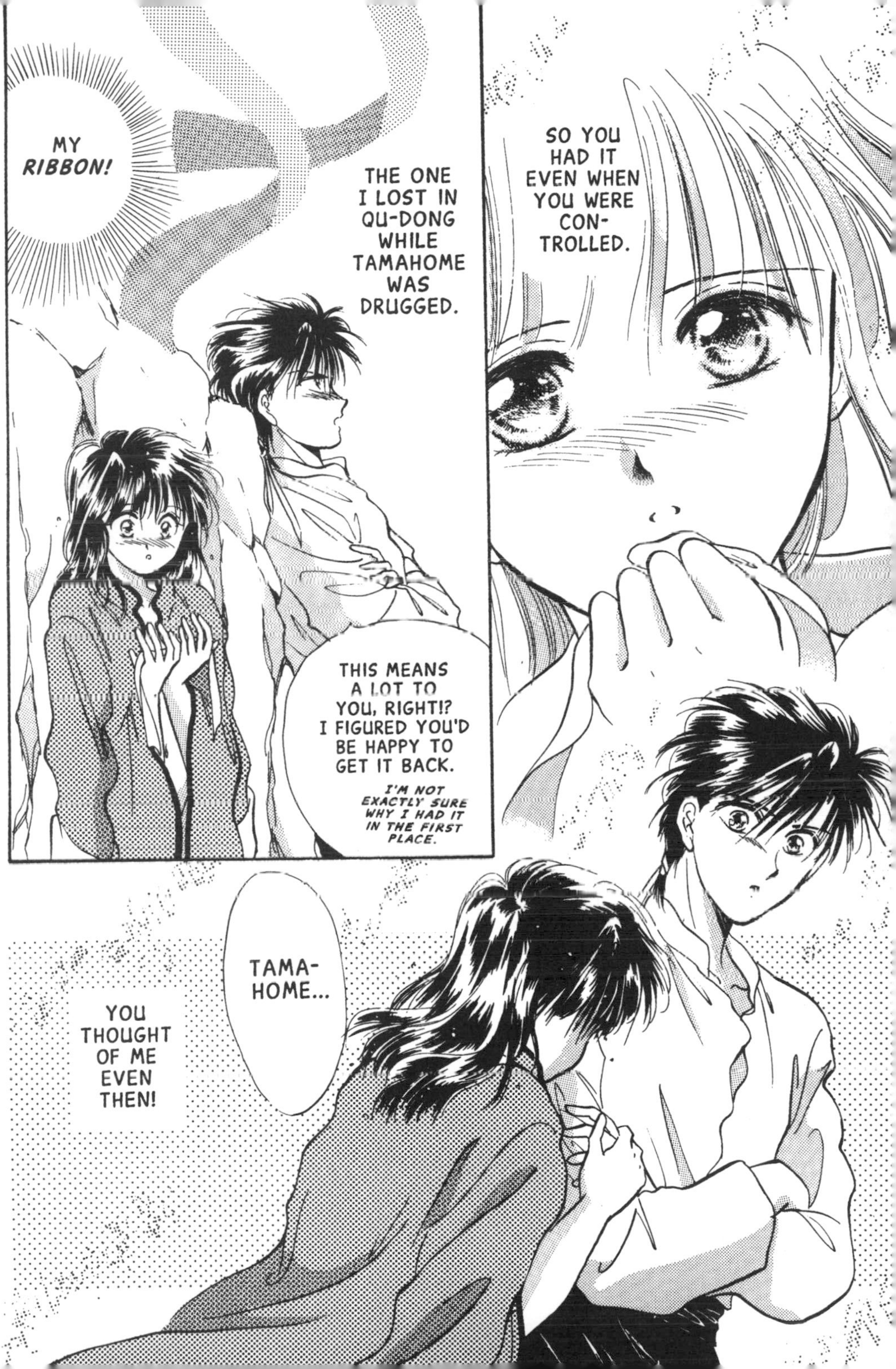

MY RIBBON!
THE ONE I LOST IN QU-DONG WHILE TAMAHOME WAS DRUGGED.
THIS MEANS A LOT TO YOU, RIGHT!? I FIGURED YOU'D BE HAPPY TO GET IT BACK.
I'M NOT EXACTLY SURE WHY I HAD IT IN THE FIRST PLACE.
SO YOU HAD IT EVEN WHEN YOU WERE CON-TROLLED.
TAMA-HOME...
YOU THOUGHT OF ME EVEN THEN!

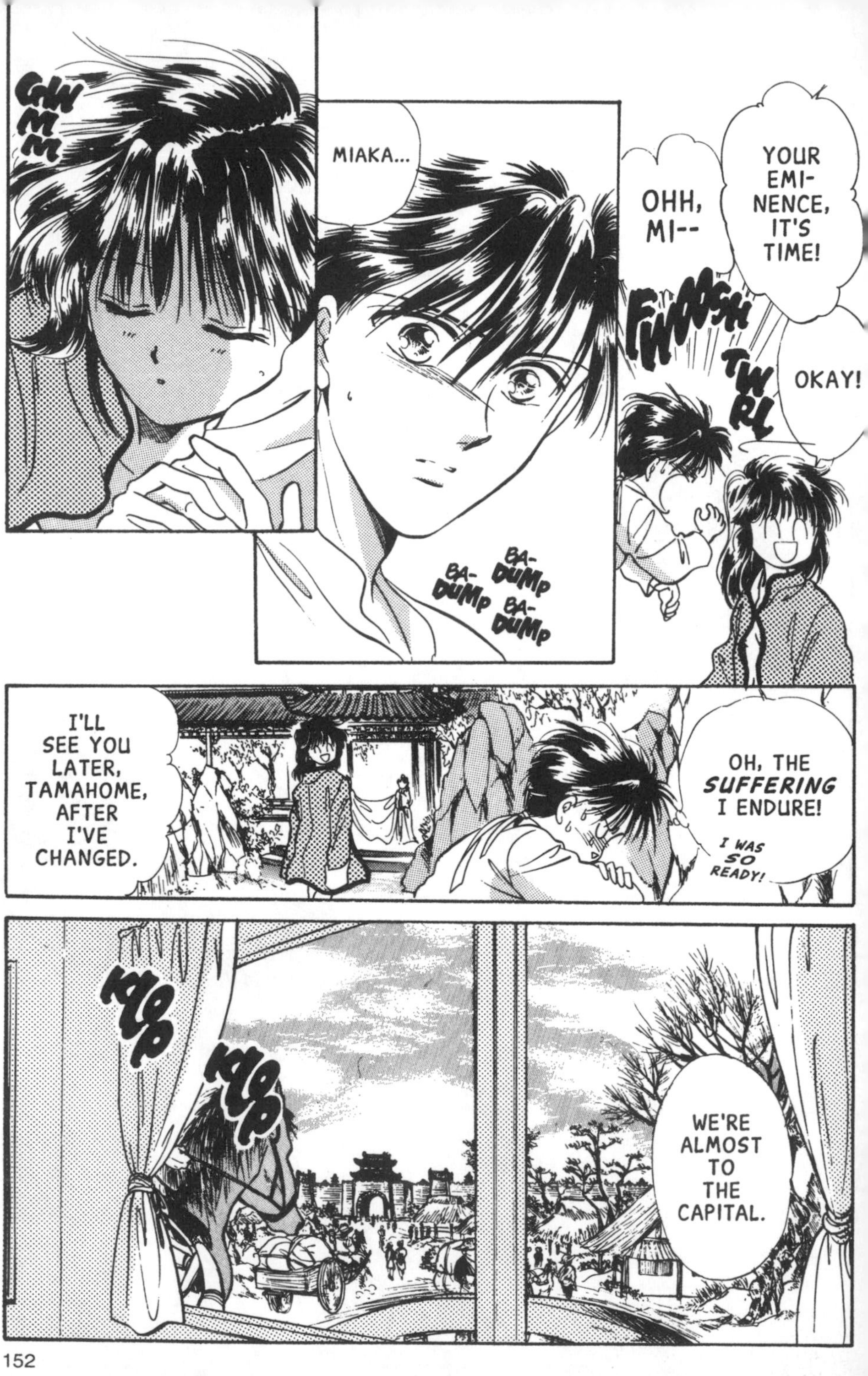
GWMMM
MIAKA...
BA-DUMP BA-DUMP BA-DUMP BA-DUMP
OHH, MI--
YOUR EMINENCE, IT'S TIME!
FWOOSH
TWIRL
OKAY!
I'LL SEE YOU LATER, TAMAHOME, AFTER I'VE CHANGED.
OH, THE *SUFFERING* I ENDURE!
I WAS SO READY!
KLOP
KLOP
WE'RE ALMOST TO THE CAPITAL.

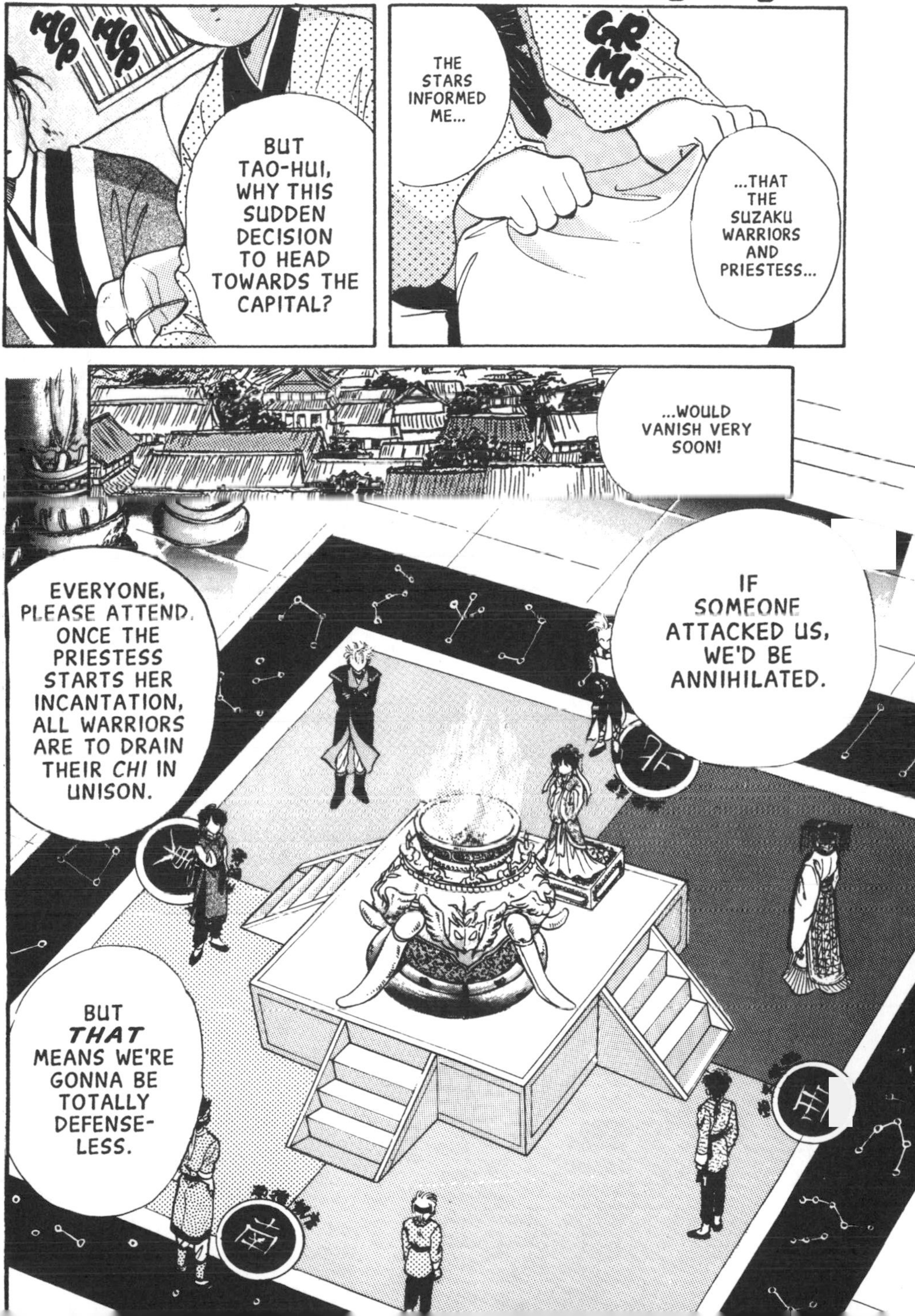
KLOP KLOP
BUT TAO-HUI, WHY THIS SUDDEN DECISION TO HEAD TOWARDS THE CAPITAL?
GRMP
THE STARS INFORMED ME...
...THAT THE SUZAKU WARRIORS AND PRIESTESS...
...WOULD VANISH VERY SOON!
EVERYONE, PLEASE ATTEND. ONCE THE PRIESTESS STARTS HER INCANTATION, ALL WARRIORS ARE TO DRAIN THEIR *CHI* IN UNISON.
IF SOMEONE ATTACKED US, WE'D BE ANNIHILATED.
BUT ***THAT*** MEANS WE'RE GONNA BE TOTALLY DEFENSELESS.

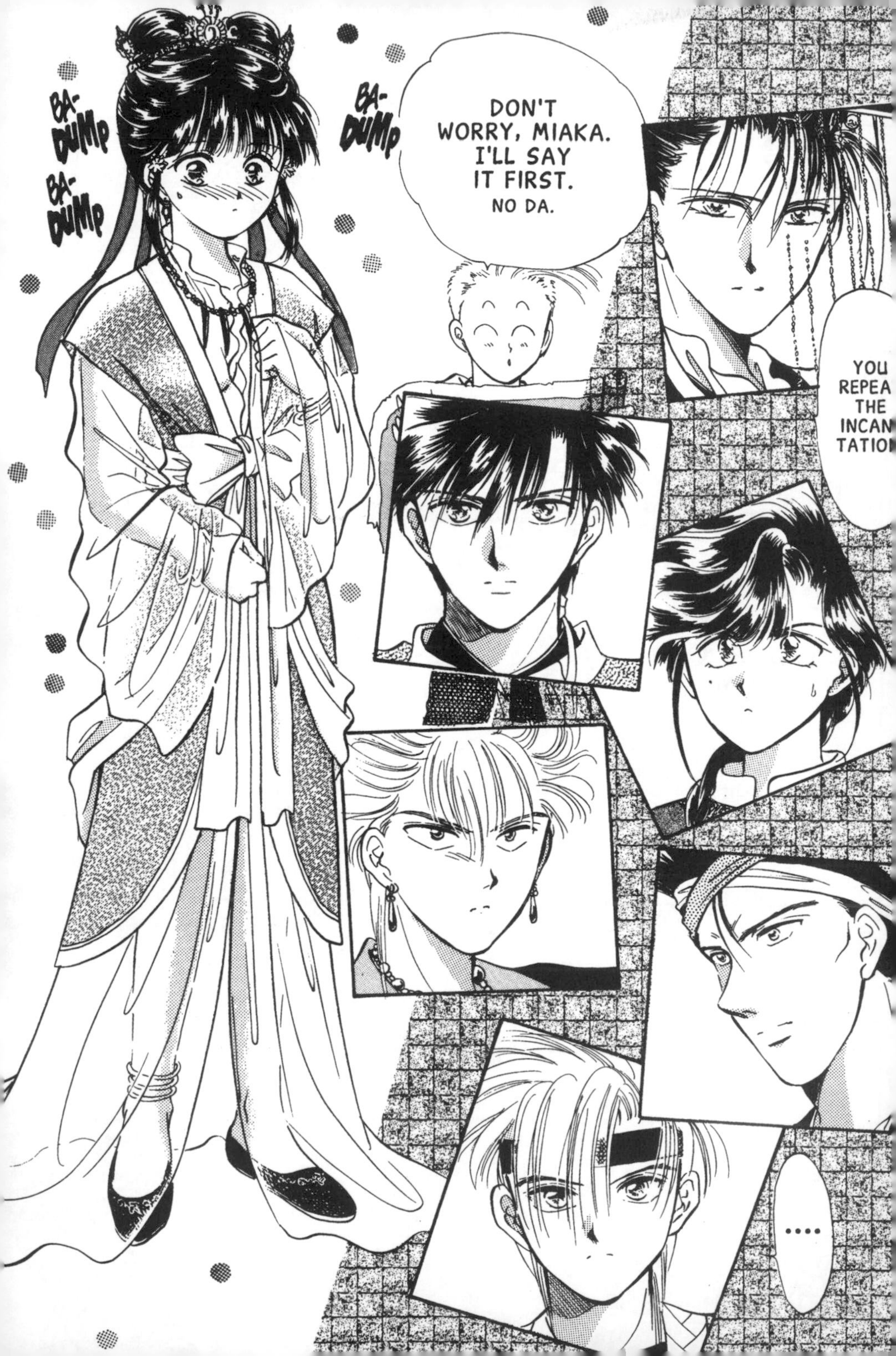
BA-DUMP
BA-DUMP
BA-DUMP
DON'T WORRY, MIAKA. I'LL SAY IT FIRST. NO DA.
YOU REPEA THE INCAN TATIO
....

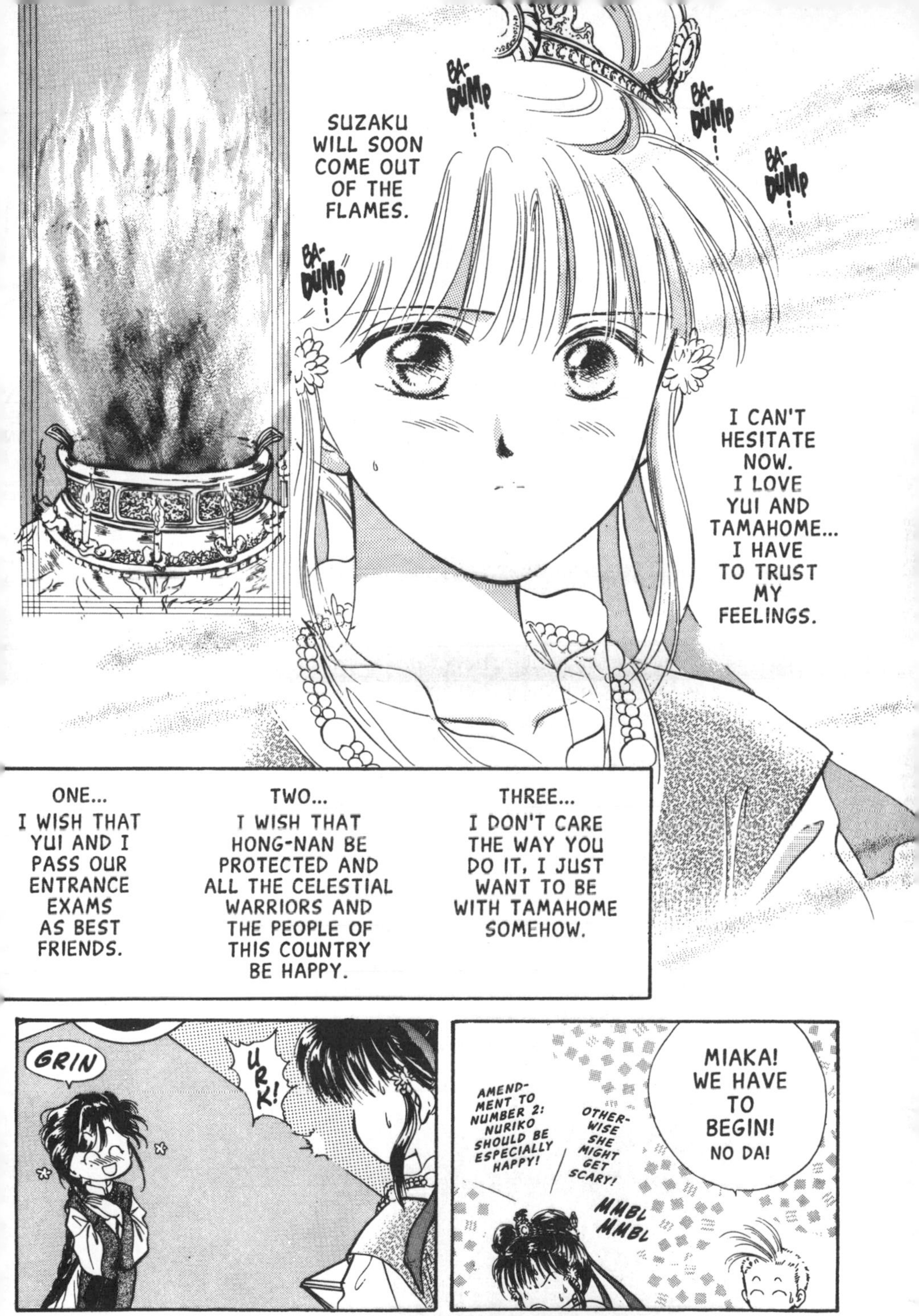
BA-DUMP
SUZAKU WILL SOON COME OUT OF THE FLAMES.
BA-DUMP
BA-DUMP
BA-DUMP
I CAN'T HESITATE NOW. I LOVE YUI AND TAMAHOME... I HAVE TO TRUST MY FEELINGS.
ONE... I WISH THAT YUI AND I PASS OUR ENTRANCE EXAMS AS BEST FRIENDS.
TWO... I WISH THAT HONG-NAN BE PROTECTED AND ALL THE CELESTIAL WARRIORS AND THE PEOPLE OF THIS COUNTRY BE HAPPY.
THREE... I DON'T CARE THE WAY YOU DO IT, I JUST WANT TO BE WITH TAMAHOME SOMEHOW.
GRIN
URK!
AMENDMENT TO NUMBER 2: NURIKO SHOULD BE ESPECIALLY HAPPY!
OTHERWISE SHE MIGHT GET SCARY!
MIAKA! WE HAVE TO BEGIN! NO DA!
MMBL MMBL

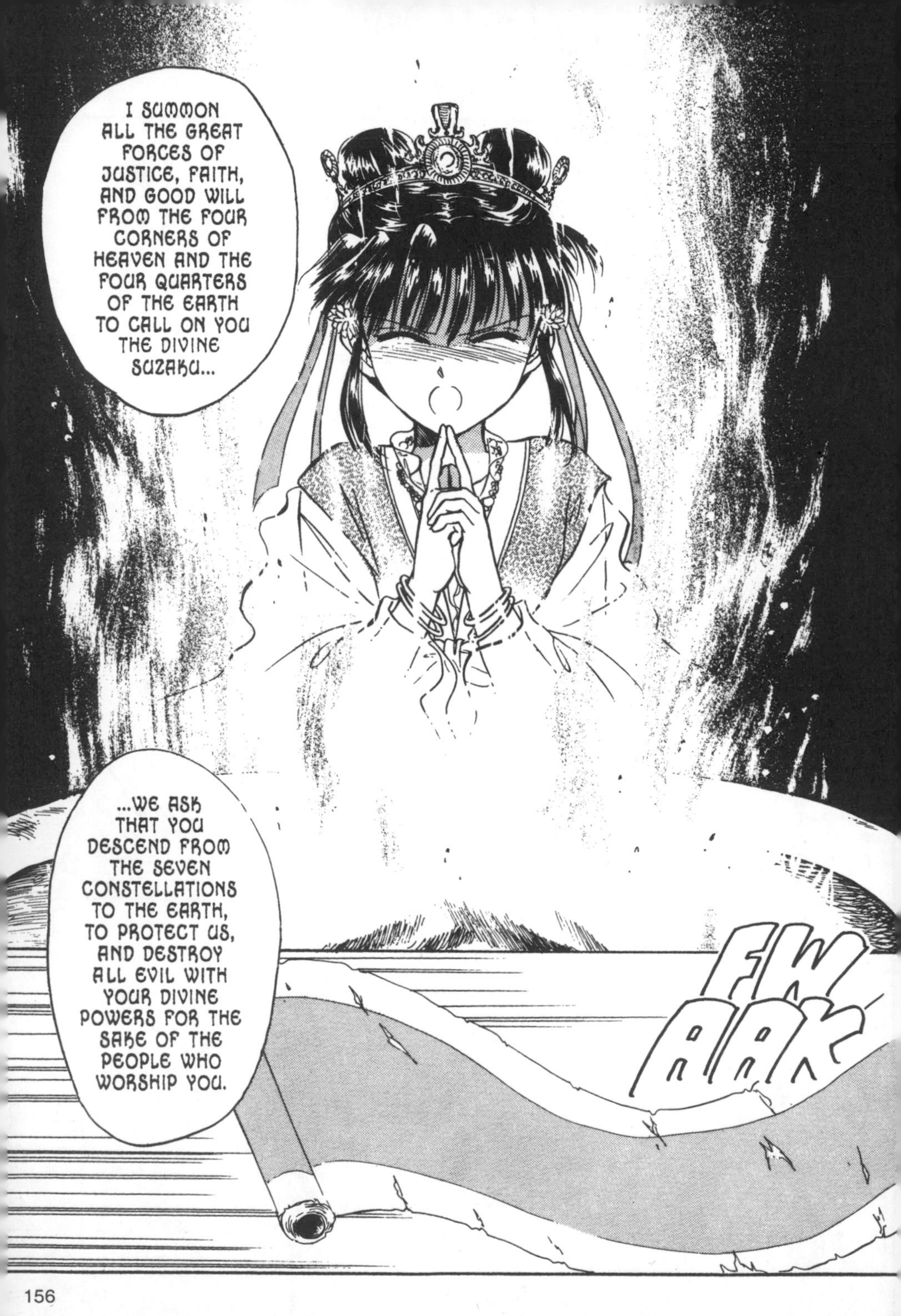
I SUMMON ALL THE GREAT FORCES OF JUSTICE, FAITH, AND GOOD WILL FROM THE FOUR CORNERS OF HEAVEN AND THE FOUR QUARTERS OF THE EARTH TO CALL ON YOU THE DIVINE SUZAKU...
...WE ASK THAT YOU DESCEND FROM THE SEVEN CONSTELLATIONS TO THE EARTH, TO PROTECT US, AND DESTROY ALL EVIL WITH YOUR DIVINE POWERS FOR THE SAKE OF THE PEOPLE WHO WORSHIP YOU.
FWAAK

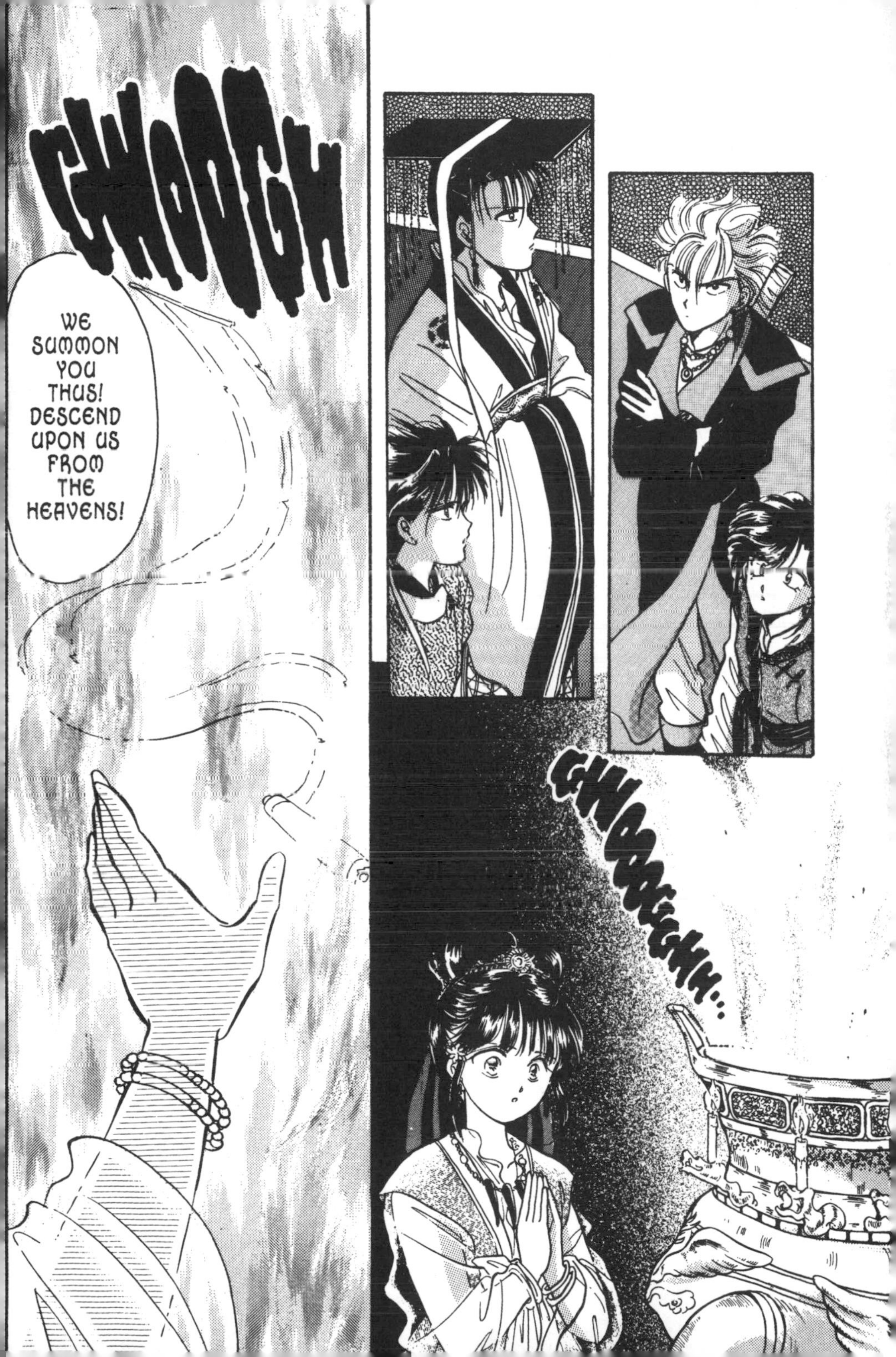
GWOOGH
WE SUMMON YOU THUS! DESCEND UPON US FROM THE HEAVENS!
GWOOOGHHH...

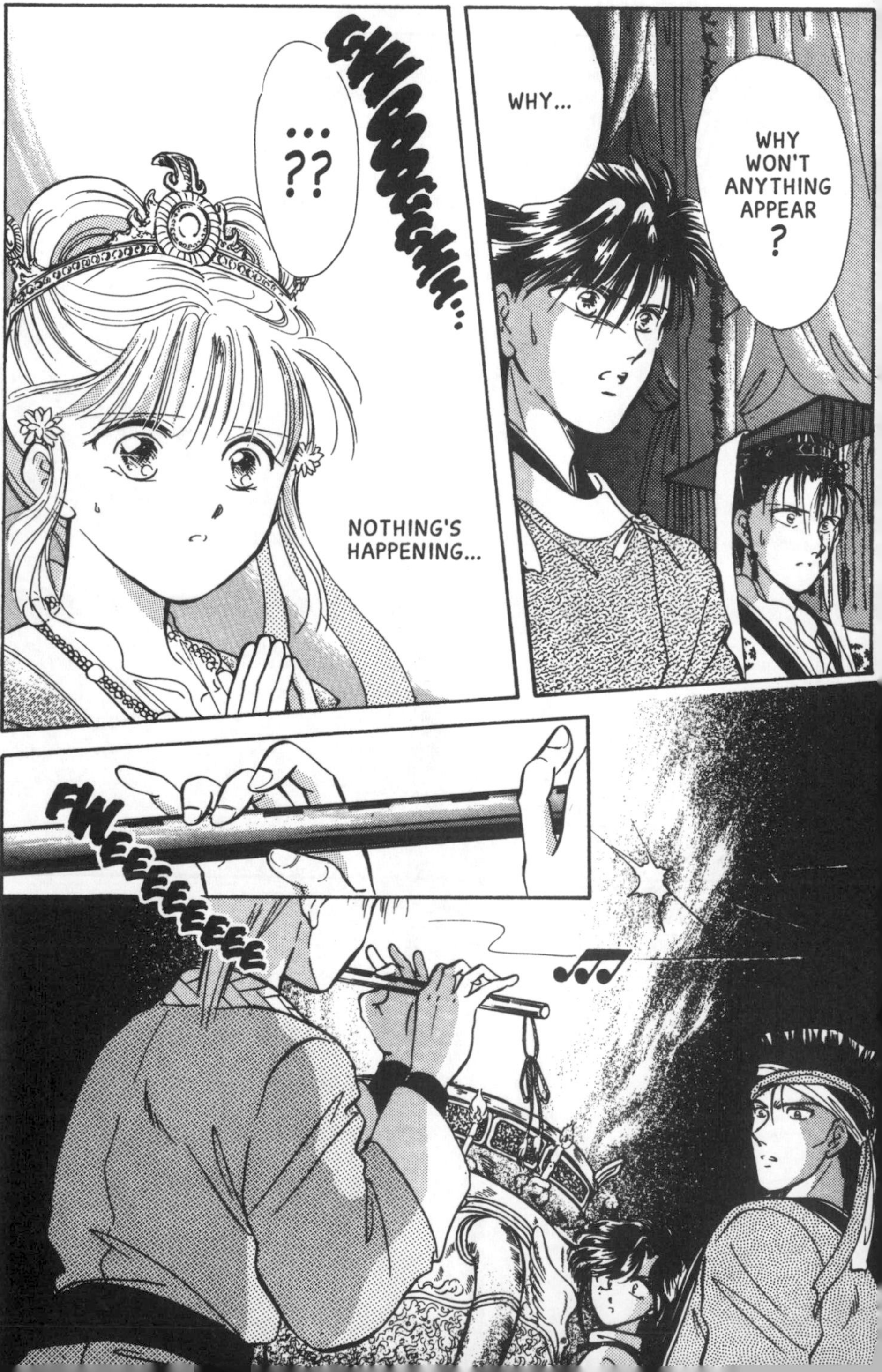
GWOOOOOOHHH...
...
??
NOTHING'S HAPPENING...
WHY...
WHY WON'T ANYTHING APPEAR?
FWEEEEEEEEE

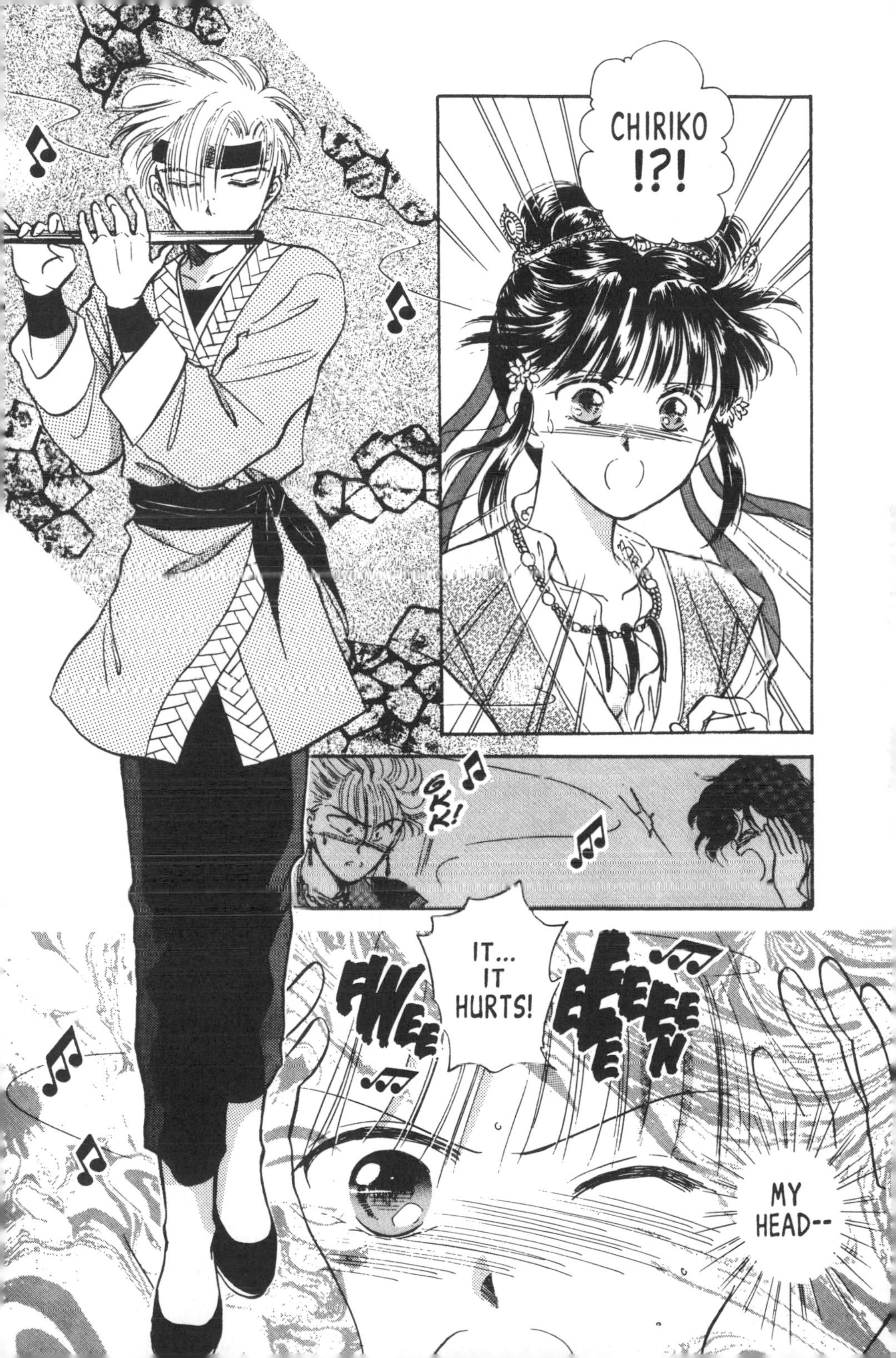
CHIRIKO !?!
GKK!
FWEE
IT... IT HURTS!
EEEEEEEN
MY HEAD--

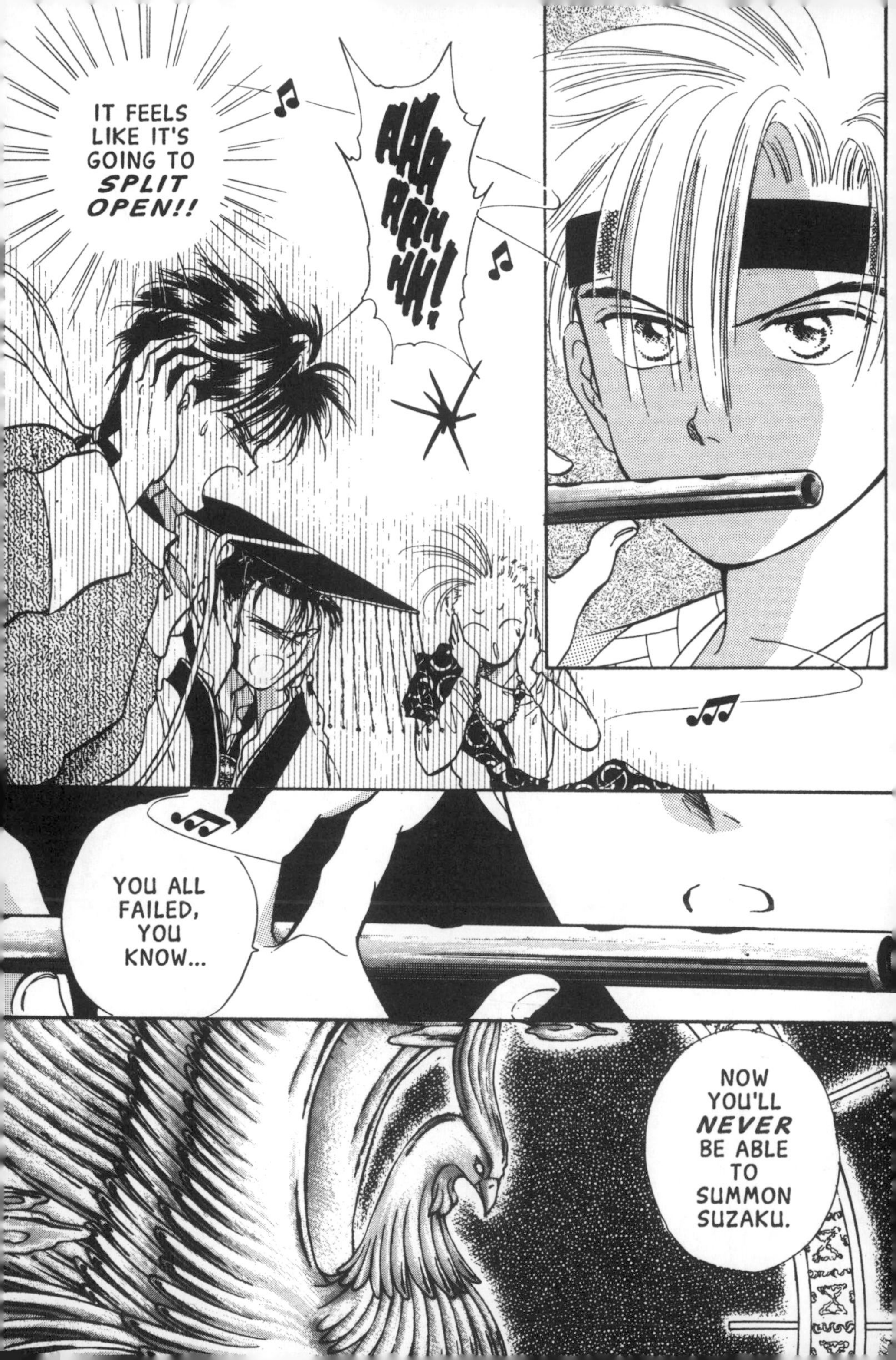
IT FEELS LIKE IT'S GOING TO *SPLIT OPEN!!*
AAAARRHHH!
YOU ALL FAILED, YOU KNOW...
NOW YOU'LL *NEVER* BE ABLE TO SUMMON SUZAKU.

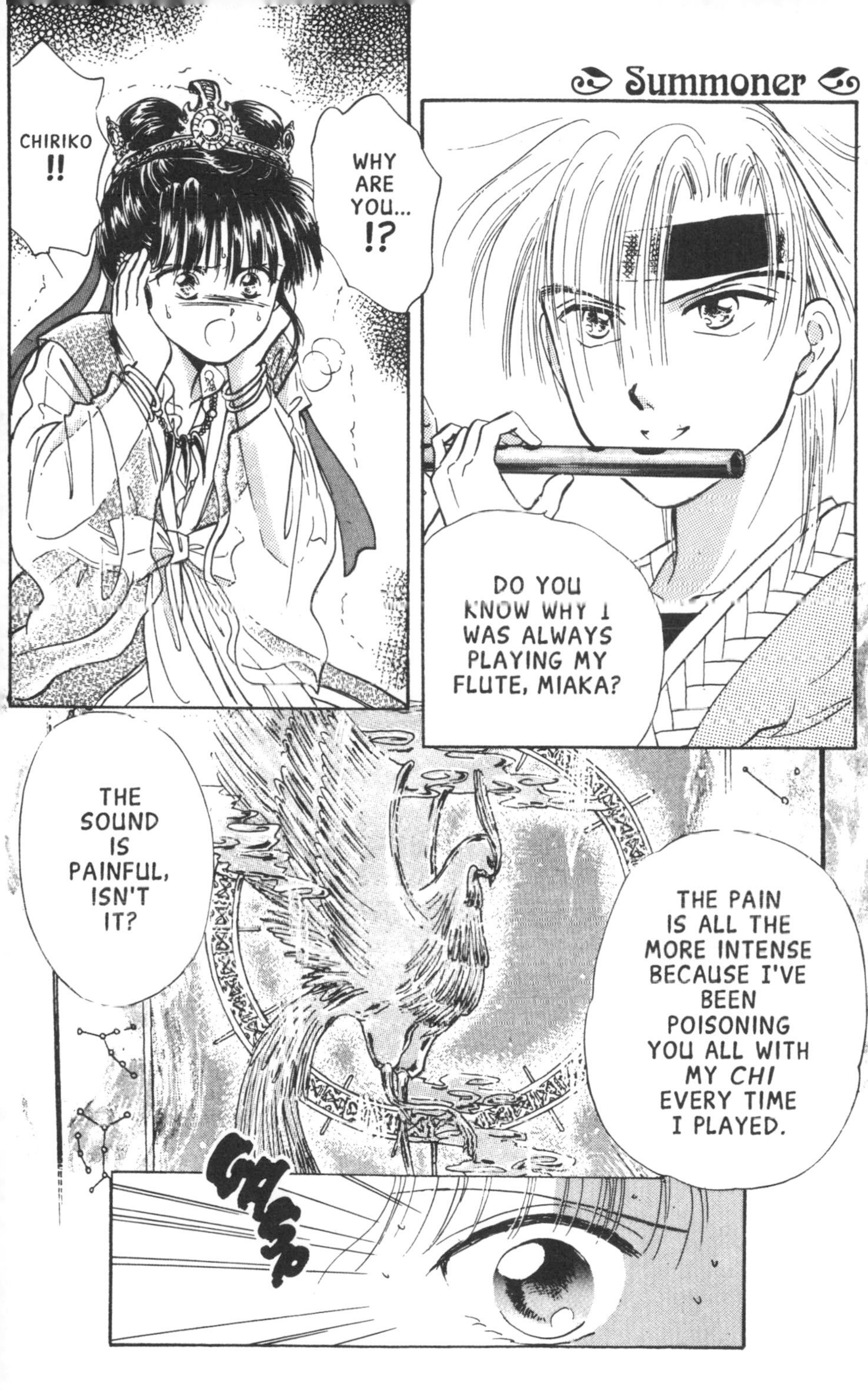
CHIRIKO !!
WHY ARE YOU... !?
DO YOU KNOW WHY I WAS ALWAYS PLAYING MY FLUTE, MIAKA?
THE SOUND IS PAINFUL, ISN'T IT?
THE PAIN IS ALL THE MORE INTENSE BECAUSE I'VE BEEN POISONING YOU ALL WITH MY *CHI* EVERY TIME I PLAYED.
GASP

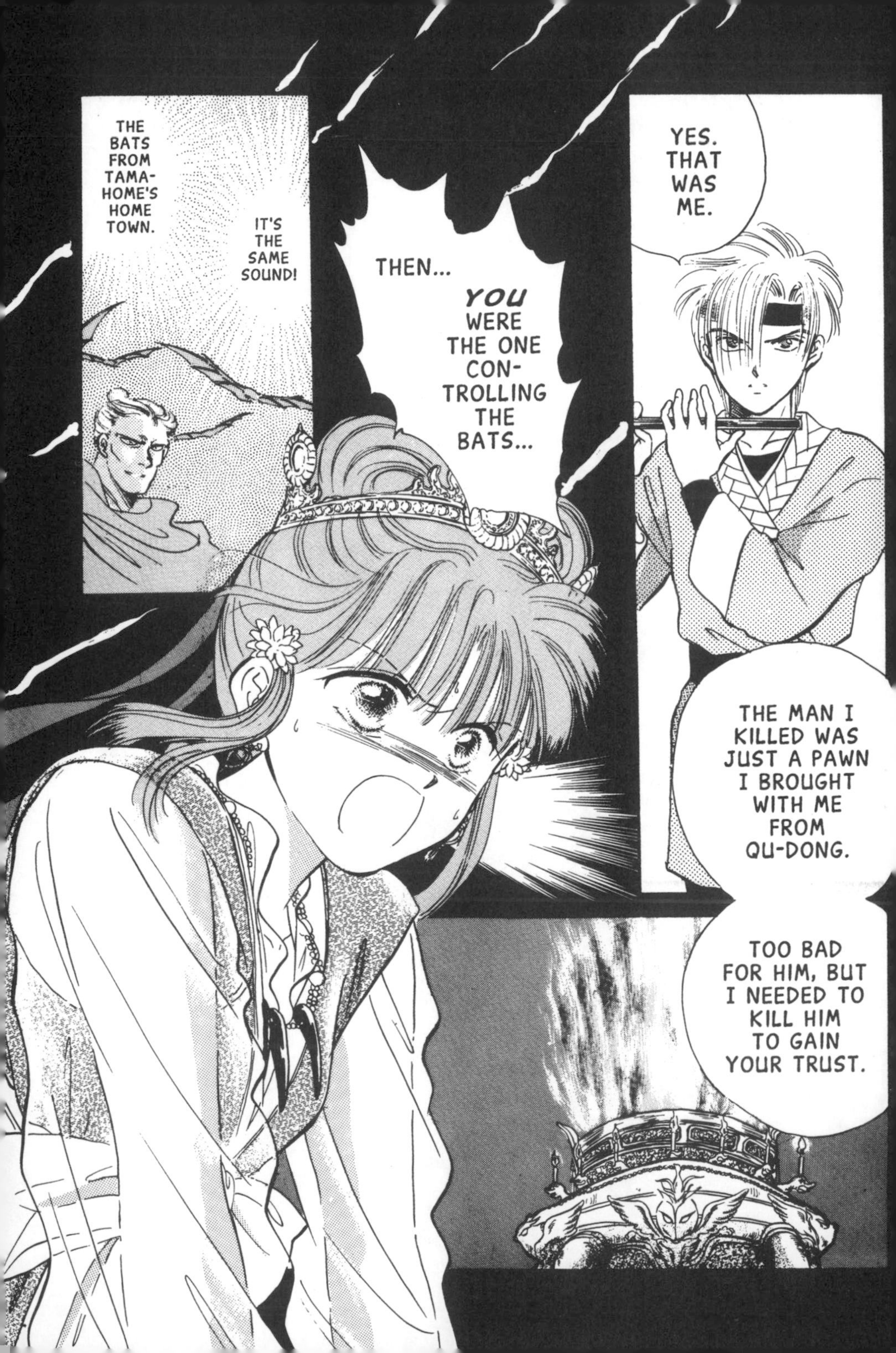
THE BATS FROM TAMA-HOME'S HOME TOWN.
IT'S THE SAME SOUND!
THEN...
YOU WERE THE ONE CON-TROLLING THE BATS...
YES. THAT WAS ME.
THE MAN I KILLED WAS JUST A PAWN I BROUGHT WITH ME FROM QU-DONG.
TOO BAD FOR HIM, BUT I NEEDED TO KILL HIM TO GAIN YOUR TRUST.

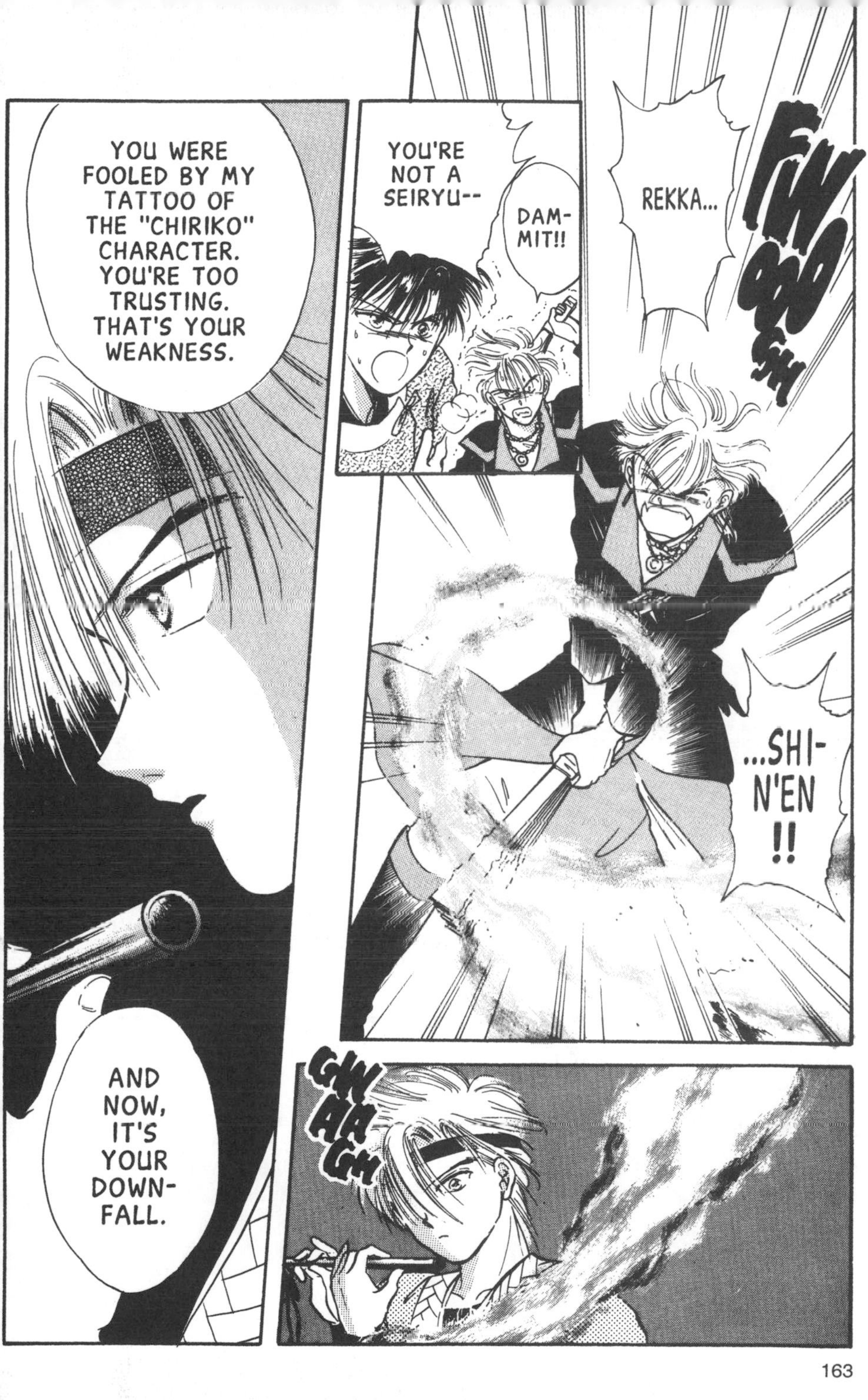
YOU WERE FOOLED BY MY TATTOO OF THE "CHIRIKO" CHARACTER. YOU'RE TOO TRUSTING. THAT'S YOUR WEAKNESS.
AND NOW, IT'S YOUR DOWN-FALL.
YOU'RE NOT A SEIRYU--
DAM-MIT!!
REKKA...
FWOOOSH
...SHI-N'EN!!
GWAAGH

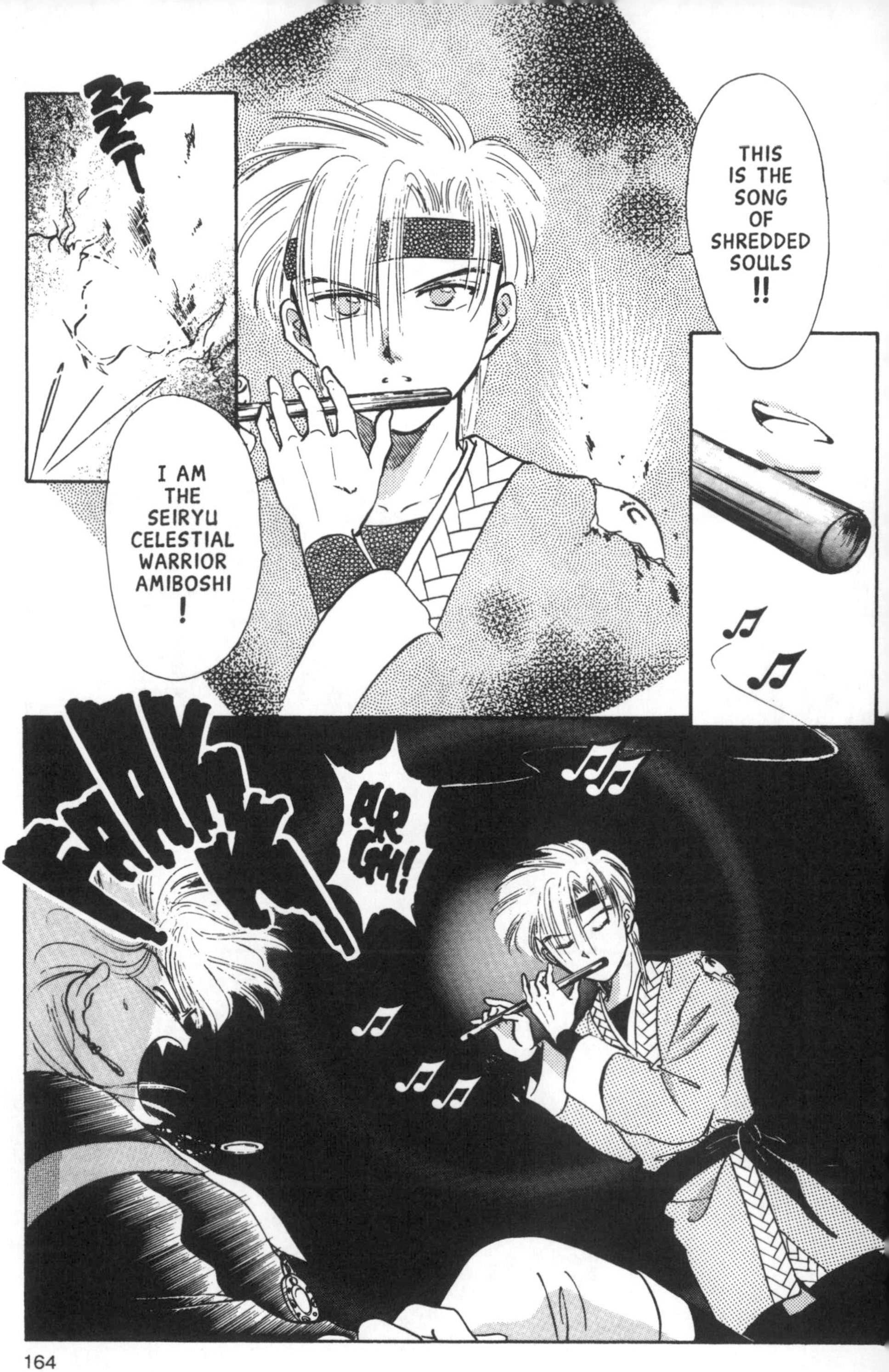
ZZZT
I AM THE SEIRYU CELESTIAL WARRIOR AMIBOSHI!
THIS IS THE SONG OF SHREDDED SOULS!!
ARGH!

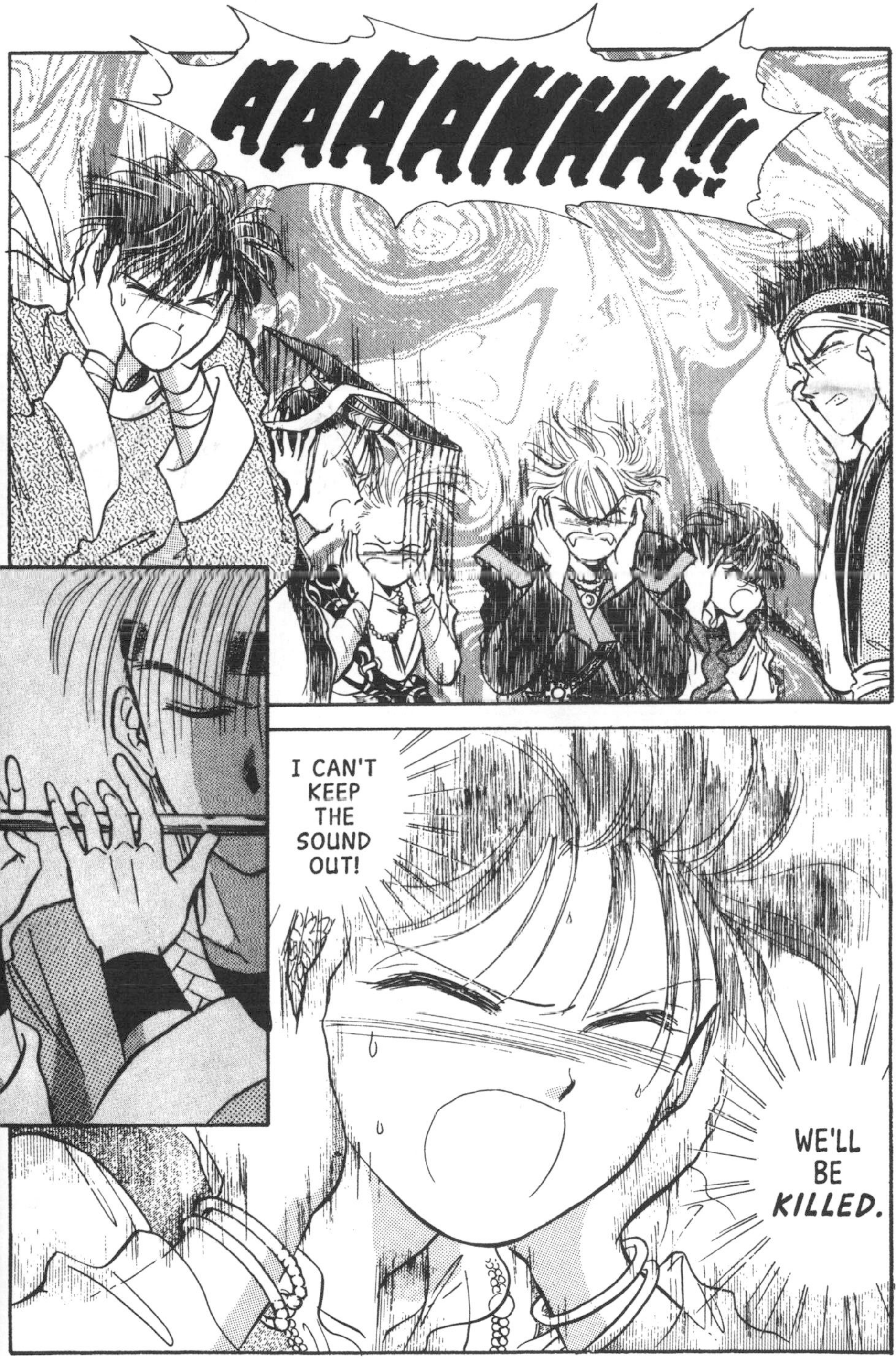
AAAAHHH!!
I CAN'T KEEP THE SOUND OUT!
WE'LL BE KILLED.

The Unexpected Illustration Corner

NO DA!!

These were drawn by my assistant M. (Who is in charge of SFX). They were so cute I had to include them. I once said that she was an animator, but it looks like she still is an animator!

But those who know anime can pretty well guess what kind of shows she worked on! (I got to look at the continuity for a show called Lamune!!)

Miaka
HIIIIIII!

MUNCH   MUNCH

KRA CKL

KRA CKL

NAKKI

This is a picture of Miaka drawn by my assistant S. Ever since around chapter six, she has been doing the highlights in the character's hair. (I won't let anybody else do Tamahome or Nuriko!) A lot of her drawings make it into the book. She's also drawn a Tamahome, but I'll save that for next time.

All right!
I filled up the page! I filled up the page!!

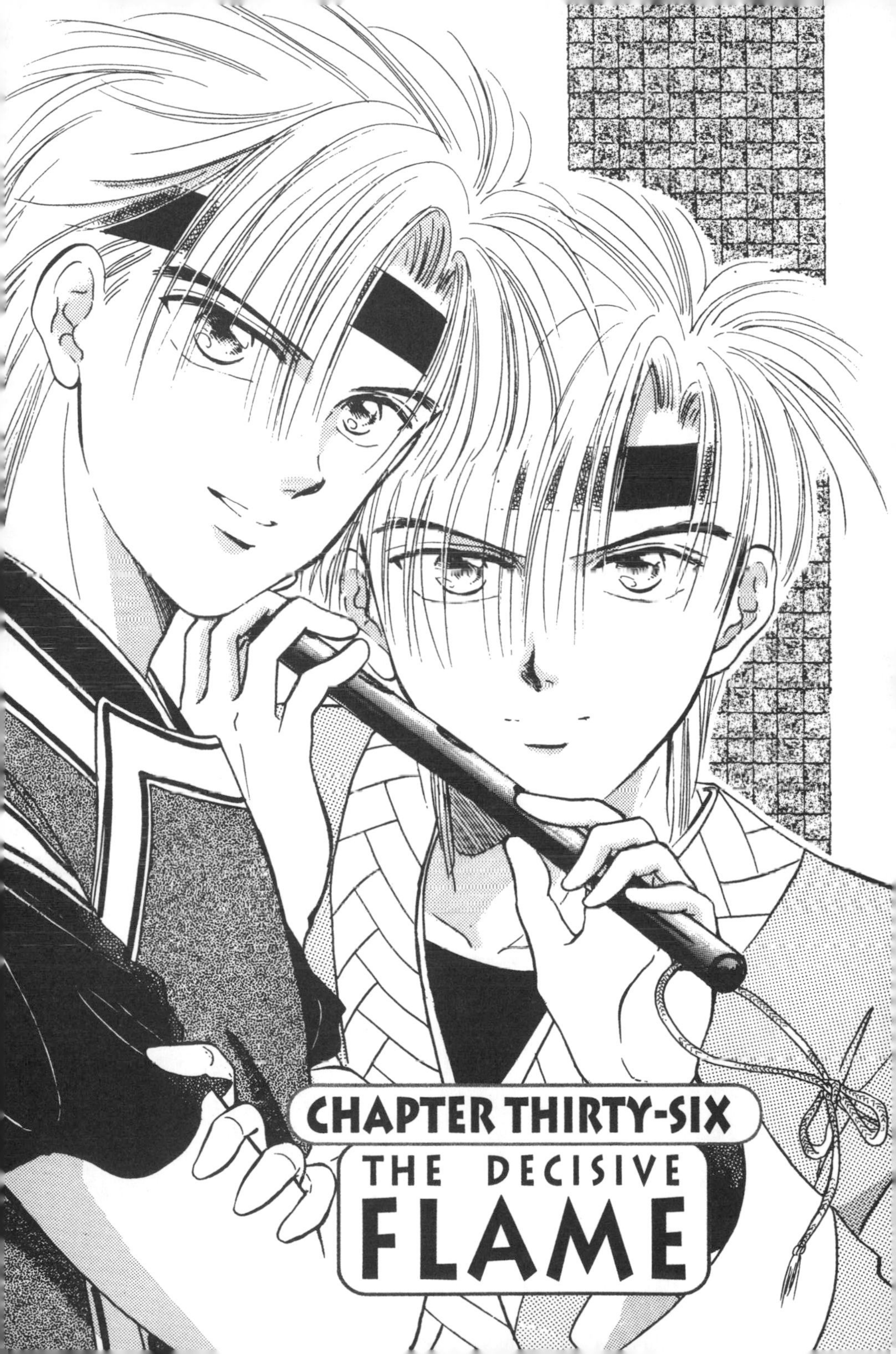
CHAPTER THIRTY-SIX
THE DECISIVE
FLAME

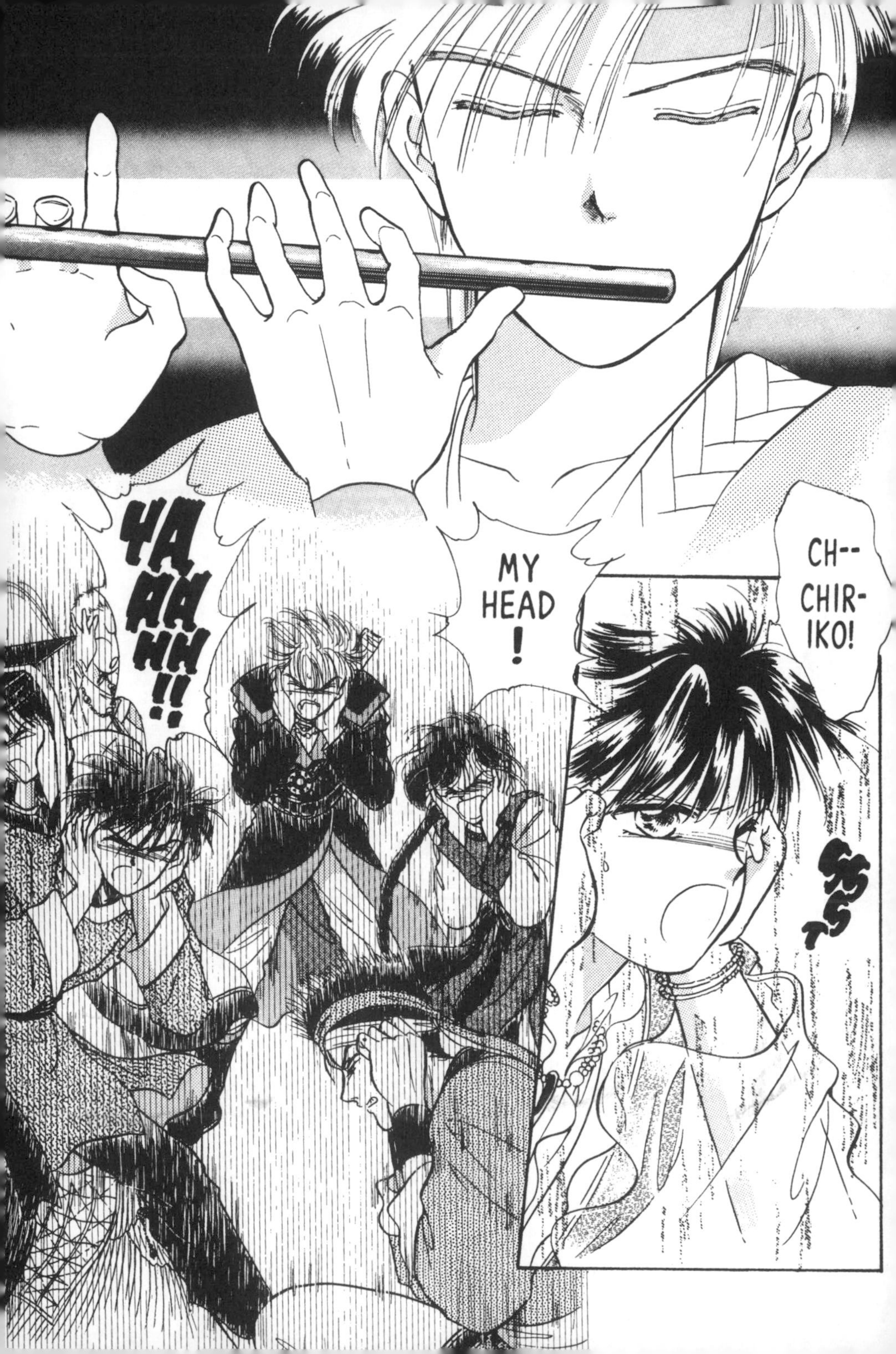
YAAAAHH!!
MY HEAD!
CH-- CHIR-IKO!
SSST

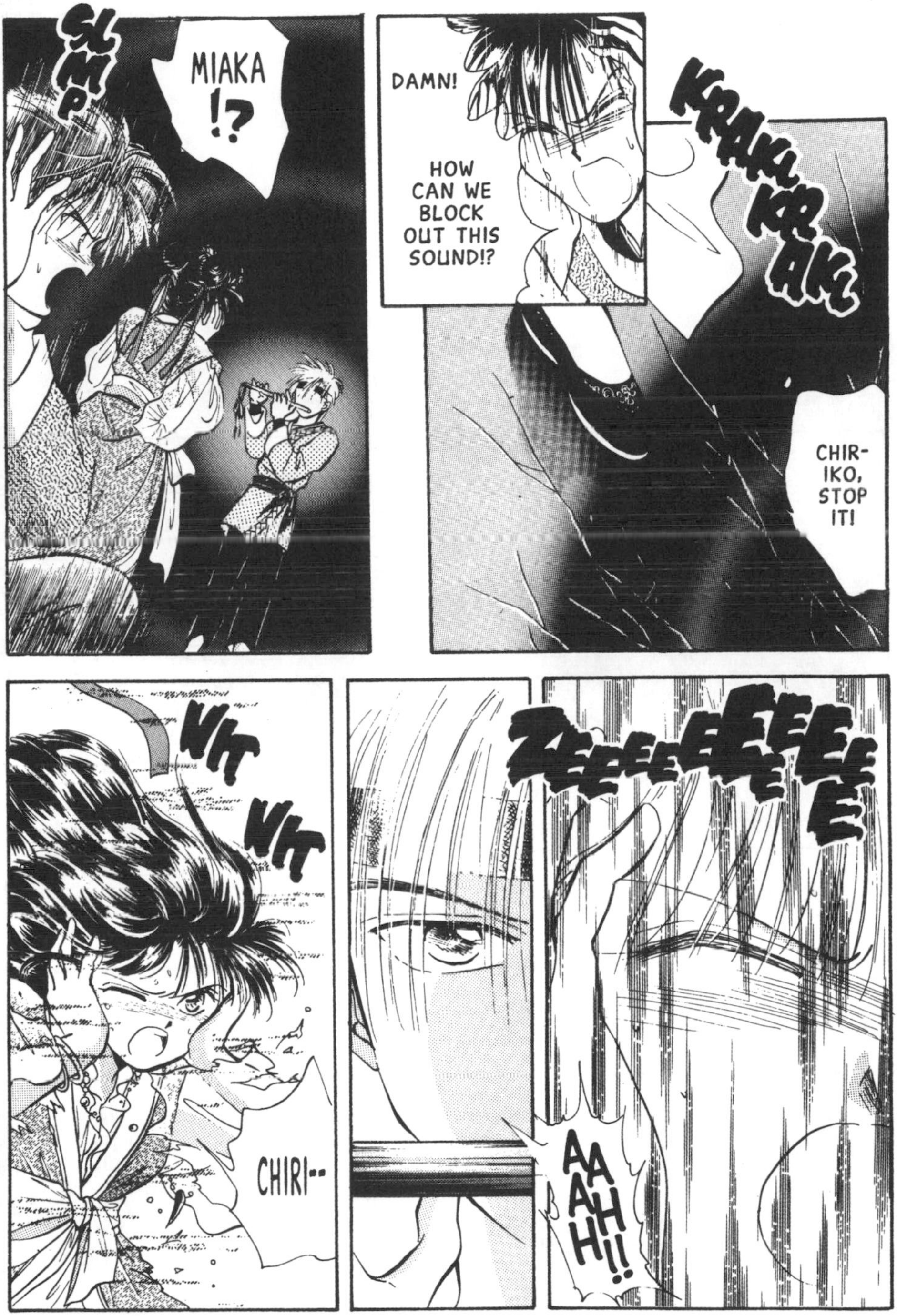
SLMP
MIAKA !?
DAMN!
HOW CAN WE BLOCK OUT THIS SOUND!?
KRAKA KRAK
CHIRIKO, STOP IT!
VIT VIT
CHIRI--
ZEEEEEEEEEEEE
AAAHH!!

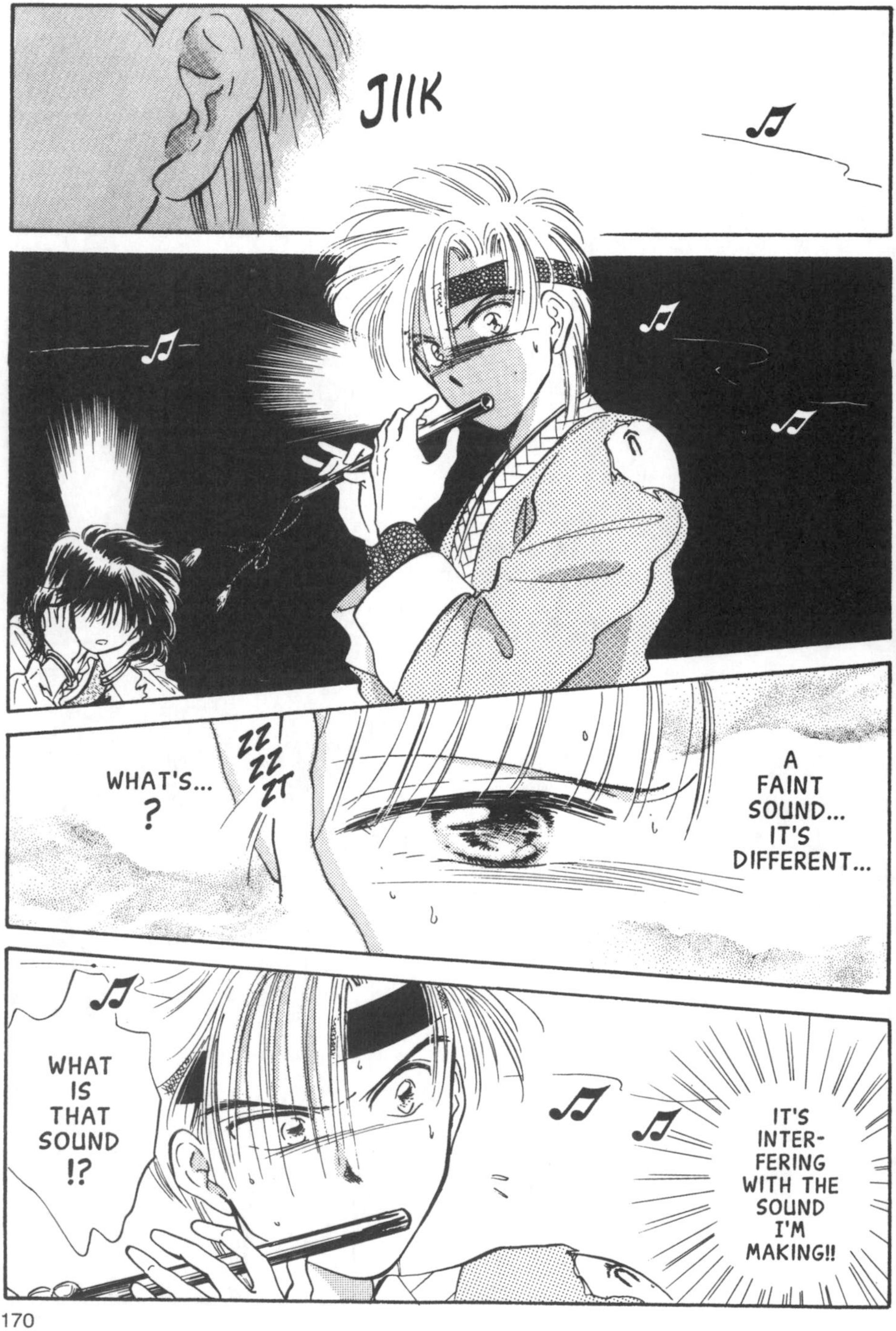
JIIK
WHAT'S... ?
ZZZZZT
A FAINT SOUND... IT'S DIFFERENT...
WHAT IS THAT SOUND !?
IT'S INTERFERING WITH THE SOUND I'M MAKING!!

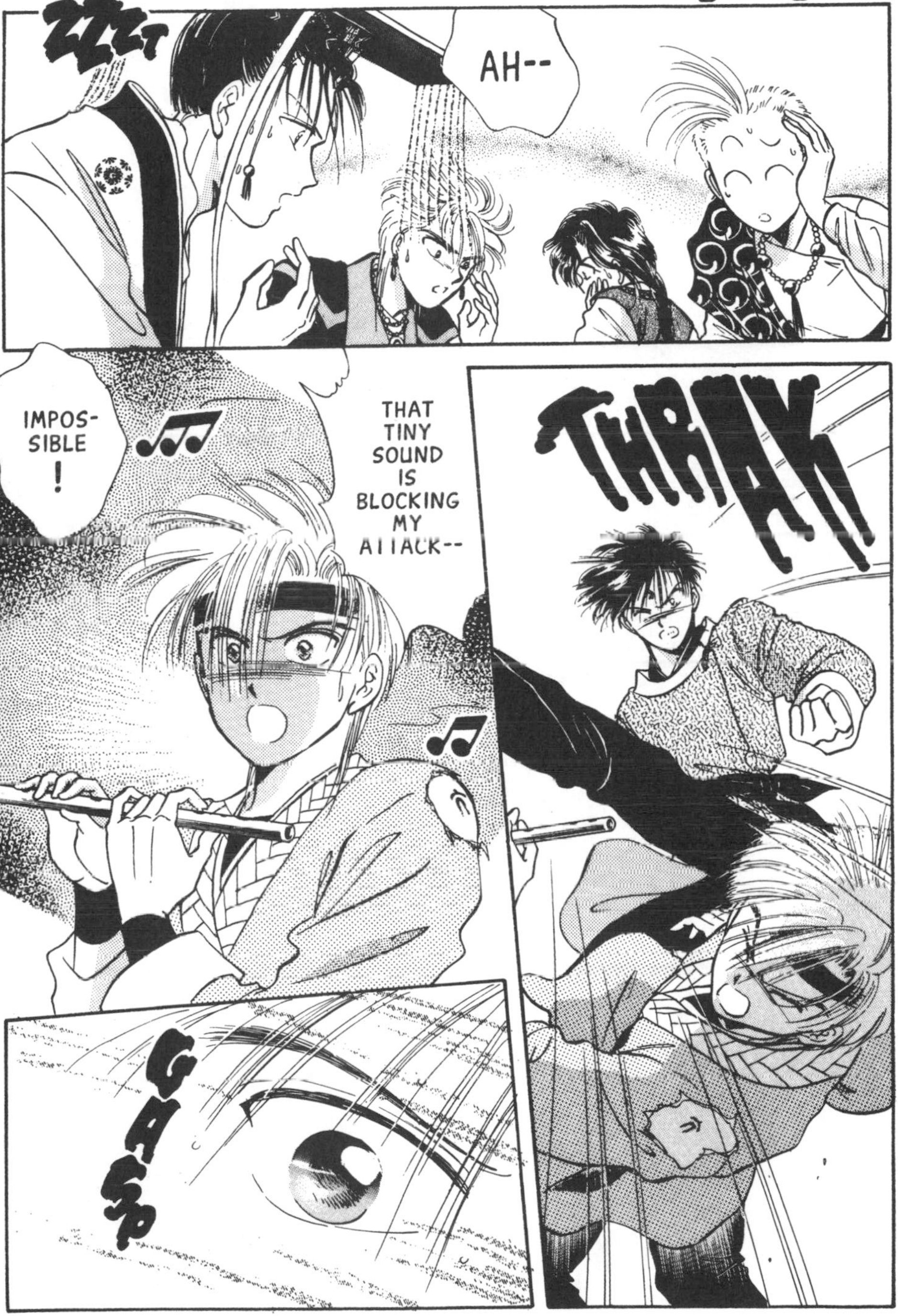
ZZZT
AH--
IMPOS-SIBLE
!
THAT TINY SOUND IS BLOCKING MY ATTACK--
THRAK
GASP

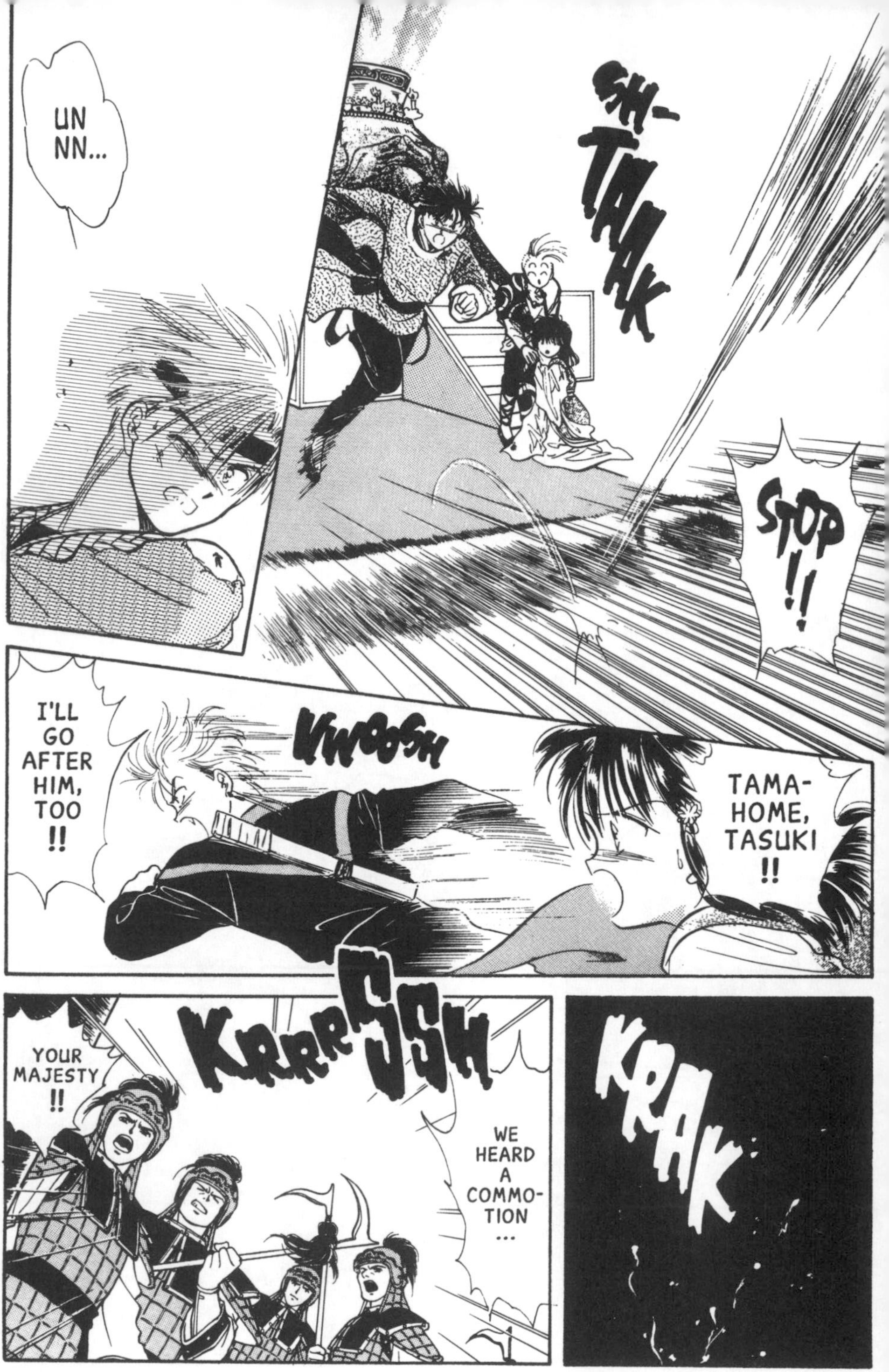
UN NN...
SH-TAAAK
STOP!!
I'LL GO AFTER HIM, TOO!!
VWOOSH
TAMA-HOME, TASUKI!!
YOUR MAJESTY!!
KRRRSSH
WE HEARD A COMMOTION...
KRAK

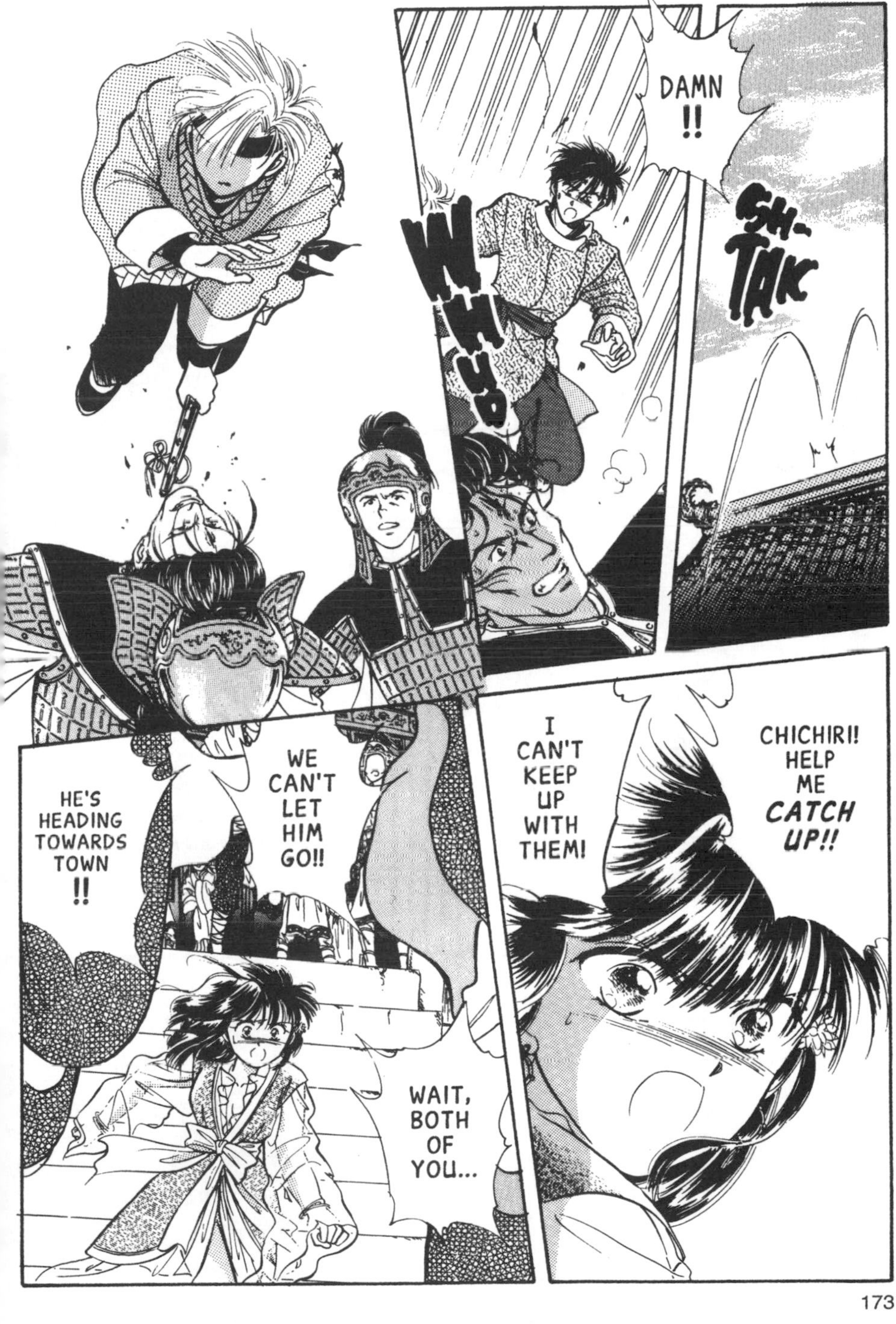
DAMN!!
WHUD
SH-TAK
HE'S HEADING TOWARDS TOWN!!
WE CAN'T LET HIM GO!!
WAIT, BOTH OF YOU...
I CAN'T KEEP UP WITH THEM!
CHICHIRI!! HELP ME *CATCH UP!!*

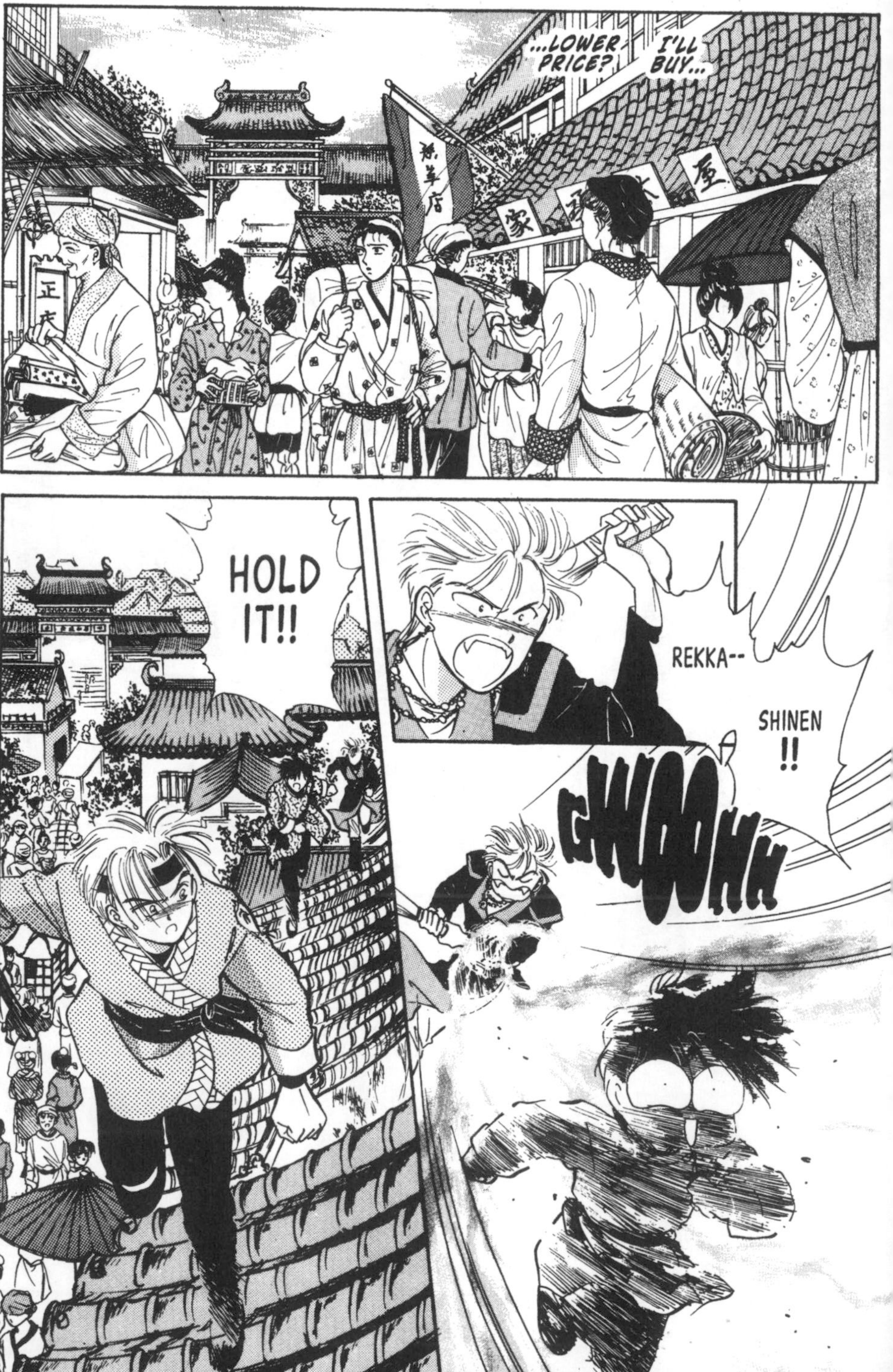
...LOWER PRICE?
I'LL BUY...
HOLD IT!!
REKKA--
SHINEN !!
GWOOHH

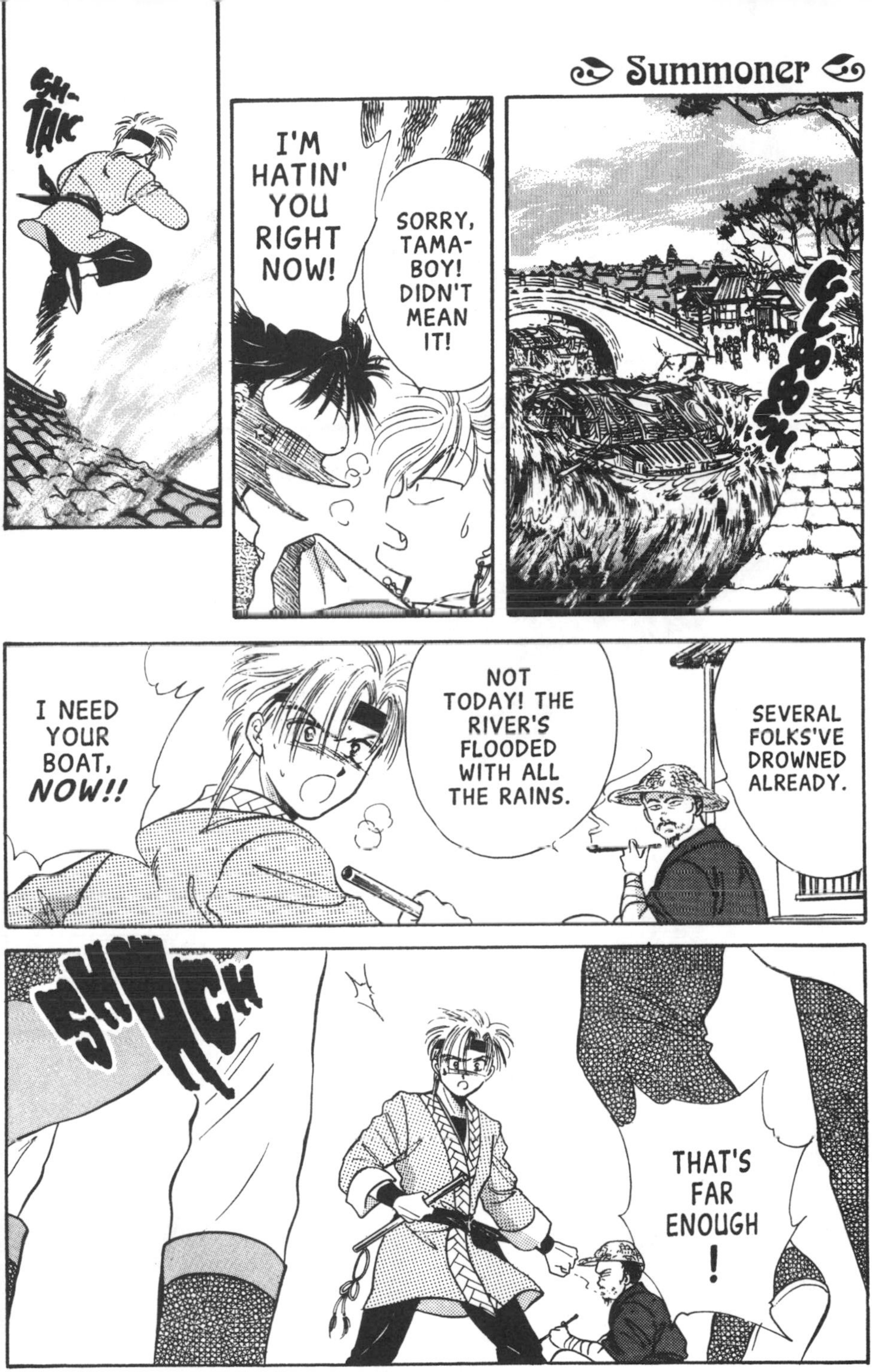
SH-TAK
I'M HATIN' YOU RIGHT NOW!
SORRY, TAMA-BOY! DIDN'T MEAN IT!
I NEED YOUR BOAT, ***NOW!!***
NOT TODAY! THE RIVER'S FLOODED WITH ALL THE RAINS.
SEVERAL FOLKS'VE DROWNED ALREADY.
SHACH
THAT'S FAR ENOUGH !

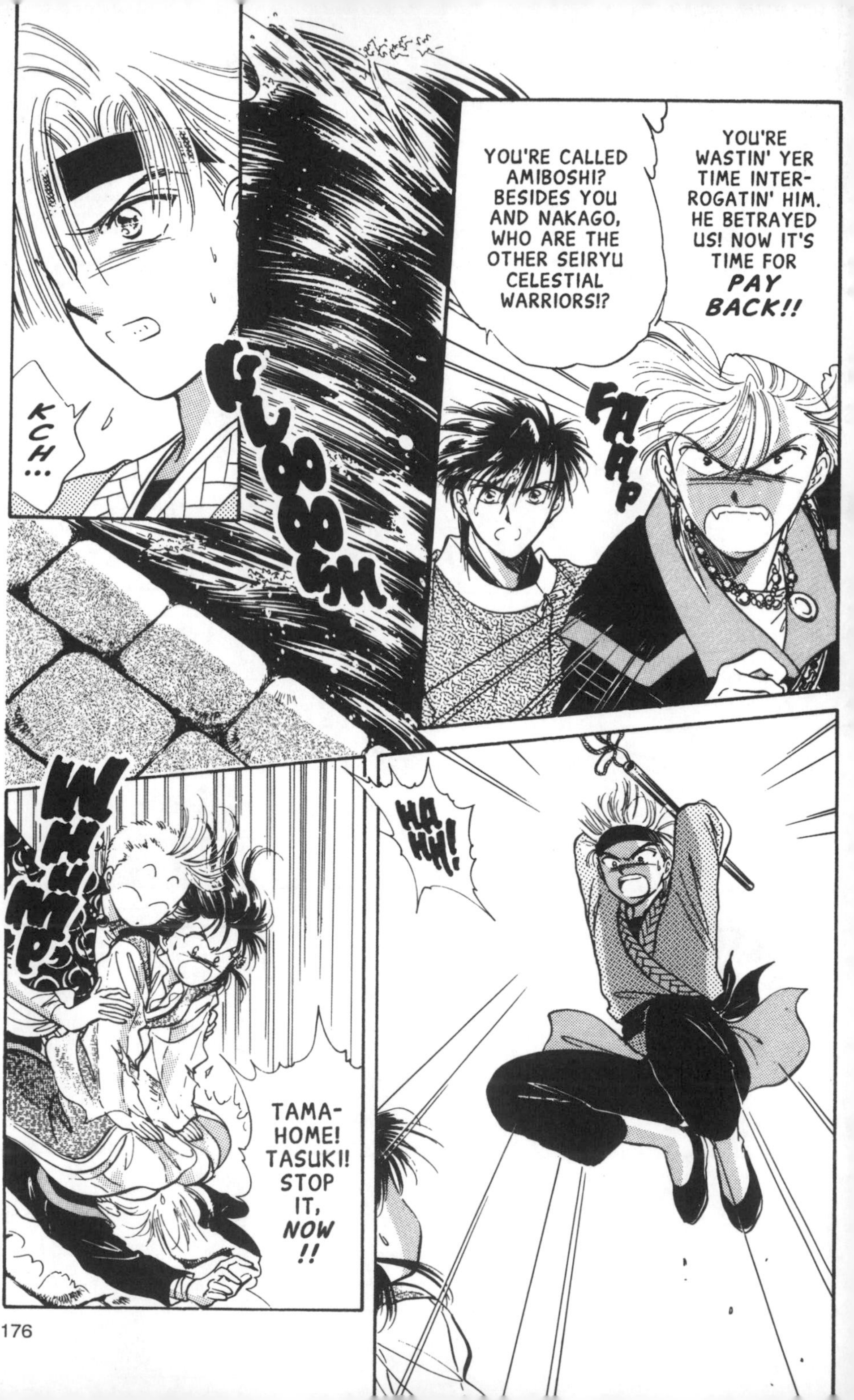
KCH...
KLOOOOM
YOU'RE CALLED AMIBOSHI? BESIDES YOU AND NAKAGO, WHO ARE THE OTHER SEIRYU CELESTIAL WARRIORS!?
YOU'RE WASTIN' YER TIME INTER-ROGATIN' HIM. HE BETRAYED US! NOW IT'S TIME FOR ***PAY BACK!!***
FAAP
WHUMP
TAMA-HOME! TASUKI! STOP IT, ***NOW!!***
HA HAH!

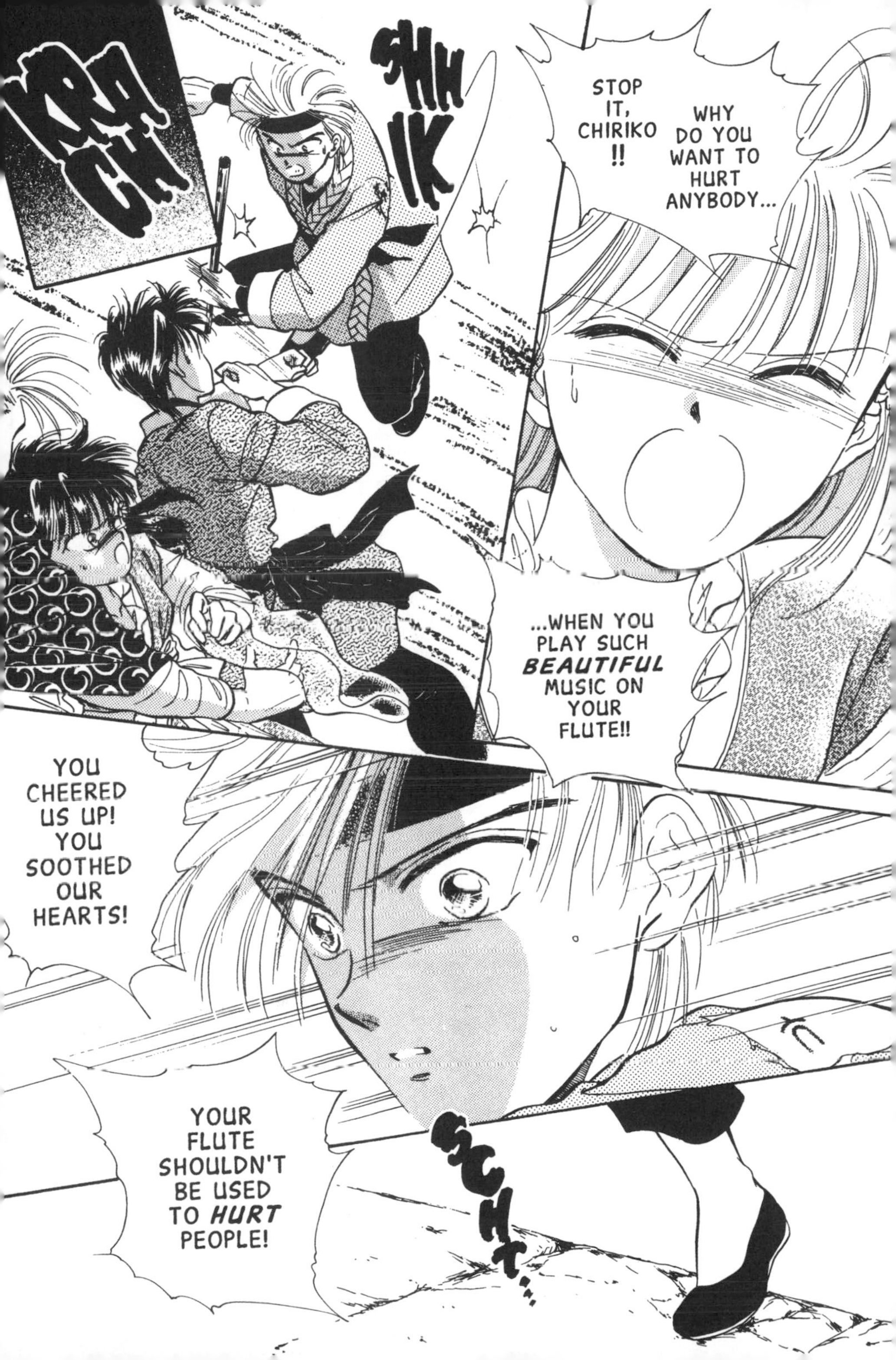
KRACH
SHHIK
STOP IT, CHIRIKO!!
WHY DO YOU WANT TO HURT ANYBODY...
...WHEN YOU PLAY SUCH ***BEAUTIFUL*** MUSIC ON YOUR FLUTE!!
YOU CHEERED US UP! YOU SOOTHED OUR HEARTS!
YOUR FLUTE SHOULDN'T BE USED TO ***HURT*** PEOPLE!
SCHT...

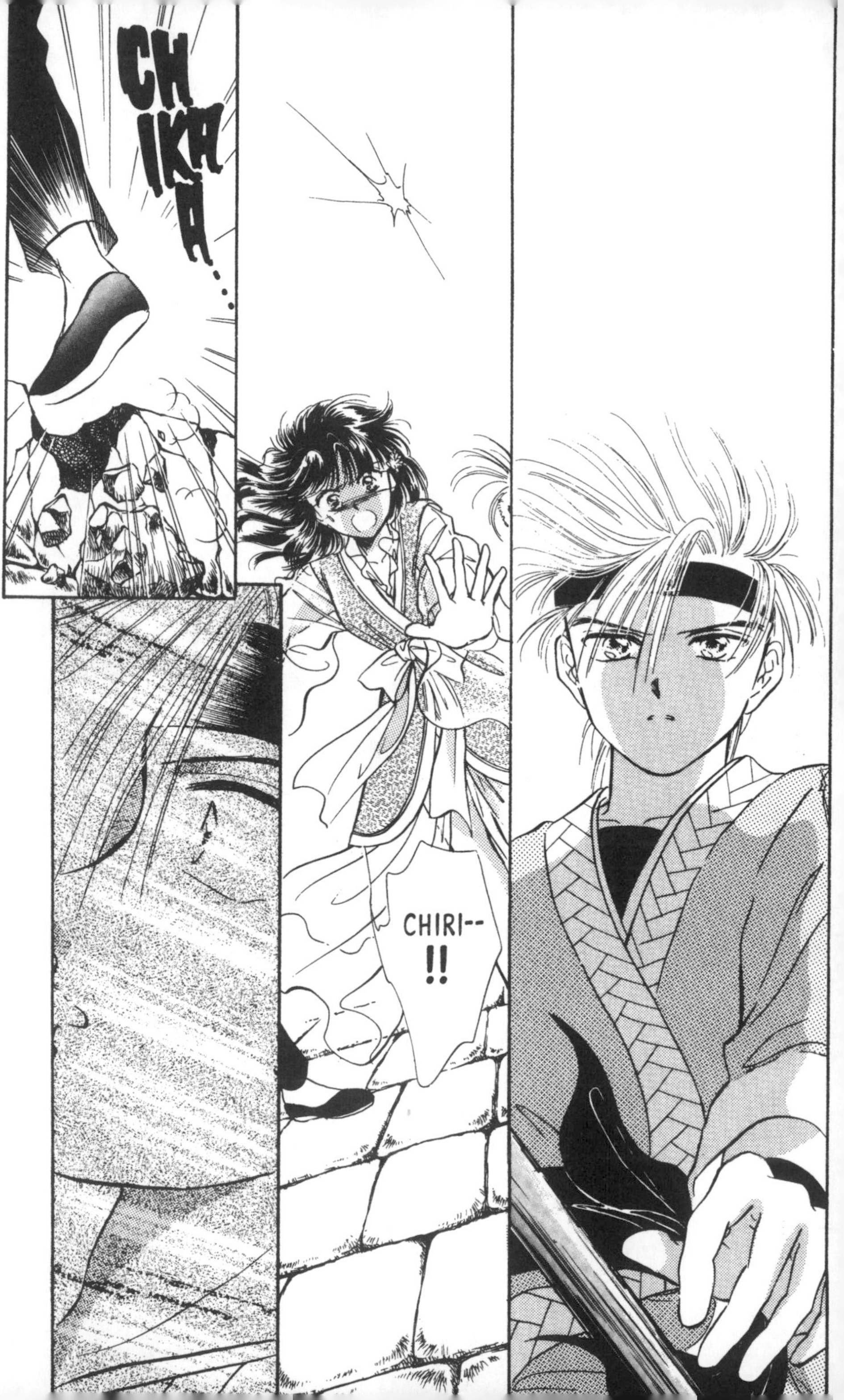
CHIKAAA...
CHIRI-- !!

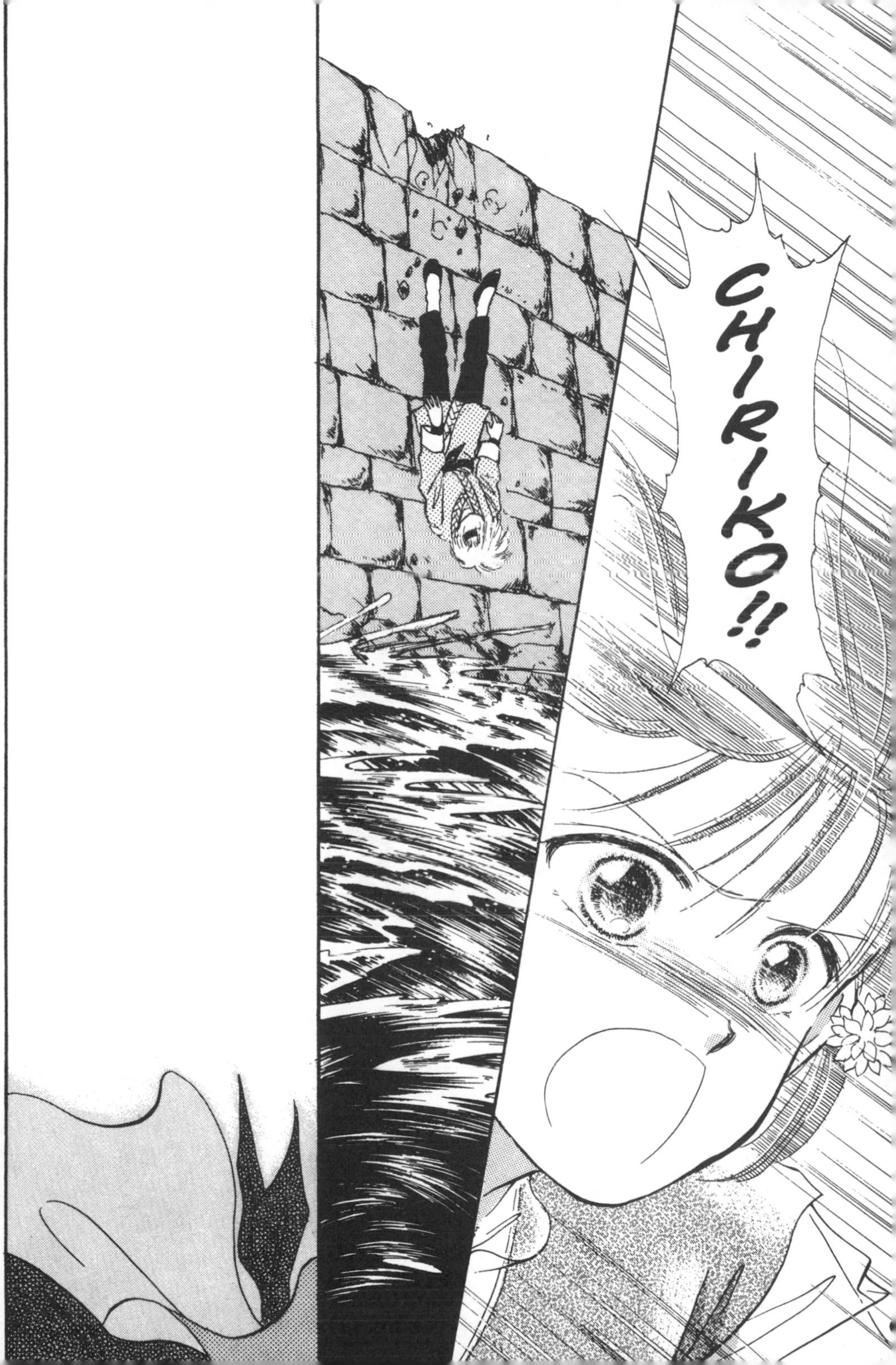
CHIRIKO!!

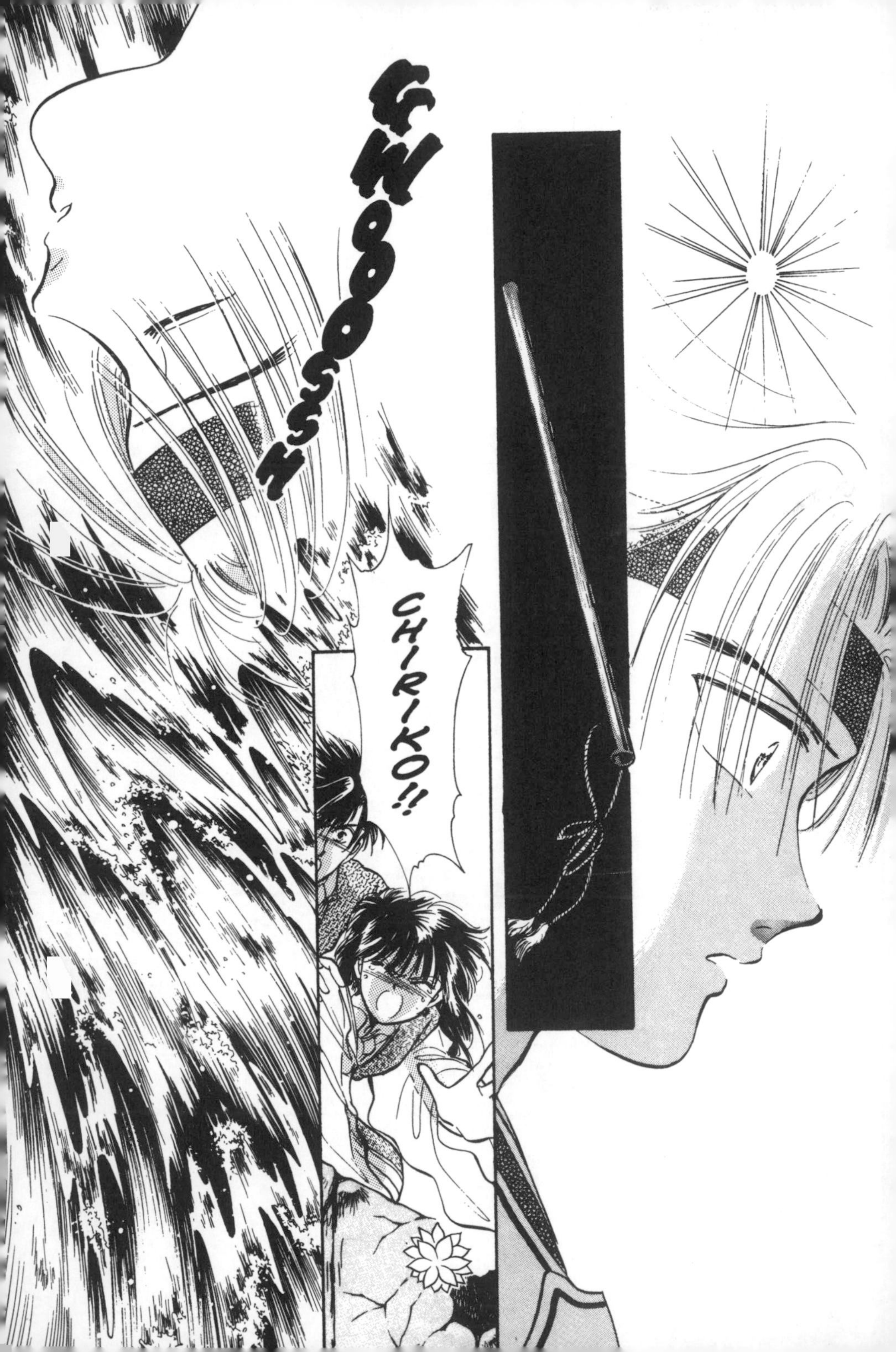
GWOOOSSH
CHIRIKO!!

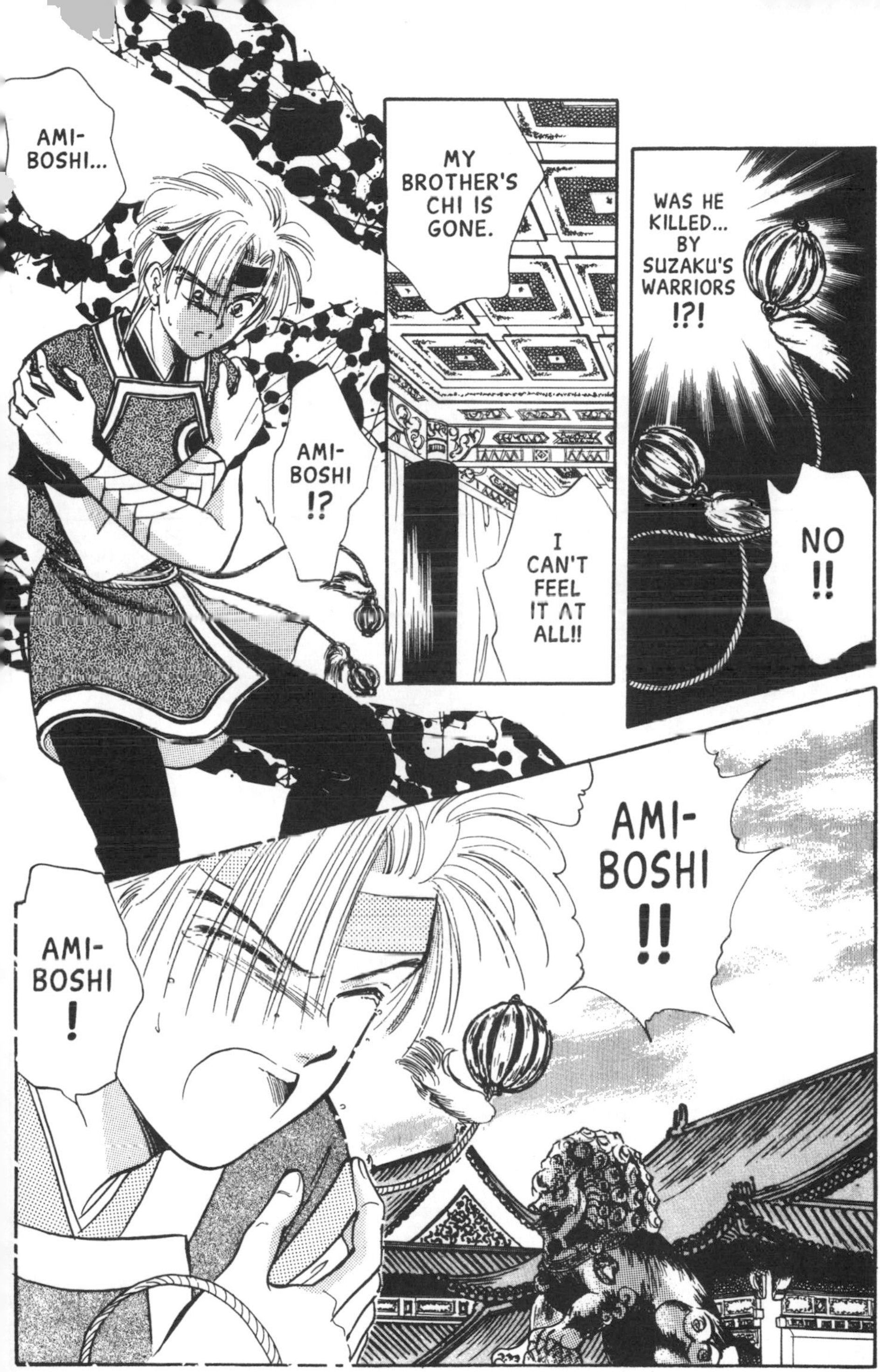
AMI-BOSHI...
AMI-BOSHI !?
MY BROTHER'S CHI IS GONE.
I CAN'T FEEL IT AT ALL!!
WAS HE KILLED... BY SUZAKU'S WARRIORS !?!
NO !!
AMI-BOSHI !
AMI-BOSHI !!

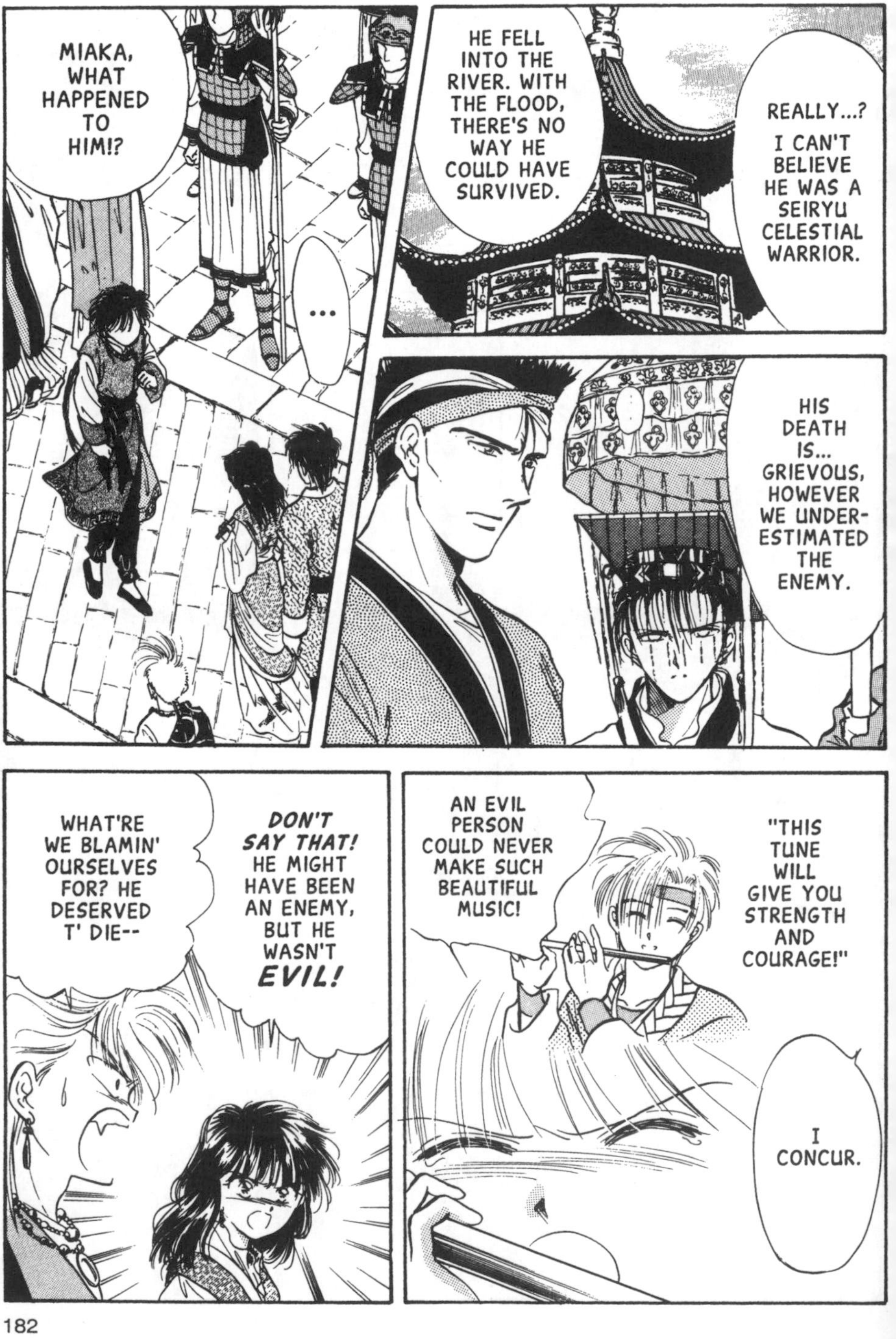
MIAKA, WHAT HAPPENED TO HIM!?
...
HE FELL INTO THE RIVER. WITH THE FLOOD, THERE'S NO WAY HE COULD HAVE SURVIVED.
REALLY...? I CAN'T BELIEVE HE WAS A SEIRYU CELESTIAL WARRIOR.
HIS DEATH IS... GRIEVOUS, HOWEVER WE UNDER-ESTIMATED THE ENEMY.
WHAT'RE WE BLAMIN' OURSELVES FOR? HE DESERVED T' DIE--
DON'T SAY THAT! HE MIGHT HAVE BEEN AN ENEMY, BUT HE WASN'T ***EVIL!***
AN EVIL PERSON COULD NEVER MAKE SUCH BEAUTIFUL MUSIC!
"THIS TUNE WILL GIVE YOU STRENGTH AND COURAGE!"
I CONCUR.

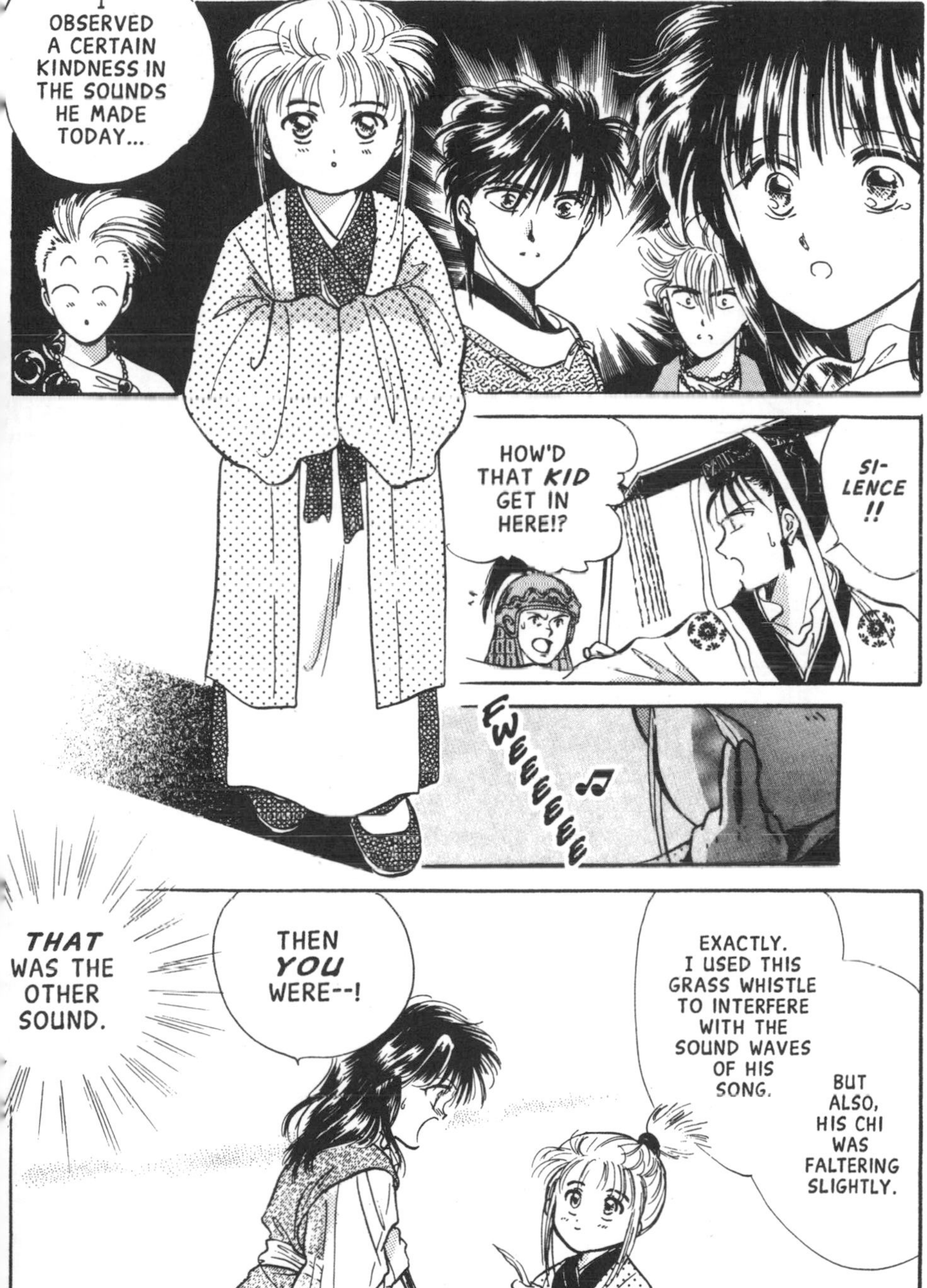
I OBSERVED A CERTAIN KINDNESS IN THE SOUNDS HE MADE TODAY...
HOW'D THAT *KID* GET IN HERE!?
SI-LENCE!!
EWEEEEEEEE ♪
THAT WAS THE OTHER SOUND.
THEN *YOU* WERE--!
EXACTLY. I USED THIS GRASS WHISTLE TO INTERFERE WITH THE SOUND WAVES OF HIS SONG.
BUT ALSO, HIS CHI WAS FALTERING SLIGHTLY.

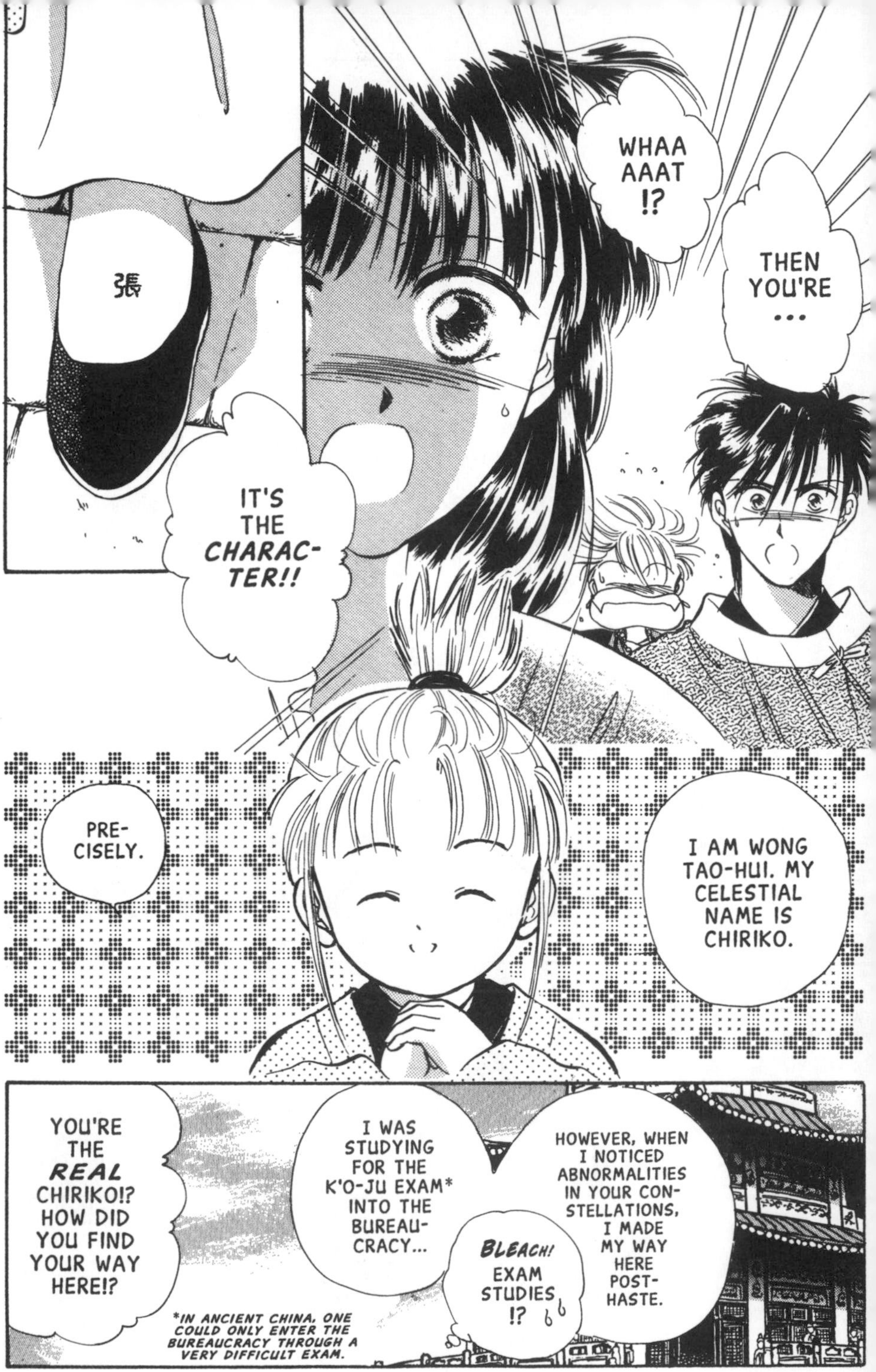
張
WHAA AAAT !?
THEN YOU'RE ...
IT'S THE CHARACTER!!
PRECISELY.
I AM WONG TAO-HUI. MY CELESTIAL NAME IS CHIRIKO.
YOU'RE THE REAL CHIRIKO!? HOW DID YOU FIND YOUR WAY HERE!?
I WAS STUDYING FOR THE K'O-JU EXAM* INTO THE BUREAUCRACY...
HOWEVER, WHEN I NOTICED ABNORMALITIES IN YOUR CONSTELLATIONS, I MADE MY WAY HERE POSTHASTE.
BLEACH! EXAM STUDIES !?
*IN ANCIENT CHINA, ONE COULD ONLY ENTER THE BUREAUCRACY THROUGH A VERY DIFFICULT EXAM.

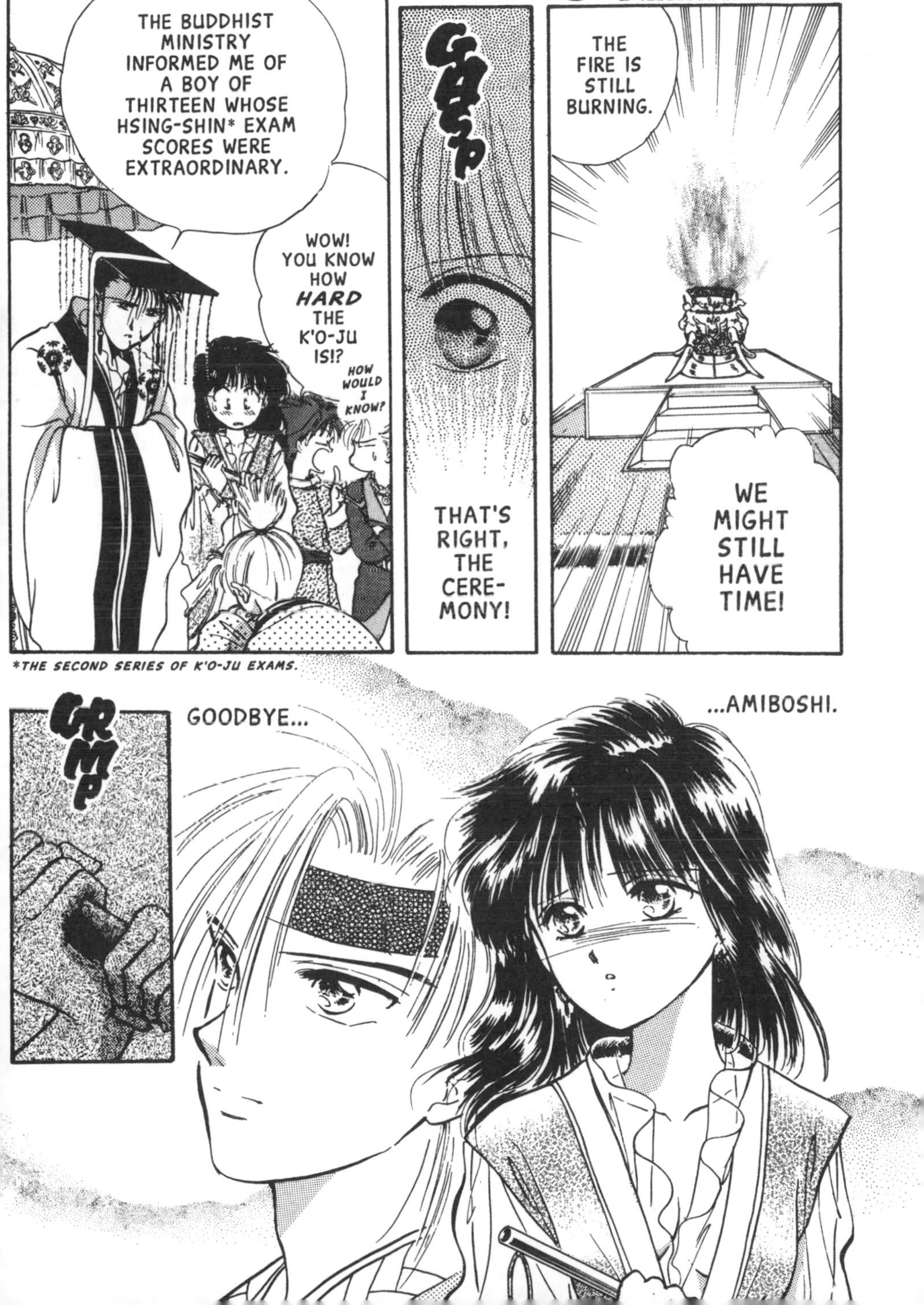
THE BUDDHIST MINISTRY INFORMED ME OF A BOY OF THIRTEEN WHOSE HSING-SHIN* EXAM SCORES WERE EXTRAORDINARY.
WOW! YOU KNOW HOW HARD THE K'O-JU IS!?
HOW WOULD I KNOW?
GASP
THAT'S RIGHT, THE CERE-MONY!
THE FIRE IS STILL BURNING.
WE MIGHT STILL HAVE TIME!
GRMP
GOODBYE...
...AMIBOSHI.

*THE SECOND SERIES OF K'O-JU EXAMS.

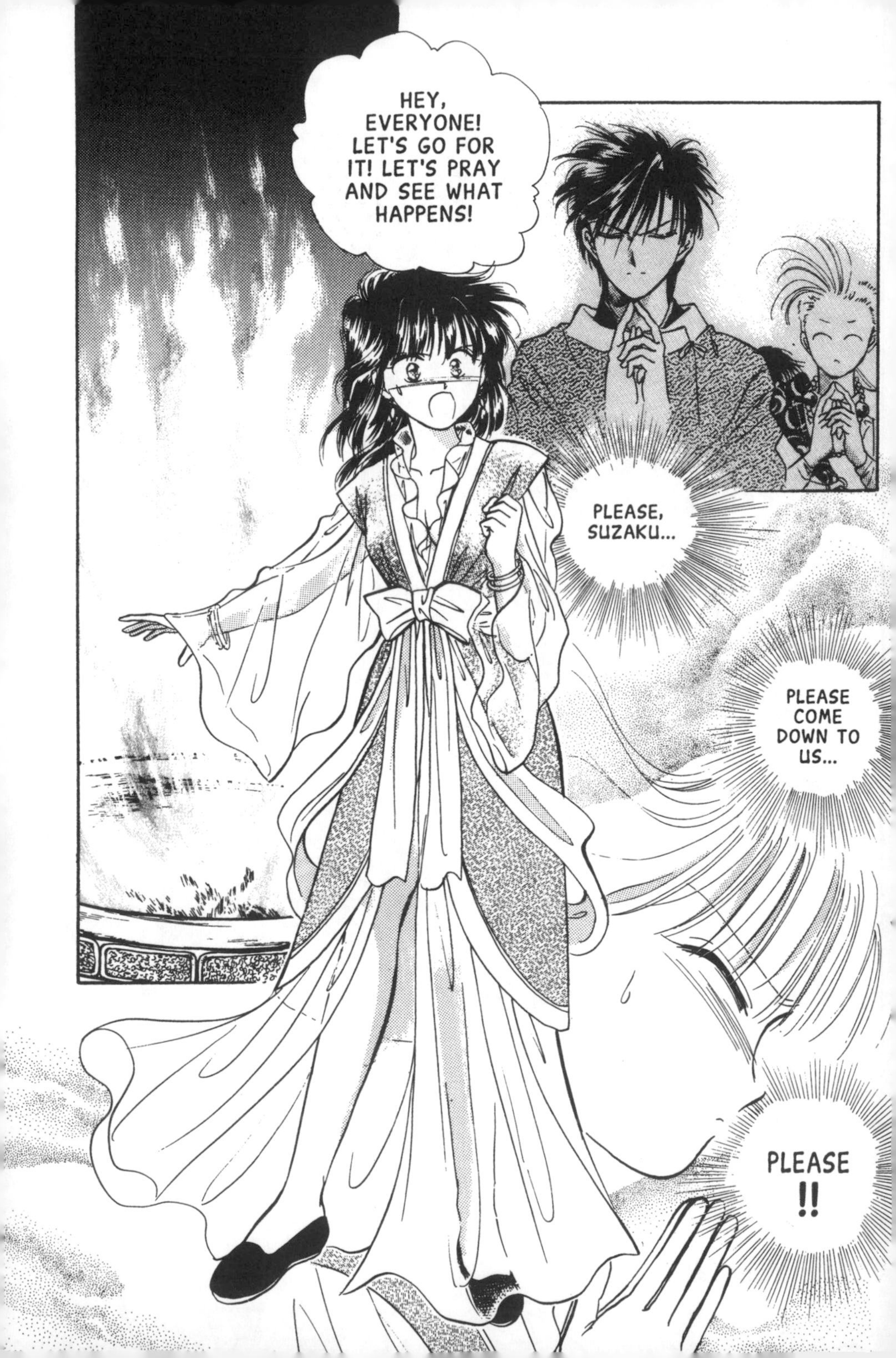
HEY, EVERYONE! LET'S GO FOR IT! LET'S PRAY AND SEE WHAT HAPPENS!
PLEASE, SUZAKU...
PLEASE COME DOWN TO US...
PLEASE !!

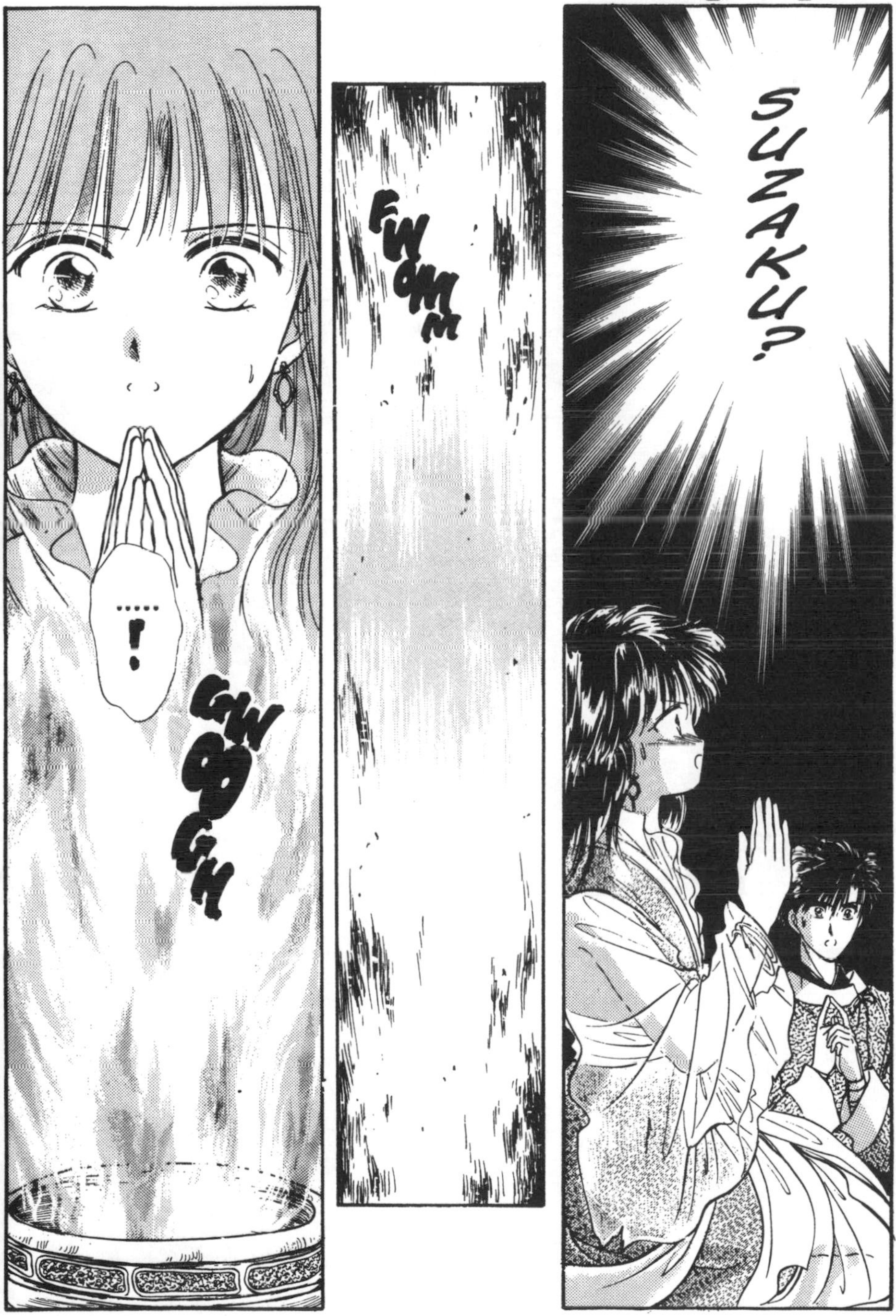
.....!
GWOOGH
FWOMM
SUZAKU?

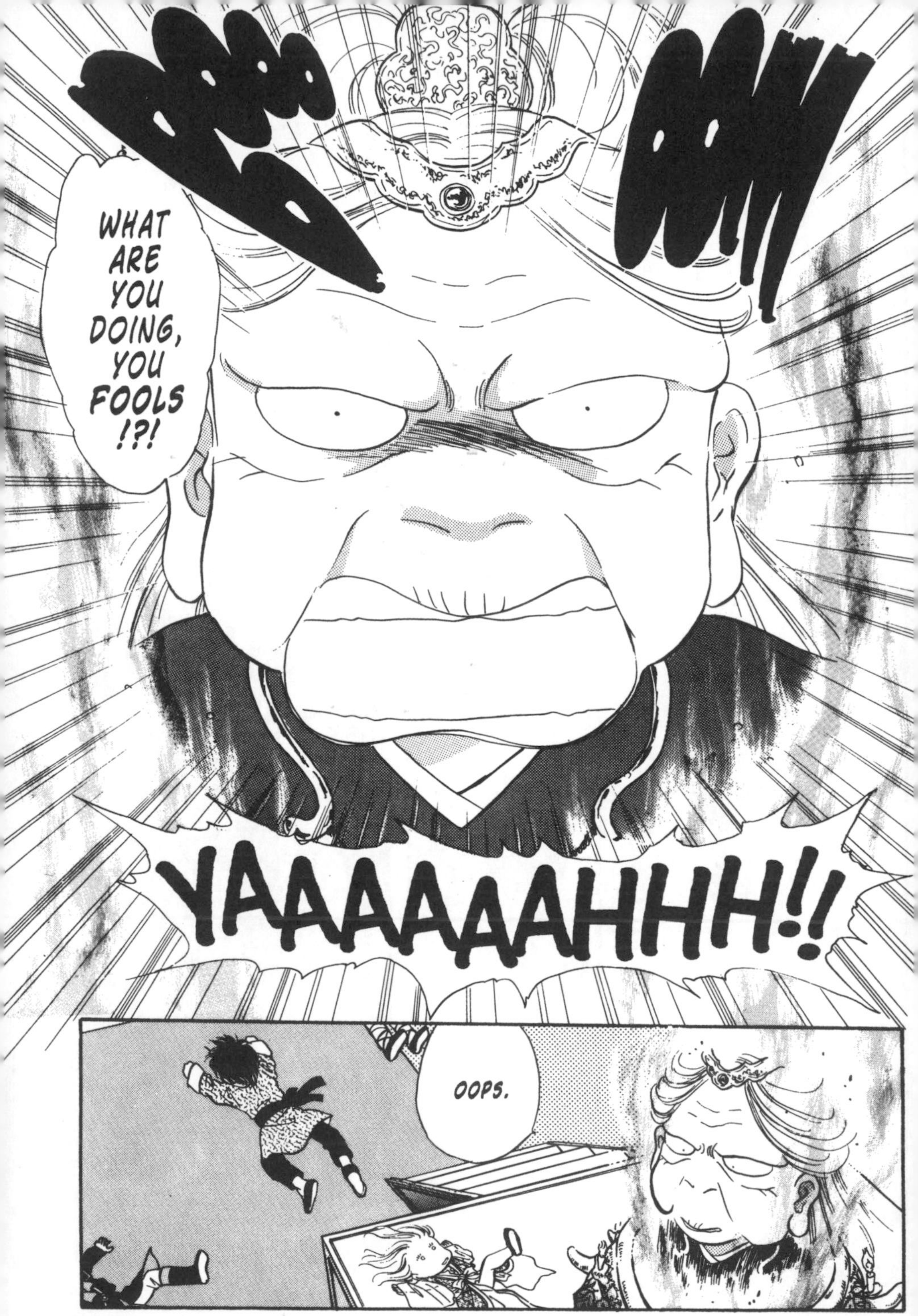
WHAT ARE YOU DOING, YOU FOOLS !?!
YAAAAAAHHH!!
OOPS.

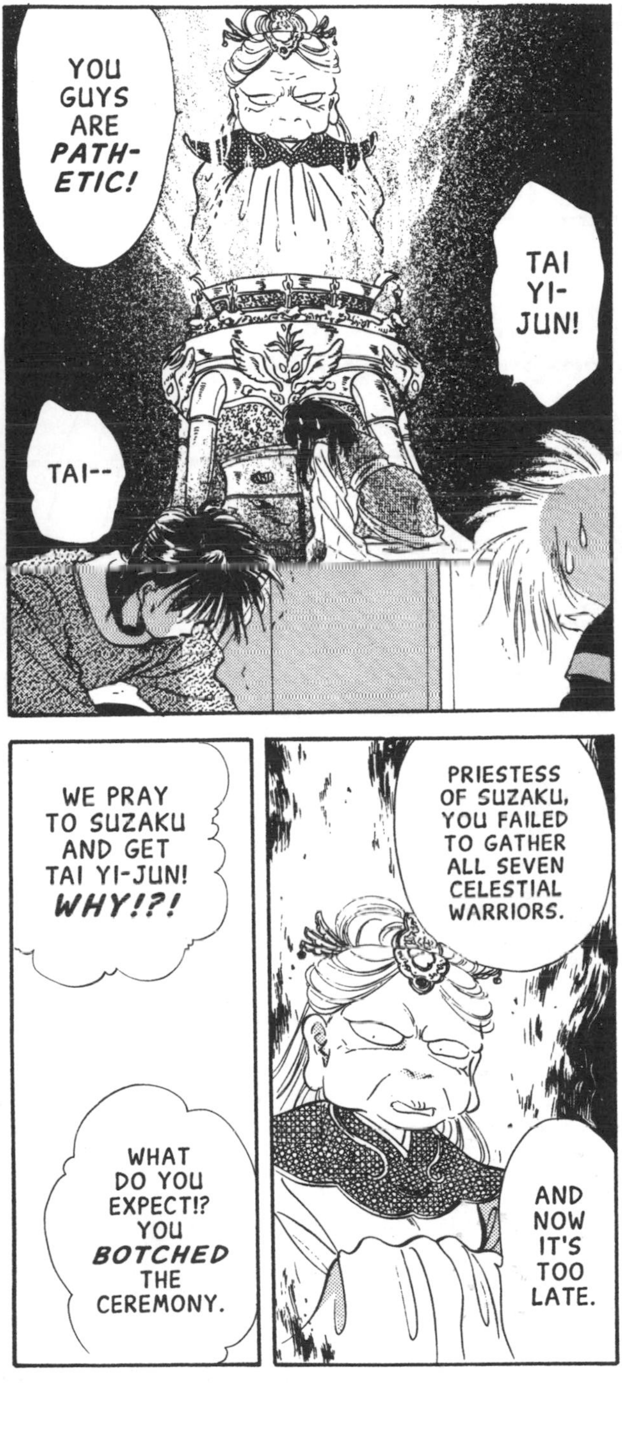
YOU GUYS ARE PATH-ETIC!
TAI YI-JUN!
TAI--
WE PRAY TO SUZAKU AND GET TAI YI-JUN! WHY!?!
WHAT DO YOU EXPECT!? YOU BOTCHED THE CEREMONY.
PRIESTESS OF SUZAKU, YOU FAILED TO GATHER ALL SEVEN CELESTIAL WARRIORS.
AND NOW IT'S TOO LATE.

Summoner

Yui was linked to Miaka by her uniform, so their entire bodies were connected. Keisuke was only linked to Miaka at his wrist (with the ribbon). Their connections are limited to the area in contact. If the ribbon were torn to shreds, it'd reach him, but no matter what bodily injuries are inflicted on Miaka, the most Keisuke would feel is a twitch on his wrist. *Do you get it now? Also, let's not forget how much stronger Yui's feelings for Miaka might be compared to Keisuke's.* Let's leave it at that for the present.

So now we finally have all seven celestial warriors. We're at the end of Part One. *It's only Part One! Titled, "The Seven Celestial Warriors."* Now, the story should go in a different direction. But we're talking about Yū Watase, so of course she has no idea where it's going. Waaaahhh!!

Hey! By the way, there's a CD book that's been released along with the Japanese edition of volume 6. It's a novelization that follows the story up to volume 7, so all the Japanese fans should give it a listen. It's all thanks to you. *Thank you so much.* Also I have the honor of illustrating Mizuchi Hayase's novel that's to be published by Shogakukan's Canvas Bunko imprint. Please take a look. *August: Volume 2 of "New Prepubescence 2" September: graphic novel of "Tiara of Sand."* Hmmm, what am I doing providing a list of my upcoming publications!? See ya later!!

135 is so great. It's Tenmai! Tenmai! I wish all the songs could be used for "Fushigi."

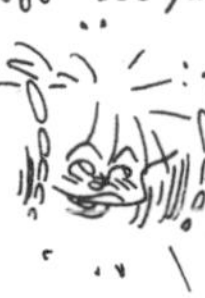

I love Yume Mirai ("Dream Future") on the Tenmai (Heaven's Dance) soundtrack! It's hard to believe this CD is game music.

Speaking of CDs my friend gave me a character album that goes with the CD of Street Fighter II.

↑

So what!? 135 is Wo Ai Ni. Wo ai ni. Fly up into the heavens, holy girl (oh yeah). I think a lot of people know the song because it was used for a tea commercial years ago...

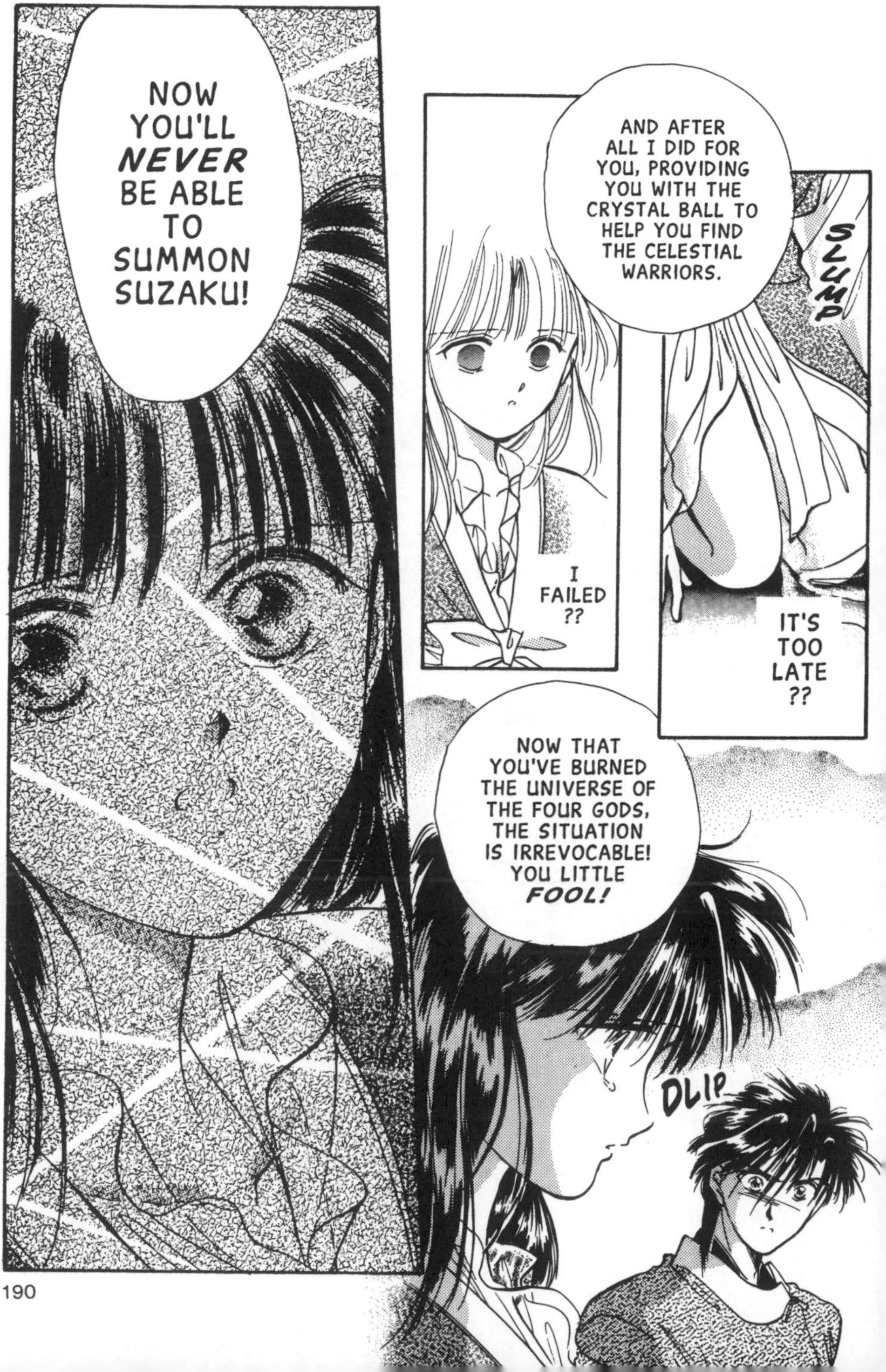
NOW YOU'LL NEVER BE ABLE TO SUMMON SUZAKU!
AND AFTER ALL I DID FOR YOU, PROVIDING YOU WITH THE CRYSTAL BALL TO HELP YOU FIND THE CELESTIAL WARRIORS.
I FAILED ??
SLUMP
IT'S TOO LATE ??
NOW THAT YOU'VE BURNED THE UNIVERSE OF THE FOUR GODS, THE SITUATION IS IRREVOCABLE! YOU LITTLE FOOL!
DLIP

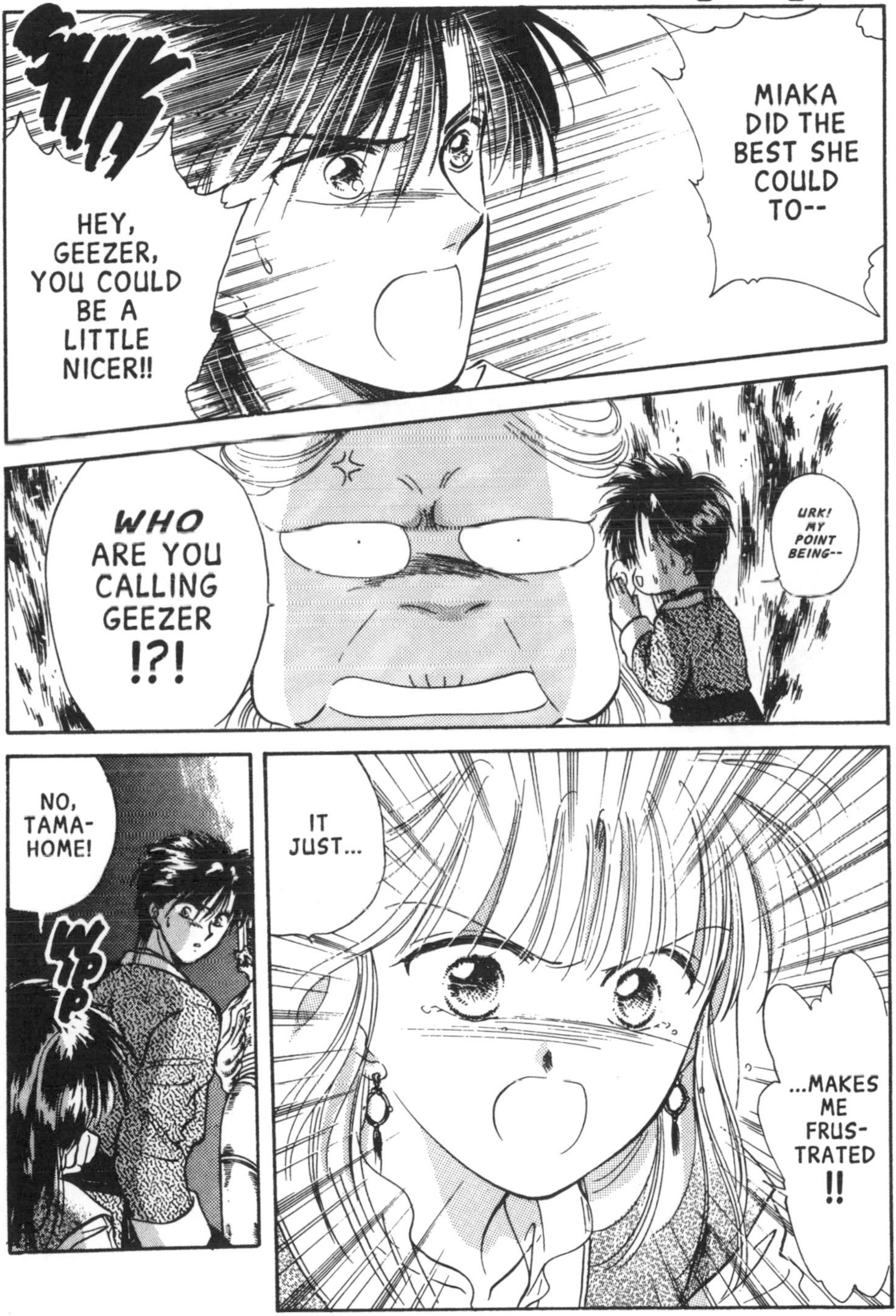
HEY, GEEZER, YOU COULD BE A LITTLE NICER!!
MIAKA DID THE BEST SHE COULD TO--
WHO ARE YOU CALLING GEEZER !?!
URK! MY POINT BEING--
NO, TAMA-HOME!
IT JUST...
...MAKES ME FRUS-TRATED !!

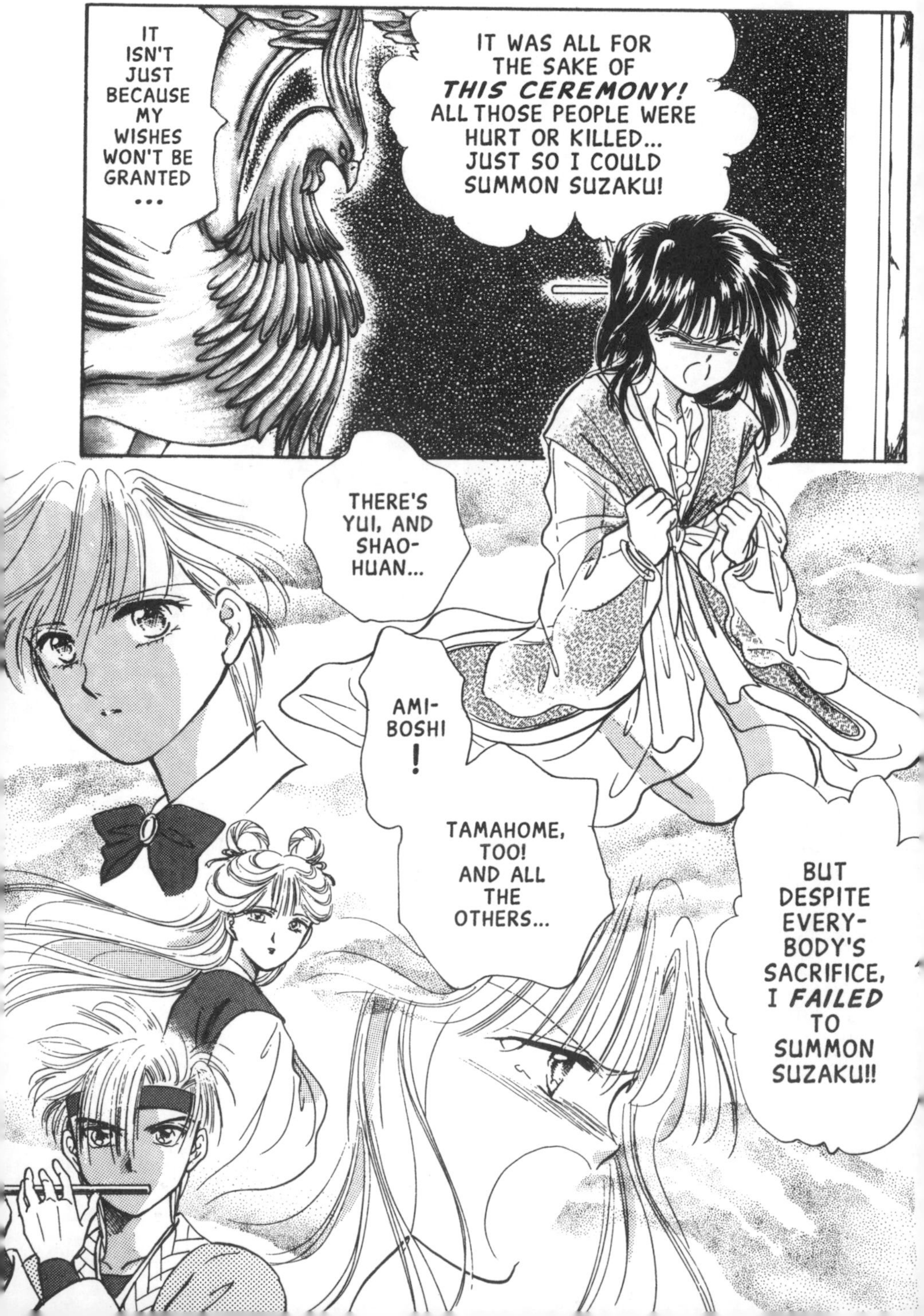
IT ISN'T JUST BECAUSE MY WISHES WON'T BE GRANTED...
IT WAS ALL FOR THE SAKE OF *THIS CEREMONY!* ALL THOSE PEOPLE WERE HURT OR KILLED... JUST SO I COULD SUMMON SUZAKU!
THERE'S YUI, AND SHAO-HUAN...
AMI-BOSHI!
TAMAHOME, TOO! AND ALL THE OTHERS...
BUT DESPITE EVERY-BODY'S SACRIFICE, I *FAILED* TO SUMMON SUZAKU!!

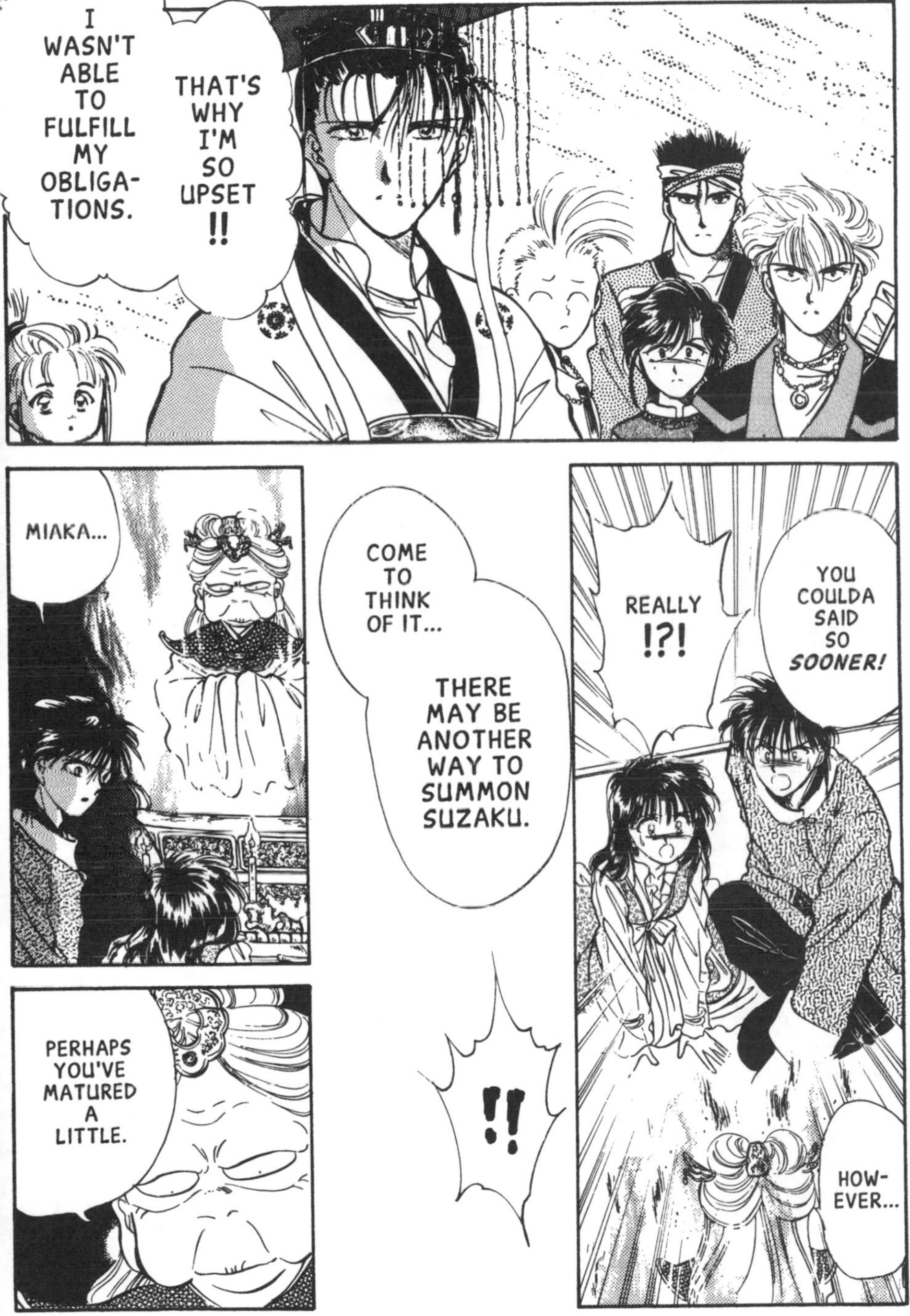
I WASN'T ABLE TO FULFILL MY OBLIGATIONS.
THAT'S WHY I'M SO UPSET!!
MIAKA...
PERHAPS YOU'VE MATURED A LITTLE.
COME TO THINK OF IT...
THERE MAY BE ANOTHER WAY TO SUMMON SUZAKU.
!!
REALLY!?!
YOU COULDA SAID SO *SOONER!*
HOW-EVER...

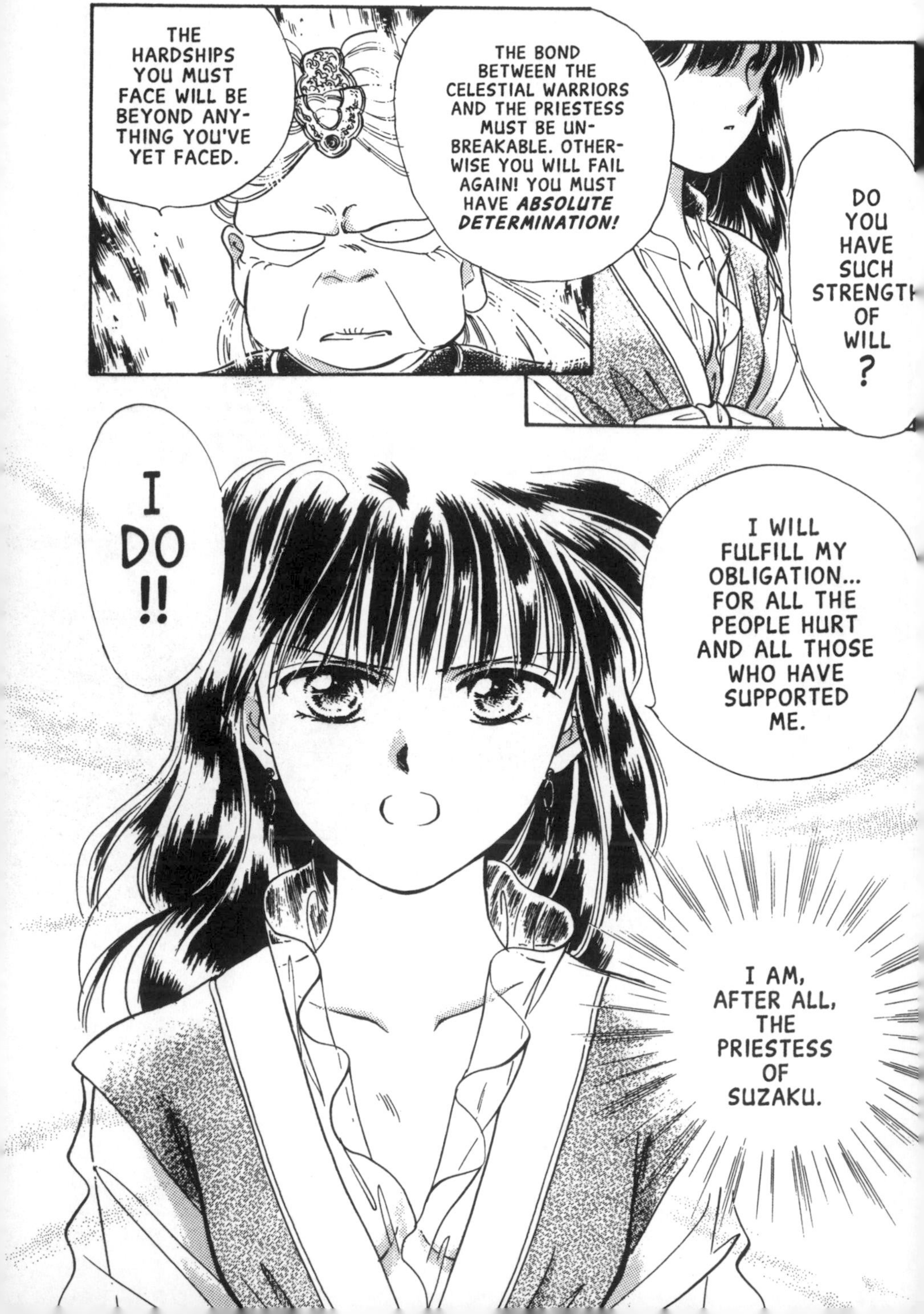
THE HARDSHIPS YOU MUST FACE WILL BE BEYOND ANY-THING YOU'VE YET FACED.
THE BOND BETWEEN THE CELESTIAL WARRIORS AND THE PRIESTESS MUST BE UN-BREAKABLE. OTHER-WISE YOU WILL FAIL AGAIN! YOU MUST HAVE *ABSOLUTE DETERMINATION!*
DO YOU HAVE SUCH STRENGTH OF WILL ?
I DO !!
I WILL FULFILL MY OBLIGATION... FOR ALL THE PEOPLE HURT AND ALL THOSE WHO HAVE SUPPORTED ME.
I AM, AFTER ALL, THE PRIESTESS OF SUZAKU.

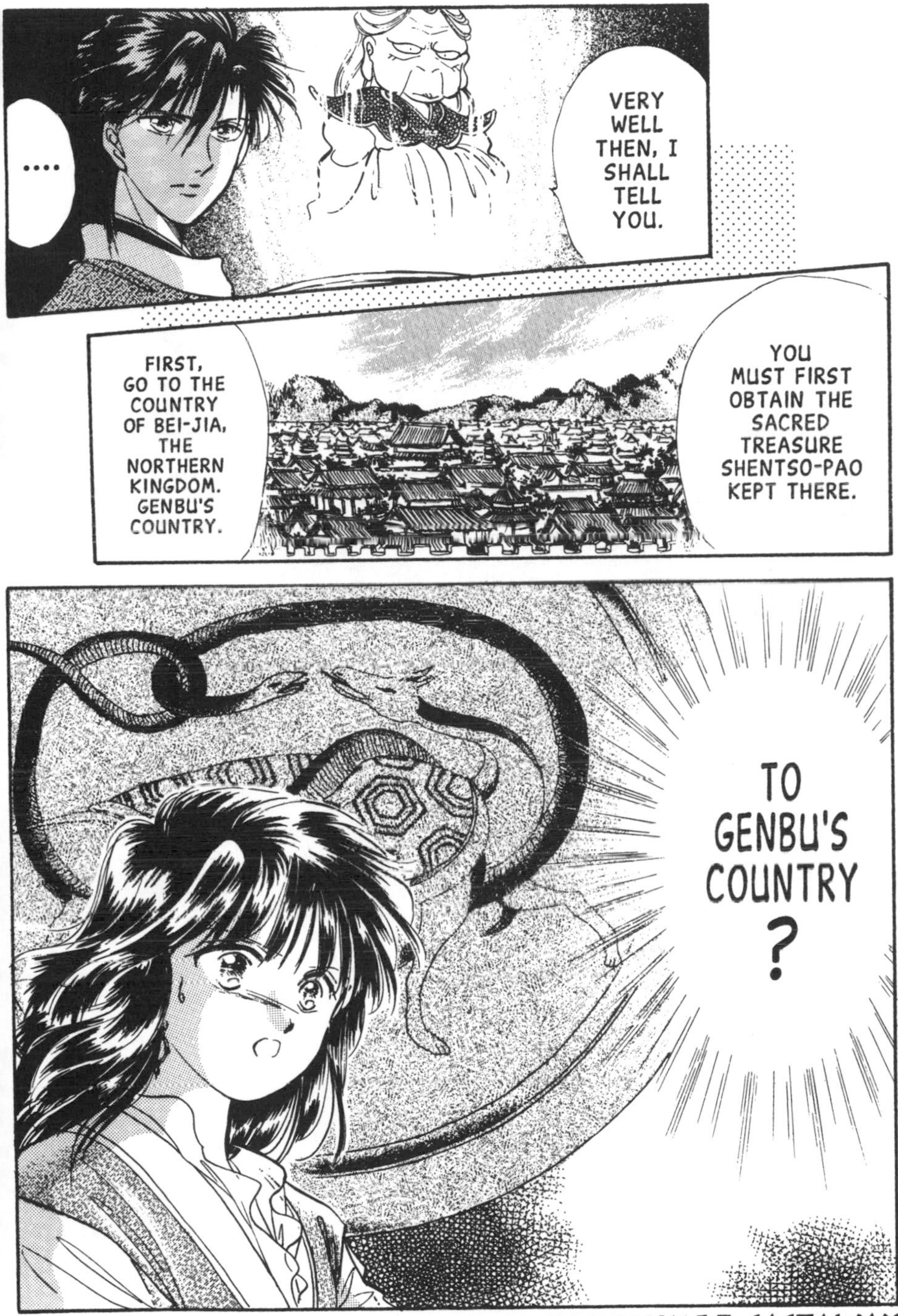
....
VERY WELL THEN, I SHALL TELL YOU.
FIRST, GO TO THE COUNTRY OF BEI-JIA, THE NORTHERN KINGDOM. GENBU'S COUNTRY.
YOU MUST FIRST OBTAIN THE SACRED TREASURE SHENTSO-PAO KEPT THERE.
TO GENBU'S COUNTRY ?

TO BE CONTINUED IN VOLUME 7: CASTAWAY

YÛ WATASE

Yû Watase was born on March 5 in a town near Osaka, and she was raised there before moving to Tokyo to follow the dream of creating manga. In the decade since her debut short story, *PAJAMA DE OJAMA* ("An Intrusion in Pajamas"), she has produced more than 50 compiled volumes of short stories and continuing series. Her latest series, *ALICE 19TH*, is currently running in the anthology magazine *SHÔJO COMIC*. Her long-running horror/romance story *CERES: CELESTIAL LEGEND* is now available in North America published by Viz Communications. She loves science fiction, fantasy and comedy.

A CELESTIAL LEGEND GIVEN FORM!

CERES
Celestial Legend

By
Yû Watase

From the acclaimed author of "Fushigi Yûgi" Yû Watase, one of the most anticipated anime series of the year! The supernatural thriller begins on the day of Aya and her twin brother Aki's 16th birthday, when their grandfather decides it's time to share a long guarded secret. The twins are summoned to the massive, mysterious Mikage House where they find thier extended family assembled and waiting. They are given a curious gift and in that instant their destiny begins to unfold... Both the video and the monthly comic unveil the secret of Aya and Ceres, the Celestial Legend

AVAILABLE MONTHLY IN COMICS, VIDEOS, AND DVDS!

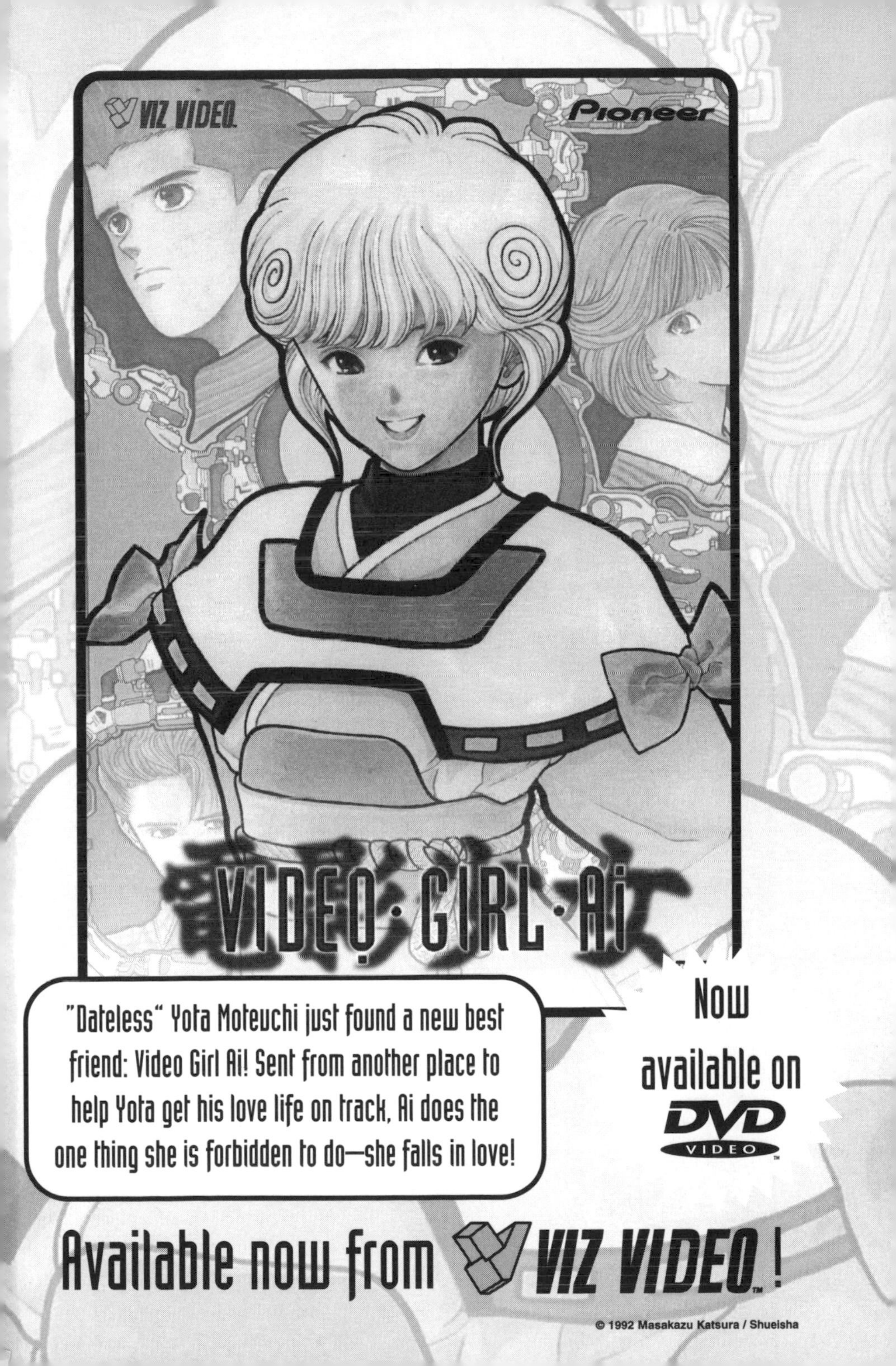
VIZ VIDEO
Pioneer
VIDEO GIRL Ai
"Dateless" Yota Moteuchi just found a new best friend: Video Girl Ai! Sent from another place to help Yota get his love life on track, Ai does the one thing she is forbidden to do—she falls in love!
Now available on DVD VIDEO
Available now from VIZ VIDEO!
© 1992 Masakazu Katsura / Shueisha